the Unofficial Guide™ to Online Investing

Henry F. Robb

IDG Books Worldwide, Inc.
An International Data Group Company
Foster City, CA • Chicago, IL • Indianapolis, IN
• New York, NY

IDG Books Worldwide, Inc.
An International Data Group Company
919 E. Hillsdale Boulevard
Suite 400
Foster City, CA 94404

ISBN: 0-02863752-6

Manufactured in the United States of America

10 9 8 7 6 5 4 3 2 1

First edition

To my wife, Satoko Chiaki-Robb

Acknowledgments

While only one name usually makes it onto the cover of a book, there is always a legion of people standing behind the author, helping him turn an idea into a reality. *The Unofficial Guide to Online Investing* is no exception.

First, I want to thank Lisa Carlson of the Bay Area Editors' Forum for her support at the outset. Many thanks to my agent, Andree Abecassis, for all her hard work and for making things go smoothly from start to finish.

I am also indebted to my acquisitions editor, Randy Ladenheim-Gil, for her support, Jessica Faust, and my development editor, John Jones, for his professionalism. I also want to thank Krista Hansing (who did a great job as copyeditor), Jena Brandt (production editor), the technical editors, and all the unsung production people and sales and marketing staff at Macmillan and IDG Books who put hours of work into this publication.

Special thanks to A.B. Watley, Inc., Elizabeth Compton and America Online, ASK Research, BigCharts, Go2Net, Charles Schwab & Co., CareerDayTrader.com, Paul B. Farrell and CBS.MarketWatch Mutual Fund Center, Sam Lockart and CNBC, Debt Counselors of America, Pete Grosz of the Dogs of the Dow, The InsiderTrader, Lisa Glass and Hoover's Online, Mark Hulbert and *The Hulbert Financial Digest*, INVESTools, MindSpring, Tom Murcko (Mayor of Investorville), James B. Stack and InvesTech Research, Carl Soderholm and The On-line Investment Center, Carl Swenlin at Decision Point, The Motley Fool, Nasdaq Stock Market, Inc., Talk City, the U.S. Department of Education, Susan J. LeClair and *U.S.News & World Report*, Bart DiLiddo and VectorVest, and Yahoo! Finance.

Finally, I want to thank my family and friends, who patiently waited for me to finish this work so we could talk again, and my wife, who had to live with me during this project.

Contents

The *Unofficial Guide* Reader's Bill of Rights

We give you more than the official line

Welcome to the *Unofficial Guide* series of Lifestyles titles—books that deliver critical, unbiased information that other books can't or won't reveal—*the inside scoop*. Our goal is to provide you with the *most accessible, useful* information and advice possible. The recommendations we offer in these pages are not influenced by the corporate line of any organization or industry; we give you the hard facts, whether those institutions like them or not. If something is ill-advised or will cause a loss of time and/or money, we'll give you ample warning. And if it is a worthwhile option, we'll let you know that, too.

Armed and ready

Our hand-picked authors confidently and critically report on a wide range of topics that matter to smart readers like you. Our authors are passionate about their subjects, but they have distanced themselves enough to help you be armed and protected, and to help you make educated decisions as you go through your process. It is our intent that, after having read this book, you will avoid the pitfalls everyone else falls into and will get it right the first time.

Don't be fooled by cheap imitations; this is the genuine article *Unofficial Guide* series from IDG Books Worldwide, Inc. You may be familiar with our proven track record of the travel *Unofficial Guides*, which have more than two million copies in print. Each year thousands of travelers—new and old—are armed with a brand new, fully updated edition of the flagship *Unofficial Guide to Walt Disney World*, by Bob Sehlinger. It is our intention here to provide you with the same level of objective authority that Mr. Sehlinger does in his brainchild.

The *Unofficial* panel of experts

Every work in the Lifestyle *Unofficial Guides* is intensively inspected by a team of three top professionals in their fields. These experts review the manuscript for factual accuracy, comprehensiveness, and an insider's determination as to whether the manuscript fulfills the credo in this Reader's Bill of Rights. In other words, our panel ensures that you are, in fact, getting "the inside scoop."

Our pledge

The authors, the editorial staff, and the Unofficial Panel of Experts assembled for *Unofficial Guides* are determined to lay out the most valuable alternatives available for our readers. This dictum means that our writers must be explicit, prescriptive, and, above all, direct. We strive to be thorough and complete, but our goal is not necessarily to have the "most" or "all" of the information on a topic; this is not, after all, an encyclopedia. Our objective is to help you narrow down your options to the best of what is available, unbiased by affiliation with any industry or organization.

In each *Unofficial Guide,* we give you:

- Comprehensive coverage of necessary and vital information

- Authoritative, rigidly fact-checked data

- The most up-to-date insights into trends

- Savvy, sophisticated writing that's also readable

- Sensible, applicable facts and secrets that only an insider knows

Special features

Every book in our series offers the following six special sidebars in the margins that were devised to help you get things done cheaply, efficiently, and smartly.

1. **Timesaver**—Tips and shortcuts that save you time.

2. **Moneysaver**—Tips and shortcuts that save you money.

3. **Watch Out!**—More serious cautions and warnings.

4. **Bright Idea**—General tips and shortcuts to help you find an easier or smarter way to do something.

5. **Quote**—Statements from real people that are intended to be prescriptive and valuable to you.

6. **Unofficially...**—An insider's fact or anecdote.

We also recognize your need to have quick information at your fingertips, and we have thus provided the following comprehensive sections at the back of the book:

1. **Glossary:** Definitions of complicated terminology and jargon.

2. **Resource Guide:** Lists of relevant agencies, associations, institutions, Web sites, and so on.

3. **Recommended Reading List:** Suggested titles that can help you get more in-depth information on related topics.

4. **Important Documents:** "Official" pieces of information you need to refer to, such as government forms.

5. **Important Statistics:** Facts and numbers presented at-a-glance for easy reference.

6. **Index**

Letters, comments, and questions from readers

We strive to continually improve the *Unofficial* series, and input from our readers is a valuable way for us to do that. Many of those who have used the *Unofficial Guide* travel books write to the authors to ask questions, make comments, or share their own discoveries and lessons. For Lifestyle *Unofficial Guides*, we would also appreciate all such correspondence, both positive and critical, and we will make our best efforts to incorporate appropriate readers' feedback and comments in revised editions of this work.

How to write us:

Unofficial Guides
Lifestyle Guides
IDG Books
1633 Broadway
New York, NY 10019

Attention: Reader's Comments

About the Author

Henry F. Robb comes from a tradition of publishing and investing. His great-grandfather, George Horace Lorimer, was the editor of the *Saturday Evening Post* and his grandfather, Graeme Lorimer, an eminent financier in Philadelphia, Pennsylvania. Robb has written and edited a dozen books, including several business and business-related titles, published in Japan. A veteran of online investing, Robb brings a wealth of knowledge and experience to bear on this new financial medium. The author graduated with honors from Tufts University in 1986.

The *Unofficial Guide* Panel of Experts

The *Unofficial* editorial team recognizes that you've purchased this book with the expectation of getting the most authoritative, carefully inspected information currently available. Toward that end, for each and every title in this series, we have selected a minimum of three "official" experts who constitute the Unofficial Panel. These experts painstakingly review the manuscripts to ensure: factual accuracy of all data; inclusion of the most up-to-date and relevant information; and insights drawn from an insider's perspective so that you are armed with all the necessary facts you need—but that the institutions don't want you to know.

For *The Unofficial Guide to Online Investing,* we are proud to introduce the following panel of experts:

Kenan Pollack Kenan Pollack is an Online Producer for Hoover's Online (http://www. hoovers.com), where he creates and manages investing content for the Money Channel and IPO Central. Prior to joining this Austin-based company, Mr. Pollack was with Washington-based *U.S.News & World Report* for six years where, most recently, he worked in the New Media division (http://www.usnews.com). There he helped develop and launch two successful sites for the national newsmagazine.

Before switching to the online world, Mr. Pollack was a general assignment reporter at *U.S.News*, as well as a freelance writer on investing and personal finance for beginners. He is the co-author of *The Real Life Investing Guide* (McGraw-Hill, 1998), a paperback for beginning investors. He currently runs a site for direct interaction with beginning investors at http://www.rlig.com. He has been a guest on CNNfn and radio, and an invited speaker on the topics of investing online.

Mr. Pollack holds a Bachelor of Arts in Political Science from Washington University in St. Louis. He lives with his wife and two cats in Austin, Texas, and can be reached at kenan@rlig.com.

Azhar M. Usman   Mr. Usman has been serving as the President of XOLIA.com since the Company's incorporation in August 1998. Previously, he was a summer associate with the law firm of Michael Best & Friedrich LLP in Milwaukee, Wisconsin, where he worked with both corporate partners and senior litigators. His major projects and research assignments focused on the areas of securities fraud litigation, secured transactions, and insurance defense. In 1998, he researched and authored a paper entitled "I Trade, You Trade, E*TRADE: The Regulatory Response to Online Investing," which traced the securities regulators' reactions to the growing trend of online trading.

Mr. Usman holds a B.A. in Communication from the University of Illinois at Chicago and earned his J.D. cum laude from the University of Minnesota Law School.

Anas Osman   Mr. Osman has served as XOLIA. com's CEO since the company's incorporation in August 1998. Previously, he was with Andersen Consulting, where he worked as a management and technology consultant in its Process Competency, focusing on Business Integration Solutions. His areas of expertise included software, computer languages, insurance certification, and business process re-engineering. In 1998, he spun off his own boutique IT consultancy, Versatile Technologies Group (VTG), specializing in Internet development and e-commerce solutions. Since then he has consulted for several Internet companies, including ApartmentZone.com. Mr. Osman holds a B.A. in Economics from Northwestern University.

William Arnold   William Arnold has spent the last two years working in marketing and corporate communications for the Manhattan-based online brokerage firm A.B. Watley Group Inc. (www.abwatley.com). Before joining A.B. Watley, he worked as an options and derivatives broker in London and Tokyo.

Introduction

More than 4 million people are regularly logging on to the Internet to check quotes, research stocks, and make investments online. And that number is growing daily. It's hard to believe that only four years ago the average person hadn't even heard of online investing. A little over two years ago, people in the brick-and-mortar financial industry scoffed at the idea that online brokers could compete with them.

Not anymore. According to some estimates, some 21 million people will have online accounts by the year 2003. E*Trade, the second largest online broker, signed on an additional 85,000 new customers in the second quarter of 1998, bringing the total to 540,000, up from only 20,000 in 1995. Two million Charles Schwab customers have online accounts; only 336,000 did three years ago. Even more impressive, Schwab's online customers now account for the majority of the company's total trading business. Online brokers handle around 253,000 trades a day, which is approximately 10 percent of all trades executed in the United States.

So why the stampede to online investing? People are making money and having fun doing it online. The Internet is allowing people to educate themselves about investing, research potential investments themselves, build portfolios that fit their individual needs, and organize their finances in a way that was previously impossible. The Internet is allowing ordinary people to reclaim control of their financial lives.

Online investing has become so much easier than it used to be. In the "old" days (a few years ago), you needed special software, a souped-up computer, and lots of time—it was a very slow process. Nowadays, all you need is a computer that meets basic standards and a modem, and you're ready to go. Investing online is also fast—faster than placing trades the old-fashioned way. You simply log on and enter your trade, and your order is off to the trading floor. No more waiting for your broker to get back from lunch—or even waiting until the next morning if you get a great idea after hours. You can place an online trade literally any time of the day or night.

With the number of online brokers (now more than 98) steadily increasing, competition for customers has become intense, leading to better services across the board. Most sites now offer research, news, stock charts, technical graphs, and an ever-expanding array of investment vehicles. Discover Direct and DLJDirect give their customers access to research that their parent companies, Morgan Stanley Dean Witter and Donaldson Lufkin & Jeanrette, respectively, once reserved for big institutional customers. But even the discount online sites such as Suretrade are now providing charts and earnings estimates. Some online brokers are even educating investors. E*Trade offers a stock-picking game designed to sharpen your stock selection skills. With everything brokerage sites are offering, in addition to the wealth of other financial sites available on the Web, online investors now have access to almost as much information as professional brokers.

Online investing has also become much cheaper. Over the past two years, commissions for Web trades have fallen 70 percent, from $52.89 a trade on average to $15.75. One deep discount online broker, Web Street Securities, even offers NASDAQ trades for free! Full-service firms, by contrast, still charge hundreds of dollars a trade. Could this be why so many investors are abandoning them? Exactly how many have left is uncertain, but at least 100,000 of Schwab's new customers in 1998 came from full-service firms. E*Trade also reports that 20 percent of its customers are defectors from other firms. This exodus has definitely grabbed the attention of the old-line brokerage houses, which are now lumbering belatedly into the online industry themselves. Merrill Lynch, the granddaddy of the full-service firms, and Prudential Securities have already taken the plunge. But many pundits feel that the move online by the big boys is designed more to stave off further losses from their customer base than to compete with true online brokerages for true online traders.

Investing for the new millennium

Online investing is the wave of the future. It is part of the general movement taking place among individuals who are assuming more responsibility for their financial lives. Gone are the days when people worked for the same company for a lifetime and retirement was simply taken care of by sizable pension checks. Now companies are incorporating 401(k) plans, and each employee has to decide for himself how to invest that money. People are also being forced to save more of their take-home pay, in part because the future of Social Security is in question. As people's responsibility for their financial security increases, so does their desire to understand and take control of their finances.

Contributing to this move toward investor independence is the concern over the ever-changing market picture. With stock prices at historically high valuations and markets exhibiting unprecedented instability, many individuals have become uncomfortable with blindly buying or selling whatever their broker recommends. This is doubly true for investors who have lost money or not done as well as they should have during the bull market of the 1980s and 1990s.

Growing distrust in financial professionals is also driving investors to take matters into their own hands. Confidence not just in the ability but also in the integrity of brokers appears to be nearing all-time lows—perhaps not without reason. In March 1999, the television program *20/20* aired a damaging exposé on the use of heroin among financial advisers working for major full-service brokerage houses on Wall Street. Interviewed were former brokers who admitted to stealing customers' money to fund their drug habit. Also interviewed were former customers whose life savings had gone up in smoke. Stories such as this fuel the flames of resentment some people already feel toward their full-service broker for charging such large commissions. More investors are waking up to the fact that even the most scrupulous of brokers, paid commissions for executing trades, have an incentive to see customers buy and sell often, even if doing so fails to improve the performance of their portfolios.

Mutual funds are also coming under scrutiny. Is everything they're telling investors the unbiased truth? Maybe not. After all, mutual funds are businesses that want investor's money. As such, they have a vested interest in shaping the investment philosophy of the general public. For example, why would a mutual fund company ever recommend that its customers sell? Think about it. What company wants its customers to dump its products? Hence the mantra we always hear coming out of the industry: History shows that buying and holding is the best overall strategy; it's best to simply ignore market fluctuations. But people are starting to realize that there is, in fact, a time to buy and a time to sell mutual funds.

Where's the beef?

The preponderance of misinformation, coupled with the inherent unpredictability of security prices, makes investing both online and offline a risky venture for the uninitiated. Much of what people have heard, read, or been told about investing is simply untrue. Much of the advice available online is also unsound or deliberately misleading. This book separates the wheat from the chaff by giving you the factual, unbiased information you need to invest online with savvy and confidence.

The key to successful investing is not just figuring out how to make money, but how to make money in a way that you're comfortable with. There simply is no single right or best investment or investment strategy for everyone. We must all find our own investment path. This is why no one can rightfully dictate what you should and shouldn't do with your money—what to buy, when to buy, what to sell, or when to sell. Online investing is about reclaiming your right to making your own investment decisions.

With that in mind, we strive in this book to teach you how to decide what kind of an investor you are and what investment vehicles and strategies are appropriate for you. We also teach you how to choose an online broker, how to execute all kinds of trades, and how to solicit advice. When you've learned how to make money, we teach you how to hold on to it with discussions on how to control risk, how to manage taxes, and how to insure yourself. A wealth of valuable Web sites related to each topic are supplied throughout. This book was written with the intention of preparing you for online investing so that your experience as an online investor will be both pleasurable and profitable.

Laying the Foundation

PART I

GET THE SCOOP ON...
The myriad advantages of online
investing ▪ Some drawbacks to online investing
▪ How safe is it? ▪ The Online Investor
Inventory

The Pros and Cons of Online Investing

Right now, at the turn of the millennium, more than 10 million people are investing online. And to hear friends, colleagues, and the media talk about it, you'd think it was a perfect world. You've doubtless heard about the guy who invested a few thousand dollars on Dell or Yahoo! only a few months ago and is tens of thousands of dollars richer for it today. You probably have a friend or a relative who has been successfully trading on the Internet for some time now. And you may have even heard about the infamous *day traders*, that new breed of investor who makes a living buying and selling stocks on his own computer several times a day. Why, day traders only have to "work" a couple times a week!

It all sounds so simple. But here's the rub: The only investment strategy that will work consistently well over a lifetime is one built on sound investment principles. Like anything else in life, making money

Chapter 1

3

consistently in the stock market is difficult and requires knowledge and discipline. But what about Uncle Harry? And the guy down the hall at work who made a bundle on high-tech stocks? And the day traders? Short-term success does not an investor make. The United States has been enjoying the greatest bull market, or period of upward price movement, in its history, starting in August 1982 and running through to the present. The past 18 years have been a time of unprecedented upward movement in market averages, a time when most investments that initially went the wrong way would eventually turn around. It doesn't take skill to invest in a market that only moves in one direction.

Unfortunately, bear markets, periods when stock prices move down, are a fact of life, and when the stock market finally does move into a downward phase, you will see many a former stock prodigy turn stooge. Truly sophisticated investors are capable of handling both up and down markets—they can play both offense and defense. *Making* money is only half the task before us; the other is holding on to it.

The medium of online investing itself is far from perfect. From September 1997 to September 1998, 1,100 people filed complaints with the Security and Exchange Commission (SEC) about problems they had trading online. This was four times as many complaints as the year before. And in the period from April 1998 to April 1999, the number of complaints to the SEC increased 330 percent. So before you rush to sign up with an online broker, you need to be apprised of both the opportunities and the risks. In this chapter, we will do just that. We will also take a look at how safe investing online really is and what areas of your personality might get in your way.

Watch Out!
Many books on investing promise to teach how to make a lot of money quickly. These get-rich-quick strategies are pure hype. Making money consistently in stocks is hard work, and getting rich takes time.

The striking advantages of online investing

The number of people investing online is taking off, and this trend will undoubtedly continue. Unlike fads that come and go with changes in popular sentiment, online investing is growing on the foundation of common sense. Let's take a look at some of the reasons for the steady growth of online investing in the next sections.

Low cost

For one thing, investing online is cheap. While placing orders to buy and sell stocks through traditional brokers can cost several hundred dollars per trade, placing trades online can cost as little as $7 per trade. These kinds of savings simply cannot be ignored.

Let's say you want to place an order to buy 10 shares of America Online (AOL) at $125 per share. That transaction, placed for you by a traditional full-service broker, could cost you $150 (indeed, some full-service firms charge considerably more). That's $150 you must pay the broker for the service of placing the trade for you (and possibly for having recommended the stock in the first place). The same trade placed online could cost you as little as $10. You save $140! Now, let's say the price of AOL increases to $165 per share, and you decide to sell. In theory, you've made $400 on the stock. But you must pay your full-service broker another $150 to sell the stock, bringing your total broker fee to $300 and reducing your net gain to $100. Making that same round trip online would have cost you just $20, saving you $280. That's money in the bank, or money that could be used to buy additional shares

Unofficially...
It is estimated
that by the year
2002, more
than 14 million
people will be
investing online,
an increase of
466 percent in
five years!

of the stock. If you're planning to own stock in 10 different companies, you'll be paying commissions to buy and sell each of these, so you can see how using an online broker could save you thousands of dollars.

Flexibility

The low cost of placing trades begets another great advantage of online investing: increased flexibility. Flexibility in investing means the ability to move in and out of positions freely. Let's say, for example, that you purchased 50 shares of Dell Computer online at $35 per share, and the stock immediately started to move down. By selling the stock at, say, $32, you would realize a net loss of about $170 ($150 in reduced stock value, plus $10 each for buying and selling). Buying and selling the same stock through a full-service broker, however, would have created a net loss of $320 (at $150 per trade). This is expensive. And the more expensive it is to place trades, the less inclined you are to sell, even if you feel that the stock has soured. Trading online allows you to get in and out of stocks quickly if you choose, without having to suffer a substantial financial penalty for doing so.

Speed and simplicity

Another terrific advantage of investing online is that it's fast and easy. There's simply no wait if you want to place a trade: Just turn on your computer, log on to your online broker, and key in the order. It's as easy as 1-2-3. With a traditional broker, you may have difficulty just reaching her—she could be on another line, out of the office, at lunch, or on vacation. Who has time for delays like that? As an online investor, you can place your trades at literally any time of the day or night.

Imagine that you come home from work, have some dinner, roll up your sleeves, and spend an hour or so on the Internet analyzing a pharmaceutical company you like. Satisfied that the company meets your criteria, you decide to purchase 100 shares of its stock at tomorrow's opening bell. But it's 9:30pm. Not a problem. As an online investor, you simply log on to your online broker's site, place the trade, and go to bed. The order will be automatically executed at tomorrow's market opening.

Selling is also a snap online. If one of your stocks turns down and you want to sell, you can place a sell order, and the trade will be executed almost immediately. Let's say you owned 25 shares of Coca-Cola, which you purchased at $50 a share in September 1997. The price rose to $75 in August 1998 and then began moving down steadily. On September 9, 1998, worried about the stock, you logged on to the Internet and watched Coke's share price drop below $60. You decided to sell, wanting to lock in profits. You placed the sell order online at 2:00pm, and the order was filled at $60 per share at 2:10pm During the time it would have taken you to reach a traditional broker and place the order, the share price might have fallen to $59 or less. As an online investor, when you make a decision to do something, it gets done.

As an online investor, there's an overriding sense that you're in control of your own destiny—you're in the driver's seat. This is a great feeling. No one is telling you what to do, or even what you *should* do. Traditional brokers not only place trades for you, but they also advise you on what trades to place. This is why their services cost so much money: You're getting expert analysis, opinion, and (supposedly) personalized advice.

Timesaver
With online accounts, there is no need to call your broker for account balances. Your account is automatically updated, if not instantly, then at the end of each market day, and you can check your holdings and balances any time.

Bright Idea
Where to get capital for your online investments? Try paying yourself first! As soon as your paycheck comes in each month, take 10% off the top and put it in your investment account. This will ensure that you don't blow all your spending money on nonessential items.

The catch is that brokers and the firms they work for don't make money when you make money; they make money only when you place a trade. This means that full-service brokers have a vested interest in convincing you to buy and sell often. They need those commissions! An unscrupulous broker might call a client and recommend selling a high-tech mutual fund only to turn around and recommend that the client buy a different high-tech fund. Why? The broker's view on the market hasn't changed; he just wants the fat commissions he'll make on the sale of one fund and the purchase of another. And if a client is reluctant to take a broker's advice, the broker will usually urge the client to do what he suggests. Online investors, on the other hand, avoid being pressured into doing anything they don't want to do with their money.

Unlimited information

Online investors also have the luxury of unlimited access to information. You can access your online account as many times as you like at any time of the day or night to see exactly how your holdings are performing. Again, no need to chase down your broker and get him to fax you something—something that may not be up-to-the-minute. As an online investor, you can get current stock quotes throughout the day. In fact, there's really no limit to the amount of financial and investment-related information you can access online: recent news about the companies you're interested in; charts showing how those companies' stocks have performed over the last day, five days, three months, year, or more; profiles of those companies, explaining what they do; statistics showing how those companies are doing; and much, much more.

Most online brokers post their research right on their Web site, so it's easy to get the information you need before placing a trade. And many sites provide research tools you can use to select investments that meet your personal criteria. In addition to all the stuff available on the brokers' sites, services such as CNET Investor, Yahoo! Finance, CBS MarketWatch, and CNNfn provide comprehensive investing information.

Here's a list are some of the great things you can access online:

- Global market news and commentary
- Economic news
- Real-time stock quotes
- Charts of stock prices
- Price histories
- Company news
- Company profiles
- Annual reports
- Stock research tools
- Educational materials
- Advice
- Financial planning tools
- Glossaries of financial terms
- Free financial software

What does unlimited access to unlimited information mean to you? It means that you can research potential investments yourself at your leisure. All the information that was previously available only to professional stockbrokers is now available to you at the click of a mouse. Let's say everyone around you has been talking about Amazon.com, the online

Unofficially...
The wide range of information available to you as an online investor empowers you to make investment decisions that are appropriate for you as an individual.

bookseller, and you've been seriously thinking about purchasing the stock. But before you do, you log on to Yahoo! Finance (http://quote.yahoo.com/), a financial Web site, where you can look closely at what kind of a stock Amazon.com really is.

A quick look at the one-year price chart shows you that this stock, while on a long-term upward trend, is also very volatile. On a particular day in the autumn of 1999, for example, the stock dropped more than $31 per share (−16.48 percent). With this in mind, you decide to stay away from Amazon.com because you know you don't have the stomach for that kind of price fluctuation. (You never did like roller coasters much.)

The disadvantages of online investing

There are two sides to every story, and though the advantages of investing online are many, the disadvantages and potential drawbacks are very real.

You're on your own

Perhaps the greatest potential negative you need to consider is that you'll be investing a lot of money—possibly your life savings—without the guidance of a professional. The various advantages of firing your broker notwithstanding, brokers actually can be very helpful, and many investors would feel lost without one. Would you? You have to be honest with yourself on this point. Are you an independent person? Do you enjoy personal finance, and are you good at it? If you bought this book, chances are good that you have at least a passing interest in taking control of your own investments. But doing this successfully requires fortitude.

One of the nice things about having a broker is being able to talk over your investment ideas with a trained professional. But as an online trader, you won't have a warm, knowledgeable person on the other end of the phone to support or disapprove of your ideas. Nor will you have anyone to help you generate ideas. And if the stocks you purchase turn down, you won't have anyone to blame, nor will there be anyone to reassure you, explain it to you, or tell you what to do. One of the most difficult decisions independent investors have to make is when to sell a stock and when to hold on. The hard reality of online investing is that you have to be emotionally prepared to lose money sometimes, and you have to be prepared to go through this, by and large, by yourself.

Fortunately, several paths are open to online investors who do not want to go it totally alone. One popular route is to join an investment club. Investment clubs are groups of independent investors who pool their assets and agree upon certain stocks to purchase. There are also numerous online investment discussion groups, where investors exchange ideas, and numerous sites that offer stock recommendations and advice. The trick, though, is to find someone who is truly talented to get advice from. (In Chapter 10, "Getting Advice Online," we'll talk more about how to get sound advice.)

Getting overconfident

A related problem with online investing is that it's easy to get carried away with the excitement of it all and make unwise decisions. Without a broker to serve as a buffer between your bright ideas and the unforgiving market, online investors are vulnerable to taking unnecessary risks and even developing a gambler's mentality. Investors with little knowledge

> 66
> You must do the thing you think you cannot do.
> —Eleanor Roosevelt
> 99

or experience (in other words, people who don't know what they're doing) are getting online, placing ill-conceived trades, and losing large sums of money.

It's not difficult to imagine how this happens. An amateur investor purchases 100 shares of a high-flying stock such as Sun Microsystems at $120 per share. The stock backs down to $110, then $100, and then skyrockets to $140. The investor sells for a nifty profit. The same pattern repeats itself with another stock, and another. Ah, the sweet taste of success and the smell of money.

Confident now in his stock-picking ability and his overall investing prowess, our hero buys 200 shares of Rite Aid Corp. at $50 a share. The stocks falls to $45, then $40 and $35, but instead of turning up again, the stock moves still lower, to $32, then $30. Convinced that the stock has bottomed, our investor buys an additional 100 shares because the stock is now "cheap." The stock languishes for the next few months in the $30–$35 range before continuing down. This investor has already lost $4,000 and has compounded the problem by buying additional shares. Frustrated with this trade and still pumped up from prior successes, our trader, on a hunch, buys 200 shares of 3Com Corp. at $45 a share. A variation of the scenario with Rite Aid repeats itself.

Certainly, these stocks may eventually turn around, but when? Time is money, and there are no guarantees. Just as important, how does our investor feel after these trouncings? Not so good, I bet.

Aside from the dangerous tendency to follow hunches about price movements, the amateur online trader can easily become addicted to the very act of buying and selling. Buy/sell, buy/sell, buy/sell—like the slot machines at the casinos, online investing approached as a game can become a form of entertainment. Some people get lucky, but most end up losing a bundle this way. When online investors fall into the gambler's trap, they often wind up losing their entire nest egg.

When the brokerages blow it

Perhaps the problem that has gained the most notoriety and attention in the press is that of online brokerage Web sites crashing. Nothing strikes fear into the hearts of online investors like not being able to log on to their broker's site, especially when they want to sell. And this does happen. Thousands of online investors with E*Trade, then the third largest online broker, received the following message when trying to access the site on February 3, 1999:

> *Your request cannot be completed. Please try again or contact E*TRADE Customer Service at service2@etrade.com. Thank you.*

Problems continued into the next day, and the next, caused the first two days by excessive trading volume (known as volume breakdown) and the third day by a software glitch. As a result of the crashes, countless investors were locked out of their accounts and could not buy or sell stocks for significant blocks of time. Many claimed that this cost them a lot of money, and one customer filed a class-action suit against E*Trade for her losses.

This was not the first time E*Trade made the news. In November 1997, unsatisfied investors hit E*Trade with a class-action suit claiming that the company took on more accounts than its system

Watch Out!
What do site crashes mean to you as an online investor? They mean that volume breakdowns and software glitches can and do occur, even to the largest online brokers; this can negatively affect your returns and throw off your trading strategy.

could handle. In the suit, the plaintiffs cited the wild trading days of October 27 and 28 of that year, when the markets posted their largest one-day drop (–554.26) and one-day gain (+337.10) in history. The trading volume on both days was astronomical, and the resultant delays in logging on to online trading sites such as E*Trade cost investors time and money.

E*Trade is certainly not alone in committing these faux pas. On February 8, 1999, the entire Ameritrade Web site—as well as its touch-tone service, which allows customers to get stock prices and make trades—crashed. And on February 24 of that year, Charles Schwab's main Web site for online investing went down, having crashed only a week before. Charles Schwab, moreover, is not a small start-up company—it's the largest online brokerage.

How are online investors compensated in such cases? After the October 1997 debacle, E*Trade sent out an apology letter, but that obviously wasn't enough to satisfy the customers who filed suit, nor was it enough to placate the customers locked out of their accounts in February 1999. These people want their money back! E*Trade has a stated policy in these cases that the orders in question will be processed based on the stock price at whatever time the order was placed, allowing for a "realistic" time to place the trade. But what (and who) defines realistic?

Some brokerage firms such as Datek, the fourth largest, have offered actual monetary compensation to customers for undue delays in executing orders. Other online brokerages have instituted similar policies, but on the whole, this is still an area where full-service brokerages outshine the new kids on the block. For example, Smith Barney will match the price of a stock purchase to the minute the order was placed, as will Merrill Lynch—no questions asked. In fact, Merrill Lynch paid close to $10 million dollars in April 1999 to customers who placed more than 3,000 trades on a particularly heavy day and suffered losses as a result of delays.

Even as online brokerages scramble to atone for failing, at times, to deliver promised service, they strenuously defend themselves. Ameritrade said in April 1999 that users who had any difficulty logging on to its site had five other options at their disposal: touch-tone phone, live brokers, fax orders, personal digital assistance connected through a direct-dial system, and a DOS-based PC system. Now, that's multilevel access! Said Ameritrade president Mike Anderson, "Look at it this way: We don't call ourselves an online firm. I consider us to be deep discounters. Only 30 percent of our trades are placed through the Internet. If I'm trading through a full-service broker, how many channels do I have? One: I have to call my broker."

The truth is that online brokerage sites go down infrequently, so this doesn't pose a major obstacle to investing online. The best way to protect yourself against all kinds of computer failure, though, is to make sure your online broker also allows you to place orders by phone, fax, or other medium, like Ameritrade. Another good strategy is to open online accounts with several brokers. That way, if one is down, you can simply log on to another (although you'll only be able to trade the securities you own in that account)

Other shortcomings of the online brokerages

Uncertainty with order confirmation can be another drawback of investing online. Depending on the broker, filled orders are confirmed by fax, phone, e-mail, or U.S. mail. The problem with any sort of a delay in receiving an order confirmation is that if a mistake has been made, it becomes more difficult and costly to correct as time goes by. Complaints about delays or difficulties in receiving confirmations are frequently received by the SEC. Before signing up with an online broker, it's prudent to check with the broker about how confirmations are sent.

Online investors must also contend with the fact that many online brokers offer only certain types of investments. While it is possible to buy and sell individual stocks with any online broker, the least-expensive brokers don't even offer mutual funds, let alone bonds, precious metals, or other investment vehicles. Of course, you can buy virtually any type of investment through a full-service brokerage. It's vital, then, that you consider what types of securities you're interested in buying, and what types of securities are available for purchase through an online broker, before you send that broker a check.

People are complaining

According to the SEC, here are the three most frequent complaints against online brokerages:

- Failure to process investors' buy or sell orders, or delays in executing trades

- Investors having trouble getting into their online trading accounts or reaching their broker by e-mail or telephone

- Errors in processing trading orders

Here's a good individual example of the first type of complaint, a delay in executing an order. A California man placed an order online in May 1998 to buy 1,000 shares of EntreMed, a biomedical company whose stock has been extremely unstable. He figured the order would be executed promptly near $13 a share, which was the price of EntreMed at the time he placed the order. Unfortunately, though, there was a delay. By the time the man's order was executed, the price was at $83 a share—and that was the price he was charged!

According to the SEC, the complaints received are evenly spread among the 100 or so online brokerage firms. Incredibly, one of the SEC's investor assistance specialists personally checks out each and every complaint by contacting the online brokerage firm involved. If you have a problem with your online broker, however, the first thing you should do is call your broker and try to resolve it directly. If that fails, you should write to the brokerage firm's compliance officer. If still no resolution is reached, you should send a copy of the complaint letter to the SEC's investor education office, and they will definitely look into it for you.

Sometimes it's the investor's fault

A very common mistake made by novice online investors is to assume that the price of a stock displayed on the computer is the current price of the stock. It's not necessarily. Although real-time quotes are becoming more common, there is often a 15- to 20-minute lag time between the stock prices you see on your screen and the actual market prices at that moment. How can this affect your profit picture? It probably won't because you will most likely be placing your trades in the evening when markets are closed and prices are no longer changing. If you are buying and selling online throughout the trading day, however, you must be aware that if you place an

Unofficially...
The SEC investor education office can be reached at 450 5th Street, NW, Washington, D.C. 20549. (The agency's Web site is www.sec.gov.).

order to buy or sell a stock at the price you see, the
order may not be filled—or, not at that price—at no
fault to the online broker.

Another common mistake online investors make
is to accidentally place an order twice, buying twice
as many shares of a stock as they had planned. This
may happen if for some reason an investor thinks
the order didn't take the first time it was placed. If
the brokerage sends trade confirmations only by
U.S. mail, the mistake may not be discovered until
well after the two trades have been executed—in
certain industries, plenty of time for the stock price
to have changed dramatically. Now, if the stock went
up, terrific! But if it went down—oh, no! And to
think that some people don't even *look* at their trade
confirmations…

The hidden costs

The final issue to consider before rushing out and
buying your online trading software is *costs*. On this
issue, it pays to read the fine print. Some online brokers actually charge extra if you call in an order
instead of placing it online, and you may have to
demand the standard commission fee if you're calling only because you were unable to log on to their
site. Some online brokers charge more for limit
orders (orders in which you specify the price at
which you want to buy or sell a stock).

The other kinds of costs to consider are opportunity costs. An opportunity cost is the cost of pursuing one opportunity at the expense of another.
For instance, there is no question that if you decide
to take over investing your nest egg, you'll be spending more of your time researching, analyzing, and
monitoring your investments than you were before.
(This is what you used to pay your broker the big

bucks for.) The time you take to do this has to come from somewhere—your sleep time, your work time, your leisure time, your family time, your TV time, your reading time, or whatever it was that you used to do before you became an online investor. Depending to a large extent on whether you'll be following someone else's advice or doing all your own research and stock-picking, the investment in the time you will need to be successful at investing online could range anywhere from 10 minutes a day to several hours.

Online investing also has opportunity costs in the form of the energy you will spend—both mental and emotional. Extensive analysis of securities can leave you feeling burned out, with little left over for your spouse and kids, who may really need your input on things. Emotionally, too, online investing can be taxing; you may find yourself on an emotional seesaw, as the prices of your holdings go up and down. It's important to limit the amount of emotional capital you spend on your newfound avocation and to keep your priorities straight. Don't let online investing become your whole life; it should always be just a part of it.

Is it safe?

The nightmare: After weeks of arduous research, you select an online broker that you feel is perfect in every way for you, and you fire off a check for $10,000 to open an account. Three days later, you receive an e-mail from your broker of choice congratulating you on successfully opening an account and wishing you well as you embark on your online investing career. After several days of research and deep thought, you log on to your account to place

> 66
> The great dividing line between success and failure can be expressed in five words: I did not have time.
> —Anonymous
> 99

you first online trade, only to discover that your account balance is zero! There must be some mistake, you think. You immediately call the broker, only to meet with repeated busy signals and, later, recordings. Finally, you get through, only to be greeted by an unfriendly, aloof computer-world guy who lacks any kind of interpersonal skills. He sounds a bit skeptical of your story, but says he'll "look into it" and "get back to you." You're stymied. What should you do?

In a world where people are wary about ordering a $20 book online, investing your nest egg sounds pretty scary. What if a hacker gets into your account and your funds simply evaporate without a trace? Why would anyone in their right mind risk their money this way? Well, because the reality is that online investing is very, very safe. Several layers of protection exist to ensure that your account and your privacy will never be violated.

Checking out the security system

Every online trading site employs three or four security mechanisms. The first level of security is the so-called firewall. A *firewall* is a special type of software designed specifically to keep intruders out. These programs are extremely sophisticated and very difficult to outsmart. Another technique employed by online brokers is to monitor account activity. When any kind of "suspicious" activity occurs, as judged by the broker, the individual using the account will be expelled and the account holder will be contacted for user verification.

Still another layer of protection comes from the use of encryption by all online brokers. Encryption is the process of changing data into a form that can be read only by the intended receiver. To read the data, the receiver must have the proper decryption key. All online brokers require that you use a secure Web browser—Microsoft Explorer, Netscape Navigator, or America Online 3.0 browser—that encrypts whatever information you send over the Net. The brokers, in turn, use secure servers, which enable them to decode the information you send.

All instructions between customers and online brokers are encrypted. This means that when you send an order to a broker, the entire message is transformed into a incomprehensible jumble of letters, numbers, and symbols. So even if a hacker were to intercept the transmission, he would not be able to decipher it. Only your broker, the intended receiver of the transmission, has the decoder. One commonly employed encryption system, data encryption standard (DES), was developed by IBM and has been certified by the U.S. government to send any material that is not classified as top secret. This encryption system provides excellent security for online trading sites.

Just to be sure, though, online brokers commonly employ still another level of security. It's the one most of us are familiar with: the good old password. Every online broker requires that you enter your secret password (and account number) to access your account. It's that simple. Unless you choose to give the information to someone else, no one but you will know your personal identification number (PIN) or your account number; without those two numbers, absolutely no one can get into your account.

PIN safety

You should think about a couple things regarding your PIN and account number, however. First, don't

Moneysaver
You do not have to pay for the most popular Web browsers— Netscape Navigator or Microsoft Explorer. Just go to their Web sites (www. netscape.com or www.microsoft. com) and download a free copy.

put them in plain view. (Incredibly, some people just write them on a Post-it and stick it on their computer!) It's best to memorize at least your password and keep a back-up hard copy in a secret place in case you forget. Second, consider not using the same password for all your accounts. If someone were to get your PIN for one account, he would hold the key to your financial universe. Third, consider choosing a password that isn't too obvious. The first numbers a hacker will try are combinations of your birthday, your phone number, your wife's birthday, or some other potentially significant numbers to you. The best passwords are random, or at least not easily guessed by someone else.

Other protocols to protect you

Your online account is also protected by certain protocols. No one—not even you—can order an online broker to send you money out of your account without providing the broker with written authorization. So, the would-be hacker also has to be able to forge your signature to get his hands on your money. But just to be sure, if your broker did receive such a letter, the broker would contact you personally to verify the transaction before it was carried out. If a hacker got into your account, then, all he could really do is buy and sell securities; he could never cash them in.

Feeling secure yet? You should be. There just haven't been any security problems to speak of with online brokerages, and for good reason: Online brokers realize that their very livelihood, like that of the airline industry, depends on their safety record. They understand that people will not trade online if there is significant doubt in their minds about the security of their funds. The general consensus is that no single security system can keep out all the hackers, but a combination of three or more definitely does the job. While no one wants to claim that their site is 100 percent secure (this would be too great a challenge for the hackers to pass up!), the reality is that the security of these sites is, for all intents and purposes, airtight.

The NASD

Before signing on with a broker, however, it can't hurt to ask about the security measures they employ. You should also confirm that they are members of the National Association of Security Dealers (NASD). NASD dealers must carry Securities Investor Protection Corporation (SIPC) coverage, which insures the value of your securities in the unlikely event that the broker goes bankrupt. The SIPC provides up to $500,000 of protection for your securities and $100,000 for cash. Some online brokerages carry additional insurance. E*Trade, for example, provides its clients with an additional $99.5 million of insurance on securities.

Do you have what it takes?

Having taken an honest look at the pros and cons of online investing, as well as the safety issues, you are now ready to take an honest look at yourself. The following test was designed to help you evaluate some of your strengths and weaknesses as they may relate to your success potential in online investing.

The ideal online investor has good money management skills and is organized. He is self-disciplined, shows emotional maturity, and has more than a passing interest in and knowledge about finance and investing. Most importantly, he is able to admit his mistakes and learn from them. If you

Watch Out! Remember, no amount of insurance protects you against a drop in the value of your investments.

don't possess all these qualities, join the club. If you have next to none of them, however, you need to be especially cautious as you move into the online realm.

THE ONLINE INVESTOR PERSONALITY INVENTORY

Instructions: Circle the number corresponding to the responses you feel best answer the questions. Answer the questions as honestly as you can.

KNOWLEDGE AND INTEREST

1. Stocks are generally riskier than bonds, but historically they produce a higher total return.
   1. Strongly agree
   2. Agree
   3. Neither agree nor disagree
   4. Disagree
   5. Strongly disagree

2. I enjoy reading books and articles related to business, finance, and/or personal finance.
   1. Strongly agree
   2. Agree
   3. Neither agree nor disagree
   4. Disagree
   5. Strongly disagree

3. It is possible to lose 100% of the money that I invest in a stock.
   1. Strongly agree
   2. Agree
   3. Neither agree nor disagree
   4. Disagree
   5. Strongly disagree

4. Financial cable channels, market news, and business stories tend to capture my interest.

1. Strongly agree
2. Agree
3. Neither agree nor disagree
4. Disagree
5. Strongly disagree

5. Mutual funds pool investors' money to invest in a large number of securities.
   1. Strongly agree
   2. Agree
   3. Neither agree nor disagree
   4. Disagree
   5. Strongly disagree

Now add up the numbers of the answers you circled to get your total score, and write this number in the space provided.   _____

The best possible score is a 5, and the worst possible score is a 25. This quiz gives some indication of your level of interest in and knowledge about finance and investing. Clearly, both interest and knowledge are important for your success as an online investor. If you scored between 5 and 10, you are probably on the right track in this department. If you scored more than a 10, however, you need to work on this area.

SELF-DISCIPLINE

1. You planned to work one evening, but you discover that a movie you really want to see is on TV. You work anyway.
   1. Strongly agree
   2. Agree
   3. Neither agree nor disagree
   4. Disagree
   5. Strongly disagree

2. You have decided to only eat sweets on weekends, but a friend offers you a piece of cake on Wednesday. You do not eat the cake.

    1. Strongly agree
    2. Agree
    3. Neither agree nor disagree
    4. Disagree
    5. Strongly disagree

3. You have decided never to spend the money in your savings account, but you find the stereo of your dreams on sale, and you need the cash. You do not buy the stereo.

    1. Strongly agree
    2. Agree
    3. Neither agree nor disagree
    4. Disagree
    5. Strongly disagree

4. You have planned to call an unpleasant client or acquaintance to discuss something important, but on the appointed day, you really don't feel like making the call. You call anyway.

    1. Strongly agree
    2. Agree
    3. Neither agree nor disagree
    4. Disagree
    5. Strongly disagree

5. You decided not to spend more than $500 on gambling in Las Vegas, but you hit your limit with a full day left in your vacation. You do not gamble on your last day.

    1. Strongly agree
    2. Agree
    3. Neither agree nor disagree
    4. Disagree
    5. Strongly disagree

Add up the numbers of the answers you circled, and write this number in the space provided. _____

If you scored between 5 and 10, you are probably a very self-disciplined person. This trait will serve you well as you move into the online trading realm, where distractions and temptations abound. If you scored more than a 10, you need to stay aware of a tendency you may have to stray from your original plans and commitments.

EMOTIONAL MATURITY

1. If I were unable to buy a stock for the price I wanted, I would accept this calmly.
   1. Strongly agree
   2. Agree
   3. Neither agree nor disagree
   4. Disagree
   5. Strongly disagree

2. If I were losing money on a stock, I would accept this calmly and stick to my original strategy.
   1. Strongly agree
   2. Agree
   3. Neither agree nor disagree
   4. Disagree
   5. Strongly disagree

3. If I won the lottery, I would carefully consider what to do with the money before making big plans, big purchases, and significant changes in my lifestyle.
   1. Strongly agree
   2. Agree
   3. Neither agree nor disagree
   4. Disagree
   5. Strongly disagree

4. If I needed a significant amount of money quickly, I would not try to make that money at the casinos or on the stock market.

1. Strongly agree
2. Agree
3. Neither agree nor disagree
4. Disagree
5. Strongly disagree

5. If friends and fellow investors alike were selling their stocks in a panic, I would calmly assess the situation and decide for myself what to do about my own stocks.
   1. Strongly agree
   2. Agree
   3. Neither agree nor disagree
   4. Disagree
   5. Strongly disagree

Add up the numbers of the answers you circled, and write this number in the space provided. _____

A score between 5 and 10 indicates a relatively high degree of emotional maturity, a quality essential to successful online investing. A higher score indicates that this is an area that you need to be aware of as a potential Achilles heel.

ADMITTING MISTAKES AND LEARNING FROM THEM

1. I am quite willing to admit that I am wrong.
   1. Strongly agree
   2. Agree
   3. Neither agree nor disagree
   4. Disagree
   5. Strongly disagree

2. When I make a mistake, I make a special effort to learn from it and change so as not to make the same mistake again.

Watch Out!
It's important not to let yourself get carried away with your emotions as an investor. The two great banes of investors through the ages have been fear and greed.

   1. Strongly agree

   2. Agree

   3. Neither agree nor disagree

   4. Disagree

   5. Strongly disagree

3. I never hear from people close to me "You never say you're sorry" or "You think you're always right."

   1. Strongly agree

   2. Agree

   3. Neither agree nor disagree

   4. Disagree

   5. Strongly disagree

4. I think it is more important to be flexible than to stick to your original decision.

   1. Strongly agree

   2. Agree

   3. Neither agree nor disagree

   4. Disagree

   5. Strongly disagree

5. I can think of at least two things I am doing better in my life now than I was a few years ago.

   1. Strongly agree

   2. Agree

   3. Neither agree nor disagree

   4. Disagree

   5. Strongly disagree

Add up the numbers of the answers you circled, and write this number in the space provided. _____

A score between 5 and 10 indicates a relatively high level of humility, an important trait for online investors. Investors who cannot admit that they have made a bad investment and dump it are destined to lose a lot of money online. If you tend to be a bit strong-headed, be careful not to let this demon wipe you out.

ORGANIZATIONAL SKILLS

1. I am a very organized person.
    1. Strongly agree
    2. Agree
    3. Neither agree nor disagree
    4. Disagree
    5. Strongly disagree

2. I never forget appointments.
    1. Strongly agree
    2. Agree
    3. Neither agree nor disagree
    4. Disagree
    5. Strongly disagree

3. I am never late for appointments.
    1. Strongly agree
    2. Agree
    3. Neither agree nor disagree
    4. Disagree
    5. Strongly disagree

4. I never misplace important documents.
    1. Strongly agree
    2. Agree
    3. Neither agree nor disagree
    4. Disagree
    5. Strongly disagree

5. I check receipts and statements for accuracy and sometimes find mistakes.
    1. Strongly agree
    2. Agree
    3. Neither agree nor disagree

4. Disagree
5. Strongly disagree

Add up the numbers of the answers you circled, and write this number in the space provided. _____

If you scored between 5 and 10, you are probably an organized person. Without a broker, it is essential that you keep good records. If your score was high on this quiz, make a special effort to get organized before you get online and start trading.

MONEY MANAGEMENT

1. I never bounce checks.
   1. Strongly agree
   2. Agree
   3. Neither agree nor disagree
   4. Disagree
   5. Strongly disagree

2. I am never late paying my bills.
   1. Strongly agree
   2. Agree
   3. Neither agree nor disagree
   4. Disagree
   5. Strongly disagree

3. I budget my expenses and live within my means.
   1. Strongly agree
   2. Agree
   3. Neither agree nor disagree
   4. Disagree
   5. Strongly disagree

4. I have not built up a large credit card debt.
   1. Strongly agree
   2. Agree

Bright Idea
Organization is crucial. If you are not organized, you will lose money as a result of stupid mistakes, oversights, and clerical errors. Stories abound of online investors who type in the wrong numbers when placing trades, don't realize what they've done until later, and end up losing lots of money.

Watch Out!
It's so easy to rack up credit card debt. By 1998, Americans owed $549.9 billion on their plastic, an increase of almost 5 percent from 1997. Be careful not to use cards with high annual fees and high interest rates.

3. Neither agree nor disagree
4. Disagree
5. Strongly disagree

5. I have a good credit rating.
   1. Strongly agree
   2. Agree
   3. Neither agree nor disagree
   4. Disagree
   5. Strongly disagree

Add up the numbers of the answers you circled, and write this number in the space provided. _____

A score between 5 and 10 indicates that you have good money management skills and probably a good sense for money. These qualities are essential if you want to make money online. If you are currently in debt or have a bad credit rating, you should be aware that you may have a tendency to borrow money you can't pay back in a timely fashion, and this tendency could get you into a lot of trouble online. For starters, make it a rule not to buy stocks with borrowed money (trading on margin). Next, take stock of your overall financial situation. It would behoove you to get out of debt before you get online.

Now, add up the total scores for the six quizzes to get your grand total for the test. Write this number in the space provided, and evaluate your score. _____

SCORE	EVALUATION
30–60	You are the kind of person who could enjoy and profit from online investing. Get to it!
61–90	You are the kind of person who could be a successful online investor, but you may have one or two areas you need to keep an eye on. Be vigilant!
91–150	You need to be aware of certain tendencies you may have that, if not changed or compensated for, could lead to serious trouble if you trade online. Exercise caution!

❝
I'm not OK;
you're not OK;
and that's OK.
—Virginia Satir
❞

Just the facts

- Investing online will save you time and money.

- As an online investor, you have access to an unlimited amount of investment-related information 24 hours a day.

- Although online brokers are generally reliable, some sites do crash from time to time.

- Online brokers employ a variety of security measures that make your online funds extremely safe.

- The ideal online investor possesses certain traits, including knowledge about and interest in investing, self-discipline, and good money management skills.

GET THE SCOOP ON...
Getting yourself a computer ▪ Modems that
make a difference ▪ An ISP is definitely not
an ISP ▪ Not all browsers are created
equal ▪ Arming yourself with key software

Everything You Need

Chapter 2

With online investing all the rage these days, the tendency is to jump in and put your money down. The fear of missing out on the next surge in America Online or Dell sometimes is greater than any concern that your stock picks just might go the wrong way. Always keep this in mind: There is no rush. There will always be opportunities to make money on Wall Street. So, if you miss out on today's rally, or this week's or next week's, it's not important. Every market and every market day offer the potential for profits.

As you move into the online investing realm, take your time and build yourself a solid foundation. The goal is not to make a lot of money this year or next; the goal is to develop an investment strategy that will work for you consistently in good markets and bad, a strategy that will generate positive returns for you for the rest of your life.

The first step in building a solid foundation is to make sure you have everything you need to succeed. You need to set up an online investing work station.

Watch Out!
If you own only
one phone line,
you won't be
able to make or
receive phone
calls while you're
on the Internet.
You might want
to consider
getting a second
line so you
don't miss any
important calls.

The essential items include a desk, a computer, a modem, a phone line, and a computer program that allows you to access the Internet. You will also need to select an Internet service provider (ISP), a company that actually connects your computer to the Internet. You really don't need all that much, but it's important that you choose the things you do need wisely because you will be depending on them.

The guiding principle in setting up your work station is this: *Keep it simple.* Sometimes less is more. Avoid buying all kinds of extraneous equipment and programs that you'll never use and that might just gum up your system. Remember: Online investing should not complicate your life—it should simplify it.

You need a computer

The first thing you need to purchase is a computer. This need not be a difficult process. While there are hundreds of computer manufacturers out there, each producing an extraordinary array of computers, it will not be difficult for you to find one that will fit your needs. If you buy a computer made by any one of the "Big 4"—Compaq, Dell, IBM, or Hewlett-Packard (or Apple)—you will no doubt be getting a quality machine. As an online investor, you won't need the most powerful computer on the market nor the most expensive. Actually, almost any computer will do just fine. But your computer *will* need to meet certain minimum requirements.

The first thing you have to consider is whether you want to buy a desktop computer, a notebook computer, or a palmtop computer. A desktop is the largest of the three and derives its name from where it is placed and remains: on your desk. A notebook computer is portable. Although sizes and weights vary, the idea is that you can fold it up and take it anywhere. Palmtops are even smaller than notebooks and can fit in your bag, your briefcase, or even your pocket.

Palmtops are generally not used independently, but they give you a way of communicating with another computer—such as the one you have at home—while you're out. Although it's possible to invest online using only a palmtop, it's not such a good idea. Palmtops are extremely small, the screens are tiny, and the amount of information you can view at any one time is severely limited. Data can be entered only by punching one key at a time. What's more, if you want to connect to the Internet, you still have to hook up the palmtop to a modem and a phone line (unless you can find a wireless palmtop), and connecting to and surfing the Net is quite slow.

The real choice before you is whether to buy a desktop or a notebook. The advantages of notebooks are that they are small, take up relatively little desk space, can be moved easily, and can be taken with you wherever you go. This means that if you go on a business trip, you can continue to monitor your investments and place trades. The disadvantages of notebooks are these:

- The screens are small.

- The screens can strain the eyes if you use them for extended periods, and they aren't as clear as desktop screens.

- The keyboards are small.

- Instead of a mouse, you move your screen pointer with a trackball device, which is harder to use.

Unofficially...
While using a palmtop for online investing in conjunction with another computer could be advantageous (you could use it to get stock quotes during the day), depending on a palmtop to do the whole job is not recommended.

- Notebooks tend to be more expensive than desktops, they're easier to drop or step on, and it's harder to find replacement parts for them when they do break.

Not sure if a notebook computer is for you? The following quiz should help you decide:

1. Are you less concerned with the overall performance of your computer than with its portability?

2. Are you comfortable with a relatively small screen (display)?

3. Do you need your computer when you travel?

4. Are you comfortable spending more money than you would for a comparable desktop system?

5. Are you comfortable with being unable to upgrade your system in the future?

If you answered yes to four or five of these questions, you should seriously consider purchasing a notebook computer instead of a desktop.

How to buy a notebook

You should consider three major things when purchasing a notebook computer: price, performance, and ergonomics. Prices of notebooks range anywhere from $1,000 or less for budget models, to more than $5,000. For online investing purposes, you probably should be looking for something in the range of $1,800–$3,000. However, you can probably pick up a used model for much less. Look in your local newspaper's classified section, and check out computer trade magazines for secondhand computers for sale by owner. The risk of buying a used computer is that it may not be operating perfectly, and you have little or no warranty. If you do go this route, check out the computer in person before you buy it. Run some programs and "surf the Net" (explore the Internet) a bit. Ask the owner if there is anything wrong with it and if the warranty is still good.

When you have determined your price range, you can compare the notebooks in that range on their merits. Notebook computers come in an amazing variety of sizes, shapes, and weights, so finding one that feels right to you should be a priority. If you're a guy with big fingers and hands, for example, you wouldn't be comfortable using some keyboards, regardless of how powerful they are, because the keyboards are too small. Look at the display. Is it too small? Is it clear? Generally, components cannot be exchanged or upgraded in a notebook, so you'll want to make sure you're happy with them when you buy it. Shop around. Visit several computer stores in your area, and look at several notebooks. Ordering one through the mail is generally a bad idea, unless you are familiar with the model.

When you've found several notebooks in your price range that you like as far as look and feel go, you need to put them through their paces. Performance will be the deciding factor in your purchase. Your goal is to get the most computer for your dollar. Here's what you should demand:

- **Speed.** Speed is how quickly a computer executes commands. This mostly depends on the computer chip, also know as the chip, the central processing unit (CPU), and the microprocessor, or the processor. The CPU is essentially the brain of your computer. It's the

Bright Idea
If you buy a
Macintosh
PowerBook, go
for a model with
either a 233MHz,
a 266MHz, or a
333MHz G3
processor.

integrated circuit that does all the work, all the serious number crunching. Technically speaking, the CPU is actually only part of the microprocessor, but for all intents and purposes, they're the same. Now, computer speed is measured in megahertz (MHz); the higher the megahertz, the faster the machine moves (within the same family of processors). You should look for 233MHz and 266MHz Pentium II–based machines—or 300MHz systems, if you want to pay a little more. Pentium II is the name of a computer chip manufactured by Intel.

- **Memory.** Memory is the capacity for the CPU to "remember" key computer programs. There are two kinds of memory: random access memory (RAM) and cache. RAM is a kind of computer short-term memory that allows you to do things on your computer. When you turn off the computer, everything you did that was not saved will be forgotten. Cache is a reservoir of memory capacity that stores the most recent data accessed by the CPU so that it can be accessed again very quickly. This saves time. The *primary cache* (L1) is built into the CPU; the *secondary cache* (L2) is contained outside the CPU. Memory capacity is measured in megabytes (MB). You should demand at least 32MB of RAM and at least 256 kilobytes (KB) of L2.

- **Storage.** Storage is the capacity for your computer to remember things, even after you turn off the computer. It's a kind of computer long-term memory. The computer stores information by recording the data you want to save on a disk, often referred to as the hard disk or hard drive (HD). Storage capacity is measured in gigabytes (GB). These days, you should insist on a hard drive with 3GB or more, unless you're planning to buy a very small notebook.

- **Screen.** The most important thing about the screen is its size. You really shouldn't buy anything smaller than a 12.1-inch screen (screen size is measured by the width). Most notebook screens now deliver crisp images, using active-matrix (TFT), liquid crystal display (LCD). Just make sure you are personally happy with the screen size and image quality before you purchase the machine.

- **Warranty.** The longer, the better, of course. Expect a 30-day, no-restocking-fee return policy, a three-year warranty on parts and labor, and technical support to be available to you over the phone. Also, see if there is a guaranteed repair turnaround time.

Other things to check depend on your personal fetishes and pet peeves. If you plan to use the laptop for computer games, as a form of R&R between lengthy sessions of stock analysis, you will want to make sure that your notebook has at least 2MB of graphics RAM—preferably 4MB.

Opting for a desktop

In spite of all the advantages of laptop computers, there are many good reasons for the online investor to buy a desktop. The biggest reason is that desktops are far more comfortable to use. The screens are larger and easier to look at for long periods of time, the keyboards are larger, and the mouse is easier to use than the trackball found on most notebooks. All

Unofficially...
If you want CD-ROM capacity, shoot for 16-speed or faster. Also, check into the estimated battery run times for the notebook, even though you will probably be plugging it in most of the time.

desktops come with CD-ROM and floppy-disk drives, while some notebook computers have only one or the other. (Floppy disks are small, plastic, portable disks you can copy files to or from.) Desktops are harder to break because they are *not* portable—and if they do break, it's easier to get them repaired because replacement parts are readily available. And don't forget the price advantage. On the whole, although desktops are larger than notebooks, they are markedly cheaper for the same amount of memory and power.

As with a notebook, the first thing you should try to determine in buying a desktop is your price range. The cheapest desktops sell for well under $1,000, while high-end systems may cost you $2,500. After determining your price range, take a look at some computers with an eye, again, to the following:

- **Speed.** For systems less than $1,000, make sure you're getting at least a 233MHz or 200MHz MMX Pentium CPU. For the $1,000–$2,200 range, insist on 233MHz or 266MHz Pentium II CPUs for PCs and on 233MHz, 266MHz, or 333MHz G3 processors for Macintosh computers. For machines in the $2,000–$2,500 range, you should get a 350MHz or 400MHz Pentium II system. Although these high-end machines are state-of-the-art, they certainly aren't required equipment for online investing.

- **Memory.** Demand at least 32MB RAM. It's preferable that the machine offer an accelerated type of RAM called SDRAM or EDO DRAM, not just DRAM. You should also insist on at least 256KB of L2.

- **Storage.** If you're trying to save money, don't settle for less than a 3.2GB hard disk. For average-price desktops, you should be able to secure as much as 4GB to 6.5GB, although 8GB or more is not out of the question.

- **Screen.** Don't settle for anything smaller than a 15-inch screen, also known as a monitor or CRT (for cathode ray tube). A 17-inch screen is ideal, but consider how much desk space you have before going larger.

- **Warranty.** As with the notebooks, expect a 30-day, no-restocking-fee return policy, a three-year warranty on parts and labor, and technical support to be available to you over the phone. Also, inquire if the store will send a technician to your home if a serious problem arises or if you'll have to ship or transport the computer back to the store or to a service center. Check to see if there's a guaranteed repair turn-around time as well.

Other things to consider are CD-ROM drive speed—again, insist on 16-speed or faster—and graphics RAM—you want 2MB–4MB.

As you survey the computer landscape and talk to people about what kind of computer they have, you may come to realize that a kind of war is going on, and that most people consider themselves to be in one of two camps. The war is between users of Macintosh computers (Macs), manufactured by Apple, and users of PCs, manufactured by everyone else. Often this war has been cast as a battle between Apple and Microsoft because Apple makes the basic program (called an operating system, or OS) that runs Macs, and Microsoft makes the OS that runs all the PCs (except for the IBM PC, which runs on a program called OS2/Warp). This battle has also been cast as one between Steven Jobs, co-founder and current interim CEO of Apple, and Bill Gates, CEO of Microsoft.

In brief, the arguments proceed as follows: PCs are less expensive than Macs, but Macs are easier to use. PCs have more software (programs) available, but Macs have *better* software available. PCs make up the vast majority of the computer universe, but Macs make up the elite in that universe. Our advice to you is this: Don't get sucked into the fray. While the opinions you encounter on what equipment you should buy may be strong, you need to make your own decision—that's why they call it a *personal* computer. First assess your needs, then determine how much you want to spend, and then go look for yourself. Buy what you like within the framework of your requirements.

Caring for your computer

When you get your new computer home, take the time to read at least some of the owner's manual and send in the warranty card. Take care of your machine. Computers work best in a clean environment. Dust and dirt are their natural-born enemies. Keep the area around your computer clean. Vacuum and dust regularly, and vacuum the computer itself, including the keyboard, casing, and vents. (The computer should be turned off when you do this.) You can occasionally wipe down the keyboard, screen, and casing with a bit of isopropyl alcohol as well. If you use the floppy disk drive often, use a cleaning disk occasionally.

You may want to consider buying a computer cover to put on your machine when you're not using it. This will help keep your computer clean and will cut down on dust buildup. But never leave the cover partially on while you are using the computer—this may block the vents, causing the computer to over-heat. Computers are temperature-sensitive, and it's best to keep them in a fairly consistent temperature setting, ideally between 65° and 85°F.

The hard drive of your computer should also be given special care. At least once a week, you should run disk diagnostic and repair software, which will be discussed a littler later. Once a month, you should run a program, found on your hard disk, that rebuilds your desktop. Here, *desktop* refers to your start-up screen, where you find the icons (picture representations) for your hard disk, printer, any files you're keeping on the screen, and a trash can. Rebuilding the desktop forces your computer to check and fix, if necessary, the icons on the desktop and how they are displayed and to correct the way the information on the desktop is being stored.

Keep an eye on loose connections, the cables going into the back of your computer, your keyboard, and the wall. Cables tend to work themselves loose over time, and this can cause the computer to stop working temporarily, and even lead to a loss of data. Periodically, check to make sure that all the connections are snug.

Finally, pay attention to what you see and hear when you start up and shut down your computer. You will notice a familiar pattern of screen displays and icons and a familiar pattern of sounds. Attune your senses to what constitutes a normal startup and shutdown routine. Any variation in the usual pattern could mean a problem, which you'll want to nip in the bud. And keep in mind that it's essential to close all programs you were using before shutting down your computer.

Moneysaver
If you're having some difficulty with your computer, troubleshoot before calling a computer service professional. Windows 95 and 98 have in-depth troubleshooting programs that can help you identify and solve problems.

What's a modem?

A modem is a machine that enables your computer to connect to the phone line, which enables you to connect to the Internet, a huge global network of computers. The modem does this by converting the digital signals from your computer into analog signals that can be transmitted over phone lines. The modem also converts analog signals it receives from other modems (hooked up to other computers) back to digital signals so that your computer can receive information. This is how computers "talk" to each other all over the world, and this is what puts the Internet at the fingertips of the average person. A modem is an essential piece of equipment for the online investor.

There are two kinds of modems: internal and external. An internal modem is either built into your computer or installed later. If the modem needs to be installed, just be sure you have an unused expansion slot inside your computer. An external modem is encased in a small box, which you connect to the back of your computer, and the modem is placed next to your computer on your desk. An external modem requires a serial port on the back of your computer. Make sure that the universal asynchronous receiver transmitter (UART) on your serial port can match or exceed the modem's top transmission speeds. Confirm this with a computer salesperson, or check your computer manual.

The main advantage of an internal modem is that it's one less piece of equipment you have to fiddle with and worry about. Another advantage is that it takes up no desk space at all. Internal modems are also thought to be cheaper. The nice things about external modems, though, are that they are easier to install, they can be transferred to other machines, and they have flashing lights, which allow you to monitor the status of your connection attempt.

Notebook computers nowadays generally do not accommodate external modems. The choice is between a built-in modem and a PC card modem. With the latter, a modem card is slipped into the notebook's card slot to allow for Internet connection. This card can be removed and replaced with other cards, such as a CD-ROM card.

What truly separates one modem from another, however, is speed. The faster, the better. Transmission speed, the speed at which one modem can exchange information with another modem, is measured in bits per second (bps) or kilobytes per second (KBps, or just K). Modems are available at speeds of 14.4K, 28.8K, 33.6K, and 56K; PC modem cards at 28.8K, 33.6K, and 56K. 14.4K modems are very slow and have largely been phased out, and the online investor should avoid them. A 28.8K modem is your minimum requirement.

The tricky thing about modems is that maximum transmission speed is dependent upon both the modems that are communicating. If you have a 28.8K modem and you are communicating with a 14.4K modem, the transmission between the two modems cannot move faster than 14.4K. Additionally, while almost all phone lines will support 28.8K connections, many will not support 33.6K or faster. Moreover, even when the lines will support it, the increase in speed from 28.8K to 33.6K is only 17 percent.

The inside scoop on 56K modems

The development of the 56K modem was based on a realization about most Internet service providers

(ISPs). Again, an ISP is a company that you connect to with your modem that in turn connects you to the Internet. Modem makers realized that most ISPs have a digital, not analog, connection to the phone company's network. This means that you can receive direct digital signals from your ISP over the phone line. On the other hand, you cannot send digital signals if you don't have a digital connection with the phone company. So, the 56K modems are hybrids, which convert analog signals to digital when you're sending, but accept digital signals directly when you are receiving. By eliminating the analog-to-digital conversion time from the ISP to the phone network, 56K speed is achievable under ideal circumstances. If your local phone lines cannot support 56K, however, you will not get 56K. In fact, many people who have these modems report only a slight increase in speed.

Other than the capacity of the phone lines, the success of 56K modems in achieving their potential speed depends on three things:

1. Your ISP does, in fact, have a digital connection with the phone network.

2. Your ISP offers 56K service.

3. The modem you're communicating with has a 56K modem *of the same type as you.*

Until 1998, no production standards existed for the production of 56K modems, and two different breeds were being manufactured: the x2 by 3Com/U.S. Robotics and the K56flex by Rockwell Industries and Lucent Technologies. Both types can communicate with all slower modems, but they cannot communicate with each other.

In 1998, however, the International Telecommunications Union approved a new standard, called V.90. This means from now on all 56K modems made will meet V.90 specs and be compatible with each other. If you buy a 56K modem, then make sure that it conforms to the new standard. If you get your hands on a pre-standard 56K modem for some reason, make sure that the manufacturer will upgrade it to the new standard for free or for very little charge.

Reaching for modem alternatives

While a standard modem is definitely sufficient for the purposes of the online investor, you may want to look into one of the modem alternatives. Integrated Services Digital Network (ISDN) is a service that uses ordinary phone lines but makes all its transmissions digitally. To access ISDN, you need a terminal adapter, which replaces your modem; the phone company also has to come in and do serious work on the lines. The setup cost will run you between $500 and $700. You then have to pay a monthly fee, which varies greatly from place to place but is significantly more than the cost of an ordinary phone line. Also, your ISP must be equipped to handle ISDN. If money is no object and your ISP is hooked up, you can achieve speeds of up to 128K using this system.

The real wave of the future, however, seems to be cable modems. Big, thick coaxial cables have tremendous potential for providing high-speed access to the Internet, and cable companies have started realizing this. In selected areas of the country, cable companies have started offering Internet access. To hook you up, they install a standard network adapter in your computer and provide you with a cable modem. Cable modems enable communications to take place at 1,000K—that's almost 20 times faster than that with 56K modems.

Watch Out!
The one inherent weakness of cable modems is that you are sharing a line with all the people in your area. If everyone in your neighborhood were to log on to the Internet at the same time, speed would decrease dramatically.

Not to be left in the dust by the cable companies, the phone companies are developing their own high-speed Internet access systems. Symmetric digital subscriber line (SDSL) technology can transmit data over standard phone lines at speeds of up to 1,500K, and asymmetric digital subscriber line (ADSL) technology can transmit data at speeds of more than 6,300K. At this time, however, these services are being offered only in a few places in the country on a trial basis.

For the purpose of online investing, insist on at least a 28.8K modem, internal or external. If you can afford it, the modem alternatives are even better.

Who needs an Internet service provider?

Now that you have a computer and a modem, you need to get yourself an ISP. The reason you need to use ISPs to connect to the Internet is that the Internet is not a single network to which you can pay for access. It is a large number of privately owned and operated networks that are all interconnected. ISPs are directly, physically connected to a network that is part of the Internet network. By connecting to your ISP and paying a fee, you gain access to their network and, by extension, to the Internet.

Things to look for in an ISP

How do you choose an ISP? The most important thing to look at is whether they have a local telephone number. Why? Remember that your modem is actually using the phone lines to call your ISP, who will then give you that coveted Internet connection. If the call to your ISP is not a local call, you will get charged by the phone company for every minute you stay on the Internet!

One way to find out if an ISP has a local phone number is simply to check your local Yellow Pages under the "Internet" entry. You can also ask your friends in the area which ISPs they use. If there are no local ISPs, make sure that you get the best long-distance rate you can. This means checking different long-distance carriers and checking out which of the closest ISPs is really the cheapest to call. In some cases, phoning out-of-state is cheaper than calling another county in the same state. Many of the large ISPs can be accessed through a 1-800 number, although this is *not* a free call. The ISP charges you by the minute, but usually at a better rate than you can get from the phone company by yourself.

Next, look at pricing. There are two basic types of ISP payment plans: hourly and unlimited access. An hourly plan may provide you with anywhere from 5 to 20 hours of access time a week for a nominal fee, and then charge you $1 to $2 an hour if your time limit is exceeded. Unlimited plans provide you with unlimited access to the Internet for a flat fee, which now stands at an industry-wide standard of $19.95 a month. ISPs charging more than this need to justify their higher rates by promising exceptionally high reliability or service. In most urban areas, competition has driven prices down to their current rates, but in some rural areas where competition is minimal, rates are a bit higher.

Hourly plans may be more economical for people who expect to be on the Internet only a certain number of hours per week. Plans with flat fees are better for people who expect to spend more time on the Internet.

Some ISPs are now offering discounts for long-term commitments, such as agreeing to pay 3, 6, or

Timesaver
A quick way to find a good ISP serving your area is to use Netscape's homepage— www.netscape. com. Click on "Computing & Internet," next click on "ISP Locator," and then enter your state.

12 months in advance. Be careful, though. If you find a price that is way below the competition, chances are good that the service provided will be below industry standards as well. Some ISPs, for example, now offer Internet connection for *free*. They make money by taking a cut of what you pay to call their number, and by advertising. Because so-called free ISPs are low-budget, however, speed can be below average, they may be inaccessible unless you have certain kinds of software, and they may charge you if you call for any kind of assistance.

The next thing you need to look for in an ISP is good customer service. What's the best way to check on this? Call them up. Are they friendly? Are they helpful? They should be. The Internet was not designed with consumers in mind, and although it has become a great deal more understandable to the average person in recent years, it can still be a bit wild and woolly. The job of your ISP is to bring the Internet to you—that's what you're paying them for. Your questions should be welcomed and your problems addressed. Find out if they will help you get started and instruct you on exactly what to do. Ask if they have a free 24-hour help line you can call once you're up and running.

Another factor to look at is the size of the ISP. The largest ISPs are national, meaning that the same company provides Internet access in virtually all parts of the country. If you have an account with one of these ISPs, you can continue to access the Internet when you travel domestically (although you will have to reset your computer to conform to the ISP's phone number in a given area). Some ISPs are even global. But the vast majority are quite small, only operating within a single area code. The advantages of going with a small ISP are that it may offer lower rates and often can provide excellent, personalized customer service. The advantage of going with a large ISP is stability. Chances are good that a large ISP won't go out of business, which is not uncommon with small ISPs.

ISP reliability and performance are the final factors to consider. Sometimes when your modem dials up your ISP, you get a busy signal; other times you get connected, but you encounter lengthy delays. While the first of these problems is definitely the ISP's fault—not having sufficient capacity to handle call volume—the second may not be. Often the computer supplying the information you want (called the *server*) on the Internet is overloaded—this is common at very popular sites.

Still, ISPs do have a history of going down. In the spring of 1997, there were many reports of problems with America Online, AT&T, Pacific Bell, Prodigy, and The Microsoft Network (MSN). Most of the problems were with the computers that processed e-mail (known as mail servers)—e-mail stopped flowing for days at a time. Many of the ISPs involved had to suspend service while they upgraded their systems. With both private and business use of the Internet growing daily, expectations for uninterrupted service are constantly rising. ISPs know this and have been working together to prevent future service failures.

When choosing an ISP for yourself, keep in mind that problems seem to occur more frequently with some ISPs than others. Ask around a bit. What's the word on the street about who's good and who's not? Talk to friends and ask the people who work at your local computer store who they think are the most reliable ISPs.

Bright Idea
In selecting an ISP, one criterion you can use is what Internet services are provided. Check to see if you can get e-mail services, access to newsgroups, and support in creating your own Web page.

Here is a list of four of the best national ISPs:

- AT&T WorldNet Service
- EarthLink
- Netcomplete
- Qwest

Commercial online services

Commercial online services are an alternative to ISPs. These companies not only connect you to the Internet, but they also provide you with a wide range of additional services not provided by ISPs. Some of the services commercial online services provide include discussion forums (where users discuss various topics of mutual interest), databases (which supply a great deal of information on selected topics), and other features, such as shopping and chat rooms, where you talk to others in real time.

While content is the main advantage of commercial online services over ISPs, another is organization. All the goodies the Internet has to offer are put right in front of you. CompuServe, the oldest of these services, provides its members with the following main menu: What's New, Table of Contents, Internet, Chat, and Forums and Communities. If you select Table of Contents, you are presented with a range of topics, including news/weather, sports, health, education, society and living, business, investing, and more. Selecting one of these categories presents you with subcategories, where you can access very specific information on topics of your choice.

The Big 3 of the commercial online services are CompuServe, America Online, and Microsoft Network (MSN). In brief, CompuServe is the most serious and the most business-oriented of the three, offering many financial resources. (It is now a subsidiary of America Online.) America Online comes across as a more friendly, family-oriented service. This may be why it eventually surpassed CompuServe and is now the No. 1 commercial online service. America Online offers many useful financial features, including stock quotes, a brokerage center, a mutual fund center, and a company research center. MSN is the newest of the three, created by Microsoft. It has much less content than CompuServe and America Online, and is not as well-organized. The advantages of MSN, though, are that it comes bundled with Microsoft's Windows OS software and, of the three services, it also works the most smoothly on the Internet.

Be careful about the tendency for commercial online services to crash or be slow. America Online is so huge and is growing so fast that it can be somewhat unreliable, with subscribers getting busy signals and slow responses more often than with national ISPs. This could be a hindrance to the serious online investor.

Another consideration is that commercial online services tend to cost more than ISPs. CompuServe charges $24.95 a month for unlimited access; America Online charges $21.95 a month. MSN, however, costs the same as ISPs, at $19.95. If you want to avoid the additional cost of the first two, you can go with an ISP and then try to access the online services content for free over the Internet. In fact, an increasing amount of the commercial online services' content is available for free on the Net—especially that of MSN. The Internet addresses you'll need to access the services are www.aol.com for America Online, www.csi.com for CompuServe, and free.msn.com/start for MSN. Other online services you might look into include Genie Online Services (www.genie.com) and Prodigy (www. prodigy.com). You will learn in the next section how to use these addresses.

What's a browser?

To actually connect your computer to your ISP through your modem and then go from place to place on the Internet, you need a computer program called a Web browser. Although the terms *Web* and *Internet* are often used interchangeably, the Web, or the World Wide Web (WWW), is not the same thing as the Internet. The Internet is the global network of computer networks; the Web is a part of the Internet that consists of interconnected "pages" of graphics and text. A Web browser enables you to move freely among this universe of pages.

Your ISP will provide you with a Web browser for free and will tell you how to set up your computer so that the browser, when activated, can connect you with the Internet through them. But which browser should you use? Just as the computer world enjoys its war between Macs and PCs, so the Internet world relishes the so-called browser war: the battle between Netscape's Communicator and Microsoft's Internet Explorer.

Which browser is better? Actually, both do a fantastic job, and the online investor will be fine using either. How to decide, then? Initially, go with whatever browser your ISP provides you with. If they send you Netscape Communicator, hook up with that. After you're on the Internet, you can obtain a free copy of Explorer and try it out. (Go to www. microsoft.com/windows/ie/default.htm if you have a PC; www.microsoft.com/mac/ie if you have a

Macintosh.) If you like Explorer better, switch. (For a free copy of Communicator, go to www.netscape. com and click on "Browsers.") Switching to a different browser than the one provided by your ISP will not affect your ability to connect with your ISP. Many of the larger ISPs actually send you *both* browsers. In this case, you can install both and try them out. Which you end up using is really just a matter of personal preference.

If you purchase a Macintosh computer, you can choose whichever browser tickles your fancy. In fact, the new iMacs come with both Communicator and Explorer. If you purchase a PC with Windows 98, the current Microsoft OS, you'll find that Internet Explorer is built-in. You cannot remove Explorer without removing the entire operating system. Many feel this is Bill Gates's way of making up our minds for us about which browser to use. It's also one reason Microsoft finds itself in court right now. Many computer manufacturers have testified that Microsoft bullied them into accepting the latest OS, with Microsoft's Web browser embedded. Gates, of course, denies this. But this and other incidents led the Justice Department to embark on an antitrust suit against Microsoft in 1998, the results of which are still pending.

There is a way around Gates's ploy. If you buy a PC with Windows 98, you can use Explorer to get on to the Internet and simply download a free copy of Communicator. If you like Communicator better, use it. You will not be able to erase Explorer, however, and it will continue to occupy a certain amount of storage space on your hard drive.

You should also be aware that a growing number of alternative browsers are available. As with

Communicator and Explorer, you can download any of these for free off the Internet. The best-known of the alternatives are Opera, Amaya, HotJava, Arachne, Lynx, and Softerm Plus+. Of these, Opera is the stand-out: It is currently the only one that can read Java script, a widely used computer language on the Internet, and the only one that can utilize plug-ins, specialized programs that add functionality to your browser.

Taking your browser out for a spin

When you've decided on a browser and hooked up to your ISP, you're ready to get your feet wet with some basic Web surfing. Surfing the Web simply means moving around the Internet, freely exploring what's out there. The way to get started is to click your browser icon once or twice. This will cause your modem to call your ISP, which will then connect you to the Internet. When your browser screen opens, you will notice a toolbar on the top of the page with commands such as Back, Forward, Reload, Home, and Search. If, using your mouse or trackball, you move your screen pointer to any of these words on the toolbar, you will notice that a border appears around the word, making it look like a button on a machine. You push the button by clicking your mouse. For example, if you click the Back button, you will go back to the previous screen you were looking at.

Below the toolbar, you will notice a white line with something like this inside: http:// home. netscape.com/. This is called a uniform resource locator (URL) or, in plain English, a Web address. When you type an address in this space and hit the Return (or Enter) key on your keyboard, your browser will take you to that location on the Web. For example, if you type in http://quote.yahoo.com/

Timesaver
Use the icons on your browser's toolbar as much as possible to save time. On Internet Explorer and Netscape Communicator, you can do things such as printing out the page you are viewing or accessing top search engines with one click of the mouse.

(the URL for a Web site called Yahoo! Finance), you will go to a very popular, useful financial Web site, where you can see how the stock market is doing.

You will soon discover that there are certain sites that you like a lot and will want to revisit often. These are the sites you should add to Bookmarks (or Favorites, if you're using Explorer). Imagine that you have, in fact, gone to http://quote.yahoo.com/, and you have decided to bookmark the site. If you look at the top of your screen, above the browser toolbar, you'll see a horizontal menu of commands. Some of the menu items are words, such as File, Edit, and View, and some are icons. Move your pointer to the word Bookmark or the symbol that represents a bookmark, and click on it. The first choice on the drop-down menu will say Add Bookmark. Move your pointer down to Add Bookmark and click again. You have just placed Yahoo! Finance in your personal collection. Click again on the bookmark icon, and you will see Yahoo! Finance listed. The next time you want to go there, simply select the bookmark icon, move your pointer down to Yahoo! Finance, and click again. Using bookmarks will save you a lot of time.

Also notice that on any Web page there are words or URLs that are colored differently than the rest of the text (often they are colored blue). These words or URLs are called *links* or *hyperlinks*. When you click them, you go to another page on the Web. If you want to go back to where you came from, either click the Back button on your browser's toolbar, or use the Go item on the upper menu. Under Go is a list of all the sites you have recently visited, and you can return to any one of them by simply clicking.

How to find anything on the Web

How do you find information about something you're interested in on the Web? You search for it, of course. The best way to conduct a search is to use a program called a search engine. Many of the most popular search engines are listed right on your browser page. Near the top of the Netscape Navigator page (or home page), for example, is a Search button. Clicking this will take you to the Lycos home page, where you'll see a blank box after the words Search For. Simply type the keywords for your topic into this box, and Lycos will produce a list of related links.

Try out various search engines. Some of the most popular are Yahoo!, Excite, Lycos, Infoseek (now part of the GO Network), WebCrawler, AltaVista, and HotBot. Search engines may also be referred to as directories or indexes. Indexes are just a collection of Web sites that have been amassed and compiled through the use of computer programs that look for new Web sites. Directories, by contrast, have been arranged by humans. Each new site located by the search program is scrutinized by people, who then decide if it should be included in their directory, and if so, under what category. Of the previously mentioned search sites, only Yahoo! is a directory. Another well-known directory is Look Smart. The advantage of directories is that they are organized. You can often start your search by clicking categories first, which narrow the search to a specific subject area, such as *computers*. This helps you find exactly what you're looking for. The advantage of indexes is that they are larger than directories. You have a good chance of being able to find at least something related to your topic.

Here is a list of "alternative" search engines to try, if you strike out with the more traditional ones:

- Direct Hit: www.directhit.com

- Google!: www.google.com

- dmoz open directory project: http://dmoz.org

- Yep.com: http://yep.com

- Ask Jeeves: www.askjeeves.com

The best way to find what you're looking for on the Web using search engines is to be as specific as you can. If you're looking for information on Treasury bonds, for instance, don't type just the word *bonds* into the search box. This might dredge up hundreds of Web sites, including ones that discuss marriage bonds, a product that bonds dentures, and even a comparison of the actors who have been deemed the best James Bonds. For more effective results, type *treasury AND bonds.* (That's AND, with all capitals.) This will limit the results of your search to the specific type of bonds you're interested in. If you're interested in the yields of Treasury bonds, you should try *treasury AND bonds AND yields.* This will generate even more useful results.

Words such as *AND, OR,* and *AND NOT* are referred to as Boolean operators. AND instructs the search engine to list only those sites that contain all the words linked by AND. OR instructs the search engine to list sites containing either of two or more words—for example, *microchip OR microprocessor.* The third Boolean operator is AND NOT. This helps you winnow out undesired documents from your search results. Most search engines let you use Boolean operators together by using parenthesis. For example: *(corporate AND bonds) AND NOT junk.* This means you're looking for information on corporate bonds, but not junk bonds. Another example: *(microchip OR microprocessor) AND inventor.* This means you want to know who invented the microchip, but you know it could be listed under the word microprocessor as well.

Most search engines will let you search for a phrase by putting quotation marks around it, such as *"consumer price index."* The results will generally be limited not only to documents containing all three of these words, but also to documents containing these three words in this order. Always search for an exact phrase like this if you can, but remember that your results may be very limited. You can combine quotations marks with Boolean operators for very powerful searches. For example *"stock market" AND "forecast"* will produce a list of sites forecasting the stock market's performance in the months to come.

Another great way to improve your search results is to use meta-search engines. Meta-search engines actually let you use several search engines simultaneously, without having to go to each search engine's Web site and re-enter your search words. Each search engine spits out its top 10 matches, and the meta-search engine compiles the results for you. Because it's often difficult to find exactly what you're looking for using only one search engine, using meta-search engines is a great way to search the Web.

One of the oldest, best-known meta-search engines is MetaCrawler (www.go2net.com/search.html), which was purchased by the meta-search engine company Go2net in early 1999. MetaCrawler searches AltaVista, Excite, Infoseek, Lycos, Yahoo!, and WebCrawler simultaneously, eliminates duplicates, and displays the results in order of probable relevance. Another meta-search engine, also bought by Go2net in 1999, is Dogpile (www.dogpile.com), which accesses 13 search engines and is a tool to use if you're determined to find as much information on a topic as you possibly can. If using the combination of Boolean operators, phrases, and meta-search engines fails to turn up useful, relevant Web sites, try changing the key words you're using in your search.

The best way to master the Web and get the most out of your browser is to explore and study. There are two philosophies here. One is to sit down and read manuals and books. The other is to learn by doing: Go as far as you can, and when you get stuck, search for the answer in your manuals, on the Internet, or from a friend. The best approach is probably some combination of the two. Setting aside a certain amount of time every week—even 15 minutes—to study one of your manuals will net a lot of benefits in terms of increased efficiency and overall competence.

Bright Idea
Keep in mind that one of the most common reasons for failing to come up with useful results is misspelling one or more of the words you're using to conduct the search.

Building up your software arsenal

In addition to your browser software, you might consider acquiring some financial software, just to keep yourself organized as you begin to invest online. Check out the following two personal finance software programs:

- **Quicken Deluxe** for Windows 99 or Quicken Deluxe for Macintosh 98. This is the most popular personal finance software currently available. Produced by Intuit, Quicken allows you to monitor your investments, check out price histories, get current prices, and do in-depth analyses of your holdings. The software sells in the $40–$60 range, depending on where you buy it. Shop around a bit. Go to www.intuit. com to find out more or to order it online.

- **Microsoft Money 99.** Microsoft Money helps you plan your finances, coaching you on everything from paying your bills to creating a budget and reducing debt. Unfortunately, Microsoft Money can be used only with PCs, not Macs. You can pick up a copy at any computer store for around $35. Go to www.microsoft.com to find out more or order it online.

You will definitely want to purchase some disk diagnostic and repair software for your hard disk, and you should run this software at least once a week. The most popular software of this kind is Norton Utilities. One of the key features of this software is Norton Disk Doctor, which repairs major and minor problems found with your hard disk and indicates which documents or programs may be interfering with the smooth running of your computer. Norton will recommend that you remove or replace these files or programs. (Disk Doctor can also be used to check and fix floppy disks.)

Another key feature of the Norton Utilities software is Speed Disk, a program that allows you to defragment your hard disk. Typically, your computer stores files that you save in a hodgepodge manner, placing parts of files at various locations on the hard disk. To open a fragmented file, then, the computer has to do some jumping around. This is inefficient and causes programs to operate much more slowly. Speed Disk defragments files by placing relevant pieces of files together and leaving the unused portion of the HD clear.

One last piece of software you might consider

buying is antivirus software. A computer virus is a program that contains instructions to damage the computer it inhabits. Yes, there are some people out there with nothing better to do than come up with ways to screw up other people's lives. Most viruses are programmed to erase all the information stored on your hard drive by endlessly replicating themselves, thereby consuming all available disk space.

With a few exceptions, viruses can be picked up only from a file that requires you to execute some kind of command, such as run or start. It is not possible to pick up a virus from a passive document such as a picture or a sound file. Nor is it possible, despite popular notions to the contrary, to pick up a virus from downloading or opening your e-mail. Opening a document does not execute a command, so it cannot initiate a virus replication. Be careful about opening attachments (files linked to e-mail messages), however, since attachments can contain dangerous executable commands, or "macros." You also might want to avoid downloading and running programs from the Internet if you're not sure of the source.

Good antivirus software can help your computer avoid infection. Virus protection software can recognize a list of known viruses and expunge them from your computer if discovered, it can erase contaminated files, and it can even kill a virus in a file without destroying the entire file. Check into the following three antivirus software programs:

- **ViruSafe,** by EliaShim (www.softseek.com/Utilities/Virus_Protection/Review_index.html).

- **McAfee VirusScan,** by McAfee (www.mcafee.com/main.asp).

- **Panda AntiVirus** for Windows 95, by Panda Software (www.pandasoftware.es)

Bright Idea
If you decide to download software from the Internet, use your antivirus software to scan it for viruses before you run it.

Just the facts

- Take your time choosing a computer that fits your personal needs and meets the online investor's basic requirements for speed, memory, storage, screen, and warranty.

- Make sure your modem is at least a 28.8bps, but buy the fastest modem you can afford.

- Find an ISP with a local phone number, and don't pay more than $19.95 a month without a very good reason.

- Commercial online services provide you with content and organization that ISPs do not, making them a viable alternative.

- Both Netscape Communicator and Internet Explorer are useful tools for browsing the Web.

- Equip yourself with some financial software, disk repair software, and antivirus software.

GET THE SCOOP ON...
Knowing your financial markets ▪ Exchanges
▪ Market indices ▪ The forces that propel the
markets ▪ Stock market fundamentals

The Basic Facts

What separates the men from the boys in the investing world is wisdom—wisdom born of both knowledge and experience. In this increasingly complex world, true understanding has become a commodity—a key, if not *the* key, to success. Knowledge begets clarity, and clarity begets power. Today's independent online investor gets the power he needs to succeed from his understanding of how markets work and which investments make the most sense at a given time.

The soundness of the specific investment decisions you make will always depend on your understanding of the fundamentals. If your fundamental understanding of markets and market forces is shaky, so will be your buy and sell decisions. The completeness of your understanding will have a direct impact on your bottom line.

A good investor is always a student. Always looking for ways to broaden his knowledge, he never assumes that he knows it all. He is humble, never one to assume that he's right, always looking for ways to learn and profit from his deeper under-standing. And so, in all humility, we begin with the fundamentals, to make sure we see the big picture, to ensure that we have a firm foundation as we jour-ney up the mountain of investment knowledge.

The financial markets

The financial markets are markets where certain kinds of securities or financial instruments are bought and sold (*traded*). Items such as stocks, bonds, and mutual funds are called *securities* because they are secured or backed by something of real value. When you buy a company's stock, for exam-ple, the value of that stock is secured by the value of the company. If you lend the U.S. government money by purchasing a U.S. Treasury bond, the bond is secured by the credibility, reliability, and financial strength of the United States government.

The Big 3: Stocks, bonds, and mutual funds

The major global financial markets include stock markets, bond markets, mutual fund "markets," futures and options markets, and currency markets. Stock markets, as the name implies, are markets where stocks are traded. Stock is actually partial ownership of a company, and the amount of stock one has in a company is expressed in *shares*, individ-ual units of stock. If a company has 200,000 shares outstanding (available for purchase), and you own 100 shares, then you own .05 percent of that com-pany, and you can go to shareholder's meetings and vote on issues affecting that company, if you choose. So, when you purchase shares in eBay or McDonald's, you become part owner.

Bond markets are markets where bonds are bought and sold. A bond is basically an I.O.U. It is a contract stating that the borrower of a certain amount of money will pay back the lender in a certain amount of time with interest. Companies need money to expand. One way they raise money is by issuing stock; another way is by issuing bonds. If you purchase a $5,000, one-year bond from General Electric (GE), with a yield (coupon) of 7 percent, it means you have lent GE $5,000 and that GE will pay you the $5,000 back in one year with 7 percent interest.

"Mutual fund markets" are markets where mutual funds are bought and sold. A mutual fund is a collection of investments in different companies, typically of one type, owned and managed by a mutual fund company. Fidelity Investments is the largest mutual fund company in the world. One of their funds is called Magellan. Magellan is a stock mutual fund, which means that the investments held in the fund are stocks (though bonds may be held there too). The fund manager selects the stocks to be held in the fund, and how well the fund performs is determined by the collective performance of all the stocks in the fund.

What you should know about futures and options

Futures and options markets are markets where futures and options are traded. Futures (a.k.a. commodities) are contracts for the purchase or sale of a commodity, such as gold, sugar, or coffee, to be delivered at a future date. Futures are linked to the fact that the price of goods fluctuates depending on season, supply, and other factors. For example, a company such as General Mills might want to lock in the price of, say, sugar, today, even though it doesn't need delivery for several months, if it thinks that the current price is likely to be as low as or lower than the price several months later. Futures contracts can be bought and sold, so if the price of that commodity rises after you've purchased such a contract, you can sell the contract at a profit. If the price falls, however, you will have to sell at a loss (or accept delivery of a lot of sugar). For this reason, futures are considered very risky and should be avoided by unsophisticated investors.

Options are contracts that allow the holder of the contract to buy or sell something at a predetermined price on or before a predetermined date. If you own 100 shares of GM, for example, but you're concerned that the stock may tumble, you can buy a put option, which gives you the option to sell a certain number of shares of GM at a given price up to a certain date. If the share price of GM does tumble, you can exercise (use) your option and sell the option shares at the better price, covering your loss. If GM continues to climb, however, you will probably choose not to exercise the option, in which case you lose only the cost of the option. Used in this way, options function as a kind of insurance (hedge) against loss.

Some people, however, sell options, and this can result in big losses. If you sell a put option on a stock, for example, you're wagering that the stock will not go down and that you will be able to walk away with the fee the buyer of the option paid you for the option. But if the buyer was right and the stock does tumble, you have to pay up on the option when the buyer exercises the option. Depending on how far the stock tumbled and how much stock was covered by the option, you could lose thousands of dollars. Selling options is very risky and should be avoided by inexperienced investors.

The reason the futures and options markets are usually lumped together is because prudent traders of futures often buy options as a hedge because they realize that they could lose a lot of money. Also, both futures and options are contracts where only a fraction of the value of the item being considered is actually needed to secure the contract—a kind of good-faith deposit. Using a small amount of money to control something of far greater value is known as leveraging or using leverage.

Futures and options markets are referred to as *derivative markets,* and the contracts as *derivatives,* because they derive their value from other financial instruments (such as stocks and bonds). A stock option, for example, derives its value from the underlying value of the stock. As opposed to derivative markets, the stock, bond, and currency markets are known as *cash markets* because the buyer pays in full (in cash) for the financial instrument in question (stock, bond, currency) at the time of purchase.

Making money in currency markets

Currency markets are markets where the currencies of various countries can be traded. The value of currencies relative to each other is always changing and is largely a product of economic and fiscal conditions within the countries. The current exchange rate of the Japanese yen to the U.S. dollar is about 120 yen per dollar. This means that $1 will buy 120 yen. If you were to purchase $5,000 worth of yen at 120 yen per dollar, you would own 600,000 yen. If the yen then strengthened to 100 yen per dollar and you converted your 600,000 yen back into dollars, you would have $6,000, for a profit of $1,000. Investors buy and sell currencies based on the direction in which they believe currencies will move.

Watch Out! Because predicting the direction of currencies is extremely hard to do, investing in currencies should generally be avoided by novice investors.

The Exchanges

So where exactly are all these trades taking place? On exchanges. An *exchange* is a marketplace where securities are bought and sold. The major U.S. exchanges are the New York Stock Exchange (NYSE), the National Stock Dealers Association Quotes or Nasdaq Stock Market (NASD), the American Stock Exchange (AMEX), the over-the-counter market (OTC), the Chicago Board of Trade (CBT), and the Chicago Mercantile Exchange (CME). The major overseas exchanges include those in Tokyo, London, and Hong Kong.

The Big Board—NYSE

In terms of the value of the companies traded, The New York Stock Exchange, also know as the Big Board, is the largest securities market in the world. More than 3,275 companies are listed, with a total market capitalization of more than $11 trillion. (Market capitalization equals the number of outstanding shares multiplied by the price per share.) Generally, the stocks traded on the NYSE are those of the oldest, largest, and best-known companies in the United States. Securities are traded in an auction-style approach, with buyers and sellers (floor brokers) haggling over prices.

The New York Stock Exchange is located at 18 Broad St. in New York City, near Wall Street, the city's financial center. In fact, the NYSE's mailing address is 11 Wall Street. The term "Wall Street" is used to refer both to the NYSE in particular and to U.S. financial markets in general. The exchange is open for trading from 9:30am to 4:00pm Eastern Standard Time, Monday through Friday, except holidays. You can access a wealth of information about the NYSE online at www.nyse.com.

The following is a list of holidays observed by the NYSE:

- New Year's Day
- Martin Luther King, Jr., Day
- Washington's Birthday
- Good Friday
- Memorial Day
- Independence Day
- Labor Day
- Thanksgiving Day
- Christmas

The Nasdaq—AMEX situation

The National Stock Dealers Association Quotes (NASD) was established in 1971 as the world's first completely electronic stock exchange. There is no physical trading floor as there is with the NYSE. Instead of individuals negotiating prices, all prices and trades are settled electronically by a nationwide network of 500 stockbrokerages, known as *market makers*, linked together by a central computer. The market makers compete for investors' trades by offering various prices for the same stocks electronically. The Nasdaq is the fastest-growing stock market in the United States, and it lists the largest number of overseas stocks. About 5,500 stocks are traded on the Nasdaq, with a total market capitalization of $1.8 trillion.

The American Stock Exchange (AMEX) is the second-largest auction-style stock market in the United States, after the NYSE. The companies listed on the AMEX tend to be smaller than those listed on the NYSE or the NASD. Unlike the NYSE and the NASD, the AMEX has always been a market where investors could trade options as well as buy and sell stocks. About 800 companies are listed on the AMEX, with a total market capitalization of $162 billion.

The Nasdaq was the second-largest stock exchange in the United States, and the AMEX was the third-largest until November 1998, when the two exchanges merged. The NASD and AMEX continue to operate as separate markets, however, under the management of the newly created Nasdaq-Amex Market Group, a subsidiary of the NASD. Of course, the Nasdaq-AMEX is the second-largest stock exchange in the United States after the NYSE, with a total market capitalization of almost $2 trillion. The two markets decided to merge in the hopes of being better able to compete with the NYSE for investors' trades. The merger benefits both exchanges. Market makers on the NASD are now able to buy options as hedges, and AMEX stocks get the wider market exposure provided by Nasdaq's electronic network. The exchange is open from 9:30am to 4:00pm (EST) weekdays, except holidays. More information can be found about the Nasdaq-Amex online at nasdaq-amex.com.

The Nasdaq-Amex now offers an after-hours trading session from 4:00pm–6:30pm (EST). This development is clearly a reflection of the impact the Internet and online investing are having on the stock market. With more individuals taking control of their investments and placing trades in the evening, there is a growing demand for markets to be open for business during these hours. The advantage of after-hours trading to the investor is the ability to place a trade and have it executed right away, rather than having to wait until the next market day.

Watch Out!
In all likelihood, there will be less liquidity in after-hours trading. *Liquidity* is the degree to which buying and selling can take place easily in a market and with a minimum disturbance of prices. At this point only sophisticated investors should be trading after hours.

The OTC and the SEC

The over-the-counter market (OTC) should not be confused with the Nasdaq. Like the Nasdaq, the OTC is an electronic market, but stocks listed on the OTC do not meet the Nasdaq's listing requirements, such as the requirement for net worth. In fact, the stocks traded on the OTC don't need to meet any real quantitative or qualitative standards, as the OTC is not actually an exchange but a bulletin board that electronically lists stock prices. The companies listed on the OTC have no direct business relationship with any exchange and have no reporting obligations. (The other exchanges make sure that all companies observe securities laws, work to prevent fraud, and look into all customer complaints.) Approximately 5,000 securities are traded on the OTC—generally these are small companies in need of capital. The OTC bulletin board continuously displays and updates OTC domestic stock prices and updates foreign stock prices twice a day. OTC trades can be placed from 9:00am to 4:30pm (EST) weekdays, except for holidays.

While OTC stocks have no reporting obligations to any exchange, this does not mean that a person who invests in OTC stocks is unprotected from fraud. The United States Security and Exchange Commission (SEC) is an independent, nonpartisan federal agency that administers federal securities laws designed to protect investors. The laws stipulate that investors have access to all current, accurate information related to publicly traded securities and the companies that issue those securities. The laws also regulate companies that buy and sell securities, companies that give investment advice, and investment companies—companies that invest in various

Unofficially...
Documents by
foreign companies
are not required
to be filed on
EDGAR, although
some of these
companies do so
anyway.

securities using the money acquired through the sale of shares in their own company, such as mutual fund companies. To learn more about the laws that protect you, check out the SEC's Web site at www.sec.gov.

The SEC maintains a massive database, called EDGAR (the Electronic Data Gathering, Analysis, and Retrieval system), that contains financial documents on all companies that are required by law to file forms with the SEC. This would include just about every company that has issued stock for purchase by the public. You can find out a great deal about a company by checking on it through EDGAR. With the exception of investment companies, companies are not required to submit annual reports to EDGAR, but they are required to submit Form 10-K or 10-KSB, which contains much of the same information. Check out EDGAR online at www.sec.gov/edgarhp.htm.

The wild exchanges in the Windy City

The Chicago Board of Trade (CBOT) is the world's largest futures and options exchange. On this exchange, investors can buy commodities and options on those commodities. It's also possible to buy and sell bonds and contracts on interest rates on the CBOT. Depending on the contract, an investor of a contract on interest rates can profit if interest rates move in one direction or another. The CBOT is an actual exchange, with a trading floor, located at 141 West Jackson Blvd. in Chicago. It's open for business from 9:00am to 4:30pm (EST) weekdays, except holidays. For more information, check out the CBOT Web site at www.cbot.com.

The Chicago Mercantile Exchange (CME) is the world's largest futures exchange, specializing in livestock, currencies, and stock index futures. A *stock index* is a group of stocks whose combined performance is used to measure the direction of an overall market. When you buy a stock index futures contract, you are wagering on the future direction of that index (or the market that index measures). It is also possible to purchase agricultural commodities, foreign currencies, and contracts on interest rates on the CME. Like the CBOT, the CME is an actual exchange. It is located at 30 South Wacker Dr. in Chicago and is open from 9:00am to 4:30pm weekdays (EST), except holidays. For more information check out the CME Web site at www.cme.com.

These exchanges are not the only exchanges in the country, but they are the major exchanges. Other important exchanges include the Philadelphia Stock Exchange (PSE), the Chicago Board Options Exchange (CBOE), and the New York Commodities Exchange (COMEX).

The major market indices

The so-called market averages or market indices are scales that measure the overall upward or downward movement of a certain group of securities. Market averages differ from market indices in that averages are not weighted for market capitalization. Indices give an indication of the overall movement of a financial market and can help investors make decisions. The lion's share of well-known market indices are used to monitor the movement of stock markets. The reasons for this include these:

1. Stocks are the most popular of investment vehicles.
2. Stock mutual funds consist of stocks.

3. Stocks are more volatile than bonds, so there is a greater need to keep a close eye on the stock market than the bond market.

The Dow, the granddaddy of averages

The most famous of the stock market indices is the Dow Jones Industrial Average, or the Dow (DJIA). The Dow is a grouping of 30 of the largest companies in the United States, with a traditional bias toward industrial companies. All the stocks that make up the Dow are called *blue chips*, indicating that they are companies of the highest quality and financial strength. As of May 28, 1999, the Dow consisted of the companies shown on the accompanying table.

Allied-Signal Inc.	(ALD)
Aluminum Co. of America	(AA)
American Express	(AE)
AT&T	(T)
Boeing Co.	(BA)
Caterpillar Inc.	(CAT)
Citigroup Inc.	(C)
Coca-Cola Co.	(KO)
Disney Co.	(DIS)
DuPont	(DD)
Eastman Kodak	(EK)
Exxon Corp.	(XON)
General Electric	(GE)
General Motors	(GM)
Hewlett-Packard Co.	(HWP)
Home Depot Inc.	(HD)
Intel Corp.	(INTC)
International Business Machines	(IBM)
International Paper	(IP)
Johnson & Johnson	(JNJ)

McDonald's Corp.	(MCD)
Merck & Co.	(MRK)
Microsoft	(MSFT)
Minnesota Mining/Mfg.	(MMM)
Morgan (J.P.)	(JPM)
Philip Morris Cos.	(MO)
Procter & Gamble	(PG)
SBC Communications Inc.	(SBC)
United Technologies	(UTX)
Wal-Mart Stores Inc.	(WMT)

Each company's name in the list is followed by the company's abbreviated name, or ticker symbol, which is used to represent the company when trades are placed on the exchanges.

The Dow was created in 1897, when it consisted of only 12 stocks. It grew to 20 stocks in 1916, and finally to 30 in 1928. Originally, the Dow was calculated by simply adding the prices of the 12 stocks and dividing by 12. So, if the sum of the prices per share of all the stocks on the Dow was 360, the Dow Jones Industrial Average that day would have equaled 30 ($360/12 = 30$). Because the 30 stocks that make up the present-day Dow sometimes change, and because a company sometimes *splits* its stock (doubles the number of outstanding shares and halves the price per share), the divisor of 30 has been changed so that the average will still accurately reflect the day-to-day ups and downs of the stocks in the Dow, not the changes in the equation used to calculate it.

As a measure of the performance of the overall stock market, the Dow is very restrictive—it includes only 30 of the more than 5,000 publicly traded stocks available. Because these 30 are among the largest companies (*large cap* stocks), the Dow tends

Timesaver
For a quick look at the Dow and how all the stocks on the Dow are doing, check out www.dbc.com/cgi-bin/htx.exe/dbcfiles/dowt.html. Detailed information about each company can be accessed by clicking the ticker symbol.

to reflect the movement of the biggest blue chips more than the movement of the overall stock market. Another problem with the Dow is that it is price weighted. This means that the higher a stock's share price is, the greater that stock's impact on the average will be. Because stocks often split, however, share price is not a good indicator of a company's worth. So why should a 10 percent move in a stock with a higher share price have a greater impact on the average than a 10 percent move in a stock with a lower share price?

Measuring up to the S&P

The most widely followed market index is the Standard & Poor's 500 Stock Index (S&P 500). The S&P 500 consists of 500 of the largest publicly traded stocks, most of which are blue chips. But while the S&P 500 is also a blue chip index, unlike the Dow, the S&P is weighted for market capitalization. The greater a stock's market capitalization, the more weight that stock is given in calculating the index. This way, the movements of larger companies have a greater impact on the index than the movements of smaller companies. The performance of most mutual fund managers and stockbrokers is compared to that of the S&P, rather than the Dow, because the S&P contains a much larger universe of high-quality stocks and because it is weighted. The S&P 100, known by the ticker symbol OEX, measures the performance of a diverse group of large company blue chip stocks chosen from the S&P 500.

Nasdaq—another index

Another frequently quoted market index is the Nasdaq Composite Index (NASDAQ). The NASDAQ Composite consists of all stocks listed on the Nasdaq

Stock Exchange—some 5,500 stocks. The NASDAQ is weighted for market capitalization. This is particularly significant in the case of the NASDAQ because only a few large cap stocks are traded on the Nasdaq Stock Exchange, and the performance of those stocks tends to dominate the index. The index is thought to be tech-heavy, reflecting the performance of the technology sector more than the market as a whole. While the entire stock market has done well throughout most of the 1990s, Nasdaq's rise has been precipitous, in large part because of the stellar performances of two tech stocks, Microsoft and Intel.

Indices for the small caps

The Wilshire 5000 Index is the least restrictive of the indices, measuring the performance of *all* publicly traded stocks in the United States (now more than 7,000). The Wilshire is weighted for market capitalization. Like the Nasdaq Composite, the Wilshire contains thousands of small companies (*small cap*), but its overall performance is dominated by the performance of the large companies.

The market index that best measures the performance of small companies is the Russell 2000. The Russell 2000 is weighted for market capitalization. This index is specifically designed to measure the performance of small caps (which we'll examine in Chapter 4) and includes 2,000 of the smallest publicly traded stocks.

There are many other stock market indices, which you might hear quoted from time to time, including: the AMEX Composite, which measures the performance of all the stocks traded on the American Stock Exchange; and the Dow Jones Transportation Average and the Dow Jones Utility

Bright Idea
If you're thinking about investing in Internet stocks, you can follow the Internet Stock Index (ISDEX) at http://fast.quote.com/groups/isdex.html or the H&Q Internet Index at www.hamquist.com/research/stats/indices/internet.html.

Moneysaver
Many local
libraries sub-
scribe to daily
newspapers with
financial sections
that provide the
performance of
market indices as
well as individual
stocks. Many
papers are also
available online
free of charge.

Average, which measure the movement of stock prices in the transportation and utilities industries, respectively. A limited number of indices measure performance in other financial markets: The performance of bonds is often gauged by the 30 Year Treasury Bond Index and the 13 Week T-Bill Index; and the performance of gold is measured by the CBOE Gold Index. Which index you pay the most attention to will depend on what kind of securities you decide to invest in.

Should you pay more attention to indices weighted for capitalization than those that are not? Well, virtually all indices, except for the Dow, are now weighted for market capitalization. Giving more weight to the price movements of large companies than to small companies means that indices such as the S&P 500 will more accurately reflect the performance of your own portfolio (the securities you own collectively) if you own more large cap stocks than small. If you own mostly small caps, however, using an index such as the S&P may not give you any idea how your stocks are doing. In this case, the Russell 2000 would be better.

Market forces to be reckoned with

In addition to a basic understanding of the financial markets and the major market indices, the online investor should have a fundamental understanding of the market forces that have an impact on financial markets. While most of us studied economics in high school or college from a theoretical point of view, it's important now to look at some of those principles with an eye to their practical applications for our investments. To be sure, what's happening in the economy at large will have an impact on your individual holdings. As Henry David Thoreau might have said, no stock is an island unto itself, but a part of the continent.

The single most important market force the online investor must be aware of is interest rates— more specifically, the *direction* of interest rates. Interest rates are the rate lenders charge borrowers to borrow money. Interest rates have a greater impact on financial markets than any other market force, to the point where all other market forces, including inflation, unemployment, and the budget deficit, are now considered in terms of how they will affect interest rates. Why is this so?

While it may sound less than frugal, if not downright irresponsible, economic growth and the growth of businesses depends on borrowing money. When a person decides she wants to start or grow a business, the first thing she does (after drawing up a good business plan) is go to the bank and ask for a loan. Why? She needs money (capital) to get her business started. She needs to rent office space, rent or buy office equipment, hire staff, make a certain amount of the product, and advertise and market the product before she makes a single sale. And if this businesswoman's business is a success, she will need to borrow more money if she wants to expand.

How rates affect stocks and bonds

Unfortunately, borrowing money isn't free. The bank will charge the borrower interest. This is how banks make money. The higher the interest rate banks charge businesses to borrow, the harder it is for businesses to borrow in the first place, to pay the money back, or to make a profit. In fact, if interest rates go up too much, many businesses go bankrupt. The lower the rates are, the easier it is for companies to borrow and profit. The more a company

> **66**
> Neither a borrower nor a lender be /
> For loan oft loses both itself and friend, /
> And borrowing dulls the edge of husbandry.
> —William Shakespeare, *Hamlet*
> **99**

profits (earns), the more it is worth; the more it is worth, the more it is valued; the more it is valued, the more people are willing to pay to own its stock. That's what drives stock prices higher. And this is why low or falling interest rates are good for stocks and the stock market, and why high or rising rates are bad.

Rising rates are also bad for bonds. Here's why. Bonds have a *price*, the amount you pay for the bond, and a *yield* (or coupon), the interest rate you are paid by the borrower. Remember, a bond is an I.O.U. from the borrower to pay back the lender the face value of the bond plus interest, but the price you actually have to pay for a bond at any given time depends on the current level of interest rates. For example, if you paid $10,000 for a bond with an 8.5 percent yield, and interest rates on similar bonds subsequently rose to 9.5 percent, you would be able to sell your bond in the new interest rate climate for only around $9,000. No one would pay for a bond like yours with a lower yield unless they could get your bond at a discount.

Another reason stock and bond prices tend to fall when rates rise is that low-risk, interest-bearing investments start looking more appealing to investors. Interest rates on money market accounts, money market funds, and CDs go up when rates do. As a result, an increasing number of people pull their money out of stocks and bonds and put it into competing investment vehicles.

The main determinant of the direction of interest rates is inflation. Inflation is the tendency for things to get more expensive, for prices to rise. Why does inflation affect interest rates? Inflation drains money of its value. If at the beginning of the year

$1 can buy a loaf of bread, but at the end of the year you need $2 (an inflation rate of 100 percent), the buying power of a dollar has been cut in half. If a bank lends you $10,000 at 10 percent interest, but inflation is at 20 percent, the bank will actually lose 10 percent on its money in real terms. To prevent this from happening, banks will raise their rates to keep pace with inflation.

Here comes the Fed

Banks themselves are huge borrowers, and much of the money they borrow comes from other banks. Borrowing between banks occurs when a bank needs additional reserves to meet reserve requirements. (Banks are required to keep between 3 percent and 10 percent of funds on hand in vaults to meet unexpected withdrawals.) The rate banks charge each other to borrow is called the federal funds rate, or the funds rate. The U.S. Central Bank (www.bog.frb.fed.us), also known as the Federal Reserve, or the Fed, determines the funds rate. When the federal funds rate increases, banks raise their prime lending rate, or prime rate, the rate they charge their corporate borrowers (companies). If banks have to pay more to borrow, they have to charge others more to borrow from them.

The Federal Reserve also controls the discount rate, which is the rate the Fed charges banks for borrowing money directly from the Fed. The amount of such borrowing is small, but while an increase in the discount rate does not have a large direct impact on markets, it can signal a change in the overall direction of interest rates or a change in monetary policy, the Federal Reserve's stance on what the economy needs at any given time. When the Fed is referred to as "tightening," it indicates a policy of raising rates

Unofficially...
Generally, banks do not raise the prime rate unless the Fed raises the Federal Funds Rate.

in an effort to stem inflation; "loosening" is a policy of lowering rates in an effort to stimulate growth.

A third way the Fed can effect a change in interest rates is by increasing or decreasing the reserve requirements of banks. Increasing the required amount of cash banks must keep on hand means that banks will have less money to lend, making money scarcer (decreasing the money supply); this will cause banks' lending rates to rise. Decreasing reserve requirements has the opposite effect, increasing the money supply and leading to lower rates.

Clearly, the Federal Reserve Board shoulders the most responsibility for determining the direction of interest rates in the economy. It is actually the Federal Reserve Board's Open Market Committee (OMC), which meets every six weeks or so, that decides whether to raise rates, lower them, or leave them unchanged. The most influential person on the Open Market Committee is the chairman of the Federal Reserve Board (a position held since 1988 by Alan Greenspan). Periodically, the chairman is asked to testify before Congress on the state of the economy and where he thinks the economy is headed. The Fed chairman is a very powerful man. One word from his lips interpreted as a change in interest-rate policy can send both domestic and overseas markets reeling.

The Federal Reserve's primary aim is to shepherd the U.S. economy (and, indirectly, the economies of the world) in the direction of steady growth and low inflation. This is a difficult task. When companies grow, they are selling more products and building more stores (or offices) so that they can sell still *more* products. To sell more products, they need to make more products, and this

requires purchasing more raw materials and supplies (computers, paper, and so on) and hiring
more people. The more companies spend, the more
the demand for things increases. And the more people companies hire, the more people there are who
have money to spend, which also increases demand.
Now, as demand increases, prices tend to rise
because sellers can charge more for their wares.
This is the rule of scarcity. The more scarce a
desired object becomes, the more it is worth. So
growth tends to beget inflation.

On the one hand, growth is good because it creates jobs and wealth and fosters increased revenues
and earnings for companies. On the other hand, it
promotes inflation. The Federal Reserve, then, has
the delicate task of promoting growth, but not so
much growth that inflation gets out of control.

While interest rates are the name of the game,
political events can also move the markets. War overseas, for example, can have a destabilizing effect on
certain economies and can cause more foreigners to
buy dollars or U.S. bonds. Increased demand, then,
could drive up prices in these markets. Recession
overseas also could have a negative impact on the
earnings of U.S. companies that sell to those markets, pushing down stock prices here.

Economic indicators tell the story

The Fed looks at a slew of economic indicators in
making its decisions about raising, lowering, or
maintaining interest rates. All these indicators are
designed to give the Fed information about the
economy's rate of growth and inflation. The financial markets also keep an eye on these indicators,
and the current levels of the markets reflect what

Unofficially...
Under the
auspices of Alan
Greenspan, the
Fed has done an
unparalleled job
in the 1990s of
achieving that
balance, and this
explains, more
than anything
else, why the
stock market has
gone through the
roof. Growth has
been steady, but
inflation has
remained tame.

the markets anticipate these reports will show. Any surprises on the day a report is released affect prices.

GDP

In making its decisions, one of the first indicators the Fed looks at is the gross domestic product (GDP). Reported quarterly, the GDP measures the total value of goods and services produced domestically by the United States in a given period. Larger-than-expected increases in the GDP are considered inflationary, having an upward influence on interest rates (and thus a downward influence on stocks).

CPI and PPI

Unofficially...
Economists tend to focus on the core CPI, which does not include the volatile food and energy sectors. Economists feel that the core rate is a more accurate measure of underlying inflationary pressures.

Another very important indicator is the Consumer Price Index (CPI). The CPI is a monthly indicator that compares the prices of a list of goods now to the same list during a base period, currently 1982–1984. A larger-than-expected rise in the CPI indicates a larger-than-expected rise in the price of things such as food, gasoline, and medical care, and is considered inflationary. Along similar lines is the Producer Price Index (PPI), also a monthly indicator, which measures wholesale prices, or what producers of goods are paying for consumer goods and capital equipment. As with the CPI, when the PPI is higher than expected, it's considered inflationary.

ECI

Another important economic indicator is the Economic Cost Index (ECI). The ECI measures the salaries and benefits companies are paying employees. As salaries increase, so does this indicator, which is bad news for inflation. Why? When this indicator goes up, it means there is an increasing number of people with more disposable income. With more money to go around, the demand for goods increases relative to the supply, and this drives prices higher.

The Employment Report

The Employment-Payroll Jobs Report, or Employment Report, is an important monthly indicator, providing various data, including information on employment, the average work week, hourly earnings, and the unemployment rate. The most important number here is the one showing the number of jobs in the United States. A higher-than-expected increase would be considered inflationary—again, because more people are making money, which will be used to buy things. The unemployment rate, which is a separate report within the Employment Report, measures the unemployment rate in the United States. When the unemployment rate is less than expected, it's considered inflationary. Most economists believe that 5.5 percent unemployment is the natural rate, or the rate at which unemployment can exist without causing inflation. If unemployment falls below 5.5 percent and remains there, economists grow increasingly concerned that inflation will flare up.

The Housing Starts Report

The Housing Starts Report is another much-watched economic indicator. The housing industry is where 27 percent of all investment spending takes place, accounting for 5 percent of the overall economy. The housing-starts data used in this report are based on information from four regions of the United States: the Northeast, the Midwest, the South, and the West. Sustained declines in housing starts can actually trigger a recession (a period of low economic activity), while increases in housing starts can lead to economic growth. Greater-than-expected increases, however, are considered inflationary.

NAPM

Another report the Fed examines carefully is the National Association of Purchasing Managers Report (NAPM). This report is based on a survey sent to more than 250 companies across the United States, covering 21 industries. The managers are asked questions about their company with regard to the following six items:

1. Production
2. Orders
3. Commodity prices
4. Inventories
5. Vendor performance
6. Employment

The managers are asked to respond to each of the questions with "up," "down," or "unchanged." The index does take into account the effects of different seasons on various businesses (seasonal changes). A reading of 50 on the index indicates that conditions remain unchanged; above 50 indicates that the economy is expanding; and below 50 indicates that it is declining. Stronger-than-expected increases in the NAPM are considered inflationary.

Other indicators

This is a list of other indicators that the Fed keeps an eye on—and that you should, too. All these indicators are released monthly; if they rise more than they were expected to, this is considered inflationary. Often the indicators send mixed signals, forcing the Fed to use its judgment about whether to raise or lower rates or to leave them unchanged.

- Retail sales
- Durable goods orders
- Personal income
- Industrial production
- Capacity utilization
- Construction spending
- Existing home sales
- New home sales
- Consumer credit
- Index of Leading Economic Indicators

While the names of most of these indicators give a pretty good idea of what they measure, two are a bit mystifying: capacity utilization and Index of Leading Economic Indicators. Capacity utilization measures the extent to which the country's capital is being used for the production of goods. Capacity utilization is measured in percentages; as the percent of capital being spent on the production of goods increases, inflationary pressures rise. The Index of Leading Economic Indicators is intended to predict how the economy will behave in the months ahead. This is why it's called an index of *leading* indicators. This index is actually a composite of 10 leading indicators:

1. Average work week (manufacturing)
2. Initial unemployment claims
3. Consumer goods orders
4. Vendor performance
5. Nondefense capital goods orders
6. Building permits

7. Stock prices (S&P 500)

8. Real M2 (a measure of the money supply)

9. Interest rate spread (a measure of the differences in interest rates among various investments)

10. Consumer expectations

Other market forces

While interest rates are the most important market force affecting the overall direction of the stock market, other factors—such as the budget deficit, the national debt, and trade imbalances—also have an impact. Every year, the White House must submit a budget to Congress, which Congress must approve or amend. The budget is the government's plan for how it will spend its projected income for the year. A budget deficit occurs when the government's budget does not balance; the budget calls for spending to exceed income. Excessive government spending is inflationary.

After many, many years of spending more than it makes (since 1969, in fact), the U.S. government has amassed a huge debt, referred to as the *national debt*. Currently, the national debt stands at more than $5.5 trillion, and the government must make timely interest payments on this borrowed money. (This is referred to as *servicing the debt*.) The U.S. government's ability to make these interest payments is why it is still able to borrow money. Interestingly, despite the apparent balancing of the budget by the Clinton Administration, the U.S. national debt continues to grow (check www.brillig.com/debt_clock/), which indicates that the Treasury is, in fact, still borrowing.

The problem with the debt is that as it grows, the amount of money the government must pay out as interest payments also grows. The larger that amount becomes, the less money the government has to spend on programs and projects and the daily expenses of running the government. It has gotten to the point now where the government is actually borrowing money to pay interest on the debt, and this is inflationary. The more money the U.S. government takes out of the system, the less that is available for corporations. As the government competes with companies for capital, capital becomes scarce, driving up the price of borrowing money (interest rates).

You've doubtless heard about the trade imbalance with Japan; the United States imports more from Japan than it exports. The United States also has a negative trade imbalance with China. Trade imbalances are not inflationary—the more overseas products we import, the greater the supply, and the more domestic industries must compete by lowering prices. Free trade is never inflationary; managed trade always is. While importing more goods than we export will not spark inflation, however, the competition from overseas can hurt domestic companies by cutting into their market share and their revenues; this exerts negative pressure on their stock prices.

This raises an important point. While the negative influence of rising interest rates on financial markets is paramount, you should not forget that companies must grow in order to show rising share prices. But while growth is good, and growth in excess of what's expected is even better, greater-than-expected growth for the overall economy is

Unofficially...
Some feel that the national debt is not a problem. Borrowing, after all, is the key to economic growth. These people would argue that what the country needs is not a reduction in the debt, but more growth.

Watch Out!
Be careful not to base your investment decisions solely on what you see in the newspapers, in magazines, or on the news. This information is dated and has already been factored into market prices.

considered inflationary for individual companies. By now you know what that means: higher interest rates.

Also keep in mind that an increase in interest rates or inflationary pressures may not translate into lower share prices—at least not right away. There have been periods when the market has risen even when interest rates were climbing. Other factors, such as trend and price momentum (which we will discuss later), may offset the interest rate variable, at least in the short run. Generally speaking, however, this is not the case.

The problem with using changes in interest rates to make decisions about how to invest is that it's difficult to predict the direction of interest rates, at least before everyone else has. Before you can even get to your computer, data from the most recently released economic indicator reports will have been gobbled up and digested by the markets and will already be reflected in share prices. Nevertheless, it is important for the savvy online investor to be aware of how rates influence the financial markets and how all other market forces seem to be viewed by markets in terms of how they will affect rates.

Some stock market basics

Before we complete our discussion of basic market knowledge, we should review a few terms and concepts. The first is *bull markets* and *bear markets*. A bull market is a period characterized by a general upward movement of prices in a financial market; a bear market is characterized by the opposite, usually defined as a drop in prices of 15 percent or more. Even though we haven't seen a bear market in quite some time, it's important to keep in mind that, historically, bear markets emerge with frightening regularity. The average decline in a bear market is 34.8 percent, and the average length is 1.5 years.

MAJOR BEAR MARKETS, 1919–1999

1919–1921	–47.6%
1923	–18.6%
1929–1932	–89.2%
1933	–37.2%
1937–1938	–49.1%
1938–1942	–41.3%
1946–1949	–24.0%
1956–1957	–19.4%
1962	–27.1%
1966	–25.2%
1969–1970	–36.1%
1973–1974	–45.1%
1978–1980	–16.4%
1981–1982	–24.1%
1987	–35.8%
1990	–21.1%

When an investor is referred to as a bull, it means that he is optimistic about the stock market; bear investors are pessimistic. A person or an indicator can also be described as bullish or bearish.

You should understand the following terms used to describe markets before embarking on your adventures in online investing:

Volume: Volume indicates the number of shares traded on a given exchange in a given time period. High volume indicates a lot of activity; this is often referred to as heavy trading. Low volume is referred to as light trading.

Volatility: Volatility is a term used to describe the extent of up-and-down movement in prices on an exchange in a given time period. Periods of high volatility are accompanied by relative instability in prices (price fluctuations) and higher-than-usual levels of risk.

Trading range: Trading range describes the range of prices—the high price and the low price—for an index or an individual security over a period of time. The daily trading range of the Dow would give the highest price and the lowest price reached during the day. Large daily trading ranges suggest high volatility. Another commonly cited trading range is the 52-week trading range. This statistic gives you the highest level and the lowest level reached by an index or security in the past year.

Breadth: Breadth is a term used to describe the number of stocks involved in a bull market or rally (upswing in prices) on a stock exchange at a given time. When a small number of stocks are responsible for the lion's share of the rise in an index, breadth is said to be narrow or poor. When a large number of stocks are involved, breadth is said to be positive or good. Narrow breadth is considered a red flag for the stock market; positive breadth is considered good. One of the most common ways to measure breadth is to look at the number of stocks that go up in price (advance) on a given day.

Advance-Decline Line: The Advance-Decline Line, used to measure breadth, is the line formed by the running total of the number of advancing stocks divided by the number of declining stocks taken on a daily basis. A rise in the A-D line means that the number of advancing stocks is increasing; a fall indicates that it is decreasing.

New highs vs. new lows: In measuring the overall health of the stock market, analysts like to compare the number of stocks hitting their all-time highs with the number of stocks hitting their all-time lows at a given time. If the market is healthy, the number of stocks hitting new highs should be greater than the number hitting new lows.

Leadership: Leadership refers to the phenomenon of a group of stocks, often in one sector, that are outperforming the rest of the market but that are also leading other stocks higher. A "lack of leadership" would refer to the absence of such a group. In the late 1990s, surging Internet stocks led the stock market as a whole to all-time highs.

Also familiarize yourself with a couple Web sites to get a good overall understanding of investing fundamentals: the American Association of Independent Investors (AAII), at www.aaii.org; and the National Association of Investors Corporation (NAIC), at www.better-investing.com.

Just the facts

- The major financial markets include the stock market, the bond market, the mutual funds market, the currency market, and the futures and options markets.

- The most important exchanges in the United States include the New York Stock Exchange, the Nasdaq-AMEX Stock Exchange, the Chicago Board of Trade, the Chicago

Timesaver
If you have a question about financial markets, the market indices, or market forces, try searching for the answer on the Web. A well-conducted search could provide you with the information you're looking for in a matter of minutes, if not seconds.

Mercantile Exchange, and the over-the-counter market.

- The market indices watched most closely are the Dow Jones Industrial Average, the S&P 500, the Nasdaq Composite, the Wilshire 5000, and the Russell 2000.

- The market force with the greatest impact on financial markets is interest rates.

- A number of terms are used to describe the state of a market, such as bull market/bear market, volume, trading range, volatility, breadth, and Advance-Decline Line.

GET THE SCOOP ON...
There's more to stocks than meets the eye
■ Making sense out of bonds ■ Mutual funds
to cover all the bases ■ Alternative
investments to explore

Plenty of Investment Vehicles to Choose From

Chapter 4

Before making an important investment decision, it's vital for you to know what your choices are. Only then can you be confident that you're making the right decision for yourself at any given time. Before laying your money down, you need to know the ins and outs of the different investment vehicles, the advantages and disadvantages of each, the risks and potential rewards, and the tax implications. Having a working knowledge of the investment vehicles available to you will also enable you to make timely changes in your portfolio when your situation changes or when market conditions call for it. Being able to move from one type of investment to another knowing full well what you're doing will save you time and money and help you avoid stress.

To the average online investor, investing online means buying and selling one of two things: stocks or mutual funds. While the bulk of online trading does revolve around these two types of investments, now it's also possible to trade bonds, options, real estate investment trusts (REITs), CDs, and other types of securities online. As the Internet continues to expand, the kinds of investments available for purchase online will surely expand as well.

Everything you need to know about stocks

Of all the major investment vehicles traded on the exchanges, stocks provide investors with the best way to make the most money in the long run. Chapter 3, "The Basic Facts," defined stocks as partial ownership of a company, but not all companies are for sale in this way. Most large companies start out as small, privately owned operations. If they are very successful locally, they expand a bit and may eventually decide to go regional, national, or even international. To do this, however, these companies need money (capital). And one way to raise the necessary funds is to "go public," issuing stock in the company for sale on one of the stock exchanges. (Another way to raise money is to sell bonds.) The hope is that droves of individual and institutional investors will buy up the stock, leaving the management flush with cash to undertake their expansion.

As a partial owner of a company, you literally own a fraction of that company's assets, including its buildings, chairs, desks, computers—everything. This means that you have some say in company policy-making, you have the right to vote on issues before the company (including the right to vote in company elections), and you have the right to attend shareholders meetings. Companies you buy stock in will send you brochures—annual reports—detailing

"
Experience keeps a dear school, but fools will learn in no other.
—Benjamin Franklin
"

their operations and performance over the past year, and even proxy ballots, which allow you to vote on issues without having to attend the shareholders meetings in person. Issues facing companies all the time, such as whether to issue more stock or who should sit on the Board of Directors, are important and could eventually affect the company's success and the value of your stock. As a partial owner, you should do whatever you can to assist in your company's success.

A *share* is a unit of a company's stock. You purchase shares of a company at a certain price per share. As this book goes to press, shares of Ford, for example, are selling at $57 per share. A company's share price is always changing, and the price is based on how much investors think the company's stock is worth at any given time. If sales and revenues fall after you buy a stock, this could have a negative impact on the share price. If interest rates rise, this also could have a negative impact. On the other hand, if the outlook for the company improves after you buy its stock, the share price will probably rise. When the share price rises, you make money. You could turn around and sell the stock and walk away with a profit; this type of profit is called a *capital gain.* If you sell stock at a loss, it's a *capital loss* and can be taken as a tax deduction.

Dividends for you and me

In addition to making money through share price increases, stock investors can make money through dividend payouts. A *dividend* is a fraction of a company's profit, paid out to investors at regular intervals (often quarterly). Hopefully, the companies you invest in will be making a profit: The amount of money they're making will exceed the amount of money they're spending. Otherwise, you won't be getting any dividends. A company's dividend payout is expressed as dividend per share or as dividend yield. Ford, for example, is currently paying a dividend of $1.84, which means that for every share of Ford you own, you're getting $1.84 a year in dividends. This equals a dividend yield of 3.26 percent. Thus, shareholders are making 3.26 percent annually on their investment in Ford, apart from any change in share price.

Dividends are paid to shareholders in one of two ways, either in cash or in stock. Cash dividends are cash payments usually sent to your broker (unless you've specified otherwise), who deposits the money into your brokerage account. After a company pays out a cash dividend, the company's share price is reduced by the amount of the total dividend payout. Share price is reduced because the pre-dividend price of the stock includes all that cash in the coffers. When the cash is paid out to shareholders as dividends, the stock price must drop accordingly.

To avoid such a dip in share price and to avoid letting go of so much cash, some companies issue stock dividends instead. With a stock dividend, the company issues shareholders additional shares of stock instead of cash. So, if you own 10 shares of a stock in a company that declares a 10 percent stock dividend, you will receive 1 additional share, giving you 11 shares. In this way, the company can avoid paying out a lot of cash, which can be used instead to help grow the company.

Do you want preferential treatment?

Two basic kinds of stock exist: common stock and preferred stock. *Common stock* represents ownership of a company. Shareholders become owners "in

Moneysaver
In distributing dividends, a company first establishes a record date, which limits the recipients of a dividend payout to those people on record as owning the stock on or before that date. If you're watching a stock, waiting for a good to time to buy, try to pick it up before its record date.

common" with other shareholders, sharing in the company's profits and losses. When a company's stock goes up, shareholders of common stock benefit from larger dividends and higher share prices. On the other hand, if things turn down, common stockholders lose the most. If the company goes bankrupt, shareholders of common stock have last claim to the company's assets, behind bondholders, creditors, and preferred stockholders.

Preferred stock gives its shareholders preference by paying them dividends first and, as mentioned, compensating them before common shareholders in a bankruptcy situation. Although preferred stockholders are owners, they have no ownership *interest* in a company; that is, they do not benefit directly from appreciation in a company's share price or increases in a company's profits, nor can they vote on issues affecting the company. Instead, preferred stockholders, like bondholders, are paid a fixed dividend on their investment. Unlike bondholders, however, preferred stockholders will continue to receive these payments for as long as they own the stock. (There is no maturity date.) So, if you bought $1,000 worth of XYZ company's preferred stock, with a 7 percent dividend, you would receive $70 a year from XYZ for as long as you owned that stock.

There is a catch, though. If XYZ were to miss a dividend payment (because the company just didn't have the money to pay you), you would have no immediate legal recourse to get your money the way a bondholder would. Nevertheless, dividend payments on preferred stock are cumulative, so if an issuer of preferred stock does miss a payment, the company must make that payment later, as soon as they can.

Another drawback of preferred stocks is that companies can force you to surrender your stock for a cash payment at any time. (This is not the case with common stock.) They might do this if the interest payments on the stock are high given the current interest rate climate. There are different classes of preferred stock (A, B, C, and so on) with different restrictions, prices, and dividend payouts. Some kinds of preferred stock can be converted into common stock.

Stocks come in all shapes and sizes

The online investor should know about eight general categories of stocks: blue chip stocks, growth stocks, value stocks, income stocks, defensive stocks, cyclical stocks, speculative stocks, and convertible securities. The next sections take a look at each of these categories in more detail.

Blue chips

Blue chip stocks are the stocks of the largest, most prestigious companies in the land. These companies exhibit financial strength and have a history of paying out dividends in both good times and bad. Blue chip stocks are relatively safe stocks, stocks that will probably continue to do well in the long run, even if they don't experience explosive growth. All the stocks on the Dow and many of the stocks on the S&P 500 would be considered blue chips, and blue chips are generally large cap stocks.

Growth stocks

Growth stocks are stocks of companies that have the potential to grow a great deal and are expected to grow faster than the average company listed on any of the exchanges. Growth stocks are often relatively new companies, or not-so-new companies in new or newly explosive industries. These companies have a tendency to put a lot of money into research and development, with the hope of enhancing their future growth. These stocks do not pay out much of a dividend, if any at all, because profits are generally reinvested. Investors in growth stocks are looking mainly for large capital appreciation (share price increases), although share prices of these stocks tend to be more volatile than those of most other kinds of stocks. Good examples of growth stocks include Intel, Dell, Microsoft, Biogen (a drug company), and Office Max.

Value stocks

Value stocks are stocks whose share prices appear to some investors to be excessively low (oversold), considering the financial strength of the companies and the strength of the industries they're in. Value stocks generally show a relatively low share price as a ratio of the company's earnings. (This ratio, known as the price to earnings ratio, or PE, is the most basic way of evaluating how expensive a company is.) Warren Buffett is a world-renowned investor who made his name and his fortune hunting out underpriced issues, buying them, and holding on to them for the long haul. Like Buffett, investors in value stocks are looking for bargains, stocks that are underpriced and that should eventually see a substantial price increase.

Income stocks

Income stocks are stocks that pay a relatively large dividend (have a high dividend yield). People who purchase income stocks are generally more interested in the income they'll receive than in capital appreciation. A company with an exceptionally high dividend yield is often one offering a better product than its competitors in an industry and that is either stable or expanding. Companies that fall into this category include utility companies, chemical stocks, and some real estate stocks.

Defensive stocks

Defensive stocks are stocks that are considered relatively safe, with share prices expected to remain fairly stable in a declining market. Stocks that meet this criteria are generally the stocks of companies whose revenues are not expected to shrink appreciably in an economic slowdown. These companies include food and beverage companies, drug companies, and tobacco companies—companies making items that people need or want regardless of what's happening with the economy.

Cyclical stocks

In contrast to defensive stocks, cyclical stocks tend to show a great deal of price fluctuation with changes in the economy. While few economists believe anymore that the economy cycles systematically between periods of growth and recession, the term *business cycle* is still used to indicate the tendency for the economy to experience both periods of prosperity and stagnation. The stock market also is said to have an investment cycle or a market cycle, indicating that the market has both periods of advance and decline. Cyclical stocks are stocks of companies that tend to do especially well in a good economy and quite poorly in a bad economy, or they tend to do well when their industry as a whole is doing well and badly when it is not. Stocks of automobile manufacturers, airline companies, and steel companies are cyclicals.

Speculative stocks

Speculative stocks are stocks of companies that have the potential for explosive growth but that may or may not be successful in the long run. These are often new companies with new ideas and may not even be making a profit yet. These stocks are called speculative because there is no hard proof that these companies will ever generate a profit. Speculative stocks have extremely volatile share prices and often sport PE ratios of 100 or more. People invest in these stocks in the hope of getting in on the ground floor of something terrific and making a great deal of money as the company expands and prospers. Good examples of speculative stocks include stocks for Internet-related companies such as Netscape, eBay, and Amazon.com.

Penny stocks are actually a type of speculative stock. They are stocks of small companies or startups (very new companies) that have little or no revenue yet. Penny stocks are generally priced for less than $1 per share. People invest in penny stocks because a price increase that is small in absolute terms can have a proportionately huge effect on the percentage increase in one's investment. For example, if you owned shares of ABC company, priced at 20 cents per share, and ABC popped up to $1 a share on some announcement, you would make 500 percent on your money. However, if the share price dropped to 15 cents, you'd lose 25 percent; if it slipped to 10 cents, you're out half of your money! Investors in penny stocks often forget that these stocks are dirt cheap for a reason—usually because the company isn't worth a hoot and may even go bankrupt. It's just as easy to lose your money in penny stocks as it is in stocks with higher share prices.

Unofficially...
Some speculative stocks have no PE at all because they have no earnings yet.

Convertible securities

Convertible securities are securities that can be converted into other types of securities. The most common convertible is preferred stock that can be converted into common stock at the investor's say-so. Convertibles are a nice way to hedge because they allow you to safely collect your interest payments without forfeiting the chance for capital appreciation. You can get into a company by buying preferred stock, for example, and convert to common stock if the company does well. If the company doesn't do so well, you can stay with your preferred stock and your comfortable interest payments.

The IPO gambit

When a company decides to raise money by issuing stock for the first time, the event is called an initial public offering (IPO). IPOs in Internet stocks have created a lot of excitement in recent history because of the overwhelming conviction that most Internet companies have a bright future. Investors in IPOs are trying to grab a stock with great future potential at a low price by buying it before anyone else. While some IPOs have done extremely well, few investors seem to know that the majority of them do not; IPOs often either decline in price on the first day or move sideways. Even an IPO that shoots up in price initially often backs down in the weeks that follow, as the excitement surrounding the IPO fades and investors start taking a cold, hard look at the company's real profit potential in a competitive marketplace.

Even if you like the sound of IPOs, it's difficult to take part in an offering. The best chance you have of making money is to buy shares of the stock before it is actually made available for purchase on an exchange (the secondary market). Generally, the company issuing the stock hires an investment bank to sell the stock. The investment bank contacts customers to see if they're interested in purchasing the new issue. The investment bank may also contact various securities dealers (stockbrokers) to help sell the shares. These stockbrokers contact their best customers, too. The process doesn't usually work the other way around, with investors contacting brokers. Investors who do want to purchase IPOs, however, *should* call their broker, find out who is selling a particular issue, contact that company, and so on. The key is to find the salesperson and buy shares before the IPO effective date, the date the stock is first made available to the general public.

That said, the Internet is making it easier for the public to participate in IPOs. The investment banking firm Wit Capital (www.witcapital.com) has broken ranks and is now using the Internet to market IPOs directly to the general public. It's possible to download a prospectus for an upcoming IPO from Wit Capital's Web site and, if you're interested, make an offer at a pre-established price. Another investment banking firm, Hambrecht & Quist (www.hamquist.com), is holding "open IPOs" (or Dutch auction IPOs) in which investors bid for shares, and a computer tracking program selects the optimal price based on the various bids made. Bids above the optimal price are filled first; bids at the optimal price are filled next with the remaining shares, often partially; and bids below the optimal price are not filled. The Internet is allowing the general public to get in on IPOs at the ground level.

Stock splits and reverse stock splits

Occasionally, companies will *split* their stock. This means that they will increase the number of shares

Moneysaver
If you receive additional shares from a stock split or a stock dividend, you have no tax liability on those shares unless or until you sell them.

outstanding and will decrease the price per share accordingly. For example, XYZ corporation may have 1 million outstanding shares, with shares currently selling for $100 each. XYZ decides to split their stock 2 for 1, meaning that the total number of shares doubles to 2 million and the price per share is halved to $50 per share. Individual shareholders end up with twice as many shares, and each share is worth half of the pre-split value. Companies may also perform what is known as a reverse stock split, reducing the number of shares and increasing the value of each share accordingly. Stock splits can be in any ratio. The most common are 2 for 1, 3 for 1, 3 for 2, and 5 for 4. Stock splits and reverse splits do not change a company's market capitalization or the value of investors' holdings.

Why do companies do this? For one reason: to make their stock more attractive to investors. In the case of a stock split, companies hope that by reducing the share price, the stock will seem more affordable to more people, leading to more buying. Companies that employ a reverse stock split are trying to make their stock look more substantial.

Sometimes stock splits and reverse splits seem to have the desired effect, but often they do not. While some investors buy a stock that has recently split because it's cheaper, and other investors buy because they think recently split stocks tend to rise, often stocks mysteriously drop after a split. Similarly, a stock that has recently undergone a reverse split often fades because the company was unable to do artificially for the stock what the markets had refused to do. Low share price may be a sign of inherent weakness—companies that perform reverse stock splits are often in trouble.

Share Buybacks

There are times, usually when a company is flush with cash, that it will buy back its own shares from shareholders. The main reason a company would want to do this is for the tax savings—the tax rates on distributions to shareholders is higher than the tax rates on interest payments to bond holders. If a company's cash flow is excellent, then, it will be inclined to buy back some of its shares. The way this usually works is the company will announce the buyback and ask shareholders interested in selling their shares to submit a price at which they would be willing to sell. If the company agrees to the shareholders offer, the shareholder walks away with a tidy profit. If the shareholder isn't interested in selling, however, he will enjoy a jump in the price of his shares following the buyback, since the reduction in the number of outstanding shares increases the value per share. Share buybacks are considered a positive omen for a company by many investors, signifying financial strength, and share prices often continue to climb after a share buyback.

How do I get my stock certificates?

When you buy a stock, you receive proof of purchase in one of three ways:

1. Have the actual stock certificate, detailing how many shares you own, mailed to you.

2. Have the actual stock certificate mailed to and kept in safe keeping by your broker.

3. Have the stock held by your broker in street name. "Held in street name" means that your broker does not actually possess the stock certificate but maintains electronic records indicating that you own the stock.

Unofficially...
Some companies buy back shares they have issued in order to support the share price by increasing demand and lowering supply for the stock. This tactic is known as a "share buyback."

Having your broker keep your stock in street name has become the most common method for maintaining records in today's financial markets. There's no need to mail things before holdings can be sold, and there's no danger that important documents will be lost or stolen. Instead of stock and bond certificates, your broker will send you regular statements, which will list your holdings. These statements should be kept in a safe place so that if there's ever a dispute over what you own, or if your broker's computers crash and data is lost, you have proof. Many markets, such as those that trade options and certain kinds of government bonds, trade *only* in street name now.

Take advantage of the bond alternative

As mentioned earlier, bonds are a kind of I.O.U. You lend money to someone, and that person (or company) pays you back in a certain amount of time with interest. The major advantage of bonds over stocks is that unless the issuer of the bond goes bankrupt, you can count on making money (unless you sell before maturity). All bonds have four vital characteristics:

- A maturity
- A face value (or par value)
- A price
- A yield (or coupon)

The *maturity* is the period at the end of which the borrower must return your original loan in full; the *face value* is the amount of money the borrower will pay you at maturity; the *price* is the dollar value of the bond now; and the *yield* is the interest you earn every year for kindly lending your money to someone you don't even know. So, if you bought a 30-year $10,000 government bond with a yield of 7 percent for $10,000, the maturity would be 30 years, the par value would be $10,000, the price would be $10,000, and the yield would be 7 percent. This means that the government would pay you $700 a year for the next 30 years—no questions asked—at the end of which time they would send you a check for your original $10,000. Pretty sweet, huh?

Of course, there is a catch or two. Many bonds have these little things called *call provisions*. A call provision allows the borrower to repay her loan to you all at once before the maturity date and cancel the bond. Why would she want to do that? If interest rates were to fall—that's why. Why should she keep paying you 7 percent if she could borrow the same dough from somebody else at 6 percent? If a bond has a call provision, the lender should get a slightly higher rate for incurring the risk that his bond will be called. Interestingly, bond investors can protect themselves in a similar way by buying bonds with *put provisions*. A put allows a lender to demand immediate repayment of an entire loan. And why would you want to do that? Well, if interests rates went up appreciably. Why lend your $10,000 to anybody for 7 percent when you could get 8 percent? If a bond has a put provision, though, you'll get a slightly lower rate for asking the borrower to carry the interest rate risk.

Some investors hold on to their bonds until they mature or until they are called; others like to buy and sell them. For example, someone who 10 years ago lent the government $10,000 at 7 percent for 30 years might find that, as much as he likes getting those 7 percent interest payments, he suddenly needs that $10,000. If he decides to sell his bond, the price he'll get for it will depend on the current level of interest rates. Let's say that since he purchased the bond, interest rates have fallen a great deal, and now similar 30-year bonds have a yield of only 4 percent. The seller's bond will be considered very valuable. After all, no one is getting 7 percent these days. Consequently, the seller will be able to sell his bond at a premium, meaning for more than the face value. He might be able to sell that bond for $13,000 now, even though he paid only $10,000 for it originally. This bond investor has done very well, indeed: He has collected $700 a year for 10 years from the original bond issuer (the borrower), and now he has turned around and sold the bond itself for a $3,000 profit.

Now, what if the very same seller had come to market and found that, unfortunately, interest rates were higher than they had been 10 years ago? In that case, similar 30-year bonds being issued now would have a higher yield than the coupon on his bond, making his bond relatively unattractive. Why would a buyer pay this seller $10,000 for a bond with a 7 percent coupon when the buyer could just as easily use his $10,000 to purchase a new bond with an 8 percent coupon? He wouldn't—not unless our seller would be willing to sell his bond at a discount. Assuming that $9,000 was fair market value at the time, the seller would probably be able to get $9,000 for his bond, but no more.

So, even as a bond's yield remains constant, its price changes to reflect changes, especially changes in interest rates. Other factors also influence bond prices. Political strife or economic crises abroad, for instance, may lead to higher demand for U.S. bonds by foreigners, pushing up prices.

Watch Out!
In the bond tables in the financial section of newspapers like the *Wall Street Journal,* the yield is listed first and the YTM is listed last under "Yield" or "Ask Yield." If you speak to a broker about bonds, he will refer to the yield as the "coupon" and the YTM as the "yield."

A bond's bottom line is its YTM

A bond's total return (the total amount you will make on the bond) is expressed as the *yield-to-maturity* (YTM) or the yield-to-call (YTC). This is the actual amount that you'll make on your bond, expressed as an annual percentage, if you hold the bond to maturity (or until it is called). The YTM takes into account the coupon, the current price of the bond, and the bond's face value.

If you paid a premium for the bond—more than the face value—you have to keep in mind that at maturity, you will get only the face value. So, even if you're getting a nice yield, your total return or YTM will be less than your yield. On the other hand, if you bought your bond at a discount, accepting a lower yield than the going rate, your total return will exceed the bond's yield because you will receive more for the bond at maturity than you paid for it.

It is generally assumed that bonds with a call provision will be called sooner or later if they were purchased at a premium. This is because if you bought a bond for more than its face value, interest rates have fallen since the bond was issued, making the rate on the bond particularly good. So, naturally, if the borrower has a call option on the bond, he will exercise it because there's no reason for him to keep paying the higher interest rate. He can simply pay you off and borrow again at the current lower rate.

Bonds galore

There are several kinds of bonds, but they all function pretty much the same way. Yields on bonds vary with length of maturity and risk. The longer you let someone borrow your money, the more they will pay you. This is in large part because, with long-term bonds, you're taking a risk that you'll miss out on the opportunity to lend your money at a better rate if rates go up in the future. Also, the more unstable the borrower, the higher the yield. This is because of the risk that the borrower will go bankrupt and will not be able to pay you back.

The government loves to borrow your money and offers an array of investment vehicles, called U.S. Treasuries, to make lending them money easy. *Treasury bonds* have maturities ranging from 10 to 30 years. Interest payments are made biannually. The minimum investment is $1,000. Of all the U.S. Treasuries, Treasury bonds have the highest yields because they have the longest maturities. They are exempt from state and local taxes, but not federal. And because they are backed by the full faith and credit of the U.S. government, they're considered virtually risk-free.

Treasury notes have maturities of between 2 and 10 years, with interest payments made twice a year. They require a minimum investment of between $1,000 and $5,000. *Treasury bills* (T-bills) have maturities ranging from 13 weeks to 1 year, with full payment of interest and principal made at maturity. You need at least $10,000 to buy a T-bill. Like Treasury bonds, Treasury notes and T-bills are exempt from state and local taxes but not Federal. Obviously, the government's debt vehicles are structured to encourage lending them money for as long as you can, with Treasury bonds offering the highest interest rates and the lowest minimum investment requirements. Just like any other kind of bond, however, U.S. Treasuries can be sold before they reach maturity.

Zero coupon bonds (or Zero coupon Treasuries or STRIPS) are another type of U.S. Treasury bond backed by the government. They generally have a face value of $5,000 but no yield (Zero coupon), so you buy them at a steep discount. The YTM is in the range of other U.S. Treasuries; it's just that you don't receive periodic interest payments, only a lump sum equaling the face value of the bond at maturity. One catch with Zeroes is that even though the owner does not receive dividends, Federal tax is owed on the implicit interest that accrues each year (unless the Zero is in a tax-sheltered account). People buy Zeroes when they anticipate needing a chunk of money at some time in the future and don't need income from a bond.

Municipal bonds (munis) are bonds issued by state and local governments or their agencies. Munis generally cost $5,000 or more. These bonds are not backed by the U.S. government because they are not issued by the federal government, but by state and local governments. Munis are available in both investment-grade (low-risk) and high-yield (high-risk) varieties. The great thing about munis is that you don't have to pay federal income taxes on them—and if you live in the state or locality that issued the bonds, you don't have to pay state or local taxes on them, either. Unfortunately, because of the tax breaks, munis also yield less than U.S. Treasuries and most other bonds. To find out if you would make more with munis than with taxable bonds, you have to compare yields of munis with the after-tax yields of taxable bonds.

Mortgage-backed bonds are bonds issued by government agencies that loan money to people to buy houses. These usually cost around $25,000, and even though you're buying the bond from a government agency, these bonds are not exempt from Federal tax, only state and local. The yields on mortgage-backed bonds are higher than the yields on U.S. Treasuries because mortgage-backed bonds are not backed by the full faith and credit of the U.S. government (although the risk is still considered minimal).

Mortgage-backed bonds do not gain much value when interest rates go down because it's at these times that people tend to refinance their mortgages (paying off their existing mortgage with a new mortgage that has a lower rate). Paying off a mortgage early is known as prepaying a mortgage. If home owners prepay their mortgages, interest payments from the bonds backed by these mortgages may decrease or disappear. Due to the unpredictability of interest rates and homeowners, mortgage-backed bonds are traded on the basis of their average life rather than maturity. The amount of time your money will be tied up in the bond depends on how quickly the mortgages backing the bond are paid off. Most mortgage-backed bonds are issued by the Federal National Mortgage Association (Fannie Mae), the Government National Mortgage Association (Ginnie Mae), and the Federal Home Loan Mortgage Corporation (Freddie Mac). The bonds themselves are referred to as Fannie and Ginnie Maes and Freddie Macs.

Collateralized mortgage obligations (CMOs) are a type of mortgage-backed security issued by a government agency such as Freddie Mac that contains three to six classes (tranches) of bonds with different maturities. The various bonds within a CMO are actually held by various investors. The funds generated from the pool of mortgages backing a CMO are used to pay interest to all the bondholders at the same time. If one or more of the underlying mortgages is paid off early, however, the holders of the bonds with the shortest maturities must accept early payoff of their bonds first. (Remember, you don't want your bond to be paid off early because you want to keep receiving those juicy interest payments.) All the bondholders in the first tranche must accept early payoff of their bonds before any bondholder in the second tranche does. The holders of the bonds with the longest maturities, then, are the most insulated against the prepayment of the mortgages underlying the CMO.

Corporate bonds are issued by companies that want to borrow money. The cost of corporates varies, but the yields are higher than those of Treasury bonds or government agency bonds. The money you make on corporate bonds is taxable. The safety of your investment is a function of the financial stability of the company you lend your money to. The greater the chance the company will go bankrupt, the higher the risk and the higher the yield. Weaker companies must offer higher yields to attract money. The safest corporates, issued by companies of good financial strength, are referred to as investment-grade corporate bonds. The riskier corporates, issued by companies with weaker financials, are referred to as high-yield corporate bonds or junk bonds.

Foreign bonds represent money lent to overseas governments or corporations. With foreign curency-denominated bonds, the issuer makes interest payments and returns the principal in the foreign currency, so the investor's final profit or loss depends greatly on what happens with the exchange rate. If the dollar goes up in value against the relevant currency, the value of the interest payments and the value of the principal decline. If it is a dollar-denominated bond, however, the opposite is true. The key to foreign bonds is currency rates.

Credit rating agencies to keep you informed

The risk of all bonds is monitored and rated by independent rating agencies, such as Moody's Investor's Service (www.moodys.com/mdymap.htm), Standard and Poor's Corporation (www.standardandpoors.com/ratings), Fitch IBCA Inc. (www.fitchibca.com/home/frame.html), and Duff and Phelps Credit Rating Co. (www.dcrco.com/). Each agency assigns its ratings of bonds based on a thorough analysis of each bond issuer's financial condition, management, debt position, business condition, and the assets or revenue sources securing the bond. The highest rating is AAA (or Aaa). Bonds rated BBB or higher are considered investment-grade. Bonds rated BB or lower are considered high-yield. You can access the bond credit ratings of the rating agencies through their ratings information desks or through many libraries and, in some cases, from their Web sites.

Bright Idea
Even after you've purchased a bond, you should check on your bond's credit rating from time to time with one of the major rating agencies. Rating agencies will signal when they are considering a rating change by placing a bond on credit watch or rating watch.

CREDIT RATINGS

	Moody's	Standard & Poor's	Fitch IBCA	DCR
Investment Grade				
Highest quality	Aaa	AAA	AAA	AAA
High quality (very strong)	Aa	AA	AA	AA
Upper medium grade (strong)	A	A	A	A
Medium grade	Baa	BBB	BBB	BBB
Not Investment Grade				
Somewhat speculative	Ba	BB	BB	BB
Speculative	B	B	B	B
Highly speculative	Caa	CCC	CCC	CCC
Most speculative	Ca	CC	CC	CC

	Moody's	Standard & Poor's	Fitch IBCA	DCR
Imminent default	C	D	C	C
Default	C	D	D	D

Chart courtesy of An Investor's Guide to Bond Basics,
www.investingbonds.com

Bonds are considered to be less risky than stocks (with the exception of junk bonds) because their value does not change as rapidly. This is primarily because the value of a bond depends almost entirely on changes in interest rates; the value of stocks, while sensitive to interest rates, also depends on the performance of the underlying companies. Stock investors are sometimes forced to accept losses. Bond investors, however, can always count on getting back the face value of the bond, unless the issuer goes bankrupt.

Mutual fund essentials

A *mutual fund* is a collection of investments managed by an expert, whose goal is to maximize return. A mutual fund can be thought of as a professional portfolio. It is an expert's selection of investments, and you invest in that selection. A stock mutual fund, for example, invests in a group of stocks picked by the fund's manager. By buying shares in the fund, you are putting your faith in the fund manager to pick good stocks rather than trying to pick stocks yourself.

Mutual funds are investment products offered by mutual fund companies, also known as investment companies or fund families. There are now hundreds of mutual fund companies offering thousands of funds. Unlike individual securities, mutual funds consist of many securities and do not have a price as

Bright Idea
The success of a fund is largely dependent on the skill of the fund manager, and many experts advise choosing a fund on the basis of the fund manager. Look for funds with good long-term track records that have had the same manager for several years. Consider exiting a fund if the star manager leaves.

such, but a net asset value (NAV). In the case of a stock fund, the NAV is calculated by adding up the value of all a fund's holdings and dividing that number by the total number of shares of all the stocks in the fund. Mutual funds calculate their NAV once a day, at the end of the day, so if you get a mutual fund's NAV during the day, that price is the price of the fund as calculated at the end of the last business day. By contrast, if you check a stock's price during the day, you'll get the most recent price the stock traded at that day.

If the aggregate value of the stocks in a fund increases, the NAV will increase, and you will make money. If the value of the stocks decreases, the NAV will decline, and you will lose money, unless dividends offset falling share prices. Yes, mutual funds do pay shareholders dividends, and the amount of the dividend payouts is dependent upon the dividend payouts of the stocks held in the fund. (Many mutual fund investors choose not to collect their dividends but to have them reinvested to buy more shares of the fund.) The fund manager can sell any stock in the fund at any time. If he sells a stock in the fund at a higher price than he bought it, he realizes a capital gain. Capital gains are also distributed to shareholders (or are reinvested). So, there are three ways that people can make money in mutual funds:

- NAV increases
- Dividend payouts
- Capital gains distributions

You will owe taxes on the dividends you receive every year, even if they're reinvested. But you will pay taxes on capital gains only when you sell a fund.

Two major categories of mutual funds exist: open-end and closed-end. Open-end funds issue additional shares of the fund when money comes into the fund and remove shares when money is withdrawn from the fund. Thus, the NAV of an open-end fund is determined only by the performance of the fund's holdings, not by supply and demand for the fund's shares. A closed-end fund, on the other hand, has a fixed number of shares, so in addition to the performance of the fund's holdings, supply and demand for the fund's shares will have an impact on the fund's NAV. Shares of open-end funds can be purchased directly from mutual fund companies; shares of closed-end funds are sold only on stock exchanges and must be bought through a broker.

A wide variety of stock funds

There are several kinds of stock funds with different levels of risk. The riskier the fund, the greater the potential for profit and loss.

Moneysaver
Most mutual fund companies will sell most of their funds directly to you so that you don't have to pay a broker.

Aggressive growth funds: These are among the riskiest of the stock funds, investing in stocks with a high potential for rapid growth—generally, small caps. Investing in small companies with future potential is considered risky because some of these companies won't survive. The emphasis in these funds is on share price increases, not on dividend income. Most of the companies in aggressive growth funds don't pay out substantial dividends, pumping almost all their profits back into research and development in an effort to expand their companies.

Growth funds: These funds are considered somewhat risky, but not as risky as aggressive growth funds. Growth funds invest in growth stocks—established companies, not necessarily small cap, that are growing or expected to grow rapidly, often in industries that are also growing rapidly. Growth funds are not as risky as aggressive growth funds because growth fund companies have already demonstrated success in terms of real profits. The risk, then, is more one of whether they will *continue* to succeed.

Growth and income funds: These funds aim to realize both an increase in share price and good dividends. Fund managers strive to achieve this in a variety of ways. Some managers invest in both growth stocks, with low or no dividend yields, and income stocks, with high dividend yields. Other managers may use preferred stocks, convertibles, money market instruments (discussed later), and even options. Growth and income funds are less risky than growth funds, showing more price stability.

Equity-income funds: These funds invest primarily in stocks with high dividend payouts. (*Equity* here means stock.) These funds are less risky than growth and income funds. Because stocks are more vulnerable to price fluctuations than bonds, however, equity-income funds are riskier than fixed-income funds, which generate income through bond investments.

Index Funds: These funds attempt to mimic the performance of well-known indexes, such as the S&P 500, by investing in all the companies that make up an index or a representative cross-section. Index funds are just as risky as the stock market (for stock index funds), no more, no less.

Sector funds: Also known as specialty funds, sector funds invest in various companies in one sector of the economy, such as healthcare, the Internet, precious metals, technology, or leisure. Sector are quite risky because if that industry runs into hard times, the fund will suffer tremendously, even if the stock market in general is thriving. These sector funds have the potential to show big gains, however, if the industry covered by the fund runs hot.

International funds and global funds: International funds invest in aggressive growth funds or growth stocks overseas. Some international funds are bond funds, which carry the added risk of currency fluctuations. Unlike international funds, global funds or world funds invest in both foreign and domestic stocks or bonds. Most global funds keep about 75 percent of their assets in the United States.

Regional funds: These funds invest in certain regions of the world, such as the Pacific Rim, Latin America, or Eastern Europe. Regional funds invest in several different countries in a region with the hope that if one country's market slumps, the other countries' markets will offset that. Investing overseas, however, is generally riskier than investing at home.

Country funds: These funds invest in a single overseas country. Funds with names such as the Japan Fund, the Russia Fund, and the Malaysia Fund are now commonplace. Risk is a function of the strength of the country's economy and the stability of its political system.

Bright Idea
Like mutual funds, unit investment trusts consist of a number of securities, but the composition of their securities is fixed for the life of the fund. Buying shares of a unit investment trust is great for investors who know exactly what they want and plan to hold—it's much cheaper than buying all the securities yourself. The drawback is that they carry big loads.

Green funds: These funds invest only in companies that do not unduly damage the environment or treat people unjustly. Green funds tend not to invest in tobacco companies, companies that sell harmful products to Third World nations, or companies with poor environmental records. Performance of these funds tends to be somewhat handicapped by the limitations placed on the fund managers as to which companies they can invest in.

Bond funds: An interesting alternative

Mutual fund companies also offer bond funds. A bond fund is a portfolio of bonds chosen and managed by an expert whose goal is to maximize total return. As with bonds, the emphasis in bond funds is on income—dividend payouts. While risk is lower than that of stock funds, bond funds tend to go down in value if interest rates rise. However, when interest rates rise, bond funds' yields gradually increase as well, which will eventually offset some of the decline in the NAV of the fund. This is because bond fund managers generally buy bonds with varying maturities. As bonds in the fund mature, the manager is able to buy new bonds at the higher rates. In addition to the interest-rate risk associated with bond funds, there is also default risk. Risk increases as the quality of the bonds in the fund decreases. So, while a bond fund consisting mainly of U.S. Treasuries carries virtually no risk, a high-yield bond fund carries a lot.

Like bond investors, bond fund investors can make money on both dividend payouts and price (NAV) increases. The yield of a bond fund is the cumulative yield generated by all the bonds held in the fund. Unlike bond investors, however, bond fund investors need not be concerned with maturity dates or yield to maturity; bond fund managers take care of all the particulars of buying, selling, and holding, and can be counted on to take the most profitable action at any given time. The one thing bond fund investors must be particularly careful about is a fund's expense ratio—the percentage of the fund's assets being used to manage and market the fund. This charge eats into your profits. An expense ratio of more than 1 percent for a bond fund is too high. Always find out what a bond fund's expense ratio is before you invest.

Bond fund investors should be aware of the differences between open-end and closed-end funds. With a closed-end fund, supply and demand for the fund will affect its NAV. If the fund is trading at a price below its NAV, the fund is said to be trading at a discount; if it's trading at a price above its NAV, it's trading at a premium. If you buy a closed-end bond fund at a discount, your interest payments will still be generated on the basis of the value of the holdings in the fund. For example, if the NAV of a fund is $10 and you buy at a discount for $9, you will still get dividends on the $10 value of the holdings in the fund. Also, if the discount gets smaller after you purchase the fund, you'll make money on capital appreciation. Because performance data of closed-end funds is reported in terms of increases in NAV (like that of open-end funds), an investor who buys at a discount can achieve a higher total return than that actually reported for a fund. Of course, the opposite could happen if the discount were to widen after purchase. It all depends on supply and demand for the fund's shares. Stay away from closed-end bond funds that are selling at a premium or close to their

NAV. Remember, you also have to pay brokerage fees to buy and sell closed-end funds. Open-end funds are generally a safer investment for investors who lack the time to analyze the discount and premium patterns of closed-end funds.

As with stock funds, there are various kinds of bond funds.

Fixed-income funds: The goal of these funds is to achieve steady income through dividends while maintaining the value of the original investment (capital preservation). These funds invest in government bonds, corporate bonds, or government-backed mortgage bonds that have a fixed rate of return. Dividends and capital gains are taxable (except for those generated from Treasuries, which are not taxable at the state or local levels). There are various types of open-end and closed-end fixed-income funds, reflecting the kinds of bonds held by the funds, including investment-grade corporate bond funds high-yield corporate bond funds ("junk bond" funds), mortgage-backed bond funds, U.S. Treasury bond funds, global and international bond funds, and multisector funds; the latter purchase mixtures of bonds from different sectors, such as government, corporate, and foreign, to moderate risk. Risk is almost entirely a function of the type of fixed-income fund you choose, with risk levels of funds determined by the risk levels of the bonds held by the funds. U.S. Treasury bond funds, then, are the safest, and high-yield corporate bond funds are the riskiest.

Municipal bond funds: Muni bond funds consist of bonds issued by cities and states. These funds are generally placed in a separate category from fixed-income funds, even though they also are fixed-income investments, because of their special tax status. Dividends from municipal bond funds are not taxed by the federal government, nor by the state if the investor resides there. Capital gains resulting from the sale of a municipal bond fund, however, would be subject to taxes. Municipal bond fund yields vary greatly, depending on the maturity and the quality of the bonds held in a fund. The longer the maturities and the lower the quality, the higher the yields.

The primary difference between individual bonds and bond funds is that, with bond funds, you could lose a significant portion of your original investment if the NAV nosedives. With an individual bond, on the other hand, you know that you will always get the face value of the bond back as long as you hold the bond to maturity, unless the issuer goes bankrupt. For example, let's say that you pay face value for a $10,000, five-year bond from AT&T, with a yield of 8 percent. Even if interest rates skyrocket over the next five years, as long as you hold your bond to maturity, you'll collect $800 a year for five years and then get your $10,000 back at the end of five years, unless AT&T goes bankrupt. On the other hand, if you put $10,000 in an investment-grade corporate bond fund and interest rates skyrocket, the decline in the NAV of the fund could cancel out the money you make on interest-payment dividends.

Timesaver
Keep all your brokerage and mutual fund statements so that you can do your taxes quickly and easily when the time comes. You are personally responsible for accurately reporting the profit and loss information on the securities you sold in the past year, as well as the dividends you received.

On the other hand, bond funds provide an investor with concrete gains when interest rates fall, reflected in an increase in NAVs. An investor in an individual bond would have to actually sell his bond to realize such a gain. In addition, a bond fund provides the investor with diversification, where owning a single individual bond would not. Buying and selling a bond fund also will not be any more expensive than trading other kinds of mutual funds, whereas buying and selling an individual bond can be costly. Obviously, there are pros and cons to both bonds and bond funds.

Mutual fund safe havens

Money market funds are funds that invest in short-term debt instruments (short-term, low-risk, low-return loans). There are really only two kinds of money market funds: taxable and nontaxable. Taxable funds invest in the short-term debt securities of U.S. government agencies, banks, and corporations. They also invest in U.S. Treasury bills. Tax-exempt money market funds invest in short-term, high-quality municipal bonds.

Money market funds maintain a NAV of $1, so the money you make from them comes only as dividends generated from the interest payments on the debt vehicles in the fund. As interest rates rise, so do those of money market funds. A money market fund is the equivalent of a bank savings account in the mutual-fund world. You put your money in a money market fund when you don't want to be in stocks or bonds; it's a safe haven where your money can rest. Historically, yields of money market funds have been slightly higher than those of bank CDs. While mutual fund money market funds are not insured by the Federal Deposit Insurance Corporation (FDIC), there has never been a case of one going under. Money market funds are safe, safe, safe.

The hybrids: A balanced approach

While stock, bond, and money market funds constitute the main types of mutual funds, two new breeds of funds have become popular lately: balanced funds and asset allocation funds. *Balanced funds* hold a mixture of stocks and bonds, and the percentage of each depends on the fund manager's judgment of current market conditions. *Asset allocation* funds contain a mixture of stock, bond, and money market funds, and the fund manager decides in what proportion to hold each at any given time. If the manager of an asset allocation fund thinks the market is at a peak, for example, he might move from a 60 percent stock, 30 percent bond, 10 percent money market position into a 10 percent stock, 10 percent bond, 80 percent money market mixture. If he thinks the market is at a bottom, he might move to 80 percent stocks, 10 percent bonds, and 10 percent money markets.

Most balanced funds actually hold a certain percentage of money market instruments, too, making many of them almost identical to asset allocation funds. Most stock mutual funds also contain a mixture of investment vehicles, with managers varying the percentage of a fund's assets that they have in stocks at any one time. But there *is* a difference between stock funds and true hybrids. Although stock funds don't have to stay fully invested in stocks at all times, they're always supposed to keep a certain minimum percentage of a fund's assets in stocks.

No such thing as a free lunch

Mutual fund companies do not provide their stock-picking and portfolio-managing services for free.

Unofficially...
Actual holdings
in funds varying
greatly from
stated param-
eters has been
a cause of
considerable
controversy in
the late 1990s.
Asset allocation
and balanced
funds, however,
have a great deal
of flexibility in
this regard. Both
types of funds
would be
considered safer
than stock funds
but riskier than
bond funds.

There are certain charges, and these charges vary greatly from one company to the next. In general, the mutual fund companies that are considered expensive are called load mutual fund companies because they charge a load (transaction fee) when you buy or sell their funds. The inexpensive fund companies are called no-load companies because they do not charge a load. Companies that charge loads justify this by saying that they provide better services to investors as well as better overall fund management and performance. Actual studies have shown, however, that in terms of total returns, no-load funds have done just as well as, if not better than, load funds.

A front-end load is a sales charge for buying a fund with a load fund company; the amount each company charges varies, from .75 percent to 8.5 percent. This is money taken out of your investment principal. Back-end loads, reaching as high as 6 percent, are taken out of your principal when you sell a fund. Some load fund companies even charge a reload fee for reinvesting your dividends, not to mention the companies that will charge you for switching your money from one of their funds to another. No-load mutual fund companies provide most or all of these services for free. For a good list of no-load fund families, check out the Mutual Fund Investor's Center at www.mfea.com/.

While no-load companies don't charge you many transaction fees, both load and no-load companies charge you for their operating expenses—what it costs them to manage and market your fund. In percentage terms, this charge is referred to as the fund's expense ratio. Fees for a fund's operating expenses are taken directly out of the fund's assets, affecting the fund's performance stats (although some companies try to inflate a fund's performance numbers by absorbing these charges rather than including them as a cost to the fund). This is great while it lasts—no charges! Frequently, though, funds absorb fees for a while to attract new investors and then reinstate the fees once they've sucked in enough greenhorns.

Operating expenses include a management fee, ranging from .25 percent to 1 percent, which is used to pay the fund manager; 12b-1 fees (sometimes called distribution fees), which can go as high as 1.25 percent and pay for marketing the fund; and miscellaneous expenses, from .25 percent to 1 percent, which pay for things such as office rent, computers, and supplies. If a stock mutual fund's expense ratio is more than 1.5 percent, or if a bond fund's expense ratio is more than 1 percent, that's too high. Shop around.

Before investing in any mutual fund, call up the fund company and ask the following questions:

1. What load does this fund carry?

2. Is there a fee for reinvesting dividends or capital gains?

3. What were the total operating expenses of the fund last year (including management fees, 12b-1 fees, and miscellaneous expenses)?

4. What is the maximum allowable 12b-1 charge for the fund?

5. Do the fund's performance results reflect all operating expenses, or are these currently being absorbed?

6. If certain fees are now being waived, how long will that last?

Timesaver
When you open an account with a mutual fund company, it's a good idea to elect phone services. This allows you to perform almost all transactions over the phone, as necessary. This can be a real time-saver, especially if there is a mix-up.

For a complete list of mutual fund companies, check out American Mutual Fund Families at www.site-by-site.com/usa/funds/fundtxt.htm and Yahoo! Finance at http://biz.yahoo.com/p/fam/a-b.html.

Are mutual funds the best way to go?

The major advantage of mutual funds over individual stocks and bonds is that it's possible to benefit from the performances of a large number of stocks with a small amount of money. Some funds require an initial deposit of only $1,000, and additional deposits of as little as $100 are usually okay. But with that $1,000, you own a piece of 10 or more securities. To buy that same group of securities on your own would cost you a lot in brokerage fees. The good thing about having a stake in a group of stocks rather than just one or two is that your money is diversified (spread out). Diversification is good because if some of the holdings in the portfolio go down, this tends to be compensated for by the holdings that go up. In bear markets, then, mutual funds tend not to decrease in value as much as many individual stocks because they are well-diversified.

What proves an advantage in declining markets can be a disadvantage in advancing markets. Because mutual funds tend to be invested in a wide array of stocks, bonds, and money market instruments, their returns tend to be somewhat less impressive than those of well-performing individual stocks. This is due to the fact that the returns of a fund's winners are somewhat offset by the negative returns of its losers. Particularly in highly selective markets, when breadth is thin, certain stocks wildly outperform mutual funds. Being invested in over-diversified mutual funds in markets such as these can leave you with poor returns.

Another apparent advantage of mutual funds is that they are professionally managed. Each fund has a fund manager, who is considered by the company to be an expert in selecting profitable investments and in deciding when to buy, sell, and hold. It would appear that the amateur should be able to rely on a fund manager's expertise. But many studies have shown that most fund managers fail to beat the market (they don't produce a return greater than the average for the overall stock market), and some reputable investment advisors actually view optimism among a large majority of fund managers as an indication of market *peak* and widespread pessimism among them as a sign of a market bottom.

A final thing to be careful about when investing in mutual funds is whether the fund invests in derivatives (futures and options). Many funds do use derivatives as hedges, but some funds use them as speculative investments, which could greatly add to the risk of the fund. Because funds often don't explain their derivative holdings in the prospectus (the brochure detailing the makeup of a fund and the rules governing it), it's a good idea to call and ask if the fund you're interested in invests in derivatives, and whether those derivatives increase or decrease the fund's riskiness.

Alternative investment vehicles you should know about

Although stocks, bonds, and mutual funds certainly make up the lion's share of investments held by the majority of investors, you also should know about a growing number of interesting alternatives.

Unofficially...
Proponents of mutual funds often cite funds' liquidity, the ability to convert investments into cash, as an advantage of funds over other investments vehicles. In fact, it's just as easy to convert stocks into cash as mutual funds. Not all bonds, however, are sold daily.

Different types of investments may provide your portfolio with greater diversification and increased gains. Depending on your individual goals and needs, there may be a place in your portfolio for one or more less common investments.

Invest in real estate at the click of a mouse

Real estate investment trusts (REITs) are corporations that invest in real estate properties and mortgages. One-third of all REITs are private, and the rest are traded on stock exchanges. The revenues generated by REITs are tax-exempt at the corporate level, as 95 percent of a REIT's earnings must be distributed to investors by law. Investors, however, must pay taxes on their REIT investment returns. Investors make money on REITs in two ways: first, through dividends coming from the profits generated by the REITs; second, from increases in the share prices of the REITs. (The latter is also a good way to lose money, of course.) REITs tend to increase in value when demand and prices in the real estate market increase. The performances of individual REITs can be compared by looking at Funds From Operation (FFOs) statistics.

Three kinds of REITs exist: equity REITs, mortgage REITs, and hybrid REITs. Equity REITs purchase, own, and manage real estate properties. They may also develop properties. Mortgage REITs purchase, own, and manage real estate loans (mortgages). For example, if a private individual has loaned another individual $100,000 to buy a house at 10 percent interest, a mortgage REIT may offer to assume the loan (and those nice juicy interest payments) by paying the lender the balance due on the loan. The third kind of REIT is known as a hybrid

REIT. Hybrid REITs purchase, own, and manage both real estate properties and loans.

DSPs and DRIPs cut out your broker

Direct stock plans (DSPs) and dividend reinvestment plans (DRIPs) are programs that allow investors to buy stock directly from companies—in other words, to bypass brokers and their fees. DSPs are offered by some companies (often utilities) to investors who don't own any of the company's stock but would like to. DRIPs, which are offered by far more companies, require that you already own some of the company's stock. (When you buy it, be sure to ask to have the stock registered in your name, not in the broker's name or in street name.) Initial investment minimums in these programs are as low as $250, and subsequent contributions can be as little as $10. Some of these companies even offer IRA accounts now. The idea behind both DSPs and DRIPs is simply to attract more investors.

Naturally, there are some things to watch out for with DSPs and DRIPs. While some of these companies allow investors to collect their dividends, many require that all dividends be reinvested. In this case, the program will not provide you with any income. (Dividends that are reinvested *are* considered income for tax purposes.) Also, DSPs and DRIPs seem to be charging more these days. Initial investment requirements are climbing, and transaction fees are up to as much as $10 (plus a few cents per share, if you're buying more stock). There are also new fees: fees to reinvest your dividends, a one-time enrollment fee of $5–$15, and an administrative fee. These companies are not trying to nickel and dime their investors; they just want to cover costs, and that's the rub: The reason not all companies offer DSPs and DRIPs is because it would cost them too much. Check out all the charges before deciding to invest in a DRIP or a DSP. All things considered, it might just be cheaper and easier to buy the stock through your broker.

Futures and options are another story

Futures and options have already been discussed in general terms. With the exception of options used to control risk (which will be covered in detail in Chapter 13, "Keeping a Lid on Risk," they should be avoided unless you have specialized knowledge. If you have or develop a strong interest in futures and options, you should embark on a thorough study of how these investment vehicles work before wagering any money.

Annuities, collectibles, and good ol' CDs

An *annuity* is actually a contract or account with a life insurance company that shelters your money from taxes. The money you put into an annuity will earn interest, and this will not be taxed until money is actually withdrawn from the annuity. Fixed annuities guarantee an interest rate for a certain period of time, after which they can change the rate but cannot lower it below a set minimum. Variable annuities offer two types of investment accounts. The fixed account offers all the features of a fixed annuity, but with fewer interest rate guarantees. The separate account allows you to invest in mutual funds on a tax-deferred basis. Annuities provide investors with a life insurance death benefit and lifetime income payments to be sent to you for the rest of your life after you've paid into the annuity for a certain number of years.

Some people invest in collectibles. A *collectible* is anything anyone thinks has value and will have greater value in the future. These items are called collectibles because they are often things collected by people with a special interest. A collectible may be considered extremely valuable by some people and of little value by others. Examples of collectibles include antiques, Barbie dolls, Beanie Babies, coins, comic books, and baseball cards.

A *certificate of deposit* (CD) is a loan to a bank or other financial institution that will be paid back to the lender with interest in a certain amount of time. CDs are available with various maturities, ranging from 3 months to 10 years. The longer the maturity, of course, the higher the yield. Like a bond investor, a CD investor assumes the risk that interest rates may go up before his CD matures; unlike a bond investor, however, if he sells before maturity, he must pay a penalty. Another difference is that there is no risk that a CD will be called before maturity. Because most CDs are sold by banks, they are also guaranteed by the government (up to $100,000). The tradeoff for their negligible risk, however, is their comparatively low yields.

Venture capital and limited partnerships

Venture capital is an investment in a start-up business that is thought to have excellent prospects but does not have access to capital markets, meaning that it's not able to issue bonds to raise money. Instead, these companies seek to attract money from investors interested in taking some risk and getting in on the ground floor of a promising new business.

Venture capital is quite risky because many start-ups fail. If you're interested in exploring venture capital investments, though, contact a venture-capital firm directly. For a list of venture-capital firms by geographical location, go to the Corporate Finance Network at www.corpfinet.com. You can also check out some Web sites that specialize in venture capital, such as The Venture Capital Resource Library: www.vfinance.com; The Venture Capital Market Place: www.v-capital.com.au; and The Venture Capital Report: www.venture-capital-report.com.

You might participate in a venture capital investment through a limited partnership. A limited partnership is business with two kinds of partners or owners: general partners, who actually manage the business, and limited partners, who provide financial backing but do not manage. A general partner has unlimited responsibility for the company's debts, but a limited partner is only liable for the debts of the company to the extent of his investment in it. In other words, a limited partner can't lose more than he invests.

Limited partnerships, like proprietorships (businesses owned by a single person), have a distinct advantage over corporations. The money made by limited partnerships flows directly to the partners (investors) and is only taxed once, at the personal level. The money made by corporations is taxed at two levels: first at the corporate level, and again at the personal level. The other attractive feature of limited partnerships is that, as a limited partner, you don't have any management headaches—you just fork over the dough and, hopefully, make the big bucks.

Limited partnerships are considered very risky. For more information about limited partnerships, go to the CCH Business Owner's Toolkit at www.toolkit.cch.com/text/p10_2140.asp.-H/.

What's offshore, and is it for me?

Offshore investments are investments offered by or through overseas investment companies and life insurance companies in locations that are beyond the jurisdiction of any taxation authority. Such locations include Switzerland, Luxembourg, Bermuda, the Channel Islands, the Isle of Man, and others. All these locations could be referred to as international financial centers because they have the infrastructure and internal regulatory authorities to support international business deals and securities transactions. Less-developed locales without such capacity, limited more to banking, would be referred to simply as tax havens. Examples include Naru, Antigua, Liberia, and the Marshall Islands.

Generally speaking, offshore investment accounts allow investors to invest in an array of international markets, including U.S. markets, under the umbrella of an offshore investment or insurance company. Only when an investor withdraws his funds and brings them back to the United States is he required by law to pay taxes on his earnings. Offshore investment companies are under no obligation to supply profit and loss data to anyone, including the IRS, so it's up to the investor to keep good records. U.S. citizens cannot open offshore investment accounts when they are residing in the United States. For Americans who happen to be living abroad, however, opportunity knocks.

Just the facts

- Individual stocks provide you with the most powerful tool to make money—through price increases and dividends—but they are also the riskiest.

- Bonds generate wealth primarily through interest payments, although bond prices are also important, especially if you sell before maturity.

- Mutual funds are collections of securities managed by a professional; they allow you to invest in a wide variety of securities with limited funds.

- REITs provide you with an easy way to invest in real estate without actually having to buy and sell properties yourself.

- DSPs and DRIPs are investment programs that allow you to bypass your broker and buy stock directly from companies.

- Depending on an your needs and goals, you may wish to explore annuities, collectibles, CDs, and offshore investing opportunities.

Self-Assessment

PART II

GET THE SCOOP ON...
Determining your net worth ▪ Squeezing
cents out of the banking system ▪ Budgeting as
the cornerstone of financial health ▪ Getting
creative about saving ▪ Navigating
the debt maze

Taking Control of Your Personal Finances

Chapter 5

You've got to get your financial house in order if you want to invest online. It won't matter how much you make buying and selling securities if your money skills are unsound. You won't get any richer—the money will just slip through your fingers. You've got to know how to manage money and how to hold on to it before you can grow your wealth. It's just that simple. Are you bouncing checks? Is your credit card debt ballooning? Are you spending more than you're making? If so, it's time to get a grip and set things right.

Keep in mind that investing always involves taking a certain amount of risk. Risk means there's a chance of *losing* your money. Risk does not equal reward—and high risk does not equal high return. High-risk investments, such as aggressive growth stocks, have the potential for greater-than-average returns *or losses*. If you're currently in debt, then investing in stocks would not be a good way to get yourself out of it. There's every chance that your stocks will go the wrong way, and you'll just find yourself deeper in the hole.

It takes discipline and skill to keep your everyday finances in order, the same qualities necessary to invest successfully online. In fact, getting your day-to-day finances under control actually provides a good training ground for developing the skills you'll need to do well online. Make sure you've got all the bases covered, and take a moment to take stock of your current financial health.

Calculate your net worth

Your net worth is the best way of gauging how wealthy you truly are. To calculate this magic number, you need to get out a piece of paper (your balance sheet) and add up the value of all the things you possess (your assets), including your savings, your home, your cars, your individual retirement account (IRA), your 401(k), your furniture—everything. In deciding on something's value, try to approximate the current fair market value of the item.

Next, calculate the total of all your expenses (your liabilities), including things such as your mortgage balance, your credit card balances, and your car balance. Just use the outstanding balances on all the items you possess that you haven't paid off yet. Now subtract the value of all your liabilities from all your assets. If the number is positive, you have a positive net worth—you're worth something! If the number is negative, you have a negative net worth; you're in debt.

Net worth can be used in various ways. First and foremost, it can be used to indicate your basic level of financial health. It should be positive. Even young adults should strive to keep their net worth in positive territory.

Another way to use net worth is to help you plan retirement. Look at how much you're worth now and how much you're probably going to need to lead a comfortable retirement, and you have some idea how much ground you still have to cover. You should calculate your net worth at least once a year to monitor your progress toward your financial goals.

Banking

Banks are the repositories for a significant chunk of most peoples' liquid assets (cash or assets that can be converted to cash quickly). They are the institutions through which we pay our bills, pay our rent or mortgage, and get cash. Because we all have a certain amount of money in banks, it's important to know about the different kinds of accounts banks offer, how to increase your interest income from banks, and how to avoid ridiculous fees.

All kinds of accounts

The major types of bank accounts include the savings account, the checking account, the CD or redeemable CD, and the money market account. All accounts give you a certain amount of interest on your money, but the interest on these accounts changes as interest rates in general change. Each type of account carries different benefits and risks, and this explains the differences in interest rates among the accounts. Interest is calculated in two ways: in terms of the interest rate and in terms of the annual percentage yield (APY). The interest rate is the percentage amount you will earn on your money in a year if you withdraw your interest payments as soon as they are made. APY is the amount you will make if you don't withdraw the interest payments but let them stay in your account, adding to the total

Bright Idea
You can use net worth to determine how much life insurance you should buy. Current wisdom dictates leaving your loved ones 10 times your annual income. To calculate how much life insurance you need, multiply your annual income by 10 and subtract your net worth, the amount you already have.

balance. If you do this, subsequent interest payments will be made on a larger balance than the original one. You'll be getting interest on your interest. This is known as compound interest, and it's a very good thing.

Let's look at an example of how compound interest works to your benefit. Say that one month ago you opened a bank account, with a 4.0 percent interest rate and a 4.10 APY, with a $10,000 deposit. Today, you check your balance and see that you have $10,034.01, which means you received $34.01 in interest. Now you're receiving interest on $10,034.01, not just the original $10,000—interest on interest. At the end of one year, you'll have $10,410, and from year two, you'll be earning 4 percent on $10,410, not just $10,000. Over a period of years compounding can net you thousands of extra dollars.

Many banks compound interest daily, which maximizes the amount of time interest money is actually sitting in your account, accruing interest of its own. These banks have the highest APYs. Always opt for accounts that offer the shortest compounding intervals: daily is the best, then monthly, and finally quarterly. Always check out both an account's interest rate and its APY. Also keep in mind that if your daily balance fluctuates, so will your interest payments.

Checking accounts are bank accounts that allow you to write checks. These are the accounts people use to pay their bills. When you write a check, the check goes to the merchant, the merchant deposits the check in his own bank, and the merchant's bank then sends the check to your bank and asks for the money. Your bank takes the money out of your checking account and sends it to the merchant's bank, and the merchant's bank then puts the money in the merchant's account, upping his balance. At this point the check is said to have "cleared."

This system works great unless there isn't enough money in your account to cover the amount of the check you wrote. In this case, the check "bounces," meaning your bank does not send the merchant's bank money; instead they send the check back to his bank with "Nonsufficient Funds" or "NSF" stamped on the front. The merchant's bank then returns the check to the merchant as "bounced," does not up his balance, and *charges him a fee* for depositing a bad check in the first place.

Do you think he's mad? You bet he is, and he'll be calling you for his money, you can be sure. When you bounce a check, your bank also charges you a fine of around $15.00.

Checking accounts are a must because they allow you to pay bills with checks. They pay minimal interest. Usually a minimum balance is required, around $100. If you fall below this amount, you'll be asked to pay a monthly fee. As part of your account, you will get an automated teller machine (ATM) card that will allow you to make deposits and withdrawals anytime.

The idea of a savings account is to have a place to save money, although many people use these accounts as spending accounts, separate from their checking account. Savings accounts often have no minimum balance requirement, and the account pays the account holder significantly more interest than a checking account. Savings account interest rates vary with the amount of money held in the account. For example, if an account holder with a balance of between $.01 and $9,999 gets 1.49 percent a year, an account holder with a balance of between $10,000 and $24,999 will probably receive

Moneysaver
One way to make sure bills get paid is to have bills deducted automatically each month from your bank account. This is a free service at most banks, and it will help you save money on checks and postage. The only drawback with automatic payment is that you can't check your bills for errors before you pay them.

about 1.99 percent. You cannot write checks on a savings account, but you will get an ATM card.

Money market accounts (MMAs) became popular in the late 1970s and early 1980s when the prime rate was actually as high as 20 percent for a while. Money market accounts offer better interest rates than checking accounts, savings accounts, and many certificates of deposit (CDs) because they are not FDIC-insured. They're riskier—but not much. Except for the rare case, money market accounts never run into problems. You can generally get limited check-writing privileges with MMAs (usually only a couple checks a month are allowed without a charge). Some MMAs also offer a debit or check card, a card that charges your bank account directly when the merchant swipes your card through the machine. Some MMAs have minimum balance requirements. An ATM card is provided.

Certificates of deposit (CDs) are short-term loans made by customers to banks for time periods ranging from 30 days to 36 months. The longer the term (and the more money in the CD), the higher the interest rate. Unlike the interest rates on checking, savings, and money market accounts, the interest rates on CDs are fixed for the term of the CD. You cannot withdraw any of the money in a CD before the CD matures, or you'll forfeit a significant part of the interest coming to you. Redeemable CDs, however, allow partial early withdrawal of principal without a penalty. Even with this option, the redeemable CD offers a higher interest rate than savings and checking accounts. All CDs are FDIC-insured. ATM cards are generally not provided with these accounts.

You also can combine different bank accounts to maximize your return. One technique is to take some of the excess cash in your savings account and use it to buy a redeemable CD. If you find that you need more money than you thought you would, you can go ahead and redeem some of the CD for no fee. This system allows you to keep most of your cash in a CD, earning much better interest than if it were all wallowing in your savings account.

Another idea is to use a money market account as your main account. Deposit everything into your MMA so that it all gets access to those high interest rates. Because the MMA allows you to write a couple checks a month, write a check off the MMA once a month to fund your checking account, from which you can pay all your bills. If you find your checking account getting a little low on cash, use your second MMA check to send additional funds to the checking account. This way you're keeping the largest percentage of funds in the highest-yielding account for the longest period of time. That's smart banking.

Sneaky fees

All bank accounts carry fees. Banks charge fees to help pay for the cost of managing accounts and just to make money. The combination of fees and interest banks make on loans generates their income. Most banks will waive the fee on your account if you maintain a certain minimum balance. Some banks offer ways to avoid fees by tying one service in with another. For example, they may waive the monthly charge on your account if you order or use their credit card. Always look for these tie-in deals to help you avoid charges.

No matter what you do, though, banks go out of their way to get you to pay them fees. They may limit the number of times you can use your ATM card in a month and charge you for every transaction over that limit. They may charge you for asking them to

Timesaver
Most banks now offer a pay-by-phone option that allows you to pay your bills over the telephone. The service costs a flat fee, usually about $5 or $6 a month, but saves you a lot of time by sparing you from having to write out checks, prepare envelopes, or mail bills. The bank guarantees that payment will be made within five business days.

use their coin-counting machine to count up your spare change. They may even charge you for giving *them* rolled money. One of the most outrageous charges is when banks send you a photocopy of your (cashed) checks instead of the originals and then charge you a $15.00 fee for the photocopy! You've got to keep your eye on banks—they're slick.

Many people say the way to beat the bank fee rap is to head for your local credit union. A credit union looks like a bank and smells like a bank, but it's not a bank. It's a cooperative; that means it's owned and operated by the people who keep their money there. It's also a nonprofit organization—the goal is to serve its members (unlike banks, which need to worry about enriching shareholders). Operating income at credit unions is returned to depositors in the form of higher interest rates for all kinds of accounts and lower fees and loan rates. As a partial owner, you have a vote in all issues affecting your credit union. Credit unions have a reputation for providing customers with excellent service.

These are the four major advantages of credit unions over banks:

- Unlike banks, only a small percentage of credit unions charge fees on economy checking accounts.

- Credit unions charge 40 percent less on average than banks when minimum balances on regular checking accounts are not met.

- Far fewer credit unions than banks charge an annual credit card fee, and credit card rates are 5 percent lower on average.

- Credit unions charge significantly lower consumer loan rates than banks.

The only drawbacks of credit unions are that they don't tend to have as many types of accounts to choose from as banks, and they don't have as many branches. Most credit unions, however, are part of a network. Check out www.creditunionsonline.com/ for a great list of credit unions all over the country.

While credit unions provide one excellent alternative to banks, savings and loans (S&Ls) provide another. A savings and loan is similar to a credit union in that an S&L is owned by depositors. It's different in that it is for profit. S&Ls were originally set up for two reasons: to provide savings accounts and to provide home loans to depositors. Although the number of S&Ls in the country has fallen dramatically since the S&L crisis of the 1980s, S&Ls have expanded their account offerings to include not only savings accounts but also checking accounts, CDs, and others. Like banks, many S&Ls also offer accounts through which you can invest in mutual funds. Many S&Ls pay better interest on checking accounts than banks and require much lower minimum balances to avoid fees. You might be able to avoid fees altogether if you have your paychecks deposited directly into your account by your employer every payday (direct deposit).

If you decide to go with a bank, however—and most people do—you really should do some comparison shopping. Call around to the different banks in your area, and make a list of yields, charges, and the services offered at the different institutions. Most banks have Web sites now, if you prefer to surf for the info. Drop by a few small, local banks. While they may not offer as wide a selection of products or services, they're often more pleasant than large banks and are easier to work with.

Unofficially...
These days S&Ls also offer loans to anyone who qualifies, not just depositors. In fact, it's often easier to get a loan from an S&L than from a bank. The main disadvantage of S&Ls is that they have fewer locations than banks.

Balance that checkbook!

Can you balance your checkbook? Well, can you? If it just ain't balancing, you've got to get it together. Otherwise, you're going to get yourself in trouble by spending money you don't have. The key to balancing your checkbook is to get into the habit of writing down in your check register every check you write, every deposit and withdrawal you make, and every debit card purchase you make. When you write a check, record it in your check register right away. When you use your ATM or debit card, put the receipt in your wallet; that very night, record the transaction in your check register. Save all your receipts. Then, the day your monthly bank statement comes, match all the items in your check register with the items on your statement.

At this point, write any interest payments, service charges, or automatic payments appearing on the statement into your check register. (Automatic payments are payments made directly out of your checking account to certain companies every month.) Your check register balance should equal the statement balance, minus any checks that haven't cleared yet. If it doesn't, check your work. If the records still don't match, get your receipts together, call or visit your bank, and get it straightened out.

To repeat, in order to keep your check register up-to-date, you need to enter the following items in your register regularly:

- Checks written
- Deposits made
- Withdrawals made
- Debit card transactions made

When your statement comes, you must enter the following additional items in your check register:

- Interest payments or dividends credited
- Automatic payments made
- Service charges exacted

If your checkbook is out of balance to the point where you're concerned about overdrawing your account (bouncing checks), the best advice is to completely stop using your checkbook for a while. Go to an all-cash system until all the checks you've written have had a chance to clear. Pay for all goods in cash, and pay all your bills by postal money order. (A money order is a check for a specific amount written by a bank or other institution, obtained only by paying up front in cash.) Postal money orders can be obtained at post offices and tend to be a little cheaper than bank money orders. Save all your ATM receipts and any other transaction receipts. Keep paying your expenses this way until the bank sends you a statement that includes the last check you wrote and all check deposits. Take this statement's account balance, and start your check register fresh with this amount, recording any transactions in your check register that have occurred after the final transaction on the statement.

A possible shortcut is to call the bank and ask for your balance now. Also, ask if they can tell you which checks have cleared and which have not—both checks you have written and checks you have deposited. (Many banks will do all this for you over the phone.) This may be enough information for you to work with. Start with the balance the bank quoted you and then add in all the outstanding checks to get your real balance. Some banks have

Unofficially...
An increasing
number of banks
let you check
your balances
through their
Web site.

phone lines that let you find out your balance and which checks have cleared automatically.

The only major weakness with getting balances over the phone is that the bank could be wrong. After all, one of the reasons for balancing your checkbook in the first place is to check the bank's math. That's right—banks do make mistakes—and usually not in your favor, I might add. And guess what? So do online brokers. You have to check people's work. Don't be deluded into thinking that because everything is computerized these days, there's no room for error. Poppycock! All the numbers computers crunch are originally entered by human beings. This is where mistakes occur: in data entry. You may have deposited a check for $100, but the bank clerk may mistakenly enter the deposit as $10. Unless you catch that error, you'll never see that $90 again. This is why you should sit down with your statements when they come and check them against your check register, making sure there are no discrepancies.

If you don't find these suggestions about how to balance your checkbook enough for you, take a look on the back of your bank statement. Most bank statements have instructions about how to balance your checkbook. A final suggestion is to buy computer software to help you with the whole process. Intuit's Quicken (www.intuit.com) and Microsoft Money (www.microsoft.com) are the most popular. (See Chapter 2, "Everything You Need," for more details.)

Budgeting made easy

A *budget* is a plan for how you're going to spend your money. It's a way of allocating your income so that money is available for all the things in your life that cost money. Having a good budget and sticking to it gives you control over your personal finances. It ensures that money will be there to cover necessary expenses and helps prevent you from blowing it all on beer or take-out meals.

The first step in creating a budget for yourself or your family is deciding what time period you're going to use. A monthly budget seems to work best for most people, probably because many people are paid by the month, but you can also create a weekly or biweekly budget, or one based on some other time period.

Cash flow

Having decided on your time frame (we'll use one month as an example), the next step is get some idea of how cash is flowing into and out of your life. You do this by putting together a personal cash flow statement. Get a piece of paper, date it, and draw a line down the middle. At the top of the left column write "Inflows"; and at the top of the right column write "Outflows." Now, for the next month, write down in the left column each and every income item that you receive, such as paychecks, dividend checks, cash gifts, alimony payments, and how much it was for. Do not include 401(k) contributions because this is not cash you have access to. In the right column, write down each and every item you spend money on and how much you spent. Some of the expenses in your life may not be monthly, quarterly, or annually. Whatever the time period, calculate what the monthly equivalent is (for example, divide an annual expense by 12), and then enter that amount on your list. If you're not exactly sure what an upcoming expense will be, guess

At the end of one month, add up the left column to determine you net monthly income and the right

Watch Out!
If you decide to use financial software to help you with your personal finances, it's a good idea to maintain written records as well, just in case your computer crashes. You should always maintain a written check register, no matter what.

column to determine your total monthly expenses. Subtract the right from the left to determine your cash flow. If the cash flow number is positive, you have a positive cash flow, and this is good; you can save and invest the surplus. If the number is negative, you have a negative cash flow, and this is bad— you need to increase income or reduce expenses to avoid going into debt.

Positive or negative, you need a budget. To do so, you next need to determine the general categories of your expenditures. Here's a list of typical categories, most of which you should include in your budget:

1. Savings

2. Rent or mortgage

3. Utilities

4. Home upkeep (such as toiletries and cleaners)

5. Transportation

6. Automobile (including gas, insurance, and tags)

7. Food (groceries and eating out)

8. Clothes

9. Books, magazines, and online services

10. Entertainment (including movies and trips)

11. Debt repayment (credit cards, school loans, and so forth)

12. Other expenses

Use this list or amend it. Now go through the list of all the things you spent money on for one month and place the number to the left of each item that corresponds to the category it falls under in your budget category list. Next, add up all the items in each category to get your monthly expenses per category. This gives you a clearer idea of where your money is going than merely recording what you bought.

Setting limits

Now it's time to set some limits—this is what budgeting is all about. Look at each category and decide how much you're going to allow yourself to spend in each area per month from now on. What's reasonable? You should definitely allocate at least 10 percent of your income for savings. This is a cardinal rule. But your overall goal is simply to create a plan where your net income minus all your expenditures is positive. Such a budget is referred to as a balanced budget.

On implementing your budget, if you find that you're exceeding spending limits in certain categories, don't give up. Keep plugging away and look for ways to cut costs in that area. If you're spending less than or equal to your limits—congratulations! This surplus should be used at first to create a cushion, an emergency fund to cover unexpected expenses that may crop up. When you have three to six months income as a cushion, budget surpluses can be added to your savings or spent as you see fit.

If an emergency were to occur before you had enough money in your emergency fund to cover it, there are several things you could do.

1. Place overdraft protection on your account. This means that if you write a check for an amount that exceeds your balance, the bank will pay it, essentially granting you a loan.

2. Open a line of credit with your bank. A line of credit is an arrangement with a bank that allows you to get an unsecured loan from your bank at any time by just going in and filling

Bright Idea
The "monthly expenses by category" total will give you an idea of what kinds of things you're spending most of your money on. This is meaningful because it tells you something about yourself and your spending tendencies, and it also may indicate where you could spend less.

out some paperwork. (An unsecured loan is one in which the lender lends you money without the right to seize a particular asset of yours if you default on the loan.)

3. Obtain a secured loan from your bank. If you had a $5,000 CD, for example, you could obtain a loan for $5,000, secured by the CD. (Your CD serves as collateral for the loan.) If you default on the loan, your bank will simply take your CD money.

4. Take out a home equity loan. If you own a home, you can borrow money, using your house to secure the loan.

5. Get a cash advance on a credit card. This should be taken only as a last resort, as banks charge high interest rates on credit card cash advances, and they also charge you a fee for the transaction.

Software such as Quicken and Microsoft Money also can a big help with setting up a budget. An alternative would be the Moola Organizer, which you can check out at www.creditech.com.

Controlling spending: The engine that runs the machine

"
Lord, make me chaste. But not just yet.
—Attributed to St. Augustine
"

Although some of the expenses in our budget are predetermined, such as car payments and mortgage payments, others are not. How much we spend and save is greatly up to us. The best way to save money on everyday items, such as paper towels and shampoo, is to take the time to comparison shop. Does this really make much of a difference? Yes! Comparison shopping can save you up to 50 percent overall on your shopping costs. Twenty percent of items make up 80 percent of sales and are competitively priced; the other 80 percent of items exhibit tremendous price variability from store to store. You need to know how much the products you use cost at all the stores around you. Make a price chart in which you list all the items you buy frequently along the left margin of the page and all the different stores selling that product along the top of the page. In each cell, write the price of each item at each store. In this way, you'll have a general sense of where to shop for specific items when you need them.

Of course, prices change, stores put different items on sale at different times, and, interestingly, items generally follow a price cycle. This means that products are promoted in cycles based on seasons, manufacturing schedules, competitive environment, marketing strategies, and so forth. And different products are on different cycles. Food products such as cereal, for example, will be more affected by seasons than nonfood products such as laundry detergent. Your goal is to buy the things you want and need when they are in their promotional cycle. One techniques is to buy items only that are on sale, even if this means changing brands occasionally or buying a generic brand. Menus can also be determined this way: Tonight we're having fish because fish was on sale today. Use coupons whenever possible. Coupons for national brands (name brands), however, rarely bring the prices down to those of store brands or generic brands.

Remember: Just because an item is on sale or you have a coupon for it doesn't mean that you should buy it. If you see a video game player on sale for 50 percent off at $100, but you don't play video games, there's absolutely no reason to buy that item. You'd be throwing your money away. Similarly, buying

Watch Out!
One way to curtail impulse buying is to never go shopping unless you know exactly what you're going to buy. If you have only a vague idea, you're leaving yourself more vulnerable to temptations. Similarly, avoid window shopping because you're bound to see something you simply "must have," even though you hadn't intended to buy anything.

more than you need because it's on sale is a waste. Let's say you need a dozen hot dogs for a cookout. One brand costs $2. Another brand costs $2.50, but you can get two packs for the price of one. Which do you buy? You buy the one pack for $2 because you save $0.50. You don't need 24 hot dogs, and you'll just end up throwing out the extra 12 when they go bad. Don't pay more for more product than you need.

You can use other various techniques to help you curtail spending if you are a bit of a compulsive shopper.

- Never shop for food when you're hungry.

- Bring only cash, and bring only enough cash to cover the items on your list. (Leave the credit cards and checkbook at home.)

- Avoid malls—there are too many temptations everywhere.

- If you must go to a mall, park as close as possible to the store you plan to shop at so that you don't have to wander past other shops on your way there.

- Ask other people to pick things up for you when they go shopping. (You can't overspend if you're not there.)

Advanced techniques for serious savings

While eliminating compulsive spending habits and learning to comparison shop cover the basics, a number of more advanced techniques can be employed by the ambitious for additional savings. Remember, savings will be fueling your online investments. Maximizing savings, then, becomes a key to increasing your wealth. How much can you add to the 10 percent of your net income that you've already budgeted for savings each month?

In advanced saving strategies, you will notice that a power triangle is at work. What is good for your wallet is also good for your health and good for the environment. Let's say, for example, that instead of driving to the store, you decide to walk. You save money on gas, the walk is good for your health, and your decision has a positive impact on air and noise pollution. Let's say you decide to cook dinner tonight instead of ordering a pizza. You save money on food, the home-cooked meal is better for your health, and there's probably less trash (no pizza box). Because no delivery was made, there was also a reduction in air and noise pollution. Take note of the triple benefits of living frugally as you begin.

Here are some things most people could do to augment their savings:

1. Send e-mail instead of phoning or writing letters. E-mail is free, after your monthly service charge is paid. And some e-mail providers don't charge at all. (For a list of free e-mail providers go to http://members.tripod.com/ jason_eng/main.html.)

2. Walk and use public transportation. No matter how you slice it, cars cost money in gas, parking, insurance, and repairs.

3. Stay home once a week when you would normally go out. This will cut down on transportation costs and on all the spending on food, drinks, and entertainment that goes with going out.

4. Use less of the products that you use. When you wash your hair, for example, use half as

Bright Idea
The next time you get a raise, decide to devote the raise to your savings. Increase the percentage of income you're putting into savings each month, and continue to live on the same amount of money you had.

much shampoo as you normally do. When you brush your teeth, use half as much toothpaste. Use half a capful of oral rinse or antiplaque rinse, not a full cap. Using less of what you use will cut your spending for your favorite products way, way down because you'll be buying them much less frequently.

5. Take care of what you already have. Taking proper care of your body will save you thousands of dollars in dental and medical bills. Taking care of the machines in your life, such as actually changing the oil in your car every 3,000 miles, will eliminate the need to replace them so often.

6. Use the telephone or the Internet to comparison shop. If you're planning to make a major purchase, call all the stores in your area that sell the item and get their prices over the phone. This will save you a ton of time and point you toward the stores with the best prices.

7. Bargain. Car dealerships are not the only places where bargaining is still viable. Opportunities for haggling exist at most privately run shops, certainly, but it can't hurt to ask for a discount anywhere you shop, even at department stores. Just ask if you can get a discount, or a discount for paying in cash, or a discount if you buy two, or whatever. If you're unsuccessful, ask if the item will be going on sale any time soon, and consider waiting to buy it.

8. Make sure you're not overcharged. Many store clerks are not very good at math. Moreover, they themselves may not be clear on exactly how much an item costs. This is particularly

Bright Idea
Create a swap group or a partnership in which members exchange various goods and services for free. A doctor, for example, might provide free consultations to a barber's children, in exchange for free haircuts for the doctor's kids.

true about sale items. Sometimes it's not clear whether an item has already been marked down or whether it will be marked down at the register. This is doubly confusing if you're choosing an item from a reduced-price rack in a department that's having a department-wide sale. Be especially careful in grocery stores and drug stores that the price being rung up by the scanner is the price listed on the shelf or price tag. Often the scanner rings in a higher price or the store forgets to program in the sale price. If you don't catch this, you'll end up paying more than you should.

Many grocery store clerks aren't perfect when it comes to ringing up produce—they just can't tell if what you selected is a Fuji apple, a Red Delicious, or some other type, and they fudge it. This is fine, as long as they don't overcharge you. Check your change, too, and always check your bills for mistakes. Hospitals are the worst when it comes to billing errors, such as double billing and just plain overcharging. Phone companies also are notorious for sneaking in charges for services such as caller ID that you did not order and did not receive, and for charging you for long-distance calls that you did not make.

9. Always consider buying something used before buying it new. You don't have to buy new books or CDs if you can get them used at used book stores and CD shops. Buying computers used also can save you a fortune.

10. Consider borrowing something instead of buying it. You can borrow books, CDs, and videos from many libraries.

Moneysaver
You can save money on food by cooking large quantities from scratch. Consider making a big pot of stew, for example—it just gets more delicious with time. Adding fresh ingredients to it occasionally can provide numerous ready-to-eat meals for days.

11. Always ask yourself if there's a free way to take care of a problem before you throw money at it. If something in your home breaks, for example, ask yourself if you might be able to fix it. If it's late and you don't have time to go grocery shopping, see if you can make a meal with what you already have on hand rather than going out for fast food.

Dealing with debt

If all budgeting, spending, and savings strategies cannot save you from the jaws of debt, you're going to need a plan to dig yourself out as quickly as possible. Even if your debt was the result of an illness or injury, job loss, divorce, or some other unexpected event, the elements of debt reduction remain the same. Being in debt is not the problem, per se. Most of us borrow to buy houses and cars and even to go to college. The problem occurs when we mismanage our debt in such a way that the debt grows instead of shrinks, interest payments get larger instead of smaller, and an ever-increasing portion of our income is taken up by payments. If it gets to the point where we're unable to make our payments on time anymore, we're in big trouble.

How do we avoid this scenario, and how do we escape from it if we've already started to sink? First, you need some clarity. Remember that your goal is to pay off your debts as quickly as possible. The faster you pay them off, the fewer interest payments you'll have to make—this is money that could and should be going to fund your online investments.

Second, resolve to cut costs and use the money you save to pay down your debt ahead of schedule. If you're spending more than you earn, you're definitely going in the wrong direction. You must increase your income or decrease your spending—ideally, both.

To increase income, consider asking for a raise, looking for a better-paying job, working a second job, or starting a home business on the side. (Don't quit your day job.)

To reduce costs, first look at your biggest expenditures, things such as your mortgage or rent, car payments, and insurance costs. Look into whether you could refinance your mortgage or car payments at a lower rate. If not, how about renting a room in your house and using the proceeds to help pay that mortgage? Look into buying cheaper insurance. Most health insurance companies, for example, offer relatively inexpensive plans with excellent coverage, if you're willing to accept a deductible of $1,000 or more.

Next, maximize your monthly payments. Don't just pay the minimums due to the companies you owe; pay the absolute maximum amount you're capable of. If you owe several companies, pay all of them the minimum amount due each month, and pay one of them—the one charging you the highest interest rate—as much as you possibly can. You want to pay that one off first and then attack the one with the second worst rate, and so on. To get organized, get a piece of paper and write down all your loans, their respective interest rates (if it's a floating rate, include the current rate), how much you have left to pay on each loan, and any special considerations, such as if there's a penalty for prepayment. This way you'll be clear about the order in which you should pay off your loans.

Be careful about bimonthly mortgage payoff plans, however. The idea of paying down your mortgage every two weeks instead of every month is to

Moneysaver
You should consider actually using your savings to pay off your debt. If you're making 3 percent on the cash sitting in a savings account, and you're paying 16 percent interest on your credit card debt, you would save money by using the savings to pay off that debt.

reduce the balance due and the amount of the interest payments more quickly. The problem is that many banks don't post the first bimonthly payment to your balance until they receive the second, nullifying any beneficial effects to you, but giving them a free two-week loan! Although the bimonthly payoff system will translate into one extra payment a year, it would be better for you to just divide the extra payment by 12 and add this fractional amount to each of your monthly payments. Paying more than is required each month on your mortgage is referred to as *accelerating* your mortgage.

You don't need to pay anyone to tell you the best way to do this, by the way. Just do it!

Finally, resolve not to borrow any more money until you are debt-free. Make one-time payments, paying for everything in cash; if you use a credit card, pay it off completely every time you get a bill.

Tackling credit cards

Credit card debt has become a huge problem for millions of Americans, especially for college students, who are running up huge credit card debts without the means to pay them off. About two-thirds of all college students have credit cards, and one-tenth of them owe $7,000 or more. The first step in conquering your credit card debt is understanding how credit cards work and how banks work hard to keep you in the hole.

Who they are

A credit card company, such as Visa or MasterCard, is really nothing more than a kind of credit rating agency for banks. Banks apply to a credit card company for permission to use its logo, and the credit card company analyzes the bank's financial strength, lending practices, and management before deciding to grant the bank permission. So, credit cards are issued by banks, not credit card companies. The banks want to be able to put the Visa or MasterCard logo on their card to give it credibility; the logo means the bank is good for the money. If a bank were to issue its own credit card without such a logo, no one would accept it. A bank signs a contract with a credit card company and pays the company for the privilege of being allowed to use its logo.

Individual banks, not credit card companies, then, determine the rates you are being charged on your credit cards. This is why the rates on one Visa card can be so much higher than the rates on another. This is also why you need to shop around when you're looking for a credit card. The best cards charge no annual fee, allow you to pay off your charges within the first billing period at no charge, charge low interest rates, and offer side benefits such as frequent flyer miles (one mile for every dollar charged). Do your research: Call various banks and ask about the cards they offer. Why should you apply for their card? There is no need for you to carry a credit card from a local bank, by the way. Apply for an out-of-state card if that's the best deal you can find. A couple of good Web sites to help you in your search are GetSmart (www.getsmart.com/creditcard) and LendingTree (https://loans.lendingtree.com).

Finding out about rates

One way to find the banks offering the best rates is to call a credit card company's national number and ask if they have a list of banks charging the lowest rates. Be careful, though. Many, if not most, banks have a low introductory or "teaser" rate you pay for the first six months before the real rate kicks in. You want to know both the introductory rate and the standard interest rate of a card. Some people move from card to card every six months to avoid paying more than the teaser rates. Also, some cards' rates are fixed, while others' are variable, moving up and down as interest rates do. Check out www.asque. com/cred-card.htm for comparisons of more than 150 cards.

Be aware, as you search, that a common ploy used by banks to rope you in is to offer all kinds of promotional benefits for getting their card; they quietly drop the benefits later. By getting a bank's credit card, for example, you might receive a certain amount of automobile insurance. However, 6 to 12 months later, you might receive a notice along with your bill, written in tiny print, that this insurance has been canceled (for no reason). Most people don't notice these notices, which is the point, and never realize that they're no longer covered—at least not until they try to use the insurance.

How they make money

Always keep in mind that banks really don't want you to pay off your credit card debt. Ideally, you would just service your debt for the rest of your life. If you continuously owed them money and continuously paid just the 16 percent interest on what you owed, they'd make a 16 percent return on their money for the length of your lifetime. That's a sweet deal. If you paid off the principal all at once, the bank wouldn't make a penny. The latest scam is shrinking the grace period, the time you have to pay off a charge before the bank starts charging you interest on it.

Many banks have reduced this period from 25 to 20 days, but others—especially with their top-of-the-line gold cards—have *eliminated* the grace period. As soon as you buy an item, the bank starts charging you interest. So, if the bank paid the merchant on the 10th for something you bought and then your credit card bill came with a due date of the 30th, you would already owe 20 days worth of interest! As outrageous as this system is, some banks are taking it one step further: They're back-dating charges to the date you purchased an item. That means they're charging you interest from a date before which they even paid the store! Oh, and if you have the gall to be late in making a payment or fail to pay the minimum amount, you will, of course, be charged a late fee. "We value your business"!

But wait, there's more! Just when you've decided not to use your card anymore (except in emergencies) and even then to pay it off right away, some banks are instituting charges *for not using your card enough.* They may set a minimum dollar amount, say $1,500, and state that if you don't charge at least that amount a year, they'll charge you an annual fee—and this is despite the fact that there was no annual fee when you got the card.

Don't be fooled by all the hype about how convenient cards are for getting cash advances, either. Banks charge you the same rate on these loans as on your charges, and they charge you a one-time transaction fee of up to 2.5 percent to boot.

Perhaps the most insidious stratagem banks use to keep you in the hole, though, is to keep the minimum payment due on your card each month at a smaller percentage of the principal than the interest rate they're charging. This means that even if you pay the minimum, your balance due will *grow.* Be careful here. Many banks promote their cards by touting very low minimum payments, but those minimums are designed to make sure you stay in debt to them.

Watch Out!
Ideally, credit card payments shouldn't come to more than about 5 percent of your net income. If they exceed 20 percent, you're headed for trouble.

Fighting back

How do you fight the banks' ploys? First, try bargaining with them. Tell the bank whose card you're interested in that you're looking at several cards right now and trying to make a decision. Ask them if they'd be willing to waive the annual fee. Some will if you ask. The same thing goes for rates. If you don't like the rates they're offering, see if you can get them to offer you a better rate. Use a better rate from a card at a competing bank as leverage. If you already have a card, ask if they'll extend the introductory rate for you. Tell them that you like their card and you don't want to switch, but that you have offers from a couple other cards with better rates, offers that will be difficult to refuse. Some banks will extend the teaser rate for you when taunted like this. If you don't get anywhere, consider calling back and talking with someone else. Ask for the manager—often your success just depends on who you speak with.

If you do decide to switch to another card with a lower rate, be careful that the bank acquiring the debt doesn't plan to charge you a balance-transfer transaction fee that would wipe out any benefit of the switch. Be particularly wary of the charges for using a transfer balance credit card check to move your balance on one card to another. Also, some of these transfer balance credit card offers are very shady. If you're late with even a single payment, they raise their rates—or even if you're never late, they raise their rates.

If your bank reduces your grace period from 25 to 20 days, call and ask them to give you 25 days again. Tell them you really need 25 days. If you find out that your gold card affords you zero grace days, call and ask for 25 days; if they say no, cancel the card. If they write to tell you they're going to start charging you an annual fee if you don't start using their card more, call and ask them not to do that. If the bank won't work with you, cancel the card and take your business elsewhere. You could also switch to a debit card, which operates like a check (or, just write checks), and avoid all the games. But if you do this, you will lose the benefit of the short-term free loan, which most credit cards provide. Debit cards allow merchants to collect their money directly from your bank account with little or no delay.

If it's any consolation, know that you're not the only one being squeezed by the banks on the credit card front. Merchants who accept credit cards are also paying the banks a charge on every credit card purchase. As a result, some stores are actually charging their customers more now if they pay with a credit card than if they pay with cash.

Other tips

The following list of tips for using credit cards is based on suggestions from the National Center for Financial Education (www.ncfe.org):

1. Reduce the number of cards you carry and use to one or two.

2. Destroy all cards you don't need or want.

3. Use credit cards only when you must.

4. Keep cards you aren't using in a safe place.

5. Keep an eye on your card when you hand it to a merchant.

6. Destroy carbon paper receipts.

7. Never lend your cards to anyone.

8. Report questionable charges right away.

Unofficially...
In some cases, banks are making in excess of 30 percent a year on their credit card business, with interest payments from customers and processing fees from merchants combined.

9. Avoid signing blank charge slips.

10. Avoid giving card numbers out over the phone, especially to people calling you about a product or service.

If someone copies your credit card number, they can try to use it to purchase things over the phone. This is why you should keep an eye on your card when you hand it to a merchant and why you should try to limit access to your credit card numbers, not just to the cards themselves. If you suspect that someone is using your number, call the issuing bank and put a freeze on the card. Then write a letter to the bank (sent by certified mail) and make a copy for yourself. When this letter is received, you are protected by law from any further liability.

If a card is lost or stolen, call the bank and put a freeze on the card right away. Also write a letter. Even though store clerks are supposed to compare the signature on the charge slip with the signature on the back of the card, they rarely do, so it isn't that difficult for impostors to use stolen cards. Most issuers have a 24-hour toll-free number you can call.

Dealing with credit card debt

Moneysaver
After you have reported the theft of a credit card, you have no further liability. Your maximum liability for unauthorized charges is only $50 per card, anyway.

If you find yourself owing banks a lot of money on your credit cards and having trouble paying off the cards, the first thing you need to do is stop adding to your debt—stop using the cards. This hits the problem at its source. Next, employ the other basic debt-reduction strategies discussed previously:

1. Pay off your debt as quickly as possible.

2. Cut costs.

3. Maximize your monthly payments.

If you owe money on several cards, pay off the card with the highest rate first (while paying the minimums on the other cards). Consider switching your debt on your expensive cards to a cheaper card, unless the fee for doing this outweighs any benefit. If you decide to switch to a cheaper card, find out how long the introductory rate will last and whether you can get it extended.

Consider calling the bank and explaining that you're having trouble paying, and see if you can get a special rate. If not, think about asking an attorney to write the bank and explain the situation and the need for a lower rate. While you will have to pay the lawyer a fee for this, depending on how much you owe, it could very well be worth it.

Along the same lines, consider contacting a debt counseling service. Many banks will be more flexible if they see that you're working with a debt counselor to pay off your debt, especially if they know the counselor. Often the counseling service bargains with the bank for lower rates. Then the service pays the bank, and you send the service a more affordable monthly payment. You fill your end of the bargain by paying the service, canceling the affected credit cards, and accepting some instruction from the service on budgeting.

Even if you do opt for debt counseling, try to salvage one card, if you can, because you really need a card for certain things, such as renting a car. Several of the better-known debt counseling services are nonprofit:

> Consumer Credit Counseling Service (CCCS)
> www.cccsintl.org
> 1-800-873-2227

> Debt Counselors of America (DCA)
> www.dca.org
> 1-800-680-3328

American Consumer Credit Counseling
www.consumercredit.com
1-800-769-3571

Credit Counseling Centers of America
www.cccamerica.org
1-800-493-2222

Credit counseling should be considered for any type of debt you can't manage, not just credit card debt.

A final idea to pull yourself out of a bad credit-card debt situation is to consolidate your debt. Get a loan from a bank or credit union at a lower rate than the rates you're paying on your current debts, and pay them all off in one fell swoop. (This idea can be used for other types of debt, too.) By doing this, you are effectively refinancing your debt at a lower interest rate. Never do this, however, unless you've decided not to use your credit cards anymore, or at least until you've paid off your entire debt, including the debt you now have with the lending bank or credit union. Without making a change at the source of the problem (your spending habits), taking out a loan could just get you into more trouble; you'll owe the credit card companies *and* the bank that gave you the loan.

This may be why debt consolidation loans are not that easy to get. Even if you have a decent credit rating, you may be denied if you owe others too much money. Also be careful about taking out a secured loan, such as a home equity loan, to consolidate your credit card debt. If you were to default, the bank would have the right to sell your house!

Big trouble

If the bank thinks you're starting to have trouble making payments on your credit card—you're paying late, or paying less than the minimum—and if you haven't contacted them about it, they're likely to increase your interest rates. They do this to compensate themselves for what they perceive to be the increased risk of their loan to you. If you continue to struggle, they will move in and try to collect the entire debt right away. They do this when they become afraid that they're not going to be able to get their money back at all. Often they will demand a portion of your wages at this point. When things reach this stage, it is definitely time to contact a debt counselor.

If the bank or creditor threatens you with legal action, don't panic. Unless the amount you owe is very large, it's unlikely that a creditor will take you to court—it's just too expensive. If you contest the charges, with or without a lawyer, this will drive costs higher for the creditor by complicating proceedings. Even if the creditor wins, he won't be awarded the money he is owed—he will just be granted expanded rights to try to seize your property and wages. Seizing property and wages can be very difficult, though, because so many laws protect an individual's property and wages from seizure.

Bankruptcy

In the worst-case scenario, you might have to declare bankruptcy. Bankruptcy is a legal procedure in which a debtor gives a court the right to sell some of his assets and distribute the proceeds among his creditors. Any remaining debts are then nullified, and he is no longer liable for any unpaid sums. The problem with declaring bankruptcy is that you lose most of your stuff, and you'll have difficulty re-establishing a good credit rating for the next 10 years. This means you won't be able to get

Unofficially...
If you can't pay your bills on time, give the creditor a call and explain the situation. Often creditors will work with you on formulating a payment plan, and this could save your credit rating.

credit cards or loans for anything—a car, a home, education, or anything else. And you won't be investing online any time soon either. Declaring bankruptcy does not wipe the slate clean and give you a fresh start. It puts a scarlet letter on your credit report that brands you a bad credit risk for years. One word of advice if you're forced to declare bankruptcy: Try to keep one credit card out of the bankruptcy proceedings. You're going to want to have one active card for practical reasons.

Restoring your credit

After you declare bankruptcy, the first thing you have to do is get yourself on a budget. Then you have to try to repair your credit rating. Your credit rating is determined by credit bureaus or agencies. Credit agencies are private companies that keep track of the credit histories of virtually all U.S. citizens with a Social Security number. These agencies have the legal right to report any negative information in your credit history that occurred within the last 7 years, and any bankruptcies that occurred within the last 10 years. Contact any of the major agencies and ask for a copy of your consumer credit report. You'll have to deal with recordings; you won't be able to speak with a human being.

This is a list of the three major U.S. credit agencies and their contact information:

Equifax
P.O. Box 740241
Atlanta, GA 30374-0241
1-800-685-1111 or 770-612-3200
For Georgia, Vermont or Massachusetts:
1-800-548-4548
For Maryland: 1-800-233-7654
www.equifax.com

Experian (Formerly TRW)
P.O. Box 949
Allen, TX 75013-0949
888-397-3742.
www.experian.com

Trans Union Corporation
Consumer Disclosure Center
P.O. Box 390
Springfield, PA 19064-0390
1-800-916-8800, or 1-800-682-7654 or
714-680-7292
www.tuc.com

When you get your report, check it for accuracy. Make sure that any debts you have paid off are recorded. Make sure any information about accounts you did keep current is on the report. Also make sure that any negative reports written more than 7 years ago, and bankruptcies more than 10 years ago, are deleted. Write a letter to the agency requesting that any errors be corrected on your report, and then request another copy of your report later to make sure the changes have been made. Any letters you write to a credit bureau explaining debt situations, by the way, will go on your credit report and could be very helpful to future creditors deciding whether to give you a loan.

Avoid credit repair agencies: There is nothing they can do for you that you can't do for yourself. Some of these companies offer to give you a new credit identity. But hiding your true credit history is against the law and could get you in *serious* trouble! You want to be especially wary of agencies that want you to pay them up front. Often these companies just disappear with your money.

For detailed information about what's contained in a credit report and why repair agencies can be bad for your financial health, check out "Credit File Correction" on the Web site of the National Center for Financial Education at www.ncfe.org/credit.html#correction.

What you really need to do, though, is rebuild your financial life, and this means learning to live within your means and trying to rebuild your credit rating. After a while, you might be able to get a card at a department store such as Macy's, although it's easier to get charge cards at some stores than others. The Sears card is particularly difficult to get. You could also get a secured card, which is a card with a credit limit equal to the amount of money you have in a bank account with the issuing bank. These accounts usually pay very low interest and charge an annual fee. You should probably avoid filling out most of the card applications that come in the mail, as some of these rejections may find their way onto your credit report, and that won't make a favorable impression. You should also consider not even trying to get a card. After all, credit cards were part of what got you into this mess in the first place.

You can avoid the tangled web of debt and bankruptcy if you stick to a budget and maximize your savings. With savings you can invest online and watch your money make money for you.

Just the facts

- Your net worth is equal to the value of all your assets minus all your liabilities.

- Banks offer savings accounts, checking accounts, CDs, and money market accounts. Many banks also now provide special accounts for investing in mutual funds.

- Budget how much money you will allow yourself to spend in each area in your life that requires money.

- It is possible to save a tremendous amount of money by making things you already have last longer, by buying things used, by borrowing and swapping, and by looking for creative ways to get what you need for free.

- The keys to getting out of debt are to stop borrowing, pay off your debt as quickly as possible, reduce costs, and maximize your monthly payments.

- Credit card debt is a particularly insidious kind of debt, where sky-high interest rates, shrinking grace periods, and outright trickery leave card holders in debt jeopardy.

GET THE SCOOP ON...
Don't get psyched out ▪ What's your risk
tolerance? ▪ Long-term investor or short-term
trader? ▪ Finding your investment
style ▪ Fundamental and technical
analysis ▪ Can you take some advice?

Inner Investing

Chapter 6

There is no right way or best way to make money on Wall Street. There are only many ways, many paths to the same goal. So the best answer to the perennial question "What should I invest in?" is this: "Only you can decide." Just as with personal finances, when dealing with investments, responsibility lies with the individual. Even if you employ an investment adviser, it is your responsibility to hire someone who understands you, not just the markets.

What you invest in and how you invest should be based on your level of understanding of the investments you're considering, your personality, your risk tolerance level, your investment philosophy, and your personal preferences. Your specific goals are a secondary consideration. We all want to maximize returns and minimize fees. What's essential is to discover your personal investment style, the way that feels right to you for getting the job done. Trying to invest in a way that you're not comfortable with will only make you miserable. You'll have trouble staying the course, and this could ultimately cost you money.

Choosing the investment style that's right for you is an integral part of successful online investing.

It's important, then, that you ignore the advice of experts and pundits who want to tell you what to do with your money—not just those who would profit from your doing things their way, but family and friends, too. The "sure thing" that your cousin recommends might be profitable, but the ride might make you crazy. You could do just as well in something else and not lose sleep at night. Successful online investors decide for themselves what they're going to do with their money based on a thorough understanding of who they are.

Psychological forces investors fall prey to

We invest to make money—a very rational aim—but we have a tendency to make irrational decisions in pursuit of that goal. Why is that? It's because we are humans, not machines. We have strong feelings about money and have a tendency to get carried away by fear, greed, pain, and pride. To be sure, we do not invest just to make money; we do it for the joy of it and the feelings of self-satisfaction it can instill. Because emotions are inextricably tied up with investing, we must examine them and analyze how they can undermine our efforts. We must not suppress or negate our emotions, though. We must come to understand them and develop an investment program that works for us emotionally as well as financially.

First, you should be aware of some of the common psychological forces that affect investors' judgment. As noted earlier, some investors avoid selling a stock at a lower price than they bought it for to

> 66
> We have seen the enemy and it is us.
> —Pogo
> 99

avoid the emotional pain of having to admit to themselves that they made a bad investment. The embarrassment they will feel at having to report this loss to the IRS, accountants, and others may further inhibit selling.

In fact, in 1979 Amos Tversky and Daniel Kahneman of Princeton University discovered that investors are much more distressed by prospective losses than they are happy about prospective gains. They found that the pain felt from a $1 loss is twice as great as the pleasure derived form a $1 gain. The result of not selling a bad investment, of course, can be still greater losses, but powerful psychological forces are at work preventing investors from selling when they should.

Research has also shown that people are willing to take greater risks to avoid losses than to realize gains. People will avoid additional risk if they think they're going to make money, but they will take more risk if they think they're going to lose. Taking greater risks when faced with potential losses, of course, often results in being saddled with even greater losses.

Many investors decide to follow the crowd and buy what everyone else is buying to avoid regret and responsibility if their investments turn down. When things do go wrong, these investors can take comfort in the fact that everyone else is losing money, too. They can also take refuge in the argument that everyone thought it was a great stock. Their decision to buy the stock "made sense" (even though it was incredibly expensive).

On the other hand, if an investor buys a stock that is out of favor and it goes down, he'll have difficulty rationalizing the loss. Why did he buy that loser in the first place? Money managers tend to fall prey to this kind of thinking, too, partly because they believe that investing in hot stocks may protect them from getting fired if the stocks go down.

Another common psychological pitfall is to start viewing investing, especially online investing, as a form of gambling. Investing then becomes a kind of entertainment, a game to be won, and this leads to unnecessary risk-taking. The investor's ego gets heavily tied in with the results; to protect his ego, the investor tends to downplay or even forget his failures and emphasize his successes. This leads to overconfidence and repetition of mistakes. At this point, investing becomes an addiction.

Perhaps the greatest psychological forces facing investors are fear and greed. Fear has the effect of paralyzing some investors, preventing them from taking any risk at all. These poor souls never seem to get their money out of cash or cash equivalents, and their portfolios languish, barely keeping pace with inflation. But fear also causes aggressive investors to do irrational things, like sell in a panic, even though their game plan calls for holding.

Greed has the opposite effect of fear. It seduces people into putting caution on hold. Greed leads some investors to take a great deal of risk, usually in attempt to make a lot of money quickly. It leads others to take only slightly more risk than they should, but risk that still runs counter to a predetermined investment strategy.

Discovering your own demons

In addition to looking out for common psychological traps that beset the majority of investors, you need to become aware of your personal demons. First, examine your level of confidence. Are you a confident person? Specifically, are you confident in your ability to handle your finances? If you lack confidence, you should spend some time studying before you start investing, and then start slowly. Be aware that indecisiveness could hurt you, and consider hiring an investment adviser. On the other hand, do you have a tendency to be overconfident? A high degree of self-assurance can lead to serious losses.

Are you a disciplined person? Or do you have a tendency to let yourself slide? Do you have good habits? Successful online investing requires discipline. You have to develop a strategy, a game plan, and stay the course. You can't let what the market does, what someone else says or thinks, or anything else throw you off track.

Are you a very optimistic person? Be careful not to let your positive outlook about people and things blind you to trickery and to the reality that some investments just don't work out. If you're overly pessimistic, however, you may have a tendency to discount real opportunities and sell too soon.

Do you have trouble admitting that you just don't understand something? The tendency many people have is to bluff it, to pretend that they know what's going on when they really don't have any idea. "Sounds good, Phil, buy me 100 shares." This is a great way to lose your money. Be honest with yourself about what you do and don't understand. Ask questions to clear things up.

Can you be objective and reasonable when it comes to money or do you get emotional? It's important that you stay cool when you're investing online and make fact-based decisions. You can't let yourself get swept away by the events of the day. Do you tend to act on impulse? Basing your investment decisions on gut instincts, unless you're psychic, is

Watch Out!
Overconfidence is a common demon for investors. While most fund managers, investment advisers, and individual investors are confident in their ability to outperform the market, very few of them ever do. Increasing levels of confidence do not correlate with increasing levels of success.

not sound methodology. Good investment decisions are deliberate. Take a minute to consider which of your personality traits could be a problem for you.

You've got personality

While you must be on guard against common psychological traps and personal demons, you must also respect your individual differences and work to develop your unique investor personality. For example, you may be a confident, decisive investor with a tendency to take substantial risks. There is nothing wrong with this. You have a well-defined investor personality and need a style to match.

All investors have their own unique personalities, but most people fall into one of five categories:

1. **Risk takers,** who like to take risks and aren't bothered by short-term losses

2. **Trend hoppers,** who like to be invested in hot stocks and are always looking for the next big thing

3. **Independents,** who tend to avoid risk, spend time researching and analyzing stocks, and go their own way

4. **Safekeepers,** who are careful, risk-averse, and keen on stable, long-term investments

5. **Team players,** who tend to invest in line with a group of like-minded people or entrust their investments to professional investment advisers

Which group would you put yourself in? Or do you show some combination of traits found in two or more groups?

Determining your tolerance for risk

One of the most important considerations in discovering your investor personality is determining

Bright Idea
Visit the Web site of the Financial Psychology Corporation at www.finpsych.com to find out which of nine money personality types you resemble. The site states that gaining insight into your own money personality will empower you to enjoy money more and make more of it.

your tolerance for market risk. While it's popular to define market risk as the tendency for an investment's price to fluctuate, market risk is actually nothing more than the chance that you will lose money. The greater the risk, the greater that chance is. Investors are enticed into taking more risk by the prospect of higher returns. For example, the greater the risk that the issuer of a bond will default, the higher the yield on the bond. If you're willing to take a chance on a B-rated bond, you could get a very high yield.

With aggressive growth stock funds, risk is not really determined by the degree prices move up and down; it's determined by the underlying financial stability and economic success of the companies in the portfolio. As with risky bonds, the risk with these stocks is that the issuing companies will fail. Unlike IBM and AT&T, these companies not solid, established operations. On the other hand, if these companies succeed, owners of the stocks will reap tremendous gains because these stocks, being young and small, have so much room to grow.

It is true, though, that the less risk you take, the smaller your returns tend to be. Again, this does not mean that high risk equals high return. It means that high-risk investments have a greater potential to generate high returns than low-risk investments do. You must keep this straight in your mind: Risk is bad, return is good. Your goal always should be to minimize risk while maximizing return, or to get the maximum return per unit of risk that you take. If someone you know made 40 percent on their money last year, but they put 100 percent of their money at serious risk to make that 40 percent, this was not a good investment. They could very easily have lost their entire nest egg, and probably will next year.

The Risk Tolerance Test

We all have different risk comfort levels. Some people climb mountains and jump out of airplanes for fun; others refuse to drive because of the associated risks. Similarly, investors have different risk-tolerance levels. What's yours? Take the accompanying Risk Tolerance Test to find out.

THE RISK TOLERANCE TEST

Instructions: Circle the number corresponding to the response you feel best answers the question for you.

1. I prefer conservative investments that minimize the risk of losing any money in a given year, even though they will also minimize my chances of making a lot of money.
    1. Strongly agree
    2. Agree
    3. Neither agree nor disagree
    4. Disagree
    5. Strongly disagree

2. I tend to sell investments that show a loss rather than hold on to them.
    1. Strongly agree
    2. Agree
    3. Neither agree nor disagree
    4. Disagree
    5. Strongly disagree

3. Investing in the stock market is like playing the lottery; the odds are stacked against you.
    1. Strongly agree
    2. Agree
    3. Neither agree nor disagree
    4. Disagree
    5. Strongly disagree

4. If I were looking to purchase stocks, I would look for old, established companies with proven track records rather than small, new companies with explosive growth potential.
   1. Strongly agree
   2. Agree
   3. Neither agree nor disagree
   4. Disagree
   5. Strongly disagree

5. I would have trouble dealing with losing between 1 percent and 5 percent of my principal in a given year.
   1. Strongly agree
   2. Agree
   3. Neither agree nor disagree
   4. Disagree
   5. Strongly disagree

6. I would not invest $10,000 in something that could be worth as little as $4,000 or as much as $80,000 10 years later.
   1. Strongly agree
   2. Agree
   3. Neither agree nor disagree
   4. Disagree
   5. Strongly disagree

7. I would rather miss out on a bull market than be invested during a bear market.
   1. Strongly agree
   2. Agree
   3. Neither agree nor disagree
   4. Disagree
   5. Strongly disagree

8. I would not invest in something that might pay off big if I knew there was a chance I could lose a chunk of my initial investment.
   1. Strongly agree
   2. Agree
   3. Neither agree nor disagree

    4. Disagree

    5. Strongly disagree

9. If my portfolio was down 10 percent, I would have trouble sleeping at night.

    1. Strongly agree

    2. Agree

    3. Neither agree nor disagree

    4. Disagree

    5. Strongly disagree

10. I would be satisfied if the total return of my portfolio consistently equaled the rate of inflation plus 1 percent, if there were no risk of loss.

    1. Strongly agree

    2. Agree

    3. Neither agree nor disagree

    4. Disagree

    5. Strongly disagree

Add the numbers of the answers you circled, and enter the total here: _____ .

Refer to the score table that follows to see what kind of an investor you are in terms of risk tolerance. These scores and categories are not exact but will give you a general idea of where you fall on the risk-tolerance continuum.

SCORE	CATEGORY
10	You are a saver, not an investor.
11–20	You are a conservative investor.
21–30	You are a moderately conservative investor.
31–40	You are a moderately aggressive investor.
41–50	You are an aggressive investor.

Now, let's define the terms in the test.

A **saver** prefers to accumulate wealth and take virtually no risk. Particularly appropriate financial instruments for savers include bank savings accounts, money market accounts, CDs, money market funds, and no-risk bonds such as U.S. Treasuries (held to maturity) and savings bonds.

A **conservative investor** is willing to take a limited amount of risk, but preservation of capital is paramount to him. Particularly appropriate investment vehicles for conservative investors include money market funds, investment-grade bonds, and preferred stocks.

A **moderately conservative investor** is willing to incur some real risk to her principal for the chance of getting a better return. Particularly appropriate investments include bonds, bond funds, equity income funds, and some U.S. large cap stocks.

A **moderately aggressive investor** is willing to incur significant risk to his principal to make double-digit returns on his money. Particularly appropriate investments include non-speculative domestic and foreign stocks and all types of stock funds.

An **aggressive investor** is willing to incur substantial risk to his principal to maximize potential profits. Particularly appropriate investments include high-yield bonds and bond funds, all kinds of stocks, and all kinds of stock funds.

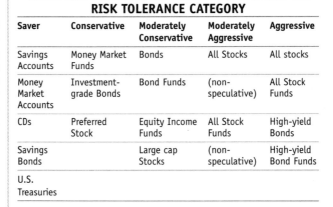

TABLE 6.1: APPROPRIATE INVESTMENTS BASED ON RISK TOLERANCE CATEGORY

Appropriate ➤ investments for each group include all the investments appropriate for lower risk-tolerance groups.

Saver	Conservative	Moderately Conservative	Moderately Aggressive	Aggressive
Savings Accounts	Money Market Funds	Bonds	All Stocks	All stocks
Money Market Accounts	Investment-grade Bonds	Bond Funds	(non-speculative)	All Stock Funds
CDs	Preferred Stock	Equity Income Funds	All Stock Funds	High-yield Bonds
Savings Bonds		Large cap Stocks	(non-speculative)	High-yield Bond Funds
U.S. Treasuries				

The truth about risk-taking

Mutual fund companies and financial professionals would have you believe that because the stock market has historically gone up, any risk you take is short-term and is purely a function of your time horizon. (Your time horizon is the length of time you have to reach your goal, the amount of time before you actually need the money you've invested.) The argument is that if you have, say, 20 years, your portfolio will surely go up and go up handsomely, no matter what you're invested in. So, the greater your time horizon, the more aggressively you should invest.

Yet, these same companies repeat like a mantra that past performance of both their funds and the market is no guarantee of future returns. Can we then rest assured that what goes down will eventually go up within our time horizon? Of course not. The Japanese stock market is still down more than 50 percent from its highs in 1989—that's 10 years later! That means if you had invested all your money in aggressive growth stocks in Japan in 1989, you would

Bright Idea
Confirm your risk tolerance by taking another test. Go to www2.valic.com/valicrsk.html, www.prusec.com/quiz.htm, or www.mackenziefinancial.com/FundInformation/Questionnaire.html for some good risk-tolerance tests.

still be down 50 percent or more. The truth is that investing aggressively is inherently riskier than investing conservatively, no matter what the time horizon, and this should not be undertaken by the faint of heart.

While risk tolerance is defined by the financial world as the maximum amount of market risk an investor can take without feeling uncomfortable, a more complete definition would include the *minimum* amount of risk an investor can tolerate as well. That is, you must not take too little risk. If you are a moderately aggressive investor but all your money is in U.S. Treasuries, you'll feel very uncomfortable. The urge to buy some stocks will be very strong, and you just might toss and turn at night over all the opportunities you feel you're missing. So, figuring out your risk tolerance level is not just about limiting the amount of risk you take; it's about finding the balance between minimum and maximum. This is not easy and may require some trial and error. As a rule of thumb, you know you're in your sweet spot when you feel comfortable during the day and you're not losing sleep at night.

Many investors who are actually conservative may invest aggressively during a bull market. This is a mistake because, when prices turn down, these investors will be extremely uncomfortable and may become irrational. They'll be out of their league. But how can you know how you'll feel about a downturn in prices before it actually happens? First, from experience. Second, use your imagination. Always consider the downside potential of an investment before you buy it, and ask yourself how you would feel if it went down, not up, and what you would do. If the downside scenario makes you uncomfortable, reconsider and think about investing in the kinds of things gen-

Unofficially...
Women investors tend to be more risk-averse than men.

erally recommended for your risk-tolerance level. It's easy to get swept up in the excitement of a raging bull market and get overextended.

More than one kind of risk

Market risk is not the only kind of risk out there. Inflation risk is the risk that the rate of inflation will outpace the return on your investments, and their value will erode. If inflation is around 7 percent, for example, and you're making 6 percent on some preferred stock, the value of your money in terms of its purchasing power is actually shrinking.

Another kind of risk you should be aware of is interest rate risk. This is the risk that you will commit your money to a fixed-income investment for a certain period of time, and interest rates will go up during that period, causing you to miss out on the higher rates and diminishing the value of your investment. For example, if you own a bond and rates rise, you miss out on the higher yields and the price of your bond drops.

Adequate assets risk is the risk that you will not have enough money to meet your needs when the time comes. If your return on investment has been extremely low for years, for instance, you may not be able to retire when you had hoped. These forms of risk help carve out the minimum levels of risk an investor can tolerate.

Liquidity risk is the risk that you will need the money you invested before its maturity but won't be able to get your hands on it without paying a penalty. This is one of the drawbacks of CDs.

There is also currency risk. When you invest internationally, the exchange rate may change in a way that will hurt your returns. If you were to purchase a U.K. stock fund that was denominated in pounds, for example, and the pound were to go down against the dollar by 5 percent, your returns would be cut by 5 percent when you converted your money back into dollars.

So when we talk about an investor's overall risk tolerance, various kinds of risk should be considered.

Long-term investors vs. short-term traders

As you begin to define your investor personality, you must also consider whether you're more of a long-term investor or a short-term trader. Long-term investors look for things to put their money in for the long haul. They carefully consider something before they buy it; once they make a purchase, they stay committed. (This is also known as the buy-and-hold.)

Long-term investors abhor buying and selling frequently. They're of the mindset that you give something time to grow. They do not concern themselves with short-term price fluctuations because they believe that over the span of 5, 10, or 20 years, their investments will definitely go up in value. The only thing that could prevent that would be selling too soon. Long-term investors are patient. Does this sound a bit like you?

Short-term traders are very different. They don't believe that any stock will necessarily go up over time. They prefer actively buying and selling stocks. They will buy a stock that is rising or that they believe is about to rise, hold the stock as it continues to go up, and sell it when it pulls back too far, with the idea of locking in a profit. If a stock goes down right off the bat, short-term traders will sell it if it goes down too much, with the idea of limiting their loss. Short-term traders are impatient and uncomfortable about holding on to under-performing stocks for long. Does this sound more like you?

Many mutual fund companies discourage short-term trading, saying that it's counterproductive. They argue that short-term traders don't do as well as long-term investors. By making frequent trades, they assert, short-term traders also increase their transaction costs, and if they're investing in a fund, the transaction costs of the fund. It would be better for them to just sit tight when a fund goes down in price, so the argument goes, because the fund is bound to recover. Investors who hold their positions during the temporary downswings, then, will be rewarded. Investors who sell at the first sign of trouble will miss out on the next surge in prices.

The problem with this logic is threefold. First, there is no guarantee that the stock market or the fund will continue to go up. Second, if the market or the fund goes down, there's no guarantee that it will recover soon. Third, how you feel is very, very important. Some people just can't stomach long-term investing.

Also, most short-term traders believe they can make more money than long-term investors, primarily by limiting their losses. In fact, both long-term investors and short-term traders can and do make good money. It's more a question of style and comfort. Before you take the word of mutual fund companies as gospel, remember that they have a vested interest in your staying fully invested at all times. (We'll explore how these two approaches stack up against each other in Chapter 11, "Venturing Out on Your Own.")

> **The style is the man himself.**
> —Georges Buffon

You've got style

The next step is to determine your basic investment style with regard to stocks and stock funds. Stock mutual fund managers also follow one or more of these approaches, so always look for funds that match your own style. Take a look at the following approaches to investing in the stock market to see which you feel most comfortable with.

Value investing

A value investor searches for companies that are undervalued. He's looking for stocks whose prices are low in proportion to things such as the company's earnings (low PE ratio) and total worth (low price-to-book value). He's looking for companies with solid fundamentals—sound financials, good management, and strong prospects, companies with an intrinsic value that is greater than their stock's current share price. Value investors reason that the share price of a value stock is low only because demand for the stock is low. The stock is out of favor, perhaps, due to setbacks at the company or in the industry not too long ago. Value investing rests on the philosophy that the stock market is not perfectly efficient in incorporating all relevant information about a stock into its price. This approach also assumes that over time, the price of a stock will gradually move toward its intrinsic value.

Growth investing

A growth investor buys stocks that are poised to grow significantly. These companies are established, successful, and well-managed, and their earnings and dividends are expected to grow faster than average. The philosophy here is that because these up-and-coming companies have already proven themselves, there is every likelihood that they will continue to succeed, growing like crazy as they do. Often these stocks have relatively high PE and price-to-book ratios because demand for them is high. Investors in

Bright Idea
You can find out a mutual fund manager's investment style by calling the fund family, checking the fund's prospectus, or checking out the style sections of mutual fund monitoring services such as *Morningstar* and *The Value Line Mutual Fund Survey*.

growth stocks believe that the prices of these stocks will rise in tandem with increases in earnings. Because the valuation of these stocks depends so heavily on earnings growth, though, they tend to exhibit more severe drops in price than average with earnings disappointments.

Momentum investing

Momentum investors invest in stocks that have been exhibiting the greatest price increases relative to other stocks in recent history, on the belief that this trend will continue. The underlying philosophy here is that the trend is your friend. People buy momentum stocks because they are going up in price, and these price increases attract more buyers, driving the prices up even higher. Many momentum investors consider themselves to be growth investors, and visa versa.

Contrarian investing

Contrarian investors invest in stocks that have performed the worst in recent history on the belief that they will turn around. The underlying philosophy here is that stock prices move in cycles, and the best way to make money is to buy a stock when it's in the cellar and hold it until it moves back up in price. (Buy low, sell high.) If a stock has already been trounced, such an investor believes, it has only one way to go—up. One common contrarian strategy is to look at all the stocks (or funds) with the worst total return for the past year and buy them. Many contrarians consider themselves to be value investors, and visa versa.

Large cap investing

Large cap investors invest in big, successful companies, such as IBM, Ford, and General Electric.

Large cap stocks are generally defined as those of companies with a total market capitalization of more than $5 billion. The philosophy behind large cap investing is simply that success begets success. These companies are successful for a reason, and they will continue to outrun the competition and pay nice dividends. There is almost zero chance that these companies will go bankrupt, and there's a reduced chance that they will show major price declines in a down market.

Small cap investing

Small cap investors invest in small companies that they expect to become big companies some day. Small cap stocks are generally defined as stocks of companies with a total market capitalization of $1 billion or less. (Some small cap investors also buy mid cap stocks, which have a market capitalization of between $1 billion and $5 billion.) The philosophy behind small cap investing is that getting in on the ground floor of even a few future McDonald's-like companies will more than make up for the risk of investing in companies destined to fail. Small cap stocks are not necessarily growth stocks because they may not be well-established companies yet, and they may not even be generating earnings. The art of small cap investing is discovering those diamonds in the rough that will be movers and shakers in the years to come.

Index fund investing

Index fund investors invest in funds that mimic the popular stock indexes. The philosophy behind this investment style is based on two points.

1. The fact that most professional fund managers (and most investors, for that matter) fail to beat the market averages in any given year.

Unofficially...
Because index funds seek to match the performance of an index, there is less buying and selling of securities based on performance and projected performance. Low turnover of securities in these funds translates into fewer capital gains distributions and reduced tax liability for investors.

2. The belief that stock prices already reflect all information available about a stock, and there is no way to predict future price movements.

The second point is based on the efficient market theory, which is backed by substantial research and accepted in most financial academic circles. The implications of this theory are that no amount of research or analysis can help an investor select stocks that will outperform the market. The most sensible thing to do, then, is invest in the stock market as a whole, which historically rises.

Ethical investing

In arriving at an investment style, you should also consider whether it is important to you to limit the universe of stocks and funds you choose from to those of companies that do not hurt people or damage the environment. This is known as ethical investing or socially responsible investing. It is possible to employ any style within this framework. The only drawback is that it can be difficult and time-consuming to find stocks that meet your financial criteria that are also ethically sound.

Variety

Of course, there is some overlap among the different styles of investing. Growth stocks in recent history have tended to be momentum stocks. Value stocks tend to be those held by many contrarian investors. Small cap investors may be purchasing several of the better-known growth stocks. Growth investors may also use value investing for a blended approach, but each of the styles can be viewed as having a unique orientation and emphasis.

All the various investment styles work—some work better at certain times than others. One-year large caps may do extremely well while small caps will lag; another year the opposite will occur. Some investors swear by value investing; others by growth. The same is true of momentum vs. contrarian approaches. Perhaps you'll come up with a combination style, such as being a contrarian, large cap investor. In fact, a well-known investment strategy follows this approach: It's called the Dogs of the Dow, which will be discussed is some detail in Chapter 11. Maybe you'll choose to be a growth, momentum investor. The most important thing is selecting an approach that makes sense to you and that you feel comfortable with. Just be sure to give your chosen style a chance—you may not make money right away.

Fundamental analysis or technical?

Two distinct but equally valid methods exist for analyzing individual stocks or funds: fundamental analysis and technical analysis. Which method is for you?

Fundamental analysis looks at things such as a company's performance, financial statements, market potential, competitors, management, and capitalization to determine its value. The idea here is to analyze a company's worth on its merits and demerits. Having done this, you're in a better position to judge whether a company is healthy and whether the current price of its stock is reasonable. The premise of fundamental analysis is that thorough research and analysis of a company's fundamentals can yield information that can indicate future prices for its stock. Fundamentalists tend to buy and hold a stock until the stocks' fundamentals change for the worse. Pure value and growth investors are fundamentalists.

Technical analysis involves looking not at a company's fundamentals, but at its stock price trend, the

Moneysaver
Be selective when it comes to choosing ethical stock funds. Some have done much better than others. Pax World Fund and Dreyfus Third Century have been around more than 25 years and have delivered consistently superior returns.

relative strength of the stock's price movement in relation to other stocks, a stock's price cycles, trading ranges, and trading volume. Technicians or technical analysts use graphs of stock prices, mathematical formulas, and computer programs to analyze stocks and make buy, sell, and hold decisions. The premise of technical analysis is that stocks do exhibit measurable price patterns that can be used as predicators of future movements. Many technicians believe that bullish and bearish periods in the markets can be identified or timed, and they adjust their exposure to the market based on signals produced by their timing indicators. Pure momentum investors are technicians.

Do you see yourself as a fundamentalist or a technician? Many investors use a combination of these two approaches, analyzing both a company's fundamentals and its stock's price action. Using both systems functions like a double filter, allowing only a select group of companies to pass through. For example, let's say you were interested in possibly buying shares of Pfizer, a major drug company. First you would look at Pfizer's fundamentals, at things such as its balance sheet, income statements, management, sales and earnings growth, competition, and capital reserves. (You'll learn how to do this kind of research in Chapter 12.) If Pfizer looked fundamentally solid, you would mark it as a buy candidate. Next, you would analyze the stock technically, looking at how Pfizer's stock price had been acting recently. If the stock met your technical criteria as well, Pfizer would be a definite buy.

Are you the do-it-yourself type?

The final major question you need to ask yourself is whether you would like to get investment advice.

Employing a professional investment adviser will cost you some money, although many advisers charge only a small fraction of your total account value. This system gives them a strong incentive to increase the value of your account. Professional investment advisers tend to be more knowledgeable about investing than the average person, and they have all day to study the markets and individual securities.

Having an investment adviser by your side can be very comforting and educational. Your adviser will tell you what he thinks you should do with your money and why—where to invest; how much; when to buy, hold, or sell; and why. If you're worried about the stock market or your investments, he will be there to reassure you. Your investment adviser also will keep you company as you venture through the investment jungle; you'll have a teammate. Relying on an investment adviser to help you make your investment decisions takes some of the pressure off.

This system works for a lot of people. As an online investor, you can secure the advice of someone you trust and simply do whatever that person recommends. The most important thing here is to choose an adviser who shares your philosophy and basic style, an adviser whose advice makes sense to you and that you feel comfortable taking. Otherwise, you'll face sleepless nights.

The other thing is to choose someone *good*. Most advisers, such as most fund managers, don't do any better than inexperienced investors. So, to a great extent, the decision of whether to use an adviser is a psychological one. Will it make you feel better? Will it give peace of mind to know you're not in this alone? Be honest with yourself.

Many people, however, cannot work with investment advisers. These investors tend to have fairly

Timesaver
Hiring a good investment adviser will save you a lot of time because all the research, analysis, and decision-making will be done by her. Depending on the relationship, she may even be able to place all your trades for you.

strong opinions and a definite sense about how they want to invest and what kinds of things they want to invest in. If this sounds like you, an investment adviser will just get in your way. You'll never be able to convince your adviser to do things your way because his job is to advise *you*. If you're not sure whether to seek the help of an adviser, you can experiment with each path. No decision is final. Real-life experience should give you enough information to reach a conclusion.

There really is no single best way for everybody to invest. And there really is no one who can tell you how you should invest your money. Good advisers should make recommendations based on *your* investor personality, not theirs. Research and empirical studies have shown that numerous different approaches to investing work.

The ultimate litmus test is comfort. If you're not comfortable with a strategy, an adjustment needs to be made somewhere. Some might counter that you don't feel comfortable because you don't understand. But you shouldn't be investing in anything you don't understand in the first place. Investing is not just about making money; it's about *how* you make that money. Successful investing increases your wealth *and* your peace of mind.

Bright Idea
You must decide what investing style best suits you. Taking an approach that doesn't fit you will cause you undue stress and may very well cost you money.

Just the facts

- Many emotional factors, such as pride, shame, and regret, influence most investors decisions and can have a negative impact on their returns.

- There are five basic investor personality types, and five basic investor types. The onus on every online investor is to find her own investor personality, with all its foibles, and adopt an investment style she is most comfortable with.

- Long-term investors buy stocks with the intent of making money over a period of years; short-term traders buy and sell stocks frequently with the idea of making numerous profitable trades over a short period of time.

- The major investment approaches are value investing, growth investing, momentum investing, contrarian investing, large cap investing, small cap investing, and index fund investing.

- Investors who lack confidence and experience may benefit from the services of an investment adviser. Investors with strong convictions and a lot of ideas of their own probably won't.

GET THE SCOOP ON...
The art of setting goals • Determining ways
to achieve your goals • Reaching financial
independence • Funding your child's
college education

Setting Goals and Formulating a Game Plan

Chapter 7

G oal-setting is the single most powerful tool we have in our possession to get the things we want in life. Having goals crystallizes in our own minds what we're striving for and helps us focus our energies on getting those things. Goals help us make decisions and eliminate the things in our lives that are pulling us off track.

Goal-setting can be viewed as a four-part process: setting the goal; developing a strategy; implementing the strategy; and evaluating the results. For goal-setting to work effectively for us, we must understand the best way to go about the four steps of this process. It's important not to set too many goals, or you'll have trouble achieving anything. You may have goals for what kind of person you want to be, your career, your health, your relationships, and your spiritual development. The goals we'll be focusing on in this chapter, however, are your financial goals.

While we all have different financial goals, most of us share two: having enough money for retirement and having enough money to pay for our children's college education. There are various strategies for achieving these goals, and we'll look at these in this chapter.

The secrets of goal-setting

Before you die, you want to achieve and experience certain things, and those things are particular to you as an individual. The unique desires that motivate you are at the very core of who you are, and the realization of these desires is at the heart of your level of happiness and self-actualization. Psychologists have found that setting goals is the best way to realize your life's desires because it forces you to make your desires concrete, putting them into a form that is specific, realistic, and attainable. Doing this helps you focus your energy and get what you want.

Step 1: Dream

The first step in goal-setting, then, is to dream. Kick back with a clipboard, a pencil, and a piece of paper, and let your mind go where it wants to go. (You should use a pencil for this exercise, not a pen.) Ask yourself what you really want to be, do, and have before you die. Some of the things you come up with might require relatively little work or preparation, such as seeing *Gone with the Wind*; others might require slightly more, such as driving across Europe. Still others might require a great deal of time and effort, such as getting a Ph.D. or building a net worth of a million dollars. Write everything down. Brainstorm—no idea is too crazy. Next, ask yourself how you think you're doing in all the areas of your life that are important to you. From this vantage point, write down additional wants on your list.

Try to avoid writing down things that don't excite you but instead give you a kind of "ugh" feeling. These are often things that you think you *should* want rather than things that you really *do* want. It comes down to what you really value. While this might seem easy, it's actually a very tricky point. We have all been put under pressure our whole lives, directly and indirectly, by family, friends, and society, to strive for certain things, even if these things are not truly what we desire.

Children of successful parents, for example, generally feel a tremendous amount of pressure to be at least as successful (in a socioeconomic sense) as their parents are. First-son syndrome is the pressure first sons feel to be as successful as their fathers, often in the same field. If your father is a successful lawyer, you may feel compelled to go into law, even though you'd rather be an architect. You're particularly vulnerable to this trap if you have no idea yet what you want to do.

If you find that you aren't producing many long-term wants and that most of the items on your list are things like "Try all of Baskin-Robbins' 31 flavors" and "Go to Reno," don't fret. Just write those things down. Don't write down noble-sounding long-term goals, like "Become a doctor," if you're really not sure about or excited about them.

Remember, goal-setting is all about who you are—there's no point in faking it. If you aren't sure what you want in certain areas of your life, then you're still in the process of discovering this, and that's a wonderful thing that can't be rushed. There's also no need to be more specific about what you want than you really are. If you think you might be interested in medicine, for example, but you're not sure, consider volunteering at a hospital. Does the idea of doing this excite you? Then write it down. If you find out, as a result of your volunteering experience, that you *don't* want to go into medicine, try something related to another field that you think you might like. There is nothing wrong with drifting laterally in this way, but trusting this process and being patient with yourself takes courage. Counseling, especially career counseling, can be helpful. Just remember to ignore those around you who tell you what you should want or who tell you that what you think you want is nuts.

Now that you've got your want list, you can begin to set your goals. (This part might be easier to do on a computer.) Look at your list and decide which of the items you really want to go after in your lifetime. The minute you commit yourself to pursuing a want, it becomes a goal. These are your lifetime goals.

Now here's the tough part: Decide which of your lifetime goals you want to go after now, keeping in mind that if you chase too many rabbits, you won't catch any. These are your current goals. Create several categories for your current goals, such as career, health, and social (don't forget financial!). Within each category, make the following time frame subcategories:

- Short-term (1–4 weeks)
- Medium-term (2–12 months)
- Long-term (more than 1 year)

Put the long-term categories first, medium-term second, and then short-term. The idea is to give priority to your long-term goals. Now enter each of your goals into its category and time frame, making the goal as specific, measurable, and realistic as you can. For example, if one of your goals is to increase the amount of money you're putting into savings, try to decide how much you want to increase the amount. For example, you might decide to increase the amount from $0 a month to $300 a month. Now prioritize your goals within each time frame category, listing or numbering the goals in order of how much you want to achieve them.

Step 2: Formulate a Strategy

Step 2 in the goal-setting process is to formulate a strategy. Like goals themselves, strategies for achieving goals should be specific, measurable, and realistic. If the goal is a permanent change in your lifestyle, the strategy for achieving and maintaining the goal will require a change in your daily, weekly, or monthly routine. For example, if your goal is to increase the amount you save every month from $0 to $300, you might decide to do this by writing your first check every fiscal month to your brokerage account. If this simple strategy works, you will need to continue to employ the strategy. It must become a habit.

Step 3: Execute

Step 3 is execution. You have your goal to increase the amount you save from $0 to $300 a month, and your strategy to write your first check of the month to yourself. But now you have to actually *do* this. Execute. Can you remember the plan? Will you continue to blow your paycheck on bills and beer? Forging new habits takes discipline. Use your daily planner to help you implement your strategies by actually entering to-do items on specific days. If

Bright Idea
Deciding what your lifetime goals are and how much time you want to devote to each would be facilitated if you knew how long you were going to live. Answer The Northwestern Mutual Life Insurance Company's "Longevity Game" questions at www. northwestern-mutual.com/ games/longevity/ longevity-main. html, and you may get some idea.

you're trying to create a new habit, such as sending a check to your brokerage account every month, make sure you schedule the next day you will perform the activity before crossing off the last entry for the activity in your planner.

Step 4: Evaluate

The final step of the goal-setting process is evaluation. You need to periodically check your progress, and a good way to keep track of how you're doing is to write everything down. Keep a log. Your log might consist of all the months of the year written out, with a check mark placed next to each month you actually performed the task in question. Decide ahead of time how often you'll evaluate yourself, perhaps quarterly.

If after three months you're on target writing those checks, congratulations! If not, ask yourself first if you've been faithfully implementing your strategy. If the reason you haven't is that you keep forgetting, you've got to work out a way to remind yourself. You could also change the strategy. See if you can arrange direct deposit from your employer or your bank to your brokerage account. Finally, evaluate the goal. Do you still want to save $300 a month? If no, then jettison the goal. If yes, but you seem to lack the motivation to implement your strategy, ask yourself if the goal is too ambitious, making you feel discouraged, or is too easy, making you lose interest.

Taking a look at your financial goals

Goal-setting is a skill that can and should be applied to our financial lives. What are your long-term, medium-term, and short-term financial goals? Maybe one of your long-term goals is to buy a sports car and own it outright in five years. Another might be to buy

"
Learn the art of patience. Apply discipline to your thoughts when they become anxious over the outcome of a goal. Impatience breeds anxiety, fear, discouragement, and failure. Patience creates confidence, decisiveness, and a rational outlook, which eventually leads to success
—Brian Adams
"

a new computer within the next year. One way to achieve such financial goals is to simply save up the money you need and then go buy the item. Another way, in the case of something as expensive as a sports car, is to finance the item, paying some of the money up front and the rest over time with interest. Both these methods can and do work well, if you stay organized and disciplined. But you should set up a savings or payment schedule for yourself and stick to it. Table 7.1 is a worksheet for setting up such a schedule.

TABLE 7.1: FINANCIAL GOALS WORKSHEET

Short-term Goals	Target Date	Total Cost	Weeks to Goal	Weekly Cost
		$		$
		$		$
		$		$
Intermediate-term Goals	**Target Date**	**Total Cost**	**Months to Goal**	**Monthly Cost**
		$		$
		$		$
		$		$
Long-term Goals	**Target Date**	**Total Cost**	**Months to Go**	**Monthly Cost**
		$		$
		$		$
		$		$

← The monthly (or weekly) cost is the total cost divided by the months (or weeks) to the goal.

The same type of planning can be used to attain larger financial goals, such as buying a home, financing college tuition, and saving for retirement. For these larger goals, however, you should consider financial planning.

Financial planners sit down with you and take a look at your entire financial situation and help you formulate goals and strategies to meet those goals. As with investment advisers, who focus on investment decisions more than your overall financial situation, financial planners can be a big help to many people. In June 1998, 92 percent of the people who sought the advice of financial planners reported that they were comfortable with their finances. Only 76 percent of those who did not receive professional advice reported the same. Of the people who sought advice, 85 percent said it was worth it, and the level of client satisfaction was directly correlated with the length of the relationship between client and adviser. The longer the relationship, the greater the client's comfort with her finances *and the likelihood of reaching her goals.*

Of the people who use financial advisers, however, only 54 percent feel that the financial benefits outweigh the lifestyle benefits, such as help with planning, peace of mind, comfort, and confidence. For the people who use financial planners, then, the advice pays off not just in dollars and cents, but also in higher quality of life. Check out the International Association of Financial Planning (IAFP) at www.iafp.org or 1-800-945-4237 for references to financial planners in your area. The IAFP is planning to merge with the Institute of Certified Financial Planners (ICFP) on January 1, 2000, to create the Financial Planning Association (FPA). Certified Public Accountants (CPAs) can also provide you with solid financial planning advice.

Achieving financial independence

One of the biggest financial goals for most of us is achieving financial independence. Financial independence can be defined as the point at which your investment income equals or exceeds your living expenses. If you had a million dollars invested in tax-free bonds earning 7 percent a year, for example,

Bright Idea
For some online help setting your financial goals, go to Charles Schwab's home page at www.schwab.com and click on "Planning."

your income from the bonds would be around $70,000 a year, enough for many people to live on. You could retire. In fact, this is what retirement is all about. It's about having enough money, or enough money coming in from investments, that you don't need to work for a living. This is a very nice thing, especially if you're old and tired of working.

Choosing a specific goal

With financial independence as your general goal, try to get more specific. At what age would you like to retire, and how much income will you need? For example, "I want to retire at age 60 with an income of $40,000." If you're not sure how much you will need, know that many financial planners estimate that you'll need between 70 percent and 100 percent of your current income in retirement. Many expenses, such as job-related expenses, will diminish, but you need to consider your personal situation. Will you be doing a lot of traveling? Do you anticipate paying more in medical costs?

Obtaining information

One good way to estimate your financial needs in retirement is to consider three categories of expenses: fixed expenses, basic living expenses, and discretionary expenses. Fixed expenses are things you can't do a lot about, such as housing, debt service, insurance premiums, and taxes. Basic living expenses are things you have some control over, such as food and utilities. Discretionary expenses are things that are totally up to you, such as gifts, travel, and recreation. Prepare a projected expense budget for your retirement by looking at your probable expenses within the framework of these categories. And take advantage of online retirement calculators, programs that assist you in estimating retirement

Watch Out!
Calculators can make mistakes. Some calculators have built-in assumptions that may not be made explicit. Some Web sites also have ulterior motives for providing calculators (such as getting your money!). For these reasons, it's always a good idea to use more than one calculator when you're trying to figure something out.

income and expenses. A good place to start is the U.S. News Retirement Calculator at www.usnews.com/usnews/nycu/money/moretcal.htm.

Find out which of your company benefits, such as medical and dental insurance, can be continued after you retire, and at what cost. One major advantage of staying with your employer's health insurance plan is that it will have a post-retirement *group* plan. Group plans usually have fewer restrictions on coverage, such as those on pre-existing conditions, than individual plans. On the other hand, you'll have to pick up the tab for the coverage, which your employer used to pay for you.

If you're 65 or older, you're eligible for Medicare, a federally administered health insurance program designed to cover some, but not all, medical expenses. You might want to buy Medigap insurance, a policy provided by private insurance companies to fill in the gaps left by Medicare. Also consider buying long-term care coverage; although it's expensive, it covers in-home care and nursing home care. In deciding how much insurance you'll need, research your options, the costs of each, and the coverage available, while taking your own as well as your family's medical history into account.

Inflation is another key consideration. If you retire today on an income of $40,000 a year, at an average annual inflation rate of just 4 percent, you'll need $59,210 only 10 years from now to have the same amount of income you do today. Don't get bent out of shape over inflation figures, though. This beast advances very unevenly, so while some things such as medical costs may skyrocket other things such as computers will probably continue to move down in price. Yes, you will need more money, but how much more will really depend on your individual spending habits and needs. Take a minute to consider what your individual income requirements will be over the duration of your retirement.

TABLE 7.2: IMPACT OF INFLATION ON INCOME NEEDS

Today	10 Years	15 Years	20 Years
		Based on 4% Inflation	
$25,000	$37,000	$45,000	$56,900
$35,000	$51,800	$63,000	$76,700
$50,000	$74,000	$90,000	$109,600
		Based on 8% Inflation	
Today	10 Years	15 Years	20 Years
$25,000	$54,000	$79,250	$116,500
$35,000	$75,500	$111,000	$163,100
$50,000	$108,000	$158,500	$233,000

Strategies for success

With a specific, measurable, and realistic goal in hand, you can now work on your strategies for achieving it. The first thing you have to do is take an inventory of your retirement sources of income. The following list includes the most common sources of retirement income:

- Company pension
- Company 401(k) or the like
- IRA
- Social Security
- Personal savings
- Non-liquid assets

If you work for a company, check into your employer's pension plan. A pension plan is a qualified retirement plan (meaning that it meets IRS requirements for favorable tax treatment) set up by a corporation, labor union, government, or other organization for its employees. Examples of pension plans include profit-sharing plans, stock bonus and employee stock ownership plans, thrift plans, target benefit plans, money purchase plans, and defined benefit plans.

If you have a pension plan with your employer, you are generally entitled to financial support from your employer for the rest of your life when you retire. The amount you can collect depends upon the number of years you were with the company, how much you made while you were there, your Social Security income, your age of retirement, and whether you want to collect a pension based on your life expectancy or on the life expectancy of you and your spouse.

Pension plans often use traditional insurance investment vehicles such as fixed annuities, which guarantee principal and a specified interest rate and may also offer dividends.

Unofficially...
Some companies will let you take a lump sum on retirement, if you choose, rather than monthly or yearly payments for the rest of your or your spouse's life. Your pension income will be taxed.

Pensions

You have four basic pension distribution options:

1. **Single life:** A monthly payment is made to you for life. With standard single life, payments stop when you die.

2. **Joint and survivor:** A reduced monthly payment is made to you for life with the guarantee that payments will continue to your survivor (spouse) for life after your death.

3. **Term certain:** A reduced monthly payment is made to you for life (or to you and your survivor for life) with the guarantee that payments will continue to be made to a beneficiary, such as a spouse or child, for a certain period after your death, such as 5, 10, or 15 years.

4. **Lump sum:** A single payment is made to you upon retirement.

You might choose to take a lump sum over monthly payments for life if you think the lump sum will exceed the total amount you will collect from monthly payments. In other words, if you have reason to believe that you're going to die soon, opting for a lump sum might make sense. When it comes right down to it, though, you don't have much control over how much income you're going to get from your pension.

As with your pension, your Social Security entitlements will depend on your age, income from other sources, and years of employment. If you're presently in your 30s or 40s, however, you may not get anything: Social Security is headed for bankruptcy. So, if you're middle-aged or younger, it would be prudent not to figure any payments from Social Security into your retirement budget. If the program is still around when you get close to retirement, you may be able to retire early and enjoy a bit of cushion during retirement.

Social Security

Unlike company pension plans, Social Security is never paid in lump sums, and the maximum annual payments are generally much smaller.

TABLE 7.3: ESTIMATED ANNUAL SOCIAL SECURITY BENEFITS

1994 Income	Early Retirement (Age 62)	Normal Retirement (Age 65)
$15,000	$5,971	$7,464
$36,000	$10,560	$13,200
$62,700	$11,981	$14,976

← Figures assume that recipients are steady earners who retired at the beginning of early 1996.

Savings plans—especially 401(k)s

The next income source you should consider in calculating your retirement income is your employer-provided savings plan. The most common of these retirement plans are 401(k)s, 403(b)s for non-profit organizations, 408(k)s or SEPs (simplified employee pension plans) for companies with 25 employees or less, and Keogh plans for self-employed individuals or unincorporated businesses. The 401(k) is used as a representative example because it is the best-known. The name 401(k) comes from the section of the tax code describing the program. Such plans allow you to put a certain amount of your pre-tax income into a retirement savings account through an automatic payroll deduction. In some cases, you're also allowed to contribute after-tax income.

Many employers will match a portion of your contributions, often 25 percent or 50 percent, and/or contribute a set dollar amount for every contribution you make. Some employers will match 100 percent of the amount you contribute! So if, for example, you defer $300 of your salary a month into your 401(k), your employer may put in an additional $150 (50 percent), raising the total contribution to $450 a month. The company may also share profits with you by contributing a fraction of company profits to your 401(k). (There are tax incentives for employers to do all these nice things.)

The IRS limits the amount of money you can contribute to your 401(k) in a year. For 1999, the limit was $10,000 of pre-tax earnings. The maximum amount that can be contributed—including money from your pre-tax and post-tax income and your employer's matching contributions—is $30,000 a year or 25 percent of your total compensation, whichever is less.

You decide how the money in your 401(k) will be invested, and you bear the investment risk. Generally, you can invest the money in three basic vehicles: a select group of mutual funds, your company's stock, or guaranteed vehicles, such as CDs. You won't pay any taxes on the principal or earnings until you start taking distributions when you retire, but not before you're age 59½. If you need to borrow some of the money before then, emergency loans are usually possible. Hardship withdrawals are also possible. Regardless of the reason, however, if you withdraw some or all of the money ahead of time, you will pay a penalty of around 10 percent in addition to taxes on the money, and you will not be allowed to redeposit the money later.

Any way you slice it, 401(k)s are a great deal. First, you're putting in pre-tax income, which means, quite literally, that you're paying fewer taxes than you otherwise would because your taxable (take-home) income is less. For example, if you make $40,000 a year and you contribute $4,000 of this to your 401(k), you will be paying taxes only on $36,000 of income.

Second, the fact that you're investing pre-tax money means that you have more to invest. For example, if you're saving 10 percent of your money, and you make $40,000 a year gross, that's $4,000 for your 401(k). If you couldn't invest your 10 percent until after taxes were taken out, you would have only $2,880 to invest (10 percent of your $28,800 take-home pay). This benefit is greatly enhanced by the fact that your employer may well be making matching contributions, so that $4,000 you put in could become $6,000. Now compare $6,000 with that $2,880. You're making out like a bandit! And your employer's contribution is free money for you—it's

Watch Out!
When you take a hardship withdrawal from your 401(k), 10–20% of the amount you withdraw will be withheld to prepay your federal income tax. Take this into account when deciding how much you're going to need to withdraw.

Bright Idea
If you want to know how much your 401(k) will probably be worth when you retire, go to www. financialengines. com or www. fplanauditors. com. For $14.95 a quarter, the first site, created under the auspices of Nobel-prize–winning economist William Sharpe, will suggest ways for you to improve your portfolio.

like a raise. The more you sink into your 401(k), the more of that free money you get.

Finally, the fact that the money in your 401(k) is invested on a tax-deferred basis allows you to make more. For example, $1,000 of pre-tax income invested in your 401(k) for 20 years (assuming that you make 8 percent a year on the money) would be worth $4,661 twenty years later. Compare this to $1,000 of post-tax income ($720), earning 8 percent a year in a taxable vehicle, which would be worth only $2,207 in 20 years. That's less than half of the 401(k) investment return! Can anyone deny that you really should be shoveling as much money as you can into your 401(k)?

Aside from the raw financial benefits of 401(k)s, these plans are convenient. For one thing, you can take your 401(k) with you from job to job, with some exceptions, by just rolling your old 401(k) into a new one with your new employer. This option keeps things simple, but it can take some time to arrange and may work against you if your new employer doesn't offer as many investment options as your previous employer did. So, if you want, you can just keep your old 401(k) with your old employer and start a new 401(k) with your new employer. If you do this, though, you can no longer borrow against your old plan, and you will have to keep track of two accounts.

Still another option is to roll your old 401(k) into an IRA and start a new 401(k) with your new employer. The advantage of this option is that an IRA may afford you a great many more investment options than your old 401(k). The negatives are that you can't take a loan from your IRA, and you have to keep track of two accounts.

The main disadvantage of the 401(k) is that your investment choices are limited. Among the typical offerings of no-risk instruments, company stock, and mutual funds, the last is the most attractive. While there may be occasions when you'll want to put your money into a CD, for slightly less interest you can park it in a money market mutual fund with no maturity requirement. Buying your company's stock is generally not such a good idea because if your company gets into trouble, you could lose your job *and* your portfolio value could go down. It's better to diversify.

Most employers offer mutual funds only through one fund family, and usually only a few funds in that family. Avoid investing in tax-free funds in your 401(k) because returns on investments in the account are already tax-deferred. You'll realize more benefit by positioning your tax-free investments outside your 401(k). If the funds or the family are subpar, however, and if your employer is not matching your contributions, you may want to reconsider contributing to your 401(k)—and by all means talk to your employer about improving the plan.

When it comes time to retire and collect your 401(k) savings, you will usually receive monthly payments, although you may be able to opt for a lump sum. If you have a choice and opt for monthly payments, however, find out if you can change your mind later. Often you cannot. You will pay income taxes on the money you receive based on the tax bracket you are in at that time. Now, you may decide to keep your money invested in your company's 401(k) even after you retire. Why would you do that? Because you realize that investing should not stop altogether when retirement starts. Most people

Timesaver
Your company's 401(k) administrator keeps track of all the contributions and investments to your 401(k), sends you quarterly statements, gives you updates, and answers your questions.

enjoy 20–25 years of retirement, and the number of years keeps growing as life expectancy continues to grow.

In addition to fixed-income investments, you may want to keep some money in stocks for a while. If you do decide to remain invested in your employer's 401(k) and wait to take distributions, make sure you'll be able to access your money easily when you do need it, and confirm that all investment options and charges will remain the same, even though you'll no longer be working at the company. Generally, you're required to begin taking withdrawals from your 401(k) by April 1 of the calendar year after you turn 70½ or by April 1 of the year following the year you retire, whichever comes later.

The IRA option

If you don't want to collect your 401(k) money right away, another option is to roll it over into a rollover IRA with a bank, mutual fund company, or brokerage firm. Doing this protects your savings from taxes and early-withdrawal penalties and preserves the option of rolling this money back into a new employer's 401(k) in the future. The only drawback is that you can't make any contributions to a rollover IRA. If you do, the rollover IRA becomes a traditional IRA, and you forfeit the right to roll that money into a new 401(k). However, you can continue to invest your 401(k) savings on a tax-deferred basis. You must have earned income (wages) to open an IRA.

The big advantage of the rollover IRA over the 401(k) is that you have more investment vehicles to choose from, including a range of mutual funds, stocks, bonds, CDs, and Treasuries. If you have multiple 401(k)s at various companies, you could roll them all into one rollover IRA, making your paperwork a lot simpler. You must begin to take the minimum required distributions from a rollover IRA in the year you turn 70½. You can't begin receiving distributions before the age of 59½. If you withdraw money before then, you'll pay a 10 percent penalty plus taxes on the money you take out. The 10 percent penalty will be excused, however, if you need the money early for any of the following reasons:

- Your disability

- Qualified higher education expenses

- First-time purchase of a home (lifetime limit of $10,000)

- Uninsured medical expenses that exceed 7.5 percent of income

- Medical insurance premiums if you have received unemployment insurance for at least 12 months

If you withdraw money from your IRA for any reason, you will have only a limited period of time, usually 60 days, to redeposit the money. After this period, your balance will be permanently reduced, and you will be limited to depositing a maximum of $2,000 a year again.

If you die before you turn 59½, your IRA money will go to your IRA beneficiary, and no penalty will be levied.

If you're sure you won't be going back to work, you would be better off rolling your 401(k) into a traditional IRA. Doing this protects your savings from taxes and early-withdrawal penalties, but once you choose this option, you cannot roll your money back into a 401(k). You're committed. A traditional IRA, also known as a contributory IRA, also provides investors with a full range of investment options to choose from and the benefits of tax deferral. The advantage of the traditional IRA over the rollover

IRA is that you can contribute up to $2,000 a year until the age of 70½, at which time you must begin taking distributions. You cannot begin receiving distributions before the age of 59½, unless you're prepared to pay a 10 percent penalty and taxes. When you begin collecting distributions, you will pay taxes on the money you receive based on the tax bracket you are in at the that time.

You don't have to contribute the $2,000 maximum to your IRA every year, but if you don't, you cannot make up the difference in later years. You may also contribute up to $2,000 a year to a separate IRA for a nonworking spouse. Your contributions may be tax deductible, depending on your adjusted gross income (AGI), a joint AGI if you and your spouse file jointly, and whether you and your spouse are eligible for company-sponsored retirement plans. Your adjusted gross income is your total income after contributions, deductions, and certain expenses, such as alimony, have been taken out. Table 7.4 shows that the income eligibility numbers are increasing.

TABLE 7.4: AGI LIMIT FOR IRA CONTRIBUTION

Tax Deduction Eligibility

Tax Year	Single	Married
1999	$31,000–$41,000	$51,000–$61,000
2000	$32,000–$42,000	$52,000–$62,000
2001	$33,000–$43,000	$60,000–$63,000
2002	$34,000–$44,000	$54,000–$64,000
2003	$40,000–$50,000	$60,000–$70,000
2004	$45,000–$55,000	$65,000–$75,000
2005	$50,000–$60,000	$70,000–$80,000
2006	$50,000–$60,000	$75,000–$85,000
2007	$50,000–$70,000	$80,000–$100,000

You may deduct your entire contribution if your income is no more than the lower dollar amount in each range. For your 1999 income, the deduction is phased out in increments of $200 for every $1,000 in income above the lower figure. For example, if you're a single filer with an AGI of $32,000 in 1999, and if you made a $2,000 contribution to your IRA, you could deduct $1,800 from your taxes. This is because $32,000 is $1,000 above the lower limit for full deduction, so $2,000–$200 = $1,800. If neither you nor your spouse is an active participant in a company-sponsored retirement plan, you may deduct your entire IRA contribution (to both your account and your spouse's account) no matter what your income.

When you withdraw money and interest from your traditional IRA, it will be taxed, except for contributions you made along the way that you weren't able to deduct from your taxes (nondeductible contributions). Because nondeductible contribution money has already been taxed, it will not be taxed again when you withdraw it. If you withdraw any money before you're 59½, the money will be subject to a 10 percent excise tax in addition to income taxes. However, you can take tax-free withdrawals for any of the same reasons that you can withdraw money early from a rollover or traditional IRA.

Now, if you roll your 401(k) money into a rollover IRA or a traditional IRA, you can convert either of these to a Roth IRA. (You cannot roll your 401[k] directly into a Roth.) You can only convert a traditional or rollover IRA to a Roth, however, if your AGI is $100,000 or less, for both single filers and married couples filing jointly. You cannot convert your traditional or rollover IRA to a Roth if you're a married person filing separately, however, no matter what your AGI is. Once your money is in a Roth IRA, as with a traditional IRA, you cannot roll the money back into a rollover IRA or a 401(k). Unlike contributions to rollover and traditional IRAs, contributions to Roth IRAs are not tax deductible. Thus, if you roll money from a rollover IRA or 401(k) into a Roth IRA, you will pay taxes on that money. However, you will never pay taxes on that money again.

After your Roth IRA has been in existence for at least five years, withdrawals made after age 59½ and investment returns are tax exempt. You cannot begin taking distributions until you are 59½ without paying a 10 percent penalty and taxes. However, you can take tax-free withdrawals for any of the same reasons that you can withdraw money early from a rollover or traditional IRA. What's more, Roth IRAs allow you to make contributions until you die; there is no age at which you have to start taking distributions. The maximum annual contribution is $2,000. If your adjusted gross income is more than $110,000 in a given year, however, or if your joint AGI is more than $160,000 and you file a joint return, or if you're married filing separately, and your income is more than $10,000, you cannot make a contribution to your Roth that year.

When deciding whether to open a traditional IRA or a Roth IRA, you have to consider whether paying the taxes on the contributions and earnings later is more advantageous to you than paying only on the contributions now. If your income makes you ineligible to deduct contributions to a traditional IRA, you should definitely open a Roth IRA. On the other hand, if you think your retirement tax bracket

Moneysaver
To determine whether you should roll your traditional IRA into a Roth IRA, go to Bank of America Investment Services, Inc. at www.acidev.com/ BofA/ira_roll.htm and fill out their online worksheet.

will be lower than your current bracket, you should consider opening a traditional account. Even if you're not rolling money into an IRA from a 401(k), open an IRA as soon as you can. Your basic strategy should be to contribute the maximum possible to your 401(k) and then contribute as much as you can to your IRA.

Other sources of retirement income

You may want to consider purchasing an income annuity with some of your retirement money. *Income annuities*, which are issued by insurance companies, are investment vehicles that allow your money to grow on a tax-deferred basis; when you start collecting the savings, they send you regular payments for the rest of your life. You give the insurance company a lump sum, usually in the case of immediate annuities, which start paying out almost immediately, or you make contributions over an extended period of time, usually in the case of deferred annuities, which start paying out when you reach retirement age.

There are three types of annuities: fixed annuities, variable annuities and equity-index annuities. *Fixed annuities* consist mainly of fixed-income investments, and pay out a set amount on a regular basis for the rest of your life. *Variable annuities* consist of stocks, bonds, and money market funds, in the proportion and of the kind that you choose, paying out varying amounts based on the performance of the underlying securities in your account. Variable annuities afford you the opportunity to grow your principle, but you also run the risk of losing it. *Equity-index annuities* are similar to variable annuities in that your payouts will vary and you're risking principle, but the decision of what to invest in has been made for you—your money is in a fund that tries to mimic the performance of a well-known index, like the S&P 500.

There are some drawbacks to annuities. First, you might make more investing the same money in stocks and mutual funds of your choice. Why? Your selection of investments is limited, and all earnings from annuities—even capital gains—are taxed as ordinary income. Second, since annuities can only be funded with after-tax money (no limit on contributions), it's always best to make the maximum contributions possible to your pre-tax retirement savings accounts, such as your 401(k) and IRA, before funding an annuity. This is doubly true in the case of variable annuities, whose high fee structures often negate the benefit of tax-deferred growth. Third, annuities are not insured by the FDIC; they are only as secure as the insurance company you buy them from. Finally, once your annuity payments begin, no withdrawals of principle are possible, and withdrawals of principle made before that time are met with stiff penalties.

Another potential source of retirement income is personal savings, savings outside your 401(k) and your IRA. Personal savings could be money you've been tucking away in a savings account for years, money you have in mutual funds, or money in stocks, bonds, and other investments. Maybe you have a certain sum of money with a brokerage firm that's being invested for you by a stockbroker you trust. That money could be a source of income for you when you retire.

Finally, consider whether you have any nonliquid assets you would like to convert into cash. You might want to sell your home and move to a smaller place, for example. The money you would make on the move could be invested to generate income. You may have old furniture you no longer need, valuable items in your attic, or even jewelry you no longer want that could be sold for cash. Take inventory of all your nonliquid assets, and see which of them you might liquidate to increase your cash base.

Bright Idea
If you'll be retiring soon, talk to your broker, and discuss the option of moving more of your money into income-generating investments.

Having looked carefully at your probable retirement expenses and your sources of retirement income, you are now in a position to create a retirement budget. Does your projected income cover your projected expenses? Table 7.5 gives an example of such a computation.

TABLE 7.5: COMPUTATION OF RETIREMENT CASH FLOW

Projected Retirement Expenses of $55,000/Yr.	
Pension Plan	$20,000
401(k)	$18,000
IRA	$5,000
Savings and Investments	$5,000
Social Security	$0
Total	$48,000
Retirement Gap	–$7,000

If your projected income is less than your projected expenses, you have what is known as a retirement gap. Table 7.5 shows an example of a retirement gap of $7,000. If your calculations show such a gap, you must look for ways to cut your retirement costs or ways to increase your retirement income, or both. Re-evaluate your retirement needs to consider which, if any, projected costs can be reduced. Modify your current cash flow to build additional savings. Adjust your investment mix to try to increase the return on the assets you're putting aside for retirement. If all else fails, consider delaying your retirement. Also bear in mind that if inflation is less than projected, you may not need as much money as you thought, and the dreaded retirement gap will vanish.

Paying for college

What is most people's greatest financial concern—funding their retirement or funding their kids' college education? Many would choose the latter. Tuitions just keep rising, and while the rate of increase has slowed somewhat in the 1990s, many private institutions now cost more than $20,000 a year; Ivy League schools cost $25,000. At current rates of increase, you will need $50,000 a year to send your newborn to a private university 18 years from now. Is it worth it? Studies show that it is. Even with the economy booming and demand for workers at all-time highs, Census Bureau data indicates that people with college diplomas continue to get better-paying jobs than those without. College graduates are also less likely to be unemployed.

While average income increases with age for both those who have a college diploma and those who do not, income increases faster for college graduates. Over a lifetime, college graduates will earn an estimated 40 percent more than those without a bachelor's degree. What's more, with the recent advances in technology revolutionizing the workplace, courses and training beyond the high school level have become essential to compete for higher-paying jobs. There's no doubt about it—a college education is, more than ever, worth the money.

Where is the money going to come from? First, before thinking about ways to save more, consider ways to spend less. Public universities are considerably cheaper than private, averaging just under $10,000 a year—half the cost of private schools. Many public universities also provide students with a quality education. If your child is interested in private schools, compare costs. Look for a combination of reasonable cost and good quality to maximize the value of the education she gets.

It's important that you begin planning and saving for your child's college education as soon as possible. Many parents procrastinate because they look at the size of the savings mountain they must scale and get disheartened. They also fear that saving for college will have a negative impact on their current lifestyle. Many parents plan to somehow pay out of their personal income when the time comes, but when you're talking about amounts like $20,000 a year, this just isn't realistic. The fact remains that your personal savings will be the cornerstone of the funding for your kid's college education—and the sooner you begin saving, the less painful paying for college will be.

Assuming that inflation averages 4 percent a year for the foreseeable future and that you invest your college savings at 6 percent a year, the following were true in 1999:

- If your child is 1, it will take about $435 invested each month for 17 years to pay for a private university.

- If your child is 10, it will take about $875 invested each year for 8 years to pay for a private university.

Moneysaver
Use the Strong College Investment Analyzer at www.educationira.com/content/gs/results.htm to help you determine how much money you're going to need for your child's college education.

Getting into the habit of putting a little away consistently is a powerful technique for accumulating the necessary funds. Budget a certain amount of your income for college savings. Also consider getting the child to contribute. You might open a "kiddie" IRA for your child, with you as the custodian. This would be either a traditional IRA or a Roth IRA.

Your child has to have some earned, taxable income (allowances, money for chores, and investment income don't count) for you to set up an IRA for him, though. All contributions must be made from his taxable income. You also cannot contribute to your child's IRA. One idea is to require your child to put half his earnings in his "college" IRA and let him spend the other half as he sees fit. Money from all IRAs can be withdrawn before the owner turns 59½ for educational expenses.

One risk of using IRAs as a vehicle for saving for college, though, is that you may make bad investment decisions and lose money instead of make it. An additional risk, if it's a kiddie IRA, is that the child will simply take the money out as soon as he gains control of the money (at 18 or 21, depending on the state), pay the early-withdrawal penalty, and use the funds for something other than college.

Buy permanent life insurance

You really should get a permanent life insurance policy, if you don't have one already. When you pay a premium to a life insurance company, they agree to pay the beneficiary of your policy a large sum of money if you die. These premium payments go to the insurance company, never to be seen again. But any money you pay into your account over and above the premiums will earn interest and/or dividends and capital returns, and this money is never taxed.

> **❝**
> The reason most people never reach their goals is that they don't define them, or ever seriously consider them as believable or achievable. Winners can tell you where they are going, what they plan to do along the way, and who will be sharing the adventure with them.
> —Denis Watley
> **❞**

Having life insurance is a must if you have kids for three reasons:

1. The policy protects your family from poverty if you die unexpectedly.

2. The policy protects that college savings fund from being spent to pay for basic necessities if you die unexpectedly.

3. The tax-deferred cash build-up in the policy can be tapped for college expenses (or anything else, for that matter) *at any time.* Because the money is coming out of a life insurance policy, you will not have to pay taxes on any of it.

You can also take loans against your policy tax-free, as long as the policy remains in force. The only sacrifice you make is paying for the life insurance itself, which you really should have anyway if you have kids.

Fixed life insurance policies generate a steady return on the money you put into your account, usually about 1 percent better than CDs, and it's tax-free. *Variable life* policies let you invest in mutual funds tax-free. (You will have to pay charges to the mutual fund companies, though.) And, importantly, life insurance policies are excluded from needs analysis by the government and colleges. Having such a policy, then, will not hurt your chances of qualifying for financial aid. Many financial planners agree that using a good life insurance policy in addition to your personal savings is the best way to finance your child's college education.

Different college investment accounts

Should you put your college savings in a savings account? That might be okay at first, but you should really consider one of several special accounts designed especially for saving for college. One of these is the Education IRA, which allows you to make nondeductible contributions of up to $500 a year per child under the age of 18. You invest these contributions on a tax-deferred basis and can withdraw the principal and the interest tax-free if you use the money for educational purposes.

That's a great deal. If you use the money for noneducation expenses, however, you will pay a 10 percent penalty plus taxes on interest. The amount you can contribute each year to an Education IRA starts to decrease for every $1,000 above $95,000 a year you make as a single filer, and for every $1,000 above $150,000 you and your spouse make combined if you file jointly.

Another option is to open a custodial account for your child—a Uniform Gift to Minors Account (UGMA) or a Uniform Transfers to Minors Account (UTMA). The first of these was established in 1956 with the passage of the Uniform Gifts to Minors Act (UGMA—same acronym as the account) as a way to transfer money and securities to minors. (Under law, minors cannot own securities, including mutual fund shares, outright. As defined by securities laws, a minor is a person under age 18 or 21, depending on the state you live in.) The second of these custodial accounts, the UTMA, was adopted in 1986 with the passage of the Uniform Transfers to Minors Act (UTMA) to expand the types of assets that could be transferred to minors. Nearly all states have enacted the UTMA, but many people still refer to the corresponding accounts as UGMAs. UTMAs and UGMAs allow an adult custodian to transfer money and securities to and invest those assets on behalf of a child, who is the beneficiary. These accounts, then, allow minors to enjoy the benefits of powerful investment vehicles without managing the investments themselves. Income generated by these investments is not heavily taxed because children have lower income tax rates than most adults (usually 15 percent), and the first $700 of their earnings is tax-exempt. Some states require that a parent or legal guardian be the custodian of the account.

There is no limit to the amount of money you can put into custodial accounts each year, although gifts from one adult of more than $10,000 in a year may be subject to a gift tax. Any concerned relative—a parent, grandparent, or aunt, for example—can open one of these accounts for a child or contribute to one that has already been established. Once you have transferred or deposited money to a custodial account, you cannot take it out. The money can be used only by the child and only when the child reaches 18 or 21 (depending on the state).

Possible drawbacks of these accounts are that the money can be used for special noneducational purposes, with the custodian's approval, while the child is a minor and can be used for any purpose, without the custodian's approval, when the child becomes an adult. There is no penalty for using the money for noneducational purposes, which increases the chances that it will be misused. Also, having a UGMA or UTMA may hurt your chances of getting need-based financial aid or may reduce the aid you are awarded. Assets owned by a child are weighed more heavily as financial resources than a parent's own assets.

You could also establish a trust fund for your child. A trust fund is an account, like a custodial

Unofficially...
Even though the "U" in UGMA and UTMA stands for "Uniform," uniform laws actually may vary from state to state. Thus, things that are true about the UGMA and UTMA in general may not be true about the acts in your state.

account, that lets you transfer assets to a child and invest them in a tax-efficient way. The child would be the beneficiary, and you or your spouse would be the trustee, responsible for investing and managing the money. These accounts, however, are more complicated than custodial accounts and more costly to set up. Very specific guidelines, based on your specific wishes, govern how the money may and may not be used. These accounts are designed to take into account your overall financial situation as well as current tax laws. Trusts provide greater tax protection and more flexibility than custodial accounts. Generally speaking, trusts are appropriate when a lot of money is involved—tens of thousands of dollars; custodial accounts are appropriate for smaller amounts.

Put the money in your name

Another option is to put the savings for your kid's college education in your name. This gives you total control over the money at all times and allows you to withdraw some or all of the money whenever you want with no penalty. This can be a big advantage if something arises where you really need cash right away. On the other hand, it means you have to have enough discipline not to use this money except in emergencies. If you want to maintain maximum control and flexibility, you should just open an ordinary investment account and earmark the funds for your child's education.

Still another way to use assets in you own name is to tap your own IRA or 401(k) money. The government has realized that the reason many parents aren't taking advantage of Education IRAs, UTMAs, and the like is that parents are having trouble just contributing to their own IRAs. As a result, the government has started allowing parents to use their IRA money for their kids' qualified higher-education expenses—things such as tuition, books, and room and board. There is no early-withdrawal penalty. Corporate America is also getting into the act. Many companies are now letting employees tap their 401(k) savings for the same purpose. Neither of these options should be pursued, however, unless you have more than enough money to support yourself in retirement—that is, no retirement gap. It will be much easier for you to get financial aid or apply for a college loan than to replace hard-earned retirement money.

Getting help

With costs skyrocketing, however, even with systematic saving, you may need help financing your child's college education. Where do you turn? First, look into the possibility of receiving financial aid from your child's schools of choice. Almost all colleges and universities offer financial assistance to students in need in the form of loans, scholarships (money provided to a student on the basis of academic merit), fellowships (money paid to support graduate students doing advanced work in some field), grants (gifts of money), and work-study programs (programs that provides part-time employment for students). Contact your child's high-school financial aid office and the financial aid office of the colleges your child is thinking of applying to.

While it tends to be difficult for middle-income families to get financial aid, some universities—especially those who need students badly—*will* award aid to middle-income families. No matter how slim you think your chances of getting aid might be, apply. You might be pleasantly surprised.

Bright Idea
To get some idea of your chances for receiving financial aid, take 5 percent of your family's total assets, including home equity, savings, and investments, add your adjusted gross income from last year's tax return, and divide the sum by the estimated annual college expense. If the resulting number is 6 or less, you may qualify for aid.

Realize, though, that even if you do qualify on a need basis, there is no guarantee that the college you child gets into will be able to help everyone who qualifies. Even if you do get financial aid, it will probably be a loan, money you'll have to pay back. Also, financial aid alone rarely covers all the costs of college. Check out the following sites for more information on financial aid:

- The Smart Student Guide to Financial Aid: www.finaid.org/

- MOLIS Scholarships and Fellowships (for minorities): www.fie.com/molis/scholar.htm

- fastWEB! Financial Aid Search: www.fastweb.com/fastweb/index.cgi/index. html?refer=studentservices-fastweb/

- Fellowship Office, National Research Council: www4.nationalacademies.org/osep/fo.nsf

After you've explored your financial aid options, look into borrowing money from a bank or credit union. You may be able to get a student loan, with special low rates and accommodating repayment terms for college students. Having to repay a large loan as soon as a student gets out of college, however, can be a real burden on a recent graduate. You could take out a personal loan or a loan on your 401(k), but try to resist actually withdrawing money from your retirement plan, unless you're absolutely sure you can afford it. Keep in mind, too, that personal loans can get quite expensive when paid back over an extended period of time. Check out Crestar Student Lending at www.student-loans.com/ or Sallie Mae: Student Loan Marketing Association (SLMA), a financial services corporation, at www.salliemae.com/.

Often a combination of things fills the bill. Personal savings, life insurance, financial aid, a student loan, and a part-time job for your child together could cover the expenses of college. Once enrolled, your child could also look into paid internships (for credit) and jobs on campus.

Uncle Sam wants to help

The U.S. government is also trying to make paying for college easier. In 1997, Congress passed the Taxpayer Relief Act (the Tax Act), which included the Hope Scholarship Credit. This tax credit gives families a tuition credit of 100 percent on the first $1,000 spent on education, and 50 percent on the second $1,000, for a maximum of $1,500 a year for the first two years of post-secondary education only. The Lifetime Learning Credit was also passed, giving families a 20 percent tax credit toward the first $5,000 they spend on qualified education expenses a year. Qualified expenses include tuition and/or educational expenses incurred to learn or improve job skills. After 2002, you'll be able to take 20 percent on the first $10,000. The Lifetime Learning Credit is available to college juniors, seniors, graduate students, and working Americans.

More importantly, though, you can apply for a number of education grants offered by the U.S. government. Again, if you think you have any chance at all of getting one of these grants or loans, you really should apply—you may qualify for more than you think. Pell Grants are among the best-known of government grants. These are awarded to undergraduates based on need and family income. The maximum award for the 1997–1998 award year was $2,700. Supplemental Educational Opportunity Grants (SEOGs) are set

Unofficially...
The money for
SEOGs comes
from the federal
government, but
the distribution
is handled by
individual
schools. The
amount of money
available through
SEOGs, then, is
limited by the
amount of
funding provided
to each school.
These grants
range anywhere
from $100 to
$4,000.

aside for undergraduates in greater need than those who receive Pell Grants.

Then there are government loans. The Federal Perkins Loans are available only to students with exceptional financial need. Being a loan, not a grant, the money (ranging anywhere from $3,000 to $15,000 a year for undergraduates) must be paid back. Interest on the loan is 5 percent. Eligible graduate students may borrow up to $5,000 a year, not to exceed $30,000 total. Payback on Federal Perkins Loans must begin no later than nine months after graduation and can extend over a period of 10 years.

Another government loan, Direct Stafford Loans, have very favorable interest rates and four flexible repayment schedules. PLUS loans (formerly Parents' Loans for Undergraduate Students) are available to parents who pass a credit check. The amount of the loan is limited to the cost of attendance for their child, minus any other financial aid that is being received. Payback of PLUS loans must begin 60 days after the final loan disbursement for the academic year. Interest on PLUS loans varies but cannot exceed 9 percent.

With the Federal Work-Study Program, payback is built in. This program provides qualified students with money for college in exchange for work. Students work 12–20 hours a week, usually at a government agency or nonprofit organization, ideally in a job related to their major. The students are paid, but the money they make goes to paying back the award money, and the student's overall compensation cannot exceed the total amount of the award money.

If you're interested in applying for a grant or a loan from the federal government, check out the following sites:

- The U.S. Department of Education:
  www.ed.gov
- The U.S. Department of Education Guide to
  Financial Aid:
  www.ed.gov/prog_info/SFA/StudentGuide/
- The National Center for Policy Analysis:
  www.ncpa.org/pi/edu/edu13.html#b

If your child isn't averse to military training while he's in college and doesn't mind serving for about eight years in the reserves, you should look into the U.S. military Reserve Officers' Training Corps (ROTC) scholarships. The Air Force, Army, Navy, Marines, and Coast Guard all have programs. The gist of these programs is that the military loans your child money for college, and your child pays the military back by serving for four years during college and four years after college—after college as an officer. Check out the following sites for ROTC information:

- Air Force: www.afoats.af.mil/rotc.htm
- Army: www-rotc.monroe.army.mil/
- Navy: http://nrotc.tamu.edu/

States are getting into the act

States offer two types of programs, known as qualified state tuition savings programs, to help parents finance their kids' college education: prepaid tuition plans and special savings accounts. The basic idea of these programs is to actually pay for your child's college tuition years ahead of time by making regular contributions to an account at a specified state college. The money you put into the plans is invested on a tax-deferred basis and is taxed at only 15 percent when you withdraw it to pay the school because it's in your child's name.

Both types of plans are convenient to use: You can arrange for automatic payments to be made directly from your bank account, and small contributions (of as little as $15 a month, in some cases) are acceptable. Anyone—parents, grandparents, and even friends—can contribute money to these plans. The plans are available to people at all income levels.

Prepaid tuition plans enable you to prepay the expenses of your child's college education in installments over a period of many years. The money you contribute earns a tax-deferred return designed to keep pace with tuition increases, although the return may be less if the child attends an out-of-state college or a private university. In the case of prepaid tuition plans, states set contribution guidelines and promise that if those are met, the total amount set aside will suffice to cover the child's tuition at a state school when the child is ready to enroll. Most prepaid tuition plans are restricted to residents of the state and can be used only for tuition, not for any of the other expenses associated with college.

The special savings account plans are better. These accounts are set up like trust funds, and anyone is free to donate as much as he likes. Some states allow total contributions to these accounts to reach $100,000. Donations to the account are considered gifts, however, so any donation by a single person of more than $10,000 in one year is subject to a gift tax. The money is invested for you on a tax-deferred basis by an investment manager such as Fidelity or Vanguard, contracted by the people running the program. The investment company charges a fee to manage your investments, but this is generally nothing next to your investment returns and what you save in taxes. There is no annual fee for these accounts.

One drawback of the special savings accounts is that you do not have any control over how your money is invested. While the investments generally do well, some people feel that the money in these accounts is invested too conservatively. In deciding whether to go with one of these plans, compare how you think you would do investing the money yourself, take out the taxes you would have to pay, and compare the return to the returns historically generated by the plan. If your hypothetical returns come out ahead and you think you can consistently outperform the plan, go for it. But realize that because the benefits of tax-deferral are cumulative in nature, the more time you have to invest in such a plan, the harder it will be to beat.

A drawback of both types of plans is that they are considered financial resources, so they lessen your chances of getting need-based (not merit-based) financial aid from colleges and the federal government. Also, the quality of the plans in terms of investment returns, flexibility, penalties, and state tax benefits varies widely from state to state—you really have to do your homework before enrolling in one. According to the National Center for Policy Analysis in January 1999, plans in Iowa and New York were among the best, and plans in Alabama, Florida, Maryland, and Michigan were among the worst.

Be aware that state schools often charge nonresidents higher tuition than residents, so if you were to move out of state, you might have to pay the difference between what your plan will cover (for residents) and your out-of-state tuition costs. Also, if you

Bright Idea
Special savings accounts with state universities that have them are available to both in-state and out-of-state residents. The money in these accounts can be used to cover all the basic expenses related to your child's college education.

put money in a plan and change your mind or find a better plan elsewhere, you may have difficulty getting out of the original plan. And if you don't end up using the funds in the plan for your child's education, you may have to pay a penalty upon withdrawal, though not more than 10 percent.

Finally, committing to one of these programs removes your child from the decision-making process of where she's going to go to college. What if she doesn't want to go to the state university? In this case, many schools will allow you to use the money in the account for tuition at another school, but you'll receive an amount equal to only the average tuition of a state school in the state where you had been saving.

On the other hand, what if your child does want to go to the school you've been saving for, but she isn't accepted? The money will be held for your child, but it's up to her to gain admission to the school—prepayment does not guarantee acceptance. Or, what if your child decides she doesn't want to go to college at all? In this case, often an amount of money equal only to the lowest tuition at a state school in that state will be refunded.

Unofficially...
To find out about the college savings plans in your state, go to the College Savings Plan Network at www. collegesavings. org/.

Like the federal government, state governments provide certain loans for education, but eligibility may depend both on academic performance and need. Generally, a recipient of a state government loan must be a resident of the state and must be enrolling in a college or university located in the state. Some states, however, have reciprocity agreements with other states. Hawaii, Idaho, Nebraska, North Dakota, South Dakota, and Georgia all have scholarship programs for state residents.

Just the facts

- There are four steps in effective goal-setting: determining the goal, deciding on a strategy, implementing the strategy, and evaluating the results.

- Financial independence or retirement is achieved when your investment income equals or exceeds your living expenses.

- Subtract your projected retirement expenses from your projected retirement income; if the number is negative, begin working now on closing that retirement gap.

- Starting to save for your child's college education early, buying life insurance, and considering special college savings accounts are the most important measures you can take to amass the necessary funds.

- Enlist your child's help in saving for his college education, apply for financial aid and for federal grants and scholarships, consider state schools, and look into state tuition savings programs to supplement your own savings for your child's college education.

Online Investing

GET THE SCOOP ON...
Taking a look at your options ▪ Selecting a
broker ▪ Comparing the online brokers ▪ The
dark side of the broker world

PART III

Choosing a Broker

Chapter 8

The broker you place your trades with can make a big difference in your bottom line. Paying a broker large commissions to buy and sell securities for you can cut substantially into your profits and add to your losses. But paying the minimum possible will mean forfeiting advice and maybe even accuracy, reliability, and efficiency, which could cost you even more. Because not all brokers are created equal, a careful analysis of who is out there and how well they deliver the goods is warranted.

Differences in commissions among brokers generally reflect the range and level of services provided. The broker you go with, then, should be based on a combination of what that broker has to offer, the quality of what's being offered, and what you need. If you're a mutual fund trader, for example, you want to avoid brokers who offer only stock trading. Choosing the right broker is an important step on the road to becoming a successful online investor.

Types of brokers

The word *broker* can be used to mean two different things:

1. A person licensed to trade securities, also referred to as a stockbroker, a registered representative, or an account executive

2. A company or firm licensed to conduct securities transactions, also known as a stockbrokerage, a brokerage, or a broker-dealer

To indicate a change in meaning, this chapter uses *stockbroker* or *stockbrokerage* once in a particular discussion, with all following usages of *broker* to carry that same meaning.

Generally speaking, stockbrokerages fall into three categories: full-service, discount, and electronic. Full-service brokers offer their clients the full spectrum of investment vehicles to choose from—everything from stocks and bonds to IPOs and futures. They also offer clients advice on exactly what and when to buy, hold, and sell, and for all this great stuff they charge a pretty penny—upwards of $300 a trade. Full-service brokers rule the roost, controlling most of the country's investments. It wasn't until 1975, when discount brokerages came along, that full-service firms had any real competition. The following list includes the biggest full-service brokers in the United States.

- A.G. Edwards
- Edward Jones
- Everen Securities
- Merrill Lynch
- Morgan Stanley Dean Witter

- Paine Webber

- Prudential

- Solomon Smith Barney

Discount brokers, such as Charles Schwab, were created to cater to the do-it-yourself crowd that doesn't need a lot of investment advice or hand-holding. Discounters offer investors almost as great a spectrum of investment vehicles to choose from as full-service firms, but no (or minimal) advice. By eliminating this labor-intensive service, discount brokers can afford to charge clients much, much smaller transaction fees than full-service brokers—in the range of $40 a trade.

The discounters themselves had little real competition until July 11, 1983, when a doctor in Michigan placed the first online trade using E*Trade. Online brokers provide investors with more limited investment offerings than discount brokers, no advice, but incredibly low transaction fees. Naturally, the lower the commissions, the more frequently investors tend to trade, so brokers charging less per trade hope to make up for it with greater trade volume.

Full-service discount brokers

Full-service discount brokers provide many of the same services as full-service brokers at a fraction of the cost. Many even offer trading of certain mutual funds for free. Full-service discount brokers offer most of the investment vehicles offered by full-service brokers as well. Like full-service brokers, they have branch offices that you can visit to get one-on-one personalized service, including financial planning. When you call a full-service discount broker,

Unofficially...
The term *discount broker* is now used to refer to virtually all brokers that are not full-service brokers, but there are actually several subdivisions.

you'll be connected with a trained representative or licensed stockbroker, who will explain investments to you and even help you decide what to do; he'll send you literature on virtually any investment topic.

Some of these discount brokers provide investment advice in the form of newsletters. Full-service discount brokers even offer services most full-service brokers do not, such as 24-hour order placement and customer service and online trading (although many full-service firms are now setting up shop online).

Discount brokers

Discount brokers provide some of the same services as full-service discount brokers, for less. They do not have local branch offices you can visit for personal services, however, nor do they provide as much literature as full-service discount brokers. Most discount brokers offer online trading.

Deep discount brokers

Deep discount brokers generally only execute trades, often at a flat fee, such as $20 for any trade of any amount. All other services are minimal. Most deep discount brokers offer online trading.

Electronic/Online brokers

Electronic brokers, also known as e-brokers, are basically the same as deep discount brokers but are designed for computer/Internet users. These brokers were the original online brokers, but the term *online broker* has come to mean any discount broker that offers online trading. Because virtually all discount brokers now offer online trading, this book uses the terms *discount broker* and *online broker* interchangeably.

TABLE 8.1: EXAMPLES OF DISCOUNT BROKERS IN EACH CATEGORY

Full-Service	Discount	Deep Discount	Electronic/ Online Discount
Charles Schwab	Aufhauser	Brown	Datek
Fidelity	Bidwell	Ceres	Suretrade
Olde	Discover	National	InvesTrade
Quick and Reilly	Jack White	Stock Mart	E*Trade
Vanguard	Waterhouse	Scottrade	Firstrade.com

The competition is fierce

The divisions among full-service brokers and discount brokers is starting to blur. Not only are discount brokers providing customers with online trading now, but full-service brokers are even starting to get into the act. In June 1999, Merrill Lynch, the No. 1 brokerage in the country, announced that it would provide online trading for its customers by December. Prudential Securities, the No. 5 brokerage, began offering online trading to its clients in May 1999.

Meanwhile, discount brokers are providing more services and advice. Charles Schwab now offers financial planning to customers, and many online brokers provide investor education pages, investor simulation games, and a plethora of research tools, including great charts and stock-picking screens. (A stock screen is a program that allows you to apply personal parameters, such as risk level, to a universe of stocks, to narrow the field to only those that meet your requirements.)

Changes of this magnitude do not come without cost. For Merrill Lynch to offer online trading, they have to accept a potentially huge drop in revenues because customers who place trades online won't have to pay as much to invest. When discount firms add more services, they also have to start charging more.

What's going on? With the Internet boom continuing pace and online trading exploding, online brokers have been growing rapidly, pulling a large number of their new customers from full-service firms. Although the full-service firms have not yet been greatly hurt by the trend, they are starting to take it seriously.

How big a threat are the upstarts to behemoths such as Merrill Lynch? Currently, online brokerage firms manage less than 2 percent of Americans' $10 trillion in assets, according to Forrester Research in Cambridge, Mass. And while these numbers are growing, full-service firms are not that anxious about it—certainly not anxious enough to become e-brokers and give up their profitable fee structures.

By offering online trading, full-service brokers are giving a nod to the online industry and are vying to hold on to their customer base; they're not trying to beat the online brokers at their own game. Merrill Lynch, for example, will not win any converts by charging $29.95 a trade *plus* an annual fee— nor will their alternative offer of charging $1,500 a year for unlimited trades and full-service features. Prudential now charges $24.95 per trade for online transactions *plus* 1.5 percent of your account's value a year. These are purely defensive strategies, designed to stem the flow of deserters.

For their part, online brokers are trying to seduce customers away from the full-service firms, as well as attract new investors, by offering more services. In addition to providing customers with an ever-increasing number of research tools to help them select profitable investments, discounters are improving customer service; working to increase online order execution, speed, and reliability; offering services such as check writing, bill paying, and credit cards; and starting to offer financial products such as insurance, mortgages, and loans.

Choosing a broker

So what type of broker should you go with—full-service or discount? Increasingly, the answer to this question depends not on whether the broker offers online trading, but on how much advice and services you want and how much you're willing to pay for them. For the most part, a full-service broker will recommend securities for you to buy; a discount broker will only place the orders you give.

The advantage of going with a full-service broker is that you'll have a professional on whom you can rely for high-quality services and professional advice. At a full-service broker, you'll also get personalized service. Your broker will work with you to design a financial plan and a portfolio that meets your needs. If you don't understand something, he'll explain it to you. These are the things that you'll be able to depend on during bear markets, when independent investors will have to survive by their wits and the advice they can get from chat rooms. Many independent investors will learn that making money—even preserving capital—is much harder during a bear market.

The main disadvantages of full-service brokers is that they're expensive, you have to give up your autonomy as an investor to employ their services, they can't guarantee superior returns, and the quality of the advice you get will depend a lot on who is handling your account. Stockbrokers cannot devote themselves to research because they are first and foremost salesman. Look into fee-based investments that link your broker's compensation to the performance of the investments.

The advantage of going with a discount broker is that you'll save a lot of money in commission fees and may get almost as many services as you would at a full-service broker. If you're the kind of person who does all your own research and just calls up your broker to place orders, you should probably go with a discount broker.

The disadvantage of a discount broker is that you're pretty much on your own. Discount brokers won't tell you what to invest in or when you should buy, hold, or sell. So, if you're not confident about or at least interested in picking your own stocks and about making your own investment decisions, you should explore other sources of advice (see Chapter 10, "Getting Advice Online"), such as financial newsletters, or go with a full-service broker. If you're determined to avoid brokers altogether, there are always DRIPs and DSPs, although fees being charged by companies for these plans are on the rise.

Whether you choose a full-service broker or a discount broker, you should make sure that the broker is registered with the Securities and Exchange Commission. You can write the SEC at Office of Consumer Affairs, Securities and Exchange Commission, Washington, D.C. 20549 (www.sec.gov). State securities regulators can also tell you whether a broker is licensed to do business in your state. In addition, you can find out about any disciplinary action taken by securities regulators and criminal authorities against any brokerage by calling the National Association of Securities Dealers, Inc. (NASD), at 1-800-289-9999 or checking their Web site at www.nasdr.com. The NASD keeps an eye on its members and takes disciplinary action when a member breaks the rules.

Finally, make sure your broker is a member of the Securities Investors Protection Corporation (SIPC). The SIPC is a nonprofit corporation established by Congress that insures securities and cash in customer brokerage accounts up to $500,000 (up to $100,000 on cash) in the event that a brokerage goes bankrupt. SIPC coverage does not insure you against trading losses, of course.

Choosing a full-service broker

If you decide to go with a full-service broker, you should call the major firms in your area and ask some questions to get an idea what they offer and what they're like. Some full-service brokers provide a wide range of services and investments; others specialize in certain securities, such as futures. Make sure the broker covers the range of securities you're interested in trading.

Charges may vary widely from broker to broker because fees are not fixed by the SEC, so it's a good idea to comparison-shop. One thing you should clarify is each broker's policies regarding agency and principal roles and the charging structures involved. When a broker buys or sells securities for a client, the broker may act as agent, simply performing the transaction on behalf of the customer (who is the real buyer or seller), or as "principal," buying and selling the securities for the brokerage's own account.

Bright Idea
You should be able to find all registered brokers and information about them on the EDGAR database at www.sec.gov/edgarhp.htm.

Statements also vary considerably from one full-service broker to the next. Some brokers will send you statements that are incomplete, confusing, and basically useless; others will prepare statements that are thorough and clear, containing useful information such as portfolio performance data. Consider asking several brokers to send you sample statements.

Part and parcel of choosing the firm you want to go with is choosing an account executive you like. The most important thing in choosing an account executive is that you feel comfortable with her. To get the best possible service, you need to be very honest with your account executive about your financial situation, goals, and investment preferences. If you're not comfortable with your account executive, you may be less open and honest than you need to be.

Also, it's important not to feel pressured to do things you don't want to do with your money. Your account executive should take the time to find out what you're comfortable with and not push you to invest in something, say, just because other clients do. So if you tell a good account executive that you don't want to invest in something, she shouldn't keep trying to get you to buy it. But if she recommends something for you that she thinks fits your goals and style, and you say no, she should try to find out why not. She may uncover a misunderstanding on your part, in which case it would be appropriate for her to continue to recommend the investment after she had explained it to you. Taking the time to explain things clearly to you and educate you about your investment choices is another quality of a good account executive.

One more thing you want to look for is whether an account executive is willing to review assets you have that are not currently under her management. Her willingness to do this demonstrates her commitment to your overall financial success. Also, look for someone who is up-to-date and who stays current with developments in the industry; these kinds of people are more likely to find new or creative solutions to your problems. You might want to check up on your account executive to see if any complaints have been filed against her. Check with the securities division of the secretary of state's office in your state. You often can obtain a list of state-registered account executives and their disciplinary history. Of course, you can also check with the NASD.

Choosing a discount broker

The most important thing in selecting a discount broker is making sure that the broker offers the investment vehicles and the services you require. Virtually all online brokers let you trade stocks, but the similarities end there. If you're interested in trading mutual funds, bonds, options, or something else, you need to be sure it's possible. Several online brokers do not offer mutual fund trading, and only a few let you trade commodities. Also make sure that if you can trade a given security with a broker, you also can trade that security over the Internet. Some brokers offer various investment vehicles, but only a few can be traded online.

For a breakdown of what you can trade online with various brokers, go to Barron's Online at www.interactive.wsj.com/public/current/articles/ SB921288085449783140.htm. Day traders want to go with brokers who offer free real-time quotes

Timesaver
Go to www.
smartmoney.
com/si/
brokermeter/ to
find out how fast
a broker is. The
site doesn't
measure trade
execution
speed—which
may vary not
only from broker
to broker, but
also from trade
to trade with the
same broker—
but measures
things such as
page download
time and
connection setup
time.

(moment-to-moment stock prices during the trading day) and quick trade executions. While many brokers say they provide real-time quotes, it's important to clarify what they mean by this. Are the quotes streaming (continual), or do you get one quote per request? Can you access real-time quotes only when you place a trade, or can you get a stock's real-time price without placing an order? Sometimes real-time quotes are offered only to customers with a cash balance over a certain amount. Will the prices of the securities in your online portfolio be updated real-time?

Next, look at cost. With fees ranging from $3 to $30 per trade, the broker you go with can make a big difference. Be careful when you comparison-shop. The size of trades affects commission rates. If you plan to place trades of only 100 or 500 shares, you may have to pay more than the broker advertises—these rates may be based on minimum trades of 1,000 or 5,000 shares. Also, check on the commissions for trading different securities. The broker's advertised rate generally applies to stock trades; brokers often charge substantially more for mutual fund trades. You also want to check if there is a minimum balance you need to keep in your account or a minimum number of trades you must make to avoid charges. Some brokers don't require any minimum balance to open an account, but you must have the necessary funds in your account before you can place a trade.

You should definitely check out the ancillary fees brokers charge as well. Some brokers charge fees for wiring money to your account or transferring funds into or out of your account. Some charge annual maintenance fees, fees to close your account, IRA fees, fees for bounced checks, fees for issuing a stock certificate, and even transaction or "postage and handling" fees on certain trades, in addition to the standard commission. Fees vary greatly from broker to broker. What you see is not necessarily what you get.

Table 8.2 shows the 11 cheapest online brokers based on what they charge for market orders, listed from lowest to highest, as of June 23, 1999. (Market and limit orders are explained in Chapter 9, "Setting Up an Account.")

TABLE 8.2: ONLINE BROKERS WITH THE LOWEST COMMISSIONS

Broker	Minimum Investment in Cash Account	Stock Trades of Less Than 1,000 Shares	Mutual Funds
Empire Financial	$1,000	$0 market	No-load: $25 plus $3 postage and handling fee $11.95 limit plus $3 postage and handling fee
Brown & Company	$15,000	$5 market $10 limit	Can't trade
Scottrade	$2,000	$7 market $12 limit	Can't trade
SureTrade	$0	$7.95 market $9.95 limit	No-load: $25 Some free
InvesTrade	$2,000	$7.95 market $11.95 limit	No-load: $29 Some free
Ameritrade	$2,000	$8 market $13 limit or stop	$18
ForbesNet	$5,000	$9.95 market or limit	$50
Trading Direct	$0	$9.95	$15.95
FirstTrade.com	$0	$9.95	No-load: $25
AB Watley	$3,000	$9.95	No-load: $40–$60
Datek	$2,000	$9.99	$9.99

Most online brokers allow you to borrow additional funds against the funds you actually have so that you can buy additional securities (called buying on margin). You might have to fill out a form to establish margin privileges or to open a margin account, and brokers usually require higher account minimums for margin accounts. Of course, the broker won't let you borrow this money for free, and the rates brokers charge (margin rates) vary widely. While you're checking on margin accounts, ask about money-market accounts as well. Most brokers have their own money market accounts and automatically sweep your uninvested cash into the account for you. For the brokers that do, find out what kind of interest your money will earn. Also ask if you can write checks on the cash in this account and if check-writing is free. Go to www.cyberinvest. com or www.xolia.com to find out which brokers sweep cash into money-market accounts.

Next, look into tools. Online brokers are offering more tools for investors to do research with. Tools on many sites now run the gamut from company profiles, earnings estimates, and stock charts to technical analysis tools, stock screening tools, analysts' research reports, and even portfolio alerts, which indicate when you should buy or sell a stock. Some brokers charge you a fee when you actually use this stuff. Even if you don't use these resources, sites that have them are often more expensive. Most research can be conducted elsewhere on the Internet for free, so if you're planning to trade frequently, you might want to go for a cheaper, no-frills broker and do your research off-site.

If you like using various types of orders, including market orders, limit orders, stop market orders, stop limit orders, and options such as Good Till Cancel (GTC), All or None (AON), and Fill or Kill, you need to make sure the broker you're considering offers these things and offers them with trades on the exchanges you will be trading. (All these types of orders are explained in Chapter 9.) Many brokers won't let you use stop orders with Nasdaq trades, and others do not accept stop orders of any kind. Only some will let you trade OTC stocks. You also want to confirm the charges for placing different kinds of orders. Several brokers charge extra for limit orders, for example.

It's also a good idea to find out how trades are executed by a broker and how trade confirmations work. When you enter a trade online, the order goes to your broker, who then sends the order to a market maker (a brokerage or bank that buys and sells securities at publicly quoted prices on the Nasdaq) or a specialist (an individual, partnership, corporation, or group of firms that stand ready to buy and sell certain securities on demand on the NYSE). Some online brokers require human brokers to review trades before they're executed. This slows things down, so make sure you know how a broker executes orders and about how long orders take to fill before you sign up.

If the process isn't clearly explained on the broker's Web site (check the FAQs link), send an e-mail asking for a detailed description of how they do it, or call them. As for trade confirmations, most online brokers send you an electronic confirmation by e-mail, but this does not necessarily mean that the order has been filled; it may just mean that your order has been received. Clarify this point.

You owe it to yourself to investigate a broker's customer service department before you send them the first check. There's nothing worse than running into a jam and not being able to reach anyone to

Bright Idea
If you want to brush up on your investment jargon, check out the glossary of investment terms located on most online brokers' sites. On Charles Schwab's Web site (www.schwab.com), for example, just click on "Getting Started" and on the next screen click "Glossary."

help you out of it. The quality of customer service varies greatly from broker to broker. Some firms really don't want to hear from their customers; after all, your relationship with them is supposed to be *online*, not over the phone.

Unfortunately, there are times when you really must speak to someone. See if you can find a phone number for customer service on the broker's Web site or in their literature. Is it a 1-800 number? Is it prominently displayed, or is it hidden away in some corner or written in small print? When you find the number, give them a call. Can you reach a person, or do you get only a prerecorded voice menu? You need to be able to speak to a person. How long does it take? When you do get someone, ask them some questions. Are they helpful, or are they short and condescending? Another way to test a broker's customer service department is to send them an e-mail and ask a question. See how long it takes to get a response.

Another thing to check is whether it's possible to place trades over the phone at the same commission rate if a broker's site crashes. Almost all online brokers charge more for broker-assisted trades, unless their Web site is down. Also ask if you actually can place a trade over the phone, if necessary. You really want to have at least the phone option in case something happens to your equipment, your ISP falters, or your broker's site goes down. Your broker should offer multiple trading channels. Can you place an order by fax?

One way to back yourself up is to have accounts at two or three online brokers (although this won't help if you need to sell something at a broker you can't reach). If you pursue this option, be sure to

Bright Idea
Ask various brokers if they offer e-mail alerts, which notify you of executed trades and expired orders, give you price information and important news affecting securities in your portfolio, and give you market updates.

open up your back-up accounts ahead of time. Don't wait until you have a problem, because you won't be able to open an account with a broker in one day.

Also, if your main account is with a popular broker, such as E*Trade, consider opening your back-up account with a smaller broker that may not be so jammed up on high-volume days. Make sure your equipment is good (see Chapter 2, "Everything You Need"), and consider hooking up a back-up computer with a different ISP, in case your first ISP goes down. Finally, if you're not a day trader, consider getting into the habit of placing trades at night, when traffic on the Internet and at broker Web sites is lighter.

Find out what perks a broker offers for trading with them. Some brokers are offering free trades, gold debit or credit cards, frequent flyer miles, and even cash. The competition among online brokers for new accounts is intense, which is a good thing for online investors.

As with discovering your investment style, choosing a broker is ultimately a question of comfort and taste. Analyze a number of brokers, but in the end listen to your feelings. Do you like the way the site looks? Is it easy to get around? Does it offer the tools you want? Don't choose a broker just because it makes the most sense. All things considered, go with the broker you like the best.

The inside scoop on the online brokers

While the number of online brokers continues to increase, those listed in Table 8.3 control more than 90 percent of the market. These are the brokers most likely to survive any shakeout in the industry (allowing for the possibility of buyouts, of course).

Timesaver
For an extensive list of online brokers and links, go to Investor Guide at www. investorguide. com/Brokerages. htm. Check out the following sites for broker ratings and evaluations: www.gomez.com, www.smartmoney. com, and www. kiplinger.com.

Unofficially...
Market share calculations are based on the total number of online trades placed, not on the total number of accounts. The number of these calculations are based on research from Piper Jaffray (as of February 4, 1999). Also, note that Jack White is now a part of Waterhouse.

TABLE 8.3: LARGEST ONLINE BROKERS BY MARKET SHARE

Broker	Market Share	Minimum Cash Investment	Stock Trades Under 1,000 Shares	Mutual Funds
Schwab	27.60%	$2,500	$29.95	$39; many free
Waterhouse	12.50%	$1,000	$12	$24
E*Trade	11.90%	$1,000 $19.95 OTC/limit/ stop	$14.95 market	$24.95; some free
Datek	10.00%	$2,000	$9.99	$9.99
Fidelity	9.80%	$5,000	$25 market $30 limit	$28.95; some free $75 for non-Fidelity
Ameritrade	7.60%	$2,000	$8 market $13 limit	$18
DLJ Direct	4.00%	$0	$20	$35; some free
Discover	3.40%	$2,000	$14.95 market $19.95 limit	$25; some free
SureTrade	2.90%	$0	$7.95 market $9.95 limit	$25; some free
NDB	1.30%	$2,000	$14.75 market $19.75 limit	$20; some free

Table 8.3 does not include the full-service brokers who are just getting into the online market. Although the full-service brokers do not currently command a significant share of the online market, they may in the future. The remaining 10 percent of online trading market share is, for the most part, spread over the following brokers:

- A.B. Watley
- Accutrade
- American Express Financial Direct
- Brown & Co.
- Bull & Bear
- CompuTEL
- Dreyfus Brokerage
- FirstTrade.com
- Mr. Stock

- Muriel Siebert
- Net Investor
- Quick & Reilly
- Scottrade
- Wall Street Access
- Wall Street Electronica
- Web Street Securities

Unofficially...
Some firms, including Schwab, can charge more because of the levels of trust and confidence they engender. Factors that determine customer confidence include capital base, Web site availability, phone response time, clarity of rules regarding trading, and reliability.

Charles Schwab

Charles Schwab (www.schwab.com/800-435-4000) is one of the more expensive online brokers, but it's also one of the best for overall service. In terms of ease of use, customer service, available investment vehicles, and tools, Schwab is hard to beat. Schwab is a great site for mutual fund investors, offering some 947 funds at no transaction fee (NTF), but you've got to hold a fund for at least 90 days before you sell it, or you'll get charged $31.

Schwab provides lots of high-quality information, including free real-time quotes, charts and graphs, and services such as e-mail alerts and trading by touch-tone phone. Schwab is a good broker for beginners, who may need some assistance in placing trades. The broker provides customer service seven days a week, 24 hours a day. Schwab is also a great broker for investors looking for one-stop shopping. Not only does Schwab provide a wide selection of investment vehicles to choose from—including bonds, options, and IPOs—but they also offer IRAs, custom financial planning, credit cards, free debit cards, online bill paying, checking, and more.

Schwab is not the place for day traders, who make frequent trades and require low commission rates. Schwab's margin rates, option charges, and other fees are also on the high side. Watch out for hidden fees, such as the $6.95 shipping charge for "free" Schwab software. Some of the other negatives include these: The site is a little hard to navigate and can be slow or hard to access on high-volume days (as can real, live brokers). Portfolio updates also are done once a day at night, not in real-time, although Schwab has plans to change that.

E*Trade

E*Trade (www.etrade.com/800-387-2331, 800-786-2575) actually offers even more services and tools than Schwab, including NASDAQ Level II quotes (real-time streaming Nasdaq quotes, available for $14.95 a month, or for free if you make 75 or more trades per quarter), Canadian stocks, penny stocks, and services such as interactive charts, reports and news, earnings estimates, IRAs, free checking, free credit cards, and more. E*Trade is a good broker for the long-term investor and the hyperactive trader, with prices in the middle range ($14.95 for NYSE market orders, $19.95 for NASDAQ and limit orders). Traders who place 75 or more trades per quarter have access to Power E*Trade service and get free access to specialized discussion groups geared toward active traders. They also can use The Pulse, a Java program with a great deal of real-time data that costs other customers $20 a month.

The major negative with E*Trade is low customer confidence. E*Trade is inconsistent, going through periods in which customers are very satisfied and periods in which many people seem disappointed. Many feel E*Trade is trying to be all things to all people and isn't succeeding. Many also complain that E*Trade is spending too much on advertising for new customers when it isn't properly servicing the ones it's already got. The company is growing fast and has been accused of not ensuring that service capacity keeps pace with the ever-expanding customer base; to be sure, E*Trade has a history of site crashes and freeze outs.

Adding insult to injury, when you call in these cases, it's often difficult to get through—and even if you *do* get through, customer service is not always very helpful. Some traders complain that the site itself is slow. Others say that it takes a very long time to set up an account. So before you climb aboard, definitely check out the site, send them an e-mail query, and give them a call.

Waterhouse

Waterhouse WebBroker (www.waterhouse.com/800-934-4410), which recently acquired Jack White, is a superb site for mutual fund investors, with 1,023 funds in its no-transaction-fee (NTF) program (more than Schwab). Unlike Schwab, Waterhouse allows five free redemptions of funds held less than six months every year. Waterhouse charges $25 per trade for buying funds outside its NTF group, much less than Schwab's $39. Waterhouse also holds its own in the products and services department. You can trade stocks, mutual funds, options, commodities, and CMOs, and you can even purchase term-life insurance and annuities. In fact, no one offers a greater variety of products for sale than Waterhouse.

The same is true of the company's services. Waterhouse offers stock screening, trading by touch-tone phone, live brokers, real-time quotes, free debit and credit cards, free check writing, and more.

The negatives are that you can't trade Treasuries, corporate bonds, or Internet stocks with Waterhouse

Unofficially...
The great thing about Waterhouse is that it's one of the few firms that doesn't charge for any of the services they offer, including things such as limit orders and setting up an IRA. Waterhouse has 116 branch offices across the country you can visit, and the customer service reps are considered very helpful.

online. The quality of service seems to depend on what region of the country you're in. Online accounts are not updated immediately following trade executions, and some people complain that trade confirmations are slow in coming.

Datek

Datek (www.datek.com/888-463-2835) provides quick, no-frills trading, decent for active short-term traders and day traders. Datek offers mutual funds, but stocks are Datek's forte. Datek has an excellent trade execution screen that utilizes convenient drop-down menus, and you can access free, unlimited real-time quotes, streaming quotes, and NASDAQ Level II quotes. Datek also provides immediate account updates and links to news and research, and it offers good margin rates.

Unlike the other online brokers, Datek does not send trade orders to the exchange floors; Datek executes trades on an Electronic Communications Network (ECN) called Island ECN. (Instinet is the oldest and largest ECN.) ECNs are computerized trading networks that match buy and sell orders entered by customers. ECNs differ from the Nasdaq in that ECNs don't have market makers, who try to make a profit on the bid-ask spread. Instead, ECNs charge a per-share fee to one or both of the parties involved in a trade. Since this fee is incorporated into Datek's transaction fee, you never see it.

Datek does not offer debit or credit cards, check writing, or touch-tone trading. The broker does not sweep uninvested cash into a money market fund for you; the money earns a flat 3.5 percent. Datek also has been somewhat unreliable, with its system down 3.6 percent of the time between January 1 and April 12, 1999, according to SmartMoney.com. The most

Moneysaver
You may get better prices ("good fills") trading with Datek than with many other online brokers because Datek has cut the middleman out of the picture.

common complaints are with non-online services, such as opening an account, transferring money, and dealing with customer service.

Broker-assisted orders cost $25 each, unless Datek's computers are down. Datek promises that if a market order is not executed in one minute, the broker won't charge a commission, but many complain that Datek cannot be counted on to honor this. Datek does not offer options trading yet, nor all-or-none orders. This means that if they can't buy all the shares you ordered, they'll buy you as many as they can rather than canceling your trade. The SEC censured Datek in 1999 because they allegedly dipped into customer funds to temporarily cover their own trading obligations.

Fidelity (Power Street)

Fidelity (www.100fidelity.com/800-544-7272) is also a great site for mutual fund investors because it sports impressive mutual fund screening tools. Fidelity provides excellent customer service, getting consistently high marks for courteous, friendly, and knowledgeable phone reps, making Fidelity a good site for beginner investors. Customer service is available seven days a week, 24 hours a day. Fidelity offers free, unlimited real-time quotes, a free debit card, and market research. The site also scores well for reliability: The trades you place get executed without much of a delay, you get quick confirmations, and there are few crashes.

The negatives are that Fidelity's fee structure is complicated, vague, and high. Make sure you research their fees thoroughly with regard to the investments you're interested in before you open an account. The only other negative is they do not provide real-time account updating.

Ameritrade

While several online brokers can boast about their mutual fund offerings, no broker offers more funds than Ameritrade (www.ameritrade.com/800-669-3900; 800-454-9272), with 4,221 different funds to choose from, according to SmartMoney.com. SmartMoney's research shows that what really puts Ameritrade in a league by itself, however, is the number of top-performing funds it has available—838, more than any other discount broker. Ameritrade also charges only $18 for a $10,000 mutual fund purchase. In fact, Ameritrade offers great rates in general: only $8 for online market orders and $13 for online limit orders, with no limit on the number of shares you can buy. Ameritrade guarantees market orders to be filled within 60 seconds, gives you access to StockQuest (which will screen more than 10,000 stocks for you using more than 50 parameters), and provides free debit cards. Generally, customers are satisfied with trade executions and customer service.

On the negative side of the ledger, online mutual fund trades with Ameritrade are seemingly accepted even if the dollar amount is below the minimum investment requirement for the fund—you don't find out until the next day that the order didn't go through. Account balances are not updated immediately following a trade. And there also have been some reports of orders not being filled or being mysteriously canceled.

DLJ Direct

DLJ Direct (www.dljdirect.com/800-825-5723) is part of the full-service brokerage Donaldson Lufkin & Jenrette. DLJ Direct has excellent mutual fund capabilities, and you can buy NYSE-listed corporate bonds at zero commission from them. This broker offers excellent Web site navigation and very convenient, informative order-entry screens, with good error-checking safeguards, such as one that makes sure you meet the minimum investment requirements for mutual funds. You get real-time quotes and news alerts on the equity order screen, your portfolio and balances are updated as soon as an order is executed, and you have access to great online research tools.

Customers with accounts of more than $100,000 can access Select Client Services, through which they can get Donald Lufkin & Jenrette research, IPOs, after-hours trading through Instinetfixed-income investments, and a special toll-free customer service number. DLJ Direct also offers free credit cards, free checking, and 24-hour customer service. It's also worth noting that this broker has not been fined or censured by NASD, or even brought to arbitration, in years.

On the negative side, much of DLJ's excellent research (and all IPOs) is available only to accounts with at least a $100,000 balance. The Web site can be slow, and the real-time quotes tend to be a bit late. Accounts are not updated immediately following a trade. Customer service is sometimes great, sometimes not. Some get the feeling that DLJ does not like day traders, and day traders might want to look for a cheaper broker anyhow.

Discover

Discover Brokerage Direct (www.discoverbrokerage. com/800-347-2683) was established by the full-service broker Morgan Stanley Dean Witter. Discover has a nicely designed Web site and offers top-notch research; before- and after-hours trading; accurate

Unofficially... Instinet is a computerized service that allows subscribers to display bid and ask prices and execute transactions, bypassing brokers.

real-time account updates; free, unlimited real-time quotes; charts; and free checking. Discover also promises to open an account for you within 72 hours of receiving the forms. Customers with more than $100,000 can access Morgan Stanley research and a special customer service line with a shorter wait. These customers can also utilize Discover's Market Baskets, which allow them to allocate a certain amount of money across a group of 10 stocks automatically.

As for the negatives, some complain that it's sometimes difficult to cancel orders online and that trade confirmations are not timely. Also, Discover charges relatively high margin rates and other fees.

SureTrade

SureTrade (www.suretrade.com/401-642-6900; toll-free number given to account holders only), a discount version of Quick & Reilly, offers excellent rates ($9.95 for market and limit orders up to 5,000 shares); only Empire Financial and Brown are cheaper. SureTrade also offers great margin rates—6.75 percent on a loan of $25,000. SureTrade's Web site also is something to cheer about. It's clear, simple, and easy to navigate, and it rarely crashes—there's no problem logging on, either. SureTrade offers good on-site resources, such as news and charts, and does a nice job providing research on holdings, allowing investors to examine various data on their stocks. Positions are updated in real time. Customer service is excellent.

No one is perfect, however. Difficulty logging on and slowness have been themes, with investors complaining that the site itself is slow, as are account updates. SureTrade is said to be particularly slow when it comes to opening, and transferring accounts. In addition, SureTrade does not transfer uninvested cash into a money market fund for you; cash earns only 1.5 percent. Finally, there are no check writing privileges at SureTrade.

NDB

National Discount Brokers (www.ndb.com/800-888-3999) is considered very good for trading OTC stocks. The broker doesn't charge more than one buy and one sell commission a day on the same stock, making NDB popular among day traders. NDB has a nice Web site, with an opening screen you can customize. The broker offers free, real-time quotes and free news and charts, and it provides generally quick executions, trade confirmations, and portfolio updates. NDB also offers free debit cards and free credit cards. NDB has a good customer service department. The naysayers complain about trade mix-ups and problems with their Web site, especially difficulty logging on and getting quotes at the beginning and end of the trading day, when volume is heavy.

The smaller brokers

A.B. Watley (www.abwatley.com/888-229-2853) provides two kinds of accounts: the A. B. Watley "Trader," which is A. B. Watley's online trading site, and the A. B. Watley "Ultimate Trader," which is a software-based system for day traders. A. B. Watley's Trader site provides free, unlimited real-time quotes, Instinet trading for all customers, market and limit orders for only $9.95, and good customer service. Real-time updates all day. Always up. Very easy to use. Fast as the wind. Some say Watley is slow to answer its e-mail, though. Accutrade (www.accutrade.com/800-454-9272) provides great research, good executions, stock screening, and fast confirmations, but they're expensive—$29.95 for limit and market orders up to 1,000 shares.

American Express Financial Direct (www.myamericanexpress.com/800-658-4677) offers free, unlimited real-time stock quotes, 220 no-fee mutual funds, and American Express rewards points. However, they suffer from complaints about inadequate customer service and high margin rates.

Brown & Co.(www.brownco.com/800-822-2021), a subsidiary of Chase Manhattan Bank, offers one of the lowest commission rates on market trades—$5 on up to 5,000 shares—a fast Web site, fast execution of trades, and excellent margin rates. But you need to make a minimum initial investment of $15,000 and have an income of $40,000 a year, a net worth of $50,000 (excluding real estate holdings), and at least five years of investing experience to open an account. Furthermore, there are no mutual funds available, there is no money market fund sweep (uninvested cash earns 2.25 percent), and there are no research tools. Customer service has a reputation for being a bit, how shall we put it, brisk.

Bull & Bear Online (www.bullbear.com/800-262-5800) offers real-time account updates and requires no minimum initial investment to open an account and no IRA annual setup fee or annual fee. However, their broker-assistance service is quite expensive, and they charge $29.95 a month for real-time stock quotes.

CompuTEL (www.rapidtrade.com/800-432-0327) offers penny stock trading, Canadian stocks, IRAs with no setup fee and no annual fee, and an excellent Web site. Some complain, however, that confirmations are slow.

Dreyfus Brokerage (www.edreyfus.com/800-421-8395), which is operated by Mellon Bank, is great for options trading; this broker boasts reasonable rates, excellent service, fast order execution, a fast Web site, and knowledgeable, helpful phone staff. Some complain about slow response to e-mail queries.

FirstTrade.com (www.firstrade.com/800-869-8800), the online division of First Flushing (Firstrade Securities), offers free real-time quotes, good customer service, and quick response to e-mail queries. However, some complain that the Web site is slow, and that it's sometimes a little hard to understand the customer service representatives.

Mr. Stock (www.mrstock/800-470-1896) is great for options trading, has a nice Web site, offers more than 3,000 mutual funds, many of which can be traded for no transaction fee, free news, charts, research, check writing, and real-time quotes when placing an order. The broker may be a little slow in establishing new accounts.

Muriel Siebert (www.msiebert.com/800-872-0711) has no minimum investment requirement to open an account, boasts excellent Web site speed and reliability, and offers lots of no-fee mutual funds, immediate trade execution confirmations, free real-time quotes, after-hours trading, and excellent customer service. The only negatives are that margin rates and broker-assisted trade rates are high, although the broker says they will negotiate lower rates for active traders and investors with large accounts.

Net Investor (www.netinvestor.com/800-638-4250), created by the well-regarded Howe-Barnes, offers options, penny stocks, free checking, and a free Visa card, but the Web site is a little hard to use.

Unofficially...
Many of the negative reports about online brokers stem from the dramatic increase in call volume they are experiencing and their frantic efforts to expand capacity fast enough to meet ever-growing demand. When the industry graduates from the explosive growth phase, consistently good service shouldn't be as hard to find.

Quick & Reilly (www.quickwaynet.com/800-837-7220) executes trades correctly and efficiently, and offers an easy-to-use Web site, lots of research, free credit cards, and decent customer service, including quick responses to e-mail queries. On the negative side, margin rates and rates for broker-assisted trades are high, and online real-time quotes cost $29.95 a month

Scottrade (www.scottrade.com) boasts a low $7 commission on market orders and has a clear, easy-to-use Web site, continuous account updates, and free real-time quotes with orders, but it's sometimes difficult to log on.

Wall Street Access (www.wsaccess.com/800-925-5781) offers free real-time quotes, very good options trading, and good customer service. However, you need $10,000 to open an account, and account balances are updated only at the end of the day.

Wall Street Electronica (www.wallstreete.com/888-925-5783) offers excellent service and real-time portfolios, but you need $5,000 to open an account. They're also a bit pricey.

Web Street Securities (www.webstreetsecurities.com/800-753-1700) offers free IRA setup and no annual fee, 10-second executions, immediate confirmations, immediate portfolio updating, market news, and quick access to customer service. Some complain that portfolios are not always updated immediately.

Brokers aren't perfect

While the majority of your investment losses (may they be few) will result from your own bad luck or mistakes, some may be the fault of your stockbroker, brokerage firm, financial planner, or investment adviser. If your brokerage firm (or investment professional) is to blame for a loss, you should demand to be compensated. If they refuse, you can take them to arbitration (settlement of a dispute by a person chosen to hear both sides and come to a decision), or you can take them to court.

Before bringing out the big guns, however, try talking to your broker and explaining the problem. Try to determine where the fault lies and what your broker told you. If the person you speak with isn't helpful, ask to speak with the manager. If this fails to produce results, write to the compliance department at the firm's main office. You should explain your problem clearly and state how you would like it resolved. Request that the compliance officer respond to you within 30 days. If you're still not satisfied, send a copy of your letter to your state securities administrator or to the Office of Investor Education and Assistance at the SEC. The SEC will research your complaint, contact the broker you've complained about and ask them to respond to you. The SEC's involvement often produces the desired result. If not, consider legal action.

But how do you know when you should pursue something and when you should let it go? The best thing to do is consult a lawyer who has some experience representing investors. Many lawyers will give you a free consultation at no obligation to help you determine if you have a claim worth pursuing. In the consultation, the lawyer will help you decide whether you should just let it go, pursue the claim and handle it yourself, or pursue the claim and hire a lawyer.

These are the questions the lawyer will be trying to answer:

> " Every kind of peaceful cooperation among men is primarily based on mutual trust and only secondarily on institutions such as courts of justice and police.
> —Albert Einstein "

Unofficially...
What's the difference between an investment adviser, broker, and financial planner? Investment advisers don't have to have *any* training. Brokers have a license to buy and sell securities and give investment advice. Financial planners give advice on finances in general. Certified Financial Planners (CFP) must complete a financial planning curriculum.

- Was there some misconduct on the part of your broker, such as lying, cheating, stealing, fraud, unsuitable recommendations, unsuitable transactions, unauthorized trades, excessive trading, or failure to follow instructions?

- Did the misconduct cause you to lose money?

- How much money are you hoping to get back?

- Do you have proof of the misconduct and the loss?

- Can you choose between arbitration and litigation?

- How much will it cost to pursue your claim?

- Has the statute of limitations expired on your ability to file a claim?

- Will you be able to collect any award if you win?

Do you have a case?

One of the ways your stockbroker can hurt you is through misrepresentations or omissions, a fancy way of saying "lies." This occurs when a broker makes predictions or even gives opinions that are not reasonably based in fact. A red flag should go up if you hear any of the following:

- **"It's a sure thing."** Nothing is a sure thing.

- **"The price will hit 70 by December."** There is no way a broker can know this, unless he has inside information, which is illegal to trade on.

- **"They're about to announce a merger/major deal with another company."** Again, there is no way your broker could know this ahead of the announcement, unless he has inside information.

- **"We are moving the price higher."** If this is false, it's misrepresentation; if it's true, it's illegal.

Your broker might also omit some information that is critical to you for making an informed decision about an investment. For example, he might recommend that you invest in a gold mining company without telling you that it's a start-up and that miners haven't actually located any of the ore yet.

Sometimes a broker will reassure you that he will closely monitor your account and sell before you lose money, if the security in question turns down. But often brokers fail to keep this promise, either because they simply forget to keep a close eye on your account or because they just aren't able to sell the security before it takes a dive. If you lose money after such a promise, your broker is liable. Also, be careful when a broker tries to sell you a "hot IPO." No one knows if an IPO will be hot or not until it actually hits the market.

Unsuitable recommendations

Your broker may also be liable if he makes "unsuitable recommendations" or "unsuitable transactions" in light of your financial situation or goals. To avoid being liable on these counts, a broker must take the time to learn about your goals and investment style, including your preferences and risk tolerance level, before recommending investments for you. But some brokers fail to do this and go on to recommend investments that are unsuitable for you or that carry more risk than you can comfortably tolerate. If you lose money on these investments, your broker may be liable.

Excessive risk

Your broker may be liable for your losses if he recommends investments that put your principal at risk when you are depending on a certain amount of investment income to live on. He also may be liable if he recommends that you put money you may need for living expenses in illiquid investments (those you can't get out of easily or without paying a substantial penalty for early withdrawal); if he recommends that you put too much of your money in a single security; if he doesn't recommend investments that protect you from taxes, if appropriate; or if he recommends tax-free investments (with lower returns) for accounts, such as IRAs, that are already tax shelters.

Unauthorized trades

In some cases a broker will make unauthorized trades or transactions in your account, and this is a big no-no. Your broker is not legally permitted to make trades on your behalf without consulting you first unless you have given him "discretionary authority" in writing. Otherwise, he must ask you for your permission on every single trade. When you agree to buy or sell a certain stock and give your broker "time and price discretion," he can decide exactly when he's going to place the trade, within reason, but he cannot decide what will be sold and how much on his own.

Your broker also isn't allowed to just call you up and state vaguely that he's going to decrease your Internet exposure. *You* have to give *him* permission as to what he can sell and how much. Even if you have a discretionary account in which you have given your broker the authority to place trades without getting your permission first, he still must operate within the parameters of your written authorization giving him this right. If your written authorization states that you don't want your broker to trade in IPOs or currency, he must abide by these restrictions.

A broker guilty of unauthorized trading may be selling some of your holdings and not reporting it to his firm, hoping to pocket the entire commission. This is known as selling away. But even if the brokerage is unaware of the broker's actions, they are liable under laws of respondent superior, controlling person liability, or negligent supervision. After all, it was the brokerage who hired the rogue and then failed to keep a leash on him.

A few brokers with discretionary authority to trade a customer's account will baldly take advantage of their position of trust by churning a client's holdings. Churning, also known as excessive trading, is buying and selling securities purely to generate commissions. A transaction is defined as churning if it is designed to profit the broker, not the client. Sometimes a broker who churns accounts will place two simultaneous or almost simultaneous transactions that cancel each other out. These are called wash transactions. For example, he might sell your 100 shares of IBM and buy 100 more shares of IBM at the same time. Such a broker might switch you out of a growth stock fund with one fund family and put you into a growth stock fund with another family.

A broker must have a very good reason to move you out of one fund and into another very similar fund, and this is why many (good) brokers use "switching letters" to confirm that their client wants to make such a switch in spite of the costs (loads). While a broker must have control over your account for you to nail him on churning, you can still win if he has de facto control. De facto control exists when

Bright Idea
The North American Securities Administrators Web site (www.nasaa.org) is useful if you have a complaint against your broker.

Watch Out!
While it's popular to be suspicious of stockbrokers, a recent investigation by the SEC determined that less than 2 percent of all the registered brokers fall into the category of problem brokers.

a customer doesn't have the knowledge or experience to make investment decisions for himself and always follows his broker's recommendations.

Failure to follow instructions

The last major claim you can win against your broker is for failure to follow instructions. Regardless of whether your broker has discretionary authority over your account, he must always follow your specific instructions. One of the most frequent situations in which this law is violated is when you have told a broker to sell a stock he has been strongly promoting. At first, he will probably try to convince you not to sell it, saying that this isn't a good time. But if you insist, he may simply not sell it. This is because he is currently trying to talk the stock's price up and doesn't want anyone to sell until after the price has risen. If he fails to pump up the stock's price, however, or if he gets you out after the price falls, you will lose big.

Another common situation in which a bad broker may not follow your instructions is when you tell him to stop using margin. The broker may not sell shares bought on margin right away because the shares may be down, and to do so would mean realizing a big loss. He stalls, hoping that the stock will turn around, and instead the stock continues to drop.

Other misconduct

There are other forms of broker misconduct that you can hold a broker responsible for. If you feel that you have been wronged in any way and you want to do something about it, call a lawyer and set up a free consultation.

If you determine that you do have grounds to make a claim against your broker, don't wait to take action. There are time limits on filing such claims in court or before an arbitral tribunal such as the National Association of Securities Dealers or the American Arbitration Association (AAA). When you open an account at a brokerage, the firms will usually require you to sign a form stating that you agree to settle any disputes by arbitration, which is cheaper for all parties concerned. To pursue a claim, you will need some capital. There will be lawyer's fees, forum fees (fees for filing the claim with the NASD or AAA) that may run around $1,000, and other cash expenses.

Instead of charging you by the hour, many lawyers will charge you only a percentage of the settlement if you win (usually 30–40 percent). If you do win, you'll be awarded damages for lawyers fees and out-of-pocket losses as well as for the profits you lost due to the wrongful investment. Arbitrators will often order the broker to reimburse you for the forum fees as well. If you lose, however, the arbitrator could make you pay the broker's forum fees. Finally, before you bring suit against a broker or a group, it's a good idea to make sure someone has the funds to pay you if you win.

Just the facts

- Traditionally full-service brokers offer investors the widest selection of investments and give advice, but they are the most expensive. Discount brokers offer fewer investment choices and no advice, but they are considerably less expensive. Electronic brokers, the original online brokers, offer the fewest investment choices and no advice, but they are the cheapest.

Moneysaver
The National Association of Securities Dealers (NASD) will send you a free report on a broker's background. Just call 1-800-289-9999.

- An online broker is any broker that allows you to trade securities over the Internet.

- Go with a full-service broker if you want professional advice and are willing to pay a premium for it. Go with a discount broker if you want to minimize commissions and make your own investment decisions.

- Ten brokers dominate 90 percent of the online market: Charles Schwab, Waterhouse, E*Trade, Datek, Fidelity, Ameritrade, DLJ Direct, Discover, SureTrade, and National Discount Brokers (NDB).

- Your broker may be liable for your losses if the losses resulted from misconduct on your broker's part, including: misrepresentations or omissions, unsuitable recommendations, unsuitable transactions, unauthorized trades, excessive trading (churning), or failure to follow instructions.

GET THE SCOOP ON...
Accounts and trading
levels ▪ Buying, selling, or selling short ▪
Market, limit, and stop orders ▪ Setting order
execution parameters ▪ Placing trades and
tracking your portfolio

Setting Up an Account

O pening an account with a broker is as simple as requesting an application, filling it out, and sending it in with your check. But what are the rules and regulations? Will your expectations be met? What kinds of trades can you place? How can you fund your account? How often will you get statements? What about trade confirmations? Is there a charge for closing you account or transferring funds?

Before placing your first trade, it's also important to look at the different types of orders you can place. There's more to trading than just buying and selling. Understanding the full range of trading options available to you will empower you to get what you want when you trade and avoid a lot of unpleasant surprises.

Types of accounts

Brokers offer investors various types of accounts. One kind of account allows you to trade securities in an individual retirement account. Others let you trade as part of a corporation, a trust, a partnership, or an investment club. The types of accounts available to you will depend on your broker, but the one account available at all brokers is the brokerage account, the standard account for investors at a stockbrokerage. Virtually anyone who is 18 or older and a U.S. citizen can open a brokerage account, and many brokers will open accounts for foreigners as well.

Cash and option brokerage accounts

Three different types of brokerage accounts exist: cash, option, and margin. A cash account is the most basic kind of brokerage account. Account holders deposit funds, and the broker uses the money in the account to pay for trades. If you have good credit or are in good standing with a broker, or both, they may let you buy securities without all the necessary cash in the account, but the money must be there by the settlement date (the date by which a purchase is actually paid for, usually three business days after the trade is executed: "T+3"). Profits from the sale of securities and dividends are deposited into your account.

Another type of brokerage account is an option account, an account that allows you to trade options. To open an option account, you fill out an application and declare that you understand the risks associated with options. Many brokers assign different margin trading privileges to different investors based on their investment knowledge and experience. The least experienced investors will be allowed to buy only puts and calls; the most experienced will be able to sell them.

Margin accounts

Margin accounts are the third major type of brokerage account. These accounts allow you to borrow money from your broker against the value of the

Unofficially...
The amount of money you need to open a cash account varies from broker to broker. Some brokers, such as SureTrade, don't require any minimum deposit; others require a $10,000 initial investment or more. The low, low commission rates you see advertised by the online brokers are for their cash accounts.

cash and securities in your account. You can also borrow securities from your broker and sell them (called *selling short*) in a margin account. Borrowing money or securities is not allowed in cash accounts. The idea of borrowing money from your broker is to invest it alongside your own money and make more than you would have otherwise. Using borrowed money to make money is called leveraging and can greatly enhance your returns.

To illustrate, let's say you bought $100,000 of Proctor & Gamble stock, and the stock went up 20 percent in one year; your gain would be $20,000. If you had borrowed an additional $100,000 at 7 percent interest and invested that money on top of your own $100,000, you would have made an additional $13,000 ($20,000 – $7,000 in interest) for a total gain of $33,000. Your account balance would be $133,000, up 33 percent for the year!

The catch with buying on margin is that it can also add to your losses—in a big way. For example, if you bought $100,000 of a stock that went down 20 percent in one year, you would lose $20,000. If you had margined $100,000 more of the stock, you would have lost an additional $20,000 + $7,000 in interest, for a total loss of $47,000. Your account value would then be $53,000, down almost 50 percent for the year. Leverage works both ways.

Because of the risks involved in buying on margin, your broker is obligated by law to require you to keep enough hard cash or assets in your account to cover your potential margin losses. To illustrate how important this is, let's look at a hypothetical situation. Suppose your total account value is $10,000, you have all $10,000 invested in one stock, and you have margined an additional $10,000 in the same stock, for a $20,000 position in the stock. Now, let's say the price of the stock drops 50 percent. How much would you be down? $5,000 on your money, $5,000 on the money you borrowed, plus interest— more than $10,000. The total asset value of your account would now be negative, and you would still have money riding on that stock. If the company went bankrupt, you might lose your entire invest- ment, all your money, and all the money you bor- rowed. Your account balance would be at —$10,000 (plus interest on the loan). And while you might owe your broker more than $10,000, they might never get their money back. After all, where are you going to come up with $10,000 if that was all you had to start with?

Brokers are not allowed to let you lose all their money. To ensure that this does not happen, they are required by law to limit the amount of stock you can buy on margin in the first place. For their own sakes, they regulate how much equity you must maintain in your account at all times as a fraction of your debt. If your investments go down far enough, they ask you to deposit more assets—and if you don't, they start selling your securities. These safe- guards ensure that you will always have enough in your account to cover your potential losses. Your account balance should never go below $0.00.

The amount you can borrow from your broker depends, first, on the initial margin requirement (IMR), which is the minimum allowable ratio of equity in your account to the total market value of your account, defined as the value of the equity plus the debt in your account. The IMR is calculated this way: total account equity / (total account equity + total debt). The IMR is set by the Federal Reserve Board and is currently at 50 percent of all marginable securities in your account. (Marginable securities are securities you can borrow against.) If the total market value (equity + debit balance) of your account equals $200,000, and if all the securities in the account are marginable, the total account equity must be equal to at least $100,000 (50 percent of $200,000). In other words, if you were to buy as many stocks on margin as you could, the value of those stocks can never equal more than 50 percent of all your securities.

Once you've bought some securities on margin, your account will be subject to a maintenance margin requirement (MMR), which is the minimum amount of equity you must keep in your account at all times as a fraction of the total market value (equity + debt) of your account. The MMR is also referred to as equity-to-debt ratio. To illustrate, let's say you bought $100,000 of XYZ company with your own money and purchased another $100,000 on margin (50 percent of your equity). And let's say that a month later the price of XYZ was down 20 percent, so the total value of your equity was $80,000, making your equity-to-debt ratio 40 percent ($80,000 / [($100,000 + $80,000)] = .4). If this ratio were to fall below a certain percentage, often 30 percent or 35 percent, you would get a "margin call" from your broker asking you to deposit more money or assets.

The MMR is set by the individual brokers and exchanges. The NYSE sets its base MMR at 25 percent, but most brokerages set it higher. The percentage set by your broker also will vary with the riskiness of the securities you are margining. If you want to margin a very volatile security, a broker might require a 70 percent MMR. Some securities

Watch Out!
If your broker gives you a margin call but you cannot or do not deposit more money or assets, he will liquidate some of your securities.

may be nonmarginable. Nonmarginable securities are those that you cannot borrow against because they are too risky (or because they're in a cash account). Because the value of these securities is unstable, they are considered unfit to serve as collateral for a loan. What one broker would consider a marginable security, another broker might not. Some brokers use the price of a security to determine whether it's marginable. A common benchmark is $5—any security priced below $5 per share would not be marginable; anything priced above that would be.

Be careful not to tie up too much of the money in your margin account in nonmarginable securities. If you ever do get into trouble, you want to be able to cash in stocks that aren't down 50 percent this week.

The interest rate you'll have to pay on your margin loan is relatively low, usually the same as or a percent or two above the prime rate. The margin rate, then, changes with changes in interest rates. The reason the rate is so low is that the loan is low-risk. It's fully collateralized by the securities in your account, and your broker can call the loan at any time, if necessary. There is no set payment schedule on the loan interest in a margin account; the interest is simply added daily to your debit balance. If things go well, you may never end up paying this interest because the value of your margined securities will always be increasing faster than your debit balance (keeping your MMR nice and low).

Not everyone can get a margin account. A broker will extend margin privileges to you only if they feel you're a good credit risk, and brokers conduct credit checks on all applicants for these accounts.

You will also have to fill out a margin account agreement. The most important part of this agreement is the "hypothecation and re-hypothecation" clause, which states that you pledge the securities in your account as collateral for the money you borrow on margin.

While having a margin account enables you to borrow money to buy more securities, you can really use the money for anything you want. Some people borrow cash for everyday expenses from their margin account so that they won't have to sell securities and pay a capital gains tax. Not having to sell securities for cash enables them to stay invested and take advantage of further increases in share prices. Some brokers facilitate using margin for everyday credit needs by issuing debit cards with a credit limit that include the margin limit on the cardholder's account.

Opening an account

Actually, opening an account with your broker of choice is not difficult. If you're going the full-service route, it would be best to set up an appointment to go into a branch office, meet your account executive, and discuss your financial goals when you open your account. You will be asked to give your name and address, as well as a certain amount of personal information, including your age, Social Security number, employer's name, work address, information about your financial resources and income, and credit references.

If you don't feel comfortable divulging all this information, you can simply refuse, but the broker can also refuse to open an account for you, especially if you don't give them the information they

Unofficially...
The interest rates on margin accounts are lower than those on even the best of credit cards.

need to comply with the laws designed to protect you. A full-service broker needs to know the basic facts about your financial situation and understand your goals and investment style to help you. Make sure you understand the forms you're asked to sign before you do. One of them may specify that you agree to settle any future disputes by binding arbitration rather than by litigation.

If you're going to invest independently, you can either call the broker you're interested in to have an application sent to you, or you can fill out an application form online. Even online applications require such information as your occupation and income. What's different about online applications is that you need to select a user name and a password for yourself, both of which you need to log on to your online account. (Some brokers assign these to you.) You will also need to indicate what type of account you want—most likely, a brokerage account—followed by the trading level: cash, margin, or option.

Now, a broker can't actually activate your account until they have a signed application form from you and until the minimum initial investment clears the bank. (Some online brokers require no initial deposit for setting up your account, but you won't be able to buy anything until you've got some money deposited there.) Legally, the broker must have your signature on a paper version of the application. This is required by the SEC to verify that it is actually you who is opening the account and that all the information about you is true. So, you can't actually open an account with a broker the same day you fill out an application form—even if it's an online broker and an online application.

Some brokers will start processing your application as soon as you fill out the online form, though, and some will even activate your account if you print out the online form, sign it, and fax it to them. But you won't be able to place any trades until your payment clears, and you won't be able to log on to your account until you receive your user name and password in the mail. (Brokers mail these because e-mail is not secure.) If you decide to fax the broker your application to speed things up, don't forget to mail them the original (along with your check, if you're paying that way); they'll close your account if they don't get a signed original within a certain period of time. If you're not in a terrible hurry to open an account, however, it's easier just to print out the online application and mail it along with your initial deposit. A week or two later, you'll receive your user name and password in the mail, and you can begin trading. If you can't print out the application for any reason, you'll have to request online (or via telephone) to have one sent by mail.

You can fund your online account in several ways. You can send checks or money orders, of course, but you can also wire money from your bank. If you want to move retirement funds from your bank to your broker, you can authorize a direct transfer. A direct transfer is not a withdrawal and does not incur any taxes or penalties. If you have funds with another broker, you can arrange to have them transferred by simply filling out an Automated Customer Account Transfer form (ACAT) with your new broker. Your new broker may also require a copy of your last account statement with your old broker, as well as some proof of identity. Transfers of brokerage accounts generally take 5–10 business

Where large sums of money are concerned, it is advisable to trust nobody.
—Agatha Christie

days; other types of accounts take 10–15 days. Some brokers charge a fee to close IRA accounts.

If you're funding your account with stock certificates, make sure that you endorse the stocks in the spaces provided. Of course, when you endorse a stock certificate, anyone who intercepts it could deposit it in his own account. To lessen the risk of this happening, you can send the certificates and the endorsement (which transfers the stock power) separately by filling out a stock power form. *Stock power* is the power of attorney that enables a person other than the owner to transfer stock ownership to another party. It's always a good idea to send stock certificates by express, certified, or registered mail.

Depending on the speed of delivery, how quickly the broker processes your application, and when your payment clears, your account will be up and running in one to three weeks. To speed up the process, some brokers will send you your user name and password as soon as they get your application, so you'll have what you need to start investing as soon as they activate your account. Other brokers mail these to you only after your account has been activated.

Types of trades

The most basic types of trade orders are buy orders and sell orders. When you buy a stock, mutual fund, or other security, you're hoping that its value, as reflected by its price, will increase. Buying securities is also known as "going long." A standard buy order is paid for with the cash you have in your account. When you sell a stock, mutual fund, or other security, you think that its value is going to decrease. If the share price is higher than when you bought it, you want to lock in your profits; if it's lower, you want to limit your losses.

Shorting

Selling short, or "shorting," is a bit more complicated than selling in the standard sense because you're selling stock you don't actually own. It's stock you've borrowed from your broker and promised to return later. Why would you want to do this? If the stock goes down in price, as you're predicting, you can buy back the shares at a lower price than you sold them for and make a profit. For example, let's say you thought shares of XYZ company were at their peak when they hit $50 a share. You could then borrow a certain number of shares of XYZ, say, 100, from your broker and sell them for a total of $5,000. Now, let's say the stock fell to $40, and you decided it had bottomed. At this point, you would buy 100 shares for a total cost of $4,000, return the 100 shares you borrowed to your broker, and pocket the $1,000 profit you made on the deal.

What happens if you're wrong, and the stock goes up instead of down? Well, you lose money, plain and simple. Let's look at how this can happen. Suppose you sell 100 shares of XYZ short at $50 per share, the price goes up to $60, and you decide to buy back the shares before they go up any further. At $60 per share, you pay $6,000 for 100 shares and suffer a loss of $1,000.

As with buying on margin, short selling is borrowing assets from your broker, and you are required to have collateral in your account—in this case equaling at least 50 percent of the total value of the securities you want to short. So, if you want to sell short 100 shares of XYZ at $50 a share ($5,000),

Unofficially...
Many brokers welcome foreign customers, even those who are not permanent residents in the United States. Foreigners should try to make deposits on checks drawn on U.S. banks, though, because foreign checks take four to six weeks to clear.

you would need at least $2,500 in your account. You also must maintain a certain amount of equity in your account relative to the value of the shorts at all times. If the price of XYZ increases to the point where your equity is equal to only 30–35 percent of the shorted stocks, your broker might ask you to deposit more assets into your account.

Generally, brokers don't put a time limit on how long you can borrow their stock. They're making money on your buying and selling, whether you're going short or long, and are happy to facilitate account activity. You usually don't have to pay the broker interest on borrowing shares for short sales because you're not actually borrowing them from your broker; you're borrowing them from another customer. You won't be able to sell a stock's shares short unless they're available from another customer at your broker.

As long as a stock's price is falling, your short sale order on the stock will not go through. For this we can thank the "uptick rule," which states that a short sale can be executed only when the price of the stock moves up a tick (a point or a fraction of a point). The rule was instituted after the stock market crash in 1929, to prevent short selling from exacerbating price declines.

How could the uptick rule affect your short sale orders? Let's say you placed an order to sell 100 shares of XYZ short, and the stock went straight down from the opening bell from $50 to $40 before moving up to 40½. Your order would go through at 40½ rather than 50, and you might be left wondering how much downside potential for the stock remained. If you had specified that you wanted to sell XYZ short at $50, you wouldn't get it unless it moved all the way back up from 40½ to 50. You can't get around the uptick rule by waiting until the next day's market opening because the rule still applies; if a stock's opening price is below the previous day's closing price, your trade will not go through.

Types of orders

The savvy online investor is familiar with different types of orders and uses them to help her get what she wants.

Market orders

The most basic type of order is the market order. A market order is a trade order in which the broker is told to buy or sell a security at the best price currently available on the market. Placing a market order is also known as "buying the market." Stock price movements, especially short-term movements, are not very predictable, so when you place a market order to buy or sell, you may not get the price you expect. For example, if you bought 100 shares of Biogen (BGEN) at $55 a share, watched it rise to $67, and then placed a market order to sell your shares, you might get out at $67, but you might also get out at $64 or $69, for that matter. You're pretty much at the whim of the market when you place a market order.

This is particularly true if you place a market order after the markets are closed. If some important news comes out about the company you're buying between trading sessions, the opening price could be way above or below the closing price, and you could end up buying the stock at a much higher or lower price than you had anticipated. (Expansion of after-hours trading could increase the frequency of wide discrepancies in opening and closing

Watch Out!
Some brokers won't let you sell short. Some brokers won't execute short sale orders placed online until the order can be confirmed with you on the phone. And some brokers charge interest on short sales! Ask your broker about these things if you're thinking of selling short.

prices.) The one thing you can definitely be sure of with market orders, though, is that your trade will be executed at some price. If you want to buy, you will buy, and if you want to sell, you will sell.

The exact price at which your market order will fill depends to a great extent on whether you're buying or selling. Securities actually have two prices: a bid price, the highest price a buyer is willing to pay for a security, and an asking (or offer) price, the lowest price at which a seller is willing to sell. The single price you see reported for a stock is actually the last price at which the stock was traded. The difference between the bid and the asking prices is called the bid-ask spread. Brokers with buy and sell orders for stocks don't actually haggle with each other over prices on the floors of the exchanges or on the Nasdaq; they trade through an agent or dealer in the stock, known as a specialist (on the NYSE) or a market maker (on the Nasdaq). The dealer buys shares from sellers of the stock and sells shares (at a slightly higher price) to buyers. This is how specialists and market makers make money—on the bid-ask spread.

The actual price at which a market order is filled is determined mostly by the bid and offer prices for the stock at the time your trade is executed. Generally, buyers will get a price at or close to the offer price, and sellers will get a price at or close to the bid price. Sometimes your broker is able to get you a price somewhere in between the bid and the ask, and this is known as price improvement. Often price improvement is just dumb luck. Your order is actually filled at a time when, due to a price fluctuation, the bid or ask price is better than the current price or is better than the price you asked for. Other times, price improvement is the result of hard work on the part of your broker.

Many stocks are traded on several exchanges; some are traded all over the world, and it's possible to get a good price if your broker shops around a bit. You have every opportunity to do this on the Nasdaq, which consists of various market makers trading many of the same securities, competing for trades by offering different bid and ask prices.

With opportunities such as this to find good prices, your broker really should be trying. Many brokers, however, actually sell their orders to other brokers, referred to as executing brokers, for a fee (called payment for order flow—PFOF). If your broker is routing your orders to another broker, you may not see any price improvement on your trades. This is because executing brokers, if they are also market makers on the Nasdaq, can make back the fees they pay for orders by executing orders at the bid or ask prices, trading their own accounts at slightly better prices and pocketing the difference.

Some brokers keep an inventory of stocks that they buy and sell directly to customers, and other brokers have computer programs that match trades from different customers, cutting off or crossing the orders before they get to the exchanges. In both of these cases, the broker gets the spread; while most brokers keep it, others, including Charles Schwab, split it between the customers who cross. It's a good idea to find out how your broker handles order flow.

Limit orders

Limit orders are an alternative to market orders. With a limit order, you specify the maximum price at which you are willing to buy or the minimum price

Moneysaver
Find out if your broker routes orders to other brokers, and if so, where your trades are being executed. Several studies have shown that you can get a better price (an eighth of a point, on average) if your trades are executed on the exchanges rather than on the third market, meaning by broker-dealers trading for their own accounts.

at which you are willing to sell a security. Let's say you've been keeping your eye on a little company named Ikon Office (IKN), whose share price, after moving down precipitously during the last month, seems to be rising. You want to buy 100 shares of the stock, but not at a price significantly higher than the current price of, say, $8 per share.

In this case, you might place a limit order to buy 100 shares of IKN at $8. This instruction requires your broker to buy the IKN shares at $8 a share *or better*. Your broker cannot buy the shares at a higher price than the limit price.

Conversely, you can place a limit order on stocks you are selling. Say that, a year later, after IKN climbs massively to $16 a share, you want to sell. To lock in that 100 percent profit, you might place a limit order to sell your shares at $16 a share. This requires your broker to sell the shares at a price of $16 *or better*. He cannot sell the shares at a lower price. Indeed, with limit orders you often do get a better price than your limit price.

Taking the idea of using limit orders to sell one step further, you might establish a goal for your stock's price and place a limit order to sell the stock at (or above) that price. Continuing with the previous example on buying IKN at $8 per share, you might turn around and place a limit order to sell IKN at $16 per share, even though the stock isn't even close to that price now. You must leave your limit order there so that it will trigger and lock in your gains as soon as it's hit.

Another technique you can use with limit orders is to place two limit orders on the same stock at the same time, one above the current price at your goal price and one below at a stop-loss price. For example, if you bought a stock for $30, you might put a limit order to sell at $45 and another limit to sell at $25. The upper limit is designed to lock in your profits, and the lower is intended to protect you from excessive losses if the stock goes the wrong way on you.

The drawbacks of limit orders

The one drawback of limit orders is that you can never be 100 percent sure that your trade will go through. Your broker may simply not be able to get the price you want for the shares. For example, if you really wanted to buy a stock at $50 and set your limit there, but the stock never dropped below $51, you would be left empty-handed as you watched the stock climb without you. Even if the stock did hit $50, you might not get it if other orders were ahead of yours and the price didn't stay at or below $50 long enough for your order to fill. You might decide to chase the stock by placing another limit order, say, at $54, in which case you would get the stock for a higher price than you probably would have if you had just placed a market order in the first place. Then again, you still might not get the stock!

The same risks with limit orders exist on the sell side. If you placed an order to sell a stock at $85, but the stock never got above $84¼ that day, you could be left holding on to a stock whose price has peaked and will continue to fall. The danger of limit orders is that your order will never be executed at all.

A good way to reduce the risk of missing the market with limit orders is to place buy orders that are above the current asking price and sell orders that are below the bid price. So, if IKN is trading around $8 a share, with an asking price of $8½ , you could

Unofficially...
When simultaneous orders are placed above and below a stock's current price, the orders are sometimes referred to collectively as an "either/or order."

place a limit order to buy at $9. With that order, you would be refusing to pay more for the stock than $9, knowing full well that you might get a better price. If you wanted to sell IKN down the road when it was trading around $16, you could place an order to sell at $15. With this order, you would be refusing to sell the stock for less than $15.

Even when you leave yourself a cushion like this, however, there is no guarantee that your limit orders will be executed. Stocks sometime gap up or down, jumping over a range of prices before settling in another. People with limit orders can be left by the wayside when this happens.

Let's look at an example: Suppose you see Amazon.com (AMZN) trading at around $115 a share, and you place a order to buy 100 shares at $116. If the stock price jumps over $116–$119 and starts trading in the $120–$125 range, your order won't be filled. Keep in mind that your limit order requires your broker to buy Amazon at $116 a share or better. The same risk exists for limit orders to sell. Where you place your limit price will definitely impact the chances of your trade going through, but a limit order is always a limit order—it's never a sure thing. If you absolutely, positively want to buy or sell a stock, place a market order. If buying or selling a stock at a decent price is a priority, use a limit order.

Limit orders on Nasdaq stocks are not always as successful as those placed on other exchanges. The reason for this is that market makers on the Nasdaq are not obligated to execute your limit order at the limit price or better when they trade for their own accounts, unless your order came from their firm. They might let your order sit. This means that often when you place limit orders on Nasdaq stocks, you won't get a better price than your limit price, and you might not even get the stock. On the NYSE, specialists are not allowed to trade for their own accounts at prices at or better than your limit order price until they execute your order.

Stop orders

Another type of order you should know how to use is the stop order. A stop order is an order to buy or sell a stock if the price hits a certain level. Unlike a limit order, a stop order does not require a broker to trade the stock at your stop price or better; it simply requires him to trade the stock for the best price he can get when the stop price is hit. For this reason, standard stop orders are also known as stop-market orders. So, if you had bought 1,000 shares of Dell (DELL) at $42 a share, you might place a stop order to sell at $35. If Dell's share price did hit $35, your stop order would be triggered, and your broker would then sell Dell at the best price he could get for it. The order to sell would be activated at $35, and it would then become a market order. You are not charged a commission for placing a stop order unless the order is actually executed.

The other kind of stop order is the stop limit order. A stop limit order is an order to sell a stock at a limit price or better as soon as the stop price is hit. To continue with the Dell example, you might place a stop limit order to sell your shares of Dell at $34 per share or better as soon as the price hits $35— that's a stop limit order with a stop at $35 and a limit at $34. As soon as Dell hit $35, then, your broker would be required to sell your shares, but not for less than $34. Stop-limit orders carry the same risks and potential rewards as limit orders, of course. For

Bright Idea
If you're interested in a defensive strategy, consider placing buy orders that are above the current asking price and sell orders that are below the bid price. This strategy is designed to improve the chances of your limit orders going through by giving up a little on the price.

example, the price dropped past your limit, the order would not be executed.

You can also use a stop order to sell a stock when it hits a price *above* its current price. For example, let's say you bought 1,000 shares of General Electric (GE) at $100 per share, and the current price was $105. You could place a stop order to sell your shares of GE when it hits $115. If you used a stop-market order, your broker would sell GE at market when GE hit $115; if you used a stop-limit, with a limit of $114, your broker would sell your shares at or at better than $114 when GE hit $115. Investors who set price goals for the stocks should consider using stops this way.

It's possible to place stop orders above and below the current price of a stock simultaneously; this is an *either/or* order. (Unless otherwise indicated, stop order means stop-market order.) If you bought a stock at $30, for example, you might place one stop at your target price of $45 and one stop at your stop-loss price of $25 to protect you to the downside. This way you're set to lock in profits if the stock rises as you expect, but you're also protected from excessive losses if it falls.

Combination orders

Some investors use a combination of limit orders and stop orders. Say you bought a stock for $50. You could place a limit order at $70 and a stop order at $42. This way, you will sell at $70 or better if the price is hit and your trade goes through, but you will definitely sell at $42 if this price is hit because the stop order triggers a market order to sell. This technique gives you excellent downside protection.

Other investors use the reverse combination. They put a stop order above the current share price and a limit order below. This technique is designed to ensure that you'll lock in some profits if your target price is hit and to put a floor on your losses if you have to get out. This system does not guarantee that you'll get out, however, because your stop-loss is actually a limit order.

You can also use stop orders to *buy* stocks. For instance, if you were interested in buying a stock currently trading at around $70 a share, if you could get it for as little as $60 a share, you could place a stop order to buy the stock at $60. If the stock were to hit $60, a market order to buy the stock would be activated. You could also set a stop-limit order to buy the stock, with a stop at $60 and a limit at $60. This order would require your broker to buy the stock for $60 or less, or not at all.

Specifying order execution parameters

In addition to deciding what kind of trade you're going to place, you need to decide how you're going to place it. First, you need to decide whether you want your order to expire at the end of one trading day, filled or unfilled, or whether you want it to remain active until you cancel it. The first type of trade is called a Day Only trade; the second is a Good Till Cancel (GTC) trade. When would you use a Day Only trade? Let's say you wanted to buy a stock at $105 a share that was trading in the $105–$108 range, and you put in a limit order GTC to buy at $105. Now, let's say you weren't able to get the stock the next day because it opened at $106 and never looked back. Imagine that over the next few weeks the stock climbed and climbed, reaching $140; at this point it suddenly turned and began dropping. As it plummeted, your buy order was filled at $105, as the stock continued downward. Is this what you

Watch Out!
With stop-limit orders, as with limit orders, you can never be 100 percent sure that your trade will go through. The advantage of using stop-market orders is that the stock will definitely be traded if the target price is hit.

wanted? If your original order had been a Day Only order, this would not have happened.

So, when would you want to use a Good Till Cancel Order? GTC orders are important to use with all stop and limit orders. Think about it. These are orders you want to be sitting there ready to trigger each and every day. If you own a stock with a current share price of $65 a share and you place a stop-market order to sell at $60, you want that order to remain active for as long as you're in the position or until you change the stop. You don't want the stop disappearing after one day! When you should use Day Only, and when GTC, depends on what you're trying to accomplish.

Another trade option you have at your disposal is Fill or Kill. When you place a trade Fill or Kill, your broker is required to trade all the shares immediately or cancel the order. If a buyer or a seller isn't found for all the shares or at the price you want, the order must be canceled.

Another timing option is Immediate or Cancel, which requires the broker to trade as many shares as he can right away or cancel the order. The difference between this and Fill or Kill is that with Immediate or Cancel, partial fills are okay. In fact, there are few uses for either of these trading options today.

Another trade order option you should consider is the All or None (AON) option. When you select AON, your broker must trade all the shares specified in your order or none at all. If you do not select AON, your broker has the right to trade as many shares as he can, which may result in a partial fill. For example, you might place an order to buy 4,000 shares of IBM, and your broker may simply not be

able to buy that many shares for you that day
(assuming this is a Day Only order). If you had
placed the order as AON, the order would be canceled; if you hadn't, your broker could buy as many
shares as he could get his hands on for you.

As a halfway measure, you may be able to specify
a Minimum Quantity of shares your broker must
trade if he can't fill your entire order. For example,
if you wanted to sell 10,000 shares of a company, you
could require your broker to sell at least 3,000
shares or none at all. But even if you don't place
trades AON or Minimum Quantity, your order will
almost always be completely filled if it's for less than
2,000 shares.

When placing a trade, also consider whether you
would be willing to reduce your asking price (limit
price) when selling a stock if the company were to
pay out a dividend while you were trying to sell it.
When companies pay out dividends, the share price
is reduced in proportion to the size of the dividend.
Unless you specify to your broker not to reduce your
asking price under these circumstances, he will. You
won't lose money, however, when your broker sells
your stock for less because the proceeds of the sale
plus the dividend you receive will equal what the
proceeds of the sale would have been at the higher
price.

For example, let's say you wanted to sell 1,000
shares of XYZ company at $85 per share. If XYZ paid
out a dividend, your broker might reduce your asking price to $80 per share, but the sum of the sale of
your shares at $80 plus your dividend would equal
the proceeds of selling your shares at $85 per share.
In spite of this, you can specify that your broker not
reduce your asking price in the event of a dividend

payout by selecting Do Not Reduce (DNR) on your trade order form.

Placing trades

To actually place a trade order, you must first go to your broker's online trading site and select the appropriate trading screen from the home page. Depending on your broker, there may be different trade order pages for stocks, mutual funds, bonds, and options. Our advice to you is to limit your online trading to stock and mutual funds. Unless you are a sophisticated bond or option trader, these instruments are best purchased over the phone in consultation with specialists at a discount or full-service brokerage.

Let's assume that you're going to place a stock trade. The most important thing to remember in filling out the trade order form is not to make any clerical mistakes when you type in the particulars of your order. More people have lost more money by simply entering the wrong information on these forms than you can imagine. If you lose money this way, your broker will *not* reimburse you. Always check everything you enter on an online trade order form before you enter the order.

The first thing you must do to trade a stock online is enter the stock's ticker symbol. Ford's ticker symbol, for example, is F; Dell Computer's ticker is DELL. If you don't know the ticker, you can use your broker's symbol lookup tool to find it, or go to http://quote.yahoo.com/ and click Symbol Lookup. With symbol lookup programs, you just type in the company name, and the program produces the ticker symbol. The next thing you need to do is select the action you want to take. This will be either buy, sell, or sell short. Next you will have to type in the number of

Unofficially...
When setting up your order execution parameters, you'll need to decide whether you want your dividends sent to you or reinvested. If you choose the former, you'll periodically receive a check from your broker. If you choose to have them reinvested, your broker will use your dividends to buy additional shares of the stock or mutual fund.

shares (quantity) you wish to trade. Be especially careful about accuracy here. One extra digit could cost you thousands of dollars! Don't worry about purchasing round lots, multiples of 100. Nowadays there are rarely penalties for buying fewer than 100 shares (odd lots), so go ahead and buy 42 shares if you want. The only time you might have to buy in round lots is with some limit and option orders. Check with your broker.

The next step in placing an online trade is to select the order type: market, limit, stop (stop market), or stop limit. If you select any of the latter three, carefully type in the stop and/or limit prices you want. (Some brokers charge more for limit and stop orders.) Next, select your trade timing parameters: Day Only, GTC, Fill or Kill, Immediate, or Cancel. Then select your nontiming parameters: AON, DNR, Minimum Quantity. (Some brokers charge more for GTC, Fill-or-Kill, Immediate, or Cancel and AON orders; some brokers, such as E*Trade, don't offer you these options at all.) Finally, select whether you want dividends reinvested.

Now check your work. Make sure you've entered everything correctly. Finally, click the Submit Order button. If the trade you have entered is valid, the online broker will then summarize your order and ask you to confirm its accuracy. Check it. Right number of shares? Buy, not sell? Ticker symbol okay? Limit price right? When you're sure, go ahead and enter the order.

Confirming your trades

After entering a trade, your online broker will flash a screen message summarizing the trade you have just placed and may give you a tracking number as well. You might want to print out this screen: It's your proof that the order was accepted by your broker.

Bright Idea
Find out if your broker has a minimum requirement for number of shares per trade and/or price per share. If you want to buy small numbers of shares of stocks with share prices less than $100, some brokers may refuse to execute your orders or may charge you more. This is true for both full-service firms and discounters.

You can also check to see if your order is actually slated to be executed and check its accuracy by checking the Order Status page in your account. If your order has been received by the broker, it will be listed on this page as either open (not yet filled), filled (may say "bought" or "sold"), or canceled (if you changed your mind and canceled the order before it was executed). Call your broker immediately if you discover any discrepancies. All pending orders will remain on this page, but filled orders will disappear by the next day's market opening, although there will be a record of your trades on the Account History or Transaction History page in your account.

When a trade is actually executed, most online brokers will e-mail you a trade confirmation, followed by a confirmation in the regular mail. Be careful, here, though. Some brokers send e-mail *order* confirmations, which indicate only that they have received your order, not that your order has been filled. With these brokers, you must check your Order Status page or Transaction History page to know whether your order has actually gone through. Unfortunately, a number of online brokers update your portfolio only once a day at the end of the day, so you won't know until the end of the day. This is why it's so nice to have real-time portfolio updating and e-mail trade confirmations.

When you receive your trade confirmations, again make sure that they are accurate. If they're not, call your broker immediately. The sooner you report a problem, the easier it will be to correct. If the error was your fault, you will have to pay for it. As you know, if you can prove that it was your broker's fault, your broker will have to pay. Sometimes you will receive duplicate confirmations. This is usually because there was some mistake or omission on the previous confirmation. The last confirmation you receive should be correct.

Do what you can to keep a handle on errors. Get into the habit of writing things down. If you place a trade over the phone, for example, write down what you tell your broker. Better still, fax your broker your order and follow up with a phone call. File the fax. Also, keep written records of all your trades. This way you can check confirmations against your own records to make sure there aren't any discrepancies. Familiarize yourself with your broker's confirmations—the way they usually look and all the information that should appear on them. This way, when something is missing or incorrect, you'll be likely to spot it.

Watch Out!
While the exchanges make every effort to ensure the accuracy of all transactions, errors still do occur. Trades get misplaced, canceled, or filled twice, and are reported out of order; prices and volume are reported incorrectly; and incorrect data gets entered at times.

Tracking your investments

In the days before everyone had a computer, monitoring your investments required checking the financial pages of newspapers and recording share prices or NAV values. Today's online investor simply doesn't have to do this. Many electronic tools available online are easier to use and are more efficient and accurate than the newspapers. Some of the tools available provide key information, such as stock quotes or mutual fund prices; others allow you to post your entire portfolio by entering things such as ticker symbols, number of shares purchased, and price per share. These portfolio tracking tools show you your portfolio's value and the value of your individual holdings.

One widely used free portfolio tracking tools is found on the Yahoo! Finance Web site (http://quote.yahoo.com/). Just log on to the site, click Customize and then Portfolios, and follow the instructions for

Moneysaver
For a top free personalized news service that gives you quotes on stocks, mutual funds, and indexes and sends you e-mail news alerts, check out InfoBeat at www.infobeat. com and click Finance.

creating your online portfolio. There are a number of other free portfolio tracking tools on the Web as well. For a good list of these sites, go to www. investorguide.com/Tracking.htm.

Many online brokers provide investment-tracking tools right on site, although you may not be able to track investments that you don't have with the broker whose portfolio tracker you're using. You can also track your portfolio online on most of the fee-based one-stop shops, such as *The Wall Street Journal* Interactive Edition (http://update.wsj.com/), Briefing (www.briefing.com/), and TheStreet.com (www. thestreet.com/). One-shops are financial sites that offer a variety of tools and information that you can use to help you with your investing. For an extensive list of one-stop shops and links, go to www. investorguide.com/OneStopShops.htm. Some custom news services, which allow you to get just the news you want, offer some portfolio tracking tools and free quotes as well. As mentioned in Chapter 2, "Everything You Need," certain financial software products, such as Quicken Deluxe and Microsoft Money, provide investors with excellent portfolio tracking tools.

Just the facts

- The brokerage account is the standard investment account used by most investors.

- The three trading levels for accounts are cash, margin, and option. Cash accounts require you to have enough cash in your account to cover all the trades you place; margin accounts allow you to borrow funds from your broker; option accounts allow you to buy (and in some cases sell) options.

- Opening an account requires that you fill out and sign an application and send a deposit. You won't be able to use the account until your payment has cleared and you have your user name and password.

- The three major types of orders are market orders, which require a trade to be placed at the best market price; limit orders, which require that an order be placed at a limit price or better; and stop orders, which require a trade to be executed once a certain price is hit. In addition, there are several trade order parameters that you should familiarize yourself with.

- When placing trades, be careful not to make typographical errors; when you get confirmations, always check them for accuracy.

- You can use many online tools, both free and fee-based, to track the performance of your investments.

Building Your Portfolio

PART IV

GET THE SCOOP ON...
Not all newsletters are created equal ▪ Joining
an investment club may be just the
ticket ▪ Surfing the Net for advice ▪ Scams
and cheats

Getting Advice Online

Chapter 10

Make a million bucks! Unbelievable investment opportunity! Over 200 percent a year—guaranteed!!! Hot Tips! Hot Tips! Hot Tips! IPOs poised for take-off! Buy today—tomorrow may be too late! For the novice online investor, venturing forth into cyberspace in search of investment advice can be a bewildering experience, fraught with peril and temptation. It seems like everyone and his grandmother has a hot stock tip for you or a sure-fire investment scheme. But do all these people know which end is up? And what's in it for them, anyway?

While there is no shortage of advice, there certainly is a lack of expertise. You've got to be careful whom you listen to. Be skeptical. Some of the advice available online is solid, some is unsound, and some is designed to bilk you. How do you know what you're getting? One way to protect yourself is to consult an independent rating service from which you can obtain data on the adviser you're interested in. Another is to get the facts on a recommended investment yourself through independent research. If you want some advice but you don't want to pay a full-service broker or an investment adviser, you have to establish some guidelines for separating the wheat from the chaff.

Investment newsletters for fun and profit

Investment newsletters are financial advice publications written, in most cases, by a single person with a specific investment philosophy and strategy. The nice thing about newsletters is that they save you a lot of time and effort. You don't have to go out searching for advice; it comes to you, in the mail. You simply open up your letter, read it, and do pretty much exactly what it tells you to. Investment newsletters are convenient.

There are thousands of investment newsletters out there, both online and off, but following the advice of many of these could be hazardous to your financial health. The advice of many tip sheets isn't worth the paper it's printed on. And if you lose money following the advice of a substandard newsletter, there's not much you can do about it. Newsletters are totally unregulated. You don't have to be a registered financial adviser to publish one; in fact, you don't even need a background in finance or any investment experience ! Anyone can start an investment newsletter, and this is why you need to be so careful about choosing one.

Word of mouth

So how do you go about finding a quality newsletter? One way is to ask other people if they follow a newsletter and if they think it's any good. How long have they followed the newsletter's advice, and how have they done? There are several problems with this approach, however. One is that many people—even people you know well—will be reluctant to tell you they've lost money following a newsletter's advice. Why? It's just human nature; people like to accentuate their victories and minimize their defeats. They may even be lying to themselves. Some people may just not have a clear idea of how they have done. They may not realize that they've actually lost money or made very little.

Short-term trial

Another approach to finding a good newsletter is to simply try out some letters on a trial basis. At first just make experimental investments on paper, to see how well you *would* be doing if you had followed the newsletter's advice. If the results are positive, put a little money behind the advice. If these investments do well, gradually increase the amount.

The only problem with this approach is that it doesn't control luck. Any letter might do well for a few weeks or months, but this could be a fluke.

Hulbert Financial Digest

One approach for choosing a top newsletter is to first subscribe to a newsletter called the *Hulbert Financial Digest.*

> *Hulbert Financial Digest*
> 888-485-2378
> or 703-750-9060
> 5051B Backlick Road
> Annandale, VA 22003
> www.hulbertdigest.com
> $135 per year

The *Hulbert Financial Digest* was founded in 1979 by editor Mark Hulbert to test the claims of newsletter writers, many of whom were promising

Watch Out!
Only long-term data showing consistent returns in good markets and bad can give you meaningful information on the value of newsletters.

extravagant gains for investors following their advice. *Hulbert* tracks the performances of more than 160 stock, mutual fund, gold, bond, and asset allocation newsletters and more than 450 portfolios over periods of 1 year, 3 years, 5 years, 8 years, 10 years, and 15 years in terms of total return and total return on a risk-adjusted basis. Total return is the sum of dividends and capital gains made on an investment over a specified period of time. Total return on a risk-adjusted basis is a way of measuring the amount of money a newsletter is making in terms of how much risk the newsletter is taking. *Hulbert* defines risk as volatility. The more pronounced a portfolio's up and down movements, the riskier it is.

Why is risk-adjusted performance important? Let's compare the results you would get from following the advice of two hypothetical investment newsletters over a five-year period: Letter A and Letter B. At the beginning of the five-year period, Letter A recommends a number of very risky investments and recommends margining as well. Over the next five years, the portfolio's value, by year, reaches +40%, –10%, +20%, –5%, +50%. Over the same period, Letter B recommends far less risky investments, and the portfolio's value goes from +10%, +20%, +30%, +40%, +50%. Letter A and Letter B produced the same results at the end of five years, but which letter do you think would be a better bet for future performance? Probably Letter B because it achieved the same results as Letter A, with much less risk. *Hulbert* suggests that the amount of return a newsletter adviser can produce for the amount of risk he takes is a measurement of skill; therefore, letters with the highest risk-adjusted performance are the most likely to do well in the future.

How many years of performance data are necessary to make a meaningful evaluation of a newsletter? *Hulbert* says five, but he also provides longer time frames. Obviously, the longer a newsletter has performed well, the more compelling the case that the adviser is skilled, not lucky. Consider this: A newsletter that returned 45 percent in its first year is not necessarily a better letter than one that returned only 16 percent in the same year if the second letter has averaged 16 percent annually over the last 15 years. Why? Because one year is not long enough to draw any meaningful conclusions about a newsletter.

True skill vs. dumb luck

Let's take a look at how luck can influence short-term performance figures. Imagine there are three newsletters, Letters A, B, and C. Letter A advises its subscribers to invest 100 percent of their money in one tiny, thinly traded penny stock, and the stock goes up 45 percent in one year. Letter B advises its subscribers to invest 100 percent of their money in a different penny stock, and that company goes bankrupt. Letter C advises its subscribers to invest in a variety of stocks, based on value and historical price stability, and that portfolio goes up 15 percent. Which is the best letter? When the stats come out about newsletters that beat the market at the end of the year, Letter A's editor will be crowned a genius; he'll be on magazine covers, and pundits will marvel at how he was able to achieve a 45 percent return in a year when the S&P 500 was up only 14 percent. Many people will rush to subscribe to his newsletter.

The only problem with these accolades is that Letter A's editor isn't necessarily a genius; he may have just gotten lucky. His only method may have

Bright Idea
When choosing a newsletter, it's important to look not only at risk-adjusted performance but also at the time period over which that performance was achieved.

been to bet the farm on an extremely risky investment and pray. Using such a strategy, he could easily go the way of Letter B next year. What's more, the luck fallacy can distort newsletter performance results for much longer periods than one year. A letter such as Letter A could get lucky for 10 years in a row before the odds finally kick in and he loses everything. Time has a way of weeding out things of low quality.

Suiting your personal style

While total return and risk-adjusted return are paramount in choosing a newsletter, you must never forget the importance of finding a newsletter that fits your individual style and needs.

Of course, if you're planning to invest in mutual funds, for example, you need a mutual fund newsletter; if you want to invest in gold, you need a gold newsletter. But there are more subtle things to look at, too. One of those is risk. No matter how highly *Hulbert* rates a newsletter, if the letter takes more (or less) risk than you feel comfortable with, it is not the letter for you. So, even if a letter is doing well on a risk-adjusted basis, you may be uncomfortable following the letter's advice. Use *Hulbert's* "Long-Term Performance Ratings" report, which comes with your subscription, to check on a newsletter's risk. Also check the report for the average length of time a security in a newsletter's portfolio is held. If the period is short—say, only a couple weeks—be prepared to trade frequently. If it's relatively long—say, a year—be prepared to hold things you buy for a while.

When you're ready to select a newsletter, subscribe for the shortest possible period of time just to try it out, or see if you can get a sample issue. Choosing a newsletter is a lot like shopping for clothes. You go to the store or section that's selling the item you're looking for, browse until you find something that catches your eye, and try it on for size. If it looks good and feels good on you, only then do you buy it. Only when you try a newsletter on for size will you know for sure if it's a fit.

First, ask yourself if you like the newsletter's philosophy and methodology. Does it make sense to you? Are you comfortable with it? Pay close attention to how easy the letter is to use, how easy it is to actually implement the letter's advice. If the letter requires that you watch intraday prices or trade frequently or call a hotline nightly, you may find the letter too difficult to use. During your trial subscription, see how religiously you're able to follow the newsletter's instructions.

When you have settled on a newsletter you like, however, it's vital that you make a commitment to follow its advice for a certain period of time, regardless of initial returns. A commitment is necessary because you might start following a letter just when it makes a couple unsuccessful recommendations (as all newsletters do from time to time). But this should not cause you to waver. You have to give a newsletter a chance to show its stuff. Make a commitment to follow a letter's advice for at least a year, or, better, two years, and have the discipline to follow through on this.

If you have trouble finding a newsletter that fits your philosophy and style perfectly, you might decide to use the newsletter's advice partially. For example, you might love a newsletter's stock picks but not feel comfortable investing 100 percent of your portfolio in stocks at all times as the newsletter does. You could utilize the letter's picks but adjust your market exposure according to how bullish or bearish you were at any given time.

Another idea is to subscribe to two top letters at the same time and invest within the framework of the recommendations made by both letters, based on your proclivities. You might subscribe to one letter that times the market and another that is always 100 percent invested in stocks, investing in the stock letter's picks only during buy signals from your timer. Whatever strategy you decide to pursue, however, it's important for you to have the discipline to follow that strategy faithfully for a predetermined period of time. This is the key to success in following the advice of investment newsletters.

The *Hulbert Financial Digest* also measures the number of securities owned by a portfolio, how clearly the letter tells you what to do, and how good the timing of the adviser's recommendations is.

The top newsletters

Hulbert ranked newsletters on a risk-adjusted basis for the last fifteen years, as of June 31, 1999. The highest-ranking newsletters are discussed below.

Systems and Forecasts

Systems and Forecasts ranked first on *Hulbert*'s list.

> Systems and Forecasts
> 516-829-6444
> 150 Great Neck Road
> Great Neck, NY 11021
> www.siesite.com
> $225 a year; $65 for three months

Systems and Forecasts showed an average annual gain of 13.8 percent for the Regular Portfolio (compared

Moneysaver
Check out *INVESTools*, which provides advice and content from more than 400 newsletters for free (at www. investools. com), and *Investors Newsletter Digest*, which costs $69 a year (at www. investornews. com).

to a gain of 17.8 percent for the Dow and the S&P for the same period). The amazing thing is that *Systems and Forecasts* achieved this return at about half the risk of the stock market. Gerald Appel, the editor of *Systems and Forecasts*, is a market timer and is famous for developing the MACD, a tool widely employed by technical analysts (see Chapter 11, "Venturing Out on Your Own").

Appel uses a market timing tool named Time Trend III to determine when investors should be in or out of the stock market. He makes specific mutual fund recommendations when Time Trend gives a buy signal, and he also recommends purchasing options on occasion, even in the Regular Portfolio, to protect against unexpected market downturns.

In addition to the Regular Portfolio, *Systems and Forecasts* has the Jack White Portfolio, which is to be traded through the Jack White brokerage firm, the Futures & Options Portfolio, and the Fidelity Select Portfolio. All these additional portfolios have done well, posting higher returns than the Regular Portfolio (except for Fidelity Select), but at higher risk. Some investors who like *Systems & Forecast*'s low risk but are dissatisfied with the total returns augment returns by buying additional shares on margin.

The Chartist

The second highest-ranked newsletter by Hulbert was *The Chartist*, edited by Dan Sullivan.

> *The Chartist*
> 310-596-2385
> P.O. Box 758
> Seal Beach, CA 90740
> $150 per year; $35 for three months

The Chartist had an average annual gain of 19.8 percent. Sullivan, who has been publishing *The Chartist* since the 1960s, bases his advice on a combination of market timing and relative strength. Relative strength is a measure of how well a stock is performing relative to other stocks, and Sullivan chooses for his portfolios stocks that have high relative strength. Sullivan's basic strategy is to be fully invested in the strongest stocks when the market is moving up and to cut back on positions, or at least not add to positions, when the market is going down. Relative strength stocks. While relative stock strengths move up faster than most when the market is climbing, they tend to move down faster than most when the market is falling, a fact that accounts for the higher-than-average riskiness of *The Chartist's* portfolios.

No-Load Fund X

Third in the rankings was *No-Load Fund X*, edited by Burton Berry.

> *No-Load Fund X*
> 415-986-7979
> 235 Montgomery St., Suite 662
> San Francisco, CA 94104
> www.fundx.com
> $129 per year

As of June 31, 1999, *No-Load Fund X* had an average annual total return of 15.4 percent. Berry ranks no-load (and some low-load) mutual funds on their performance over the past one month, places them into different risk categories, and recommends that you purchase the top-rated fund in the risk category of your choice, if you're not already holding a fund. The strategy calls for you to sell a fund when it drops out of the top five and then purchase the top-rated fund in your category at that time. Only the Class 3 port-folio is ahead of the Wilshire 5000 on a risk-adjusted bases over the last 15 years.

Investor's World

Fourth in the rankings is *Investor's World*, edited by John Dessauer.

> *Investor's World*
> 800-804-0942
> 7811 Montrose Road
> Potomac, MD 20854
> $195 per year; $35 for two months

Investor's World had an average annual total return of 15.6 percent over the last 15 years. Dessauer provides buy, hold, and sell recommendations on domestic and international securities, although he does not tell you how much of your portfolio should be invested in anything he recommends—he leaves that up to you. Dessauer is a buy-and-hold investor; the average holding time of securities in the portfolio is more than two years (737 days).

Value Line Investment Survey

Fifth in the rankings is the legendary *Value Line Investment Survey*, edited by Value Line Publishing.

> *The Value Line Investment Survey*
> 800-634-3583
> Value Line Publishing
> 220 East 42nd St.
> New York, NY 10017
> www.valueline.com.
> $570 per year ($260 per year to renew)

Value Line has an average annual return of 15.9 percent over the last 15 years. Published since the 1930s, *Value Line* developed a stock rating system in the 1960s in which a rating from 1 to 5 was assigned to all the stocks in its pool of 1,700. Stocks receiving a rating of 1 for timeliness are those expected to perform the best over the next 12 months. *Value Line* also ranks stocks on the basis of a number of other factors, including safety, timeliness of industry, highest and lowest PEs, and highest projected three- to five-year annual returns.

Value Line subscribers can use the plethora of data available on individual stocks and the various rankings to construct their own portfolios. One classic approach, however, is to construct a portfolio of stocks ranked 1 for timeliness and to replace a stock that drops to a lower ranking with another level 1 stock. This way, your portfolio always consists of level 1 stocks. Another classic approach is to create a portfolio of level 1 stocks and hold it for a year, at which time all stocks whose ratings have dropped are replaced with new level 1 stocks. *Value Line* has three model portfolios you can follow: one for conservative investors, one for long-term investors, and one for aggressive investors.

Investment clubs are all the rage

An investment club is a group of individual investors who pool their funds and invest as a team in agreed-upon securities, usually individual stocks or DRIPs. The average initial amount you must contribute to join an investment club is in the range of $200–$500. After that, you contribute $20 or $25 a month on average. Club income and expenses are distributed among members according to how much each has contributed. Members convene—usually once a month—to learn about investing, discuss possible investments for the club, and discuss, argue about, and vote on investment proposals. Some clubs require a consensus for a go-ahead; most

66

No man is so foolish but he may sometimes give another good counsel, and no man so wise that he may not easily err if he takes no other counsel than his own. He that is taught only by himself has a fool for a master.
—Ben Johnson

99

CHAPTER 10 ■ GETTING ADVICE ONLINE   335

require a simple majority. There are now around 40,000 investment clubs in the United States, up about 300 percent since 1993.

Most investment clubs put a real emphasis on studying investing and investments and provide excellent support for beginner investors. Members actively participate in what happens to their money. Usually, at a meeting each member is assigned to research a certain stock or industry and present at the next meeting a stock report and give a recommendation whether to buy the stock. Studying, learning about, and researching investments—and being supported by a group whose collective wisdom is much greater than their own—gives members a feeling of safety and comfort. As their knowledge and confidence build, many inexperienced investors become quite seasoned and start individual portfolios of their own.

Many clubs belong to the National Association of Investors Corporation (NAIC), which provides clubs with invaluable guidelines for investing as a group. Membership costs $35 a year for a club, plus $14 a year per club member.

> National Association of Investors Corporation
> 877-275-6242
> or 248-583-6242
> P.O. Box 220
> Royal Oak, MI 48068
> fax: 248-583-4880
> www.better-investing.org

Legally, most investment clubs are partnerships. A partnership is a business organization in which two or more people join together by contract and share in the profits and losses of a business. With partnerships, the individual members pay taxes on their

Watch Out!
If your invest-
ment club has
more than 100
members, or if
some members in
the club are
passively
benefiting from
the efforts of the
other members
rather than
actively
participating in
the research and
decision-making,
you may have to
register your
club with the
SEC as an
investment
company,
creating a tax
liability for the
club as a whole.

investment returns individually. So, the club files a partnership return with the IRS, and then each member reports his or her earnings from club investments on their own tax returns (using a K-1 form).

So, are investment clubs any good? Actually, investment clubs have done quite well historically. The NAIC reports that on average its members outperform the S&P 500, which is more than most professional mutual fund managers can say! One of the reasons for this could be that investment clubs have lower costs than mutual funds. The returns mutual fund managers achieve are always truncated by the fund's fees, which reduce the fund's total return numbers. Another reason may be that clubs tend to trade less frequently than fund managers, which also minimizes expenses. The turnover of the average mutual fund is 80 percent—that means four out of five stocks in a fund at any given time were not in the fund a year prior.

One of the great strengths of most investment clubs is the diversity of their members. Doctors, construction workers, housewives, pilots, college students, and engineers can all be represented in a single club. Having individuals from all walks of life in a club brings different perspectives to investments and decision making. A housewife, for example, may know what household products are superior, and this may give the club a lead on which companies in the household products industry the club should research. An engineer might be aware of a company making outstanding hydraulic equipment. Individual club members generate creative investment ideas that help clubs build diversified portfolios. Go to Investment Club Central at www.iclubcentral.com/ for lots of information on investment clubs.

Joining an investment club

If you don't know of any investment clubs near you, or if you're just not interested in joining any of the ones you know about, see how the NAIC can help you. While the NAIC is not allowed to refer people to clubs, they have more than 100 councils nationwide that hold investor workshops and other events every year. Your best bet is to attend an NAIC-sponsored event near you and talk to people there about clubs and your interest in joining one. Network.

You can also search online for online clubs. Check out About.com at http://investmentclub. miningco.com/mlibrary.htm for lists of Internet clubs all over the country. Incidentally, don't expect to see any ads for investment clubs—SEC regulations actually prohibit investment clubs from advertising for new members.

Before joining a club, it's important to determine whether the club's investment philosophy jibes with your own. Are they contrarian investors? If so, are you? Does the group consist of short-term traders who want to buy and sell mostly Internet stocks? If it does, will you be comfortable with that? One of the most common conflicts arising in investment clubs concerns how long securities should be held. Some investors are much more comfortable with long-term investments, preferring to buy and hold; others prefer buying and selling more frequently. Try to find out where a club stands on issues of philosophy and style before you commit.

Another important consideration is whether you like the people in the group and think you can work with them. An investment club can last a lifetime, and you certainly wouldn't want your money tied up with a bunch of people you can't stand for that long. Of course, you could always cash out, but you might

Unofficially...
Even when markets are going down, investment clubs invest a set amount in the market, but mutual fund managers may have less cash to work with at these times because of increased shareholder redemptions. Having capital available to invest when prices are depressed may be one reason why the historical returns of investment clubs compare favorably with those of mutual funds.

be reluctant to do this if the club is doing reasonably well. Better to tie your fortunes to a group you like from the start.

Not all clubs last long, however. Eighteen months seems to be the cut-off point. If a club stays together longer than that, it usually means that the members share a similar investment philosophy and enjoy each other's company.

How to start an investment club

It's often easier to start your own investment club than find a compatible club that already exists. Existing clubs—especially good ones—have limited memberships and low turnover rates. If you decide to start your own club, you first need to learn the basics of investment clubs yourself. Buy the NAIC's book *Starting & Running a Successful Investment Club,* available from the NAIC or at many bookstores. Also visit the NAIC's Web site and seriously consider joining.

While the NAIC does a great job providing you with the guidance and materials you need to start your own club, you might not want to stop there. Consider consulting a business adviser and some brokers about your plan, too. You may get some valuable suggestions and advisories. This may seem like a lot of work, but research has shown that the more carefully you plan your club, the greater your chances are for success.

With a basic understanding of investment clubs under your belt, you should start talking to people whom you think might be interested in joining your club. You may find people who would be interested at your church, at a club you belong to, at work, or in your neighborhood. When you have a few people who are interested, ask them to talk to a few of their friends.

Timesaver
In addition to all the instructional materials you'll get with your NAIC membership, you'll receive the magazine *Better Investing,* which is full of investment ideas and educational material. The NAIC also offers investing software, an advisory service, and a low-cost investment plan to get you started in DRIPs.

You should aim to have about 12 people, a minimum of 10 and a maximum of 20. If you choose a number that falls outside these parameters, you should still establish an upper and a lower limit. If you have too few people, you'll lack the funds you need to create a diversified portfolio, and you may also lack a diversity of ideas. If you have too many people, it will be hard to have productive discussions and hard to find a place to meet. Also, you should be looking for people with various backgrounds— try not to draw all your people from the same place. At the same time, you want the members in your club to be people you like and can trust.

The next step in forming your own club is to distribute basic information about investment clubs to all the people who have expressed interest and then you set a time, date, and place for a preliminary meeting. Make sure people know that coming to the first meeting is not a commitment to join. At the preliminary meeting, discuss how the club will be run, and try to get a feel for whether you can all work together. Are you compatible? Do you all have similar investment goals and philosophies?

Differences in investment philosophy do not mean that the club cannot work, but it is best if all members can agree on some basic principles. For example, you might agree to invest within the framework of the NAIC's guidelines for investing, or some other approach. Ideally, you would all agree to use certain written materials to back up this standard. In the case of the NAIC, you could use *Starting & Running a Successful Investment Club*. But if the majority are interested in gradual, low-risk wealth accumulation, the unapologetically aggressive investors present should probably look elsewhere for a club, or form their own.

In this preliminary meeting you also need to make it clear that being in a successful investment club is hard work. All members of the club should be interested in investigating and analyzing securities and making reports to the rest of the group. In fact, it's a good idea to require prospective members to go through a trial membership period to see if they're really going to do their part. Before going any further with this process, every potential member of your investment club must also understand that it's possible to lose money investing with a club, even with careful investing, and that most investment clubs don't start showing a profit until two or three years after they start up.

Once the major considerations are out of the way, you'll need to talk about a number of particulars. First, how much will the monthly contribution be? Many clubs start small—say, at $20 or $25—and gradually increase. Others keep the amount constant but allow individual members to contribute more if they so choose. Members should be advised not to put all their money in the club; they should have their own separate savings or investment accounts to do with as they please. A checking account at a bank, S&L, credit union, or brokerage should be opened in the club's name, not a member's, and the club should get its own taxpayer ID number from the IRS.

Last on the financial agenda is choosing a broker and deciding who's going to place trades with the broker. Many brokerages offer club accounts, but these are really no different than individual accounts, for all intents and purposes.

Next, where and how often will you meet? Clubs meet anywhere and everywhere—living rooms, coffeehouses, and unused meeting rooms in office buildings. Wherever you meet, try to hold meetings at a regular time and place so that they become a part of everyone's routine. (Most clubs meet once a month.) Also decide on the format for your meetings—there should be a regular agenda. Most investment club meetings run between one and three hours.

Other things that have to be discussed before you adjourn your preliminary meeting are picking a club name and establishing the minimum and maximum number of members, how officers will be selected, and how to deal with departing and incoming members. When all the issues have been discussed and agreed upon, you'll need to draw up a written agreement that includes all these items.

Keys to success

So how can you be sure you'll make money with an investment club? How can you tell a good club from a bad one? Well, there are no guarantees, nor is there an independent entity, such as the *Hulbert Financial Digest*, to evaluate different clubs. But successful clubs have certain qualities in common.

One is hard work. The odds of success of an investment club are largely determined by how much effort club members put into it. Regular meetings and attendance by all members is essential, as is thorough research of potential investments. "Do your homework!" say the Beardstown Ladies, an investment club consisting of septuagenarians in Beardstown, Illinois.

In addition to the importance of good old hard work, having an investment strategy and sticking to it are also key. Many of the successful clubs invest according to a set of four basic principles established by the NAIC:

Bright Idea
In selecting a broker for your investment club, first ask if any of the members have a broker they would like to recommend. Also, call some brokers and ask if they have a person who specializes in investment clubs.

1. Invest regular sums of money once a month in common stock. This helps you obtain a lower average cost on your investments.

2. Reinvest all earnings, dividends, and capital gains. Your money grows faster if earnings are reinvested. This way, compounding of your money is at work for you.

3. Buy growth stocks, companies whose sales and earnings are increasing at a rate faster than the industry in general. They should have good prospects for continued growth—in other words, they should be stronger, larger companies five years from now.

4. Invest in different industries. Diversification helps spread both risk and opportunity.

The NAIC has also established guidelines for individual stock selection, which are contained in the NAIC's *Stock Selection Guide.* These include studying a stock's earnings per share, price per earnings ratio, dividend yield, and sales growth. The guide provides formulas for establishing buy and sell zones for a stock based on your research data.

To be successful, your club needs to avoid certain things. One is short-term trading. Because clubs meet only periodically and make decisions as a group, it's difficult for them to buy and sell frequently and make the quick decisions necessary for successful short-term trading. For the same reasons, momentum investing is not a good idea. Technical analysis, which requires a great deal of study to understand and necessitates keeping an eye on the markets at all times, also isn't practical for clubs. In addition, clubs should avoid selling options or investing in commodities—investments that could backfire and put members in debt.

Unofficially...
Remember: Even if your investment club does everything right, it may take a few years before you're really making money.

The two most common reasons for a club's demise are conflict of personalities or investment philosophies, and trouble finding anyone who is willing to be the treasurer. The treasurer must spend an average of 10 hours a month crunching numbers, tracking money, paying bills, calculating dividend payouts, and putting together detailed charts of each stock's performance. The treasurer is also the one who often does the club's taxes. Most members don't want this thankless job; they just want to watch the share prices of the club's holdings climb. But the job of treasurer is vital.

Perhaps the most famous investment club in the world, The Beardstown Ladies, became world-famous, wrote a best-selling book, and sparked a huge growth in investment clubs nationwide because of the legendary 23 percent annual return they achieved over a 10-year period. Then it was discovered that the treasurer had made a mistake and inflated the club's returns by some 150 percent! The treasurer is a key to your club's success.

According to Kara K. Choquette of *USA Today*, there are several things you can do to support your treasurer.

- Rotate treasurers. Every few years, elect a new treasurer so that one person doesn't get stuck with the job for life and so that more people learn how to balance the club's books.

- Require all club members to be at every meeting, and insist that everyone scrutinize the treasurer's charts for errors.

- Require the incumbent treasurer to train a new treasurer for a set period before resigning the post.

Watch Out!
Since 1951 the NAIC has recorded 21 cases of investment club fraud. The cases typically involve a club official, usually the treasurer, stealing the club's money. One of these cases involved a family investment club!

- Select a couple members to audit the books every year.

- Buy computer software to make the treasurer's job easier.

As hard as they work, treasurers are usually the ones who, when it happens, abscond with the club's money. One way to prevent this is to set up the club's bank account so that withdrawals or checks of more than $25 require two signatures. You can also have duplicate copies of statements sent to other club officers. Some clubs make it a rule to check a person's references and credit history before appointing the person treasurer. It's also possible to purchase fidelity bonds from the NAIC, which provide limited coverage for the club's funds in case of embezzlement.

What about online clubs?

Believe it or not, some investment clubs meet only online. Members of online clubs log on at a preset time and go through the meeting agenda—online. The key difference between online clubs and live clubs is that even when meetings are over, members continue to correspond and float ideas. Many online investment clubs have their own private message boards.

Online clubs have a number of advantages. One is that there are no geographic boundaries separating potential members. Members can come from all over the country or the world! Also, membership in the club is not restricted to the people you or your friends know. Members can be recruited from the depths of cyberspace. Online clubs also are convenient. No traveling to and from a meeting place—you just jump on your computer, and you're there.

There are some disadvantages to online investment clubs. Setting up an online club can be more difficult than setting up an offline club, in part because everything has to be done through writing messages. There's no substitute for good old real-time, face-to-face dialogue. It's also harder to maintain interest in online clubs, perhaps because less bonding occurs between members in an online environment. And because you won't necessarily meet all or any of the members in the club before you join, there could be an unsavory character or two among the bunch.

If you don't decide to join an online club, you can still make use of online resources for the benefit of your club. E-mail provides a great way for members to communicate with each other between meetings, as do message boards. The Motley Fool, a famous investment Web site, will actually provide message board space for your club for free. Go to www.fool.com/InvestmentClub for information. You can also set up a Web page for your club for free through StockCentral. Go to www.investmentclubs. com and send an e-mail to editor@stockcetral.com. Having your own message board gives you a perfect place to discuss stock ideas with other members between meetings, talk about news affecting your club's stocks, exchange information, and plan the agenda for your next meeting. And as always, the Internet is a great place to research stocks and can be a source of investment ideas for your club.

Discussion groups

Many independent investors forgo newsletters and investment clubs and get their investment advice from various kinds of online discussion groups. The advantages of this approach are that it's free, it's convenient, and there's no commitment in terms of time or money. People come and go as they please in discussion groups; there is no limit on the number of people in the group, nor are there necessarily any core members. Discussions are free-flowing, and there is rarely a preset agenda.

The most significant difference between discussion groups and investment clubs, however, is that participants in discussion groups don't pool their investment funds, so there is no built-in commitment to other members in the group. As a result, there is much less consistency in the quality of the advice and information about investments that floats freely in discussion groups. One person might be a guru, and the next a dunce.

The best way to separate the geniuses from the dolts is to hang out at a few discussion groups and follow along without participating (called lurking). After a while, you should start to sense who knows what they're talking about and who doesn't. If you can establish an online relationship with some of the folks who are more in tune and are making money, you may be able to get some profitable advice.

Bulletin board systems

One source of online investment discussion groups is electronic bulletin board systems (BBSs). A BBS is an online exchange center for messages and other files between computer users connected to a central computer. Many BBSs are actually run off small home computers that have the necessary software to keep track of messages, files, and users. Some BBSs are devoted to one topic, such as medicine, dogs, or cars; others are more general. BBSs originated and generally operate independently of the Internet,

Watch Out!
Whatever you do, don't buy the first thing you hear someone recommend on some discussion group somewhere on the Web. Wait, observe, and see how useful the advice is before investing.

although many BBSs now have their own Web pages. Before the Internet and the Web became popular, computer users exchanged e-mail and posted and responded to messages on BBSs. There are currently some 40,000 BBSs worldwide.

The Usenet is essentially the world's largest BBS, and there are thousands of newsgroups on the Usenet where people discuss thousands of different topics, including investing. Newsreader software (a news client) is required to download and read articles from newsgroups, but many ISPs provide access, as long as you have fairly recent browser software (later than Navigator 3.1). If you don't, go to www.forteinc.com and download Free Agent. If you do, open your browser, click your mail icon, and then double-click Discussion Groups or Newsgroups. If you get an error message, your news client may not be installed, or you may just need to reconfigure your browser for newsgroup access. Follow the instructions provided by your news client software manual, or give your ISP a call. Otherwise, the newsreader software will create a database of all the newsgroups available, which may take a minute or two.

Using key words, you can search newsgroups for those dealing with the subject matter you're interested in by clicking on the Search tab at the top of your newsgroup page and entering a key word, such as "invest." Because newsgroup names are abbreviated, you may not get a hit on your search if you use longer words. Your search may turn up several groups related to your topic. If you want to take a look at a group, you need to subscribe to the group by clicking the Subscribe button. Then go back to your e-mail page and click that discussion group's icon, which will now be on the page under the news icon. You can also unsubscribe by selecting the discussion group icon and hitting Delete. For an excellent list of investment newsgroups, go to the Syndicate Web site at www.moneypages.com/syndicate/finance/newsgrps.html. Also take a look at the following investment newsgroups:

- misc.invest
- misc.invest.stocks
- alt.invest
- misc.invest.funds

While newsgroup participants largely exchange interesting and useful information on investing, there is a great deal of spam to sift through. *Spam* is an unsolicited message, often commercial in nature, sent or posted to a large number of people or to newsgroups. Spam has become a huge problem in newsgroups—more than 50 percent of the content of some newsgroups is spam. Be especially wary of get-rich-quick spam (scam spam). Newsgroups with a lot of spam or off-topic discussion are said to have a low signal-to-noise ratio. if you want to avoid that, seek out moderated newsgroups, which have gatekeepers who filter out the noise. Many BBSs have Web pages now. For a list of these, go to http://dir.yahoo.com/Computers_and_Internet/Communications_and_Networking/BBSs/. Users of online commercial services such as AOL and CompuServe will have access to commercial newsgroups not available to nonsubscribers. AOL calls its proprietary newsgroups message boards, and CompuServe calls its newsgroups forums.

For all the information you'd ever want about how newsgroups work, go to www.cs.indiana.edu/docproject/zen/zen-1.0_6.html#SEC31.

Mailing lists

Mailing lists are similar to newsgroups in that they both focus on a particular topic. The difference is that a new posting is sent directly to everyone on the mailing list by e-mail, but no one else has access to it. Mailing lists are an attractive alternative to newsgroups because they eliminate spam. Many mailing lists have a moderator who receives all the mail first, screens it, and decides which messages to pass on to the mailing list subscribers. The moderator can expel members who regularly post objectionable material. Other mailing lists are unmoderated, and any and all messages are automatically sent to all subscribers.

The major drawback of mailing lists is that some generate hundreds of postings a day, and subscribers are bombarded with more e-mail than they can possibly read. There are two kinds of mailing lists: participatory and nonparticipatory. With the former, your responses and input are encouraged; with the latter, you just read what you receive.

Here's a list of some good investment mailing lists:

- U.S., Canadian, and overseas stocks. Participatory. E-mail the message SUBSCRIBE INVESTORS to boock@ix.netcom.com.

- Investing in general. Participatory. E-mail the message SUBSCRIBE INVESTMENT-TALK to Majordomo@mission-a.com.

- Mutual funds. Participatory. E-mail the message SUBSCRIBE INVESTORS to Majordomo@shore.net.

- Investment information. Nonparticipatory. E-mail the message SUBSCRIBE to bobbose@stockresearch.com.

Moneysaver
Before putting money down on an online investment tip, check it out with your financial adviser, broker, or attorney.

Web-based discussion groups, also known as message boards or forums, are another popular medium for the exchange of investment ideas and information online. The central difference between newsgroups and message boards is that the latter are linked to Web sites, and the former—at least those that don't have their own Web sites—are not. Spam also seems to be less of a problem for message boards. Some decent investment forums can be found at or through the following sites:

- www.investorville.com/ubb/Forum1/HTML/000015.html

- www.investorville.com/cgi-local/Ultimate.cgi

- http://boards.fool.com/

Chat rooms

Chat rooms provide online investors with yet another way to get investment ideas and advice online. Chat rooms are virtual rooms where a number of users can convene and discuss a topic in real time on the Internet, BBSs, and other online locales. In fact, a chat room is a computer (chat server) that allows a number of people to log on at the same time. This is what makes it possible for people to send each other messages in real time.

The software that enables you to access chat rooms is called a chat client. Many chat clients are available, but all fall into one of three categories: Internet Relay Chat (IRC), Web-based chat, and hybrid chat.

Internet Relay Chat (IRC) supports text-only chat for the Internet. It's very efficient, but the commands can be a little difficult to master. One of the most popular IRC clients is

Unofficially... While the medium of communication in chat rooms is, for the most part, typed messages, software is now available to allow users to send audio and video messages back and forth and to use graphics in conjunction with typed text.

mIRC; you can download it for free from the mIRC home page at www.mirc.co.uk/ or from TUCOWS at www.tucows.com/.

Web-based chat uses HTML and Java programming language, enabling you to chat on Web site chat rooms. As the Web has become more popular, so have these clients. They're easy to use, and they allow you to send graphics in addition to text, although they tend to be a bit slow. You download the chat client appropriate for the chat room you want to enter at the Web site.

Hybrid chat clients combine the speed of IRC with the user-friendliness of Web-based clients. Hybrid clients allow you to surf the Net as you chat, but they don't really provide real-time chat, and they require a lot of memory to run. The three most popular hybrid clients are AOL Instant Messenger (www.aol.com/aim/), AOL's ICQ (www.miabilis.com), and Jamsoft NetPopup www.vtoy.fi-malo/netpopup.html), all of which can be downloaded for free from the Web sites for these clients.

So how do you find chat rooms that discuss investing? Many Web sites have their own chat rooms; go to or search for popular Web sites that relate to your topic and see if they have any chat rooms. Another option is to explore an online community. Online communities are sites on the Web designed to link people with common interests, and they often provide users with free services such as e-mail and space for personal Web pages, in addition to information and chat rooms. Check out Tripod at www.tripod.com/ and Talk City at www.talkcity.com/.

Watch Out!
One thing to keep in mind when you download chat clients is the possibility of picking up a virus. Always scan clients you download with your virus software before you use them.

As fun as chatting and sending messages back and forth to online partners can be, following the advice of online advisers is risky because there's no objective way to evaluate their expertise or their intentions. Whether you're participating in newsgroups, mailing lists, message boards, or chat rooms, it's prudent to get a second opinion and do some research of your own before putting your money down.

Scams and Cheats

Questionable ability is not the only reason you need to be wary of the investment advice you get over the Internet. All too often, the source of the advice has an ulterior motive. The Internet provides an almost ideal environment for scam artists, allowing them to reach thousands of unsuspecting individuals through fraudulent (though often professional-looking and attractive) Web sites, bogus messages on message boards, and other tactics.

Newsletters

The first area to be wary of is online investment newsletters. Unlike the newsletters tracked by Hulbert, online letters have no publicly disclosed and verifiable track record. Some of these letters are legit, but many of them, which claim to offer investors free, unbiased stock tips, are a scam. They're being paid by the very companies whose stocks they are promoting!

Although this is not illegal, the SEC requires that newsletters tell you this—who is paying them, how much, and in what form. But many don't. Instead, they position themselves as independent and declare their picks to be based on a great deal of in-depth research. Often the editors of these newsletters buy the stock they're hyping themselves and sell it when the price goes up (called pump and dump).

The unwitting investors, of course, are left holding the stock when the price plummets. Crooked online newsletters have a funny tendency to lie about their track records as well.

Newsgroups

Newsgroups, message boards, mailing lists, and chat rooms are commonly frequented by con artists. As with rogue online newsletter advisers, chat room and message board scammers like to use the pump and dump method. It's also often hard to tell if a person advocating an investment on an online forum is working for that company. What appears to be an open discussion between fellow investors could be a thinly disguised sales pitch. Unlike online newsletter editors, these people can legally hide their identity behind aliases, so you really have no idea whom you're dealing with.

Pump and dump

A red flag should go up when any person recommending a stock says he has "inside" or "confidential" information about upcoming announcements, "hot" new products, mergers, and the like. Also be cautious if this person urges you to buy quickly— "Tomorrow May Be Too Late!!" Investing right away wouldn't give you time to investigate the stock for yourself, and that may be the point. Another tip-off that an investment may not be on the up and up is the wording used to describe it: "Unbelievable Opportunity!" "Killer Stocks Ready for Blastoff!!" Any kind of hype title could indicate a scam. You should be particularly wary if someone is recommending a small, thinly traded stock.

Pump and dump scams on the Internet are widespread. On October 28, 1998, the SEC announced measures taken against 44 stock promoters for failing

Timesaver
Before investing in or even researching a tip received from an online newsletter, check with the SEC or your state securities regulator to see if the newsletter has a bad history. You can check the SEC's Enforcement Division's home page for this information at www.sec.gov/ enforce.htm, or call the SEC at 202-942-8090.

to disclose that they were being paid by the companies whose stock they were promoting.

Pyramid schemes

While the pump and dump is probably the most popular scam, you also need to watch out for others. The pyramid scam is one in which participants make money by recruiting new participants. Watch out for messages saying things like, "Make a Fortune Working at Home!" or "Big Bucks From Your Home Computer!" What these programs generally involve is you sending in money for an instructional packet that tells you how to get people to send you money for instructional packets. If it's an envelope-stuffing program, you'll probably be stuffing envelopes containing the same promotional material you originally read on the Internet.

"Risk-free" frauds

You've also got to be on the lookout for "risk-free" frauds. These messages often suggest that your principal is "protected," that the investment is "as safe" as a certificate of deposit, or that "profits are guaranteed." That guaranteed return also is often promised to be high, if not spectacularly high. Remember, with any legitimate investment, the higher the potential return, the *greater* the risk. These scams often involve unusual or exotic-sounding investments like "prime bank securities," "ostrich farms," "gemstones," and "wireless cable television." And there's usually hype: "Once In A Lifetime Opportunity!" or "Limited Time Offer!" If it sounds too good to be true, it probably is.

Offshore frauds

Then there are the offshore frauds. Foreign scam artists populate cyberspace, peddling exotic-sounding, high-return vehicles that just don't exist.

> 66
>
> I owe my success to having listened respectfully to the very best advice, and then going away and doing the exact opposite.
> —G. K. Chesterton
>
> 99

When they entice enough people to send them their money, they just disappear. ("We're sorry, this number is no longer in service.") Being overseas gives these hooligans a huge advantage over U.S.-based swindlers: It's harder to trace your money when you send it abroad, and it's much more difficult for U.S. authorities to track down foreign crooks and bring them to justice. Distance previously insulated U.S. citizens from overseas scam artists, but with the advent of the Internet, the buffer has disappeared.

Misrepresented rates of return

Another scam that you should be aware of, one that might be more appropriately labeled a trick, revolves around the way many mutual fund companies are reporting fund performance. Instead of reporting a fund's compounded annual return, which reflects the true performance of the fund, they report its "average annual gain," a grossly inflated number. For example, if an account that started with a value of $100,000 rose to a little over $300,000 in five years, the unscrupulous fund company would report that the fund had an "average annual gain" of 40% ($200,000/5 years = $40,000/year or 40 percent). But this calculation does not take into account the effect of compounding, the fact that each year all dividends and capital gains were reinvested. So the actual average yearly gain for the fund is closer to 24.6 percent. How do you figure this for yourself? Well, do the math. Year 1: $100,000 × 24.6 percent = $124,600; Year 2: $124,600 × 24.6 percent = $155,251.60; Year 3: $155,251.60 × 24.6 percent = $193,443.49; Year 4: $193,443.49 × 24.6 percent = $241,030.58; Year 5: $241,030.58 × 24.6 percent = $300,324.10. In short, beware of "average annual gain" numbers. What you want to know is the compounded annual return.

Mutual fund companies also like to report the most favorable periods of fund performance to make a fund look better than it is. A fund company might report that such-and-such fund rose 60 percent from, say, 6/97–6/99, leaving out the fact that prior to 6/97 the fund lost money, as it did after 6/99. Moreover, they don't tell you that the fund's lifetime compounded annual return is only 5.8 percent. Watch out for those short-term performance figures. Even if they're not skewed, short-term strength does not a stellar fund make.

How to avoid being taken

The overriding rule of thumb in utilizing investment advice you get online is never to invest in something based solely on what someone tells you. Take the time to check it out for yourself before you hand over your money. When you see an investment idea that looks interesting, first print out the page or message promoting the investment. Make sure you get the URL or e-mail address, and note the date. Next, ask the person recommending the investment how much they were paid to promote it and in what state the company he's recommending is incorporated.

Bright Idea
Assume that any investment tip you get online is a scam until proven otherwise. If you're excited about something you hear about online, investigate it independently and get all the facts before you actually put your money down.

Next, make sure the company being recommended is registered with the SEC, and read its reports. You can access these from the SEC's EDGAR database at www.sec.gov/edgarhp.htm. Some companies that make less than $5 million a year may be exempt from registering their securities or filing their reports on EDGAR. But they still have to file financial statements and other information with the SEC. If you can't find a company on EDGAR, call the SEC at 202-942-8090 and find out if the company filed an offering circular under

Regulation A or a Form D. Also ask to have a copy sent to you. While you have the SEC on the phone, ask if they have received any complaints about the company, its management, or its promoters. Also ask if the broker handling the stock is registered with the SEC.

After you talk to the SEC, call up your state securities regulator and ask if they have any information about the company being recommended and the people who run it. Your state securities regulator can also check the Central Registration Depository (CRD) to see if the broker handling the stock is registered to do business in your state, if the broker has a disciplinary history, and if the stock has been cleared for sale in your state. You can also check on the broker, as mentioned in Chapter 8, "Choosing a Broker," by calling the National Association of Securities Dealers, Inc., (NASD) on their toll-free public disclosure hotline: 800-289-9999.

If things check out so far, the next thing to do is to get the promoter or company in question to send you the company's annual report, financial statements, and a prospectus. When these come, analyze them. Do the facts and figures about the company as reflected in the materials you were sent match what the SEC has online? You should be able to dig up additional information about the company at the library, including payment analysis, credit reports, lawsuits, liens, and judgments. If the company is reluctant to send you anything or simply refuses, stay away!

The SEC recommends that you also check out claims about new products and big contracts, call the company's suppliers and find out if they're really doing business with the company, and make sure

Watch Out!
If you see an advertisement on the Internet for free stock, don't believe it. These ads are just designed to get you to visit the underlying Web site and divulge personal information. If the site offers you any "stock," it will surely be worthless.

Timesaver
A good place to start if you're suspicious about an investment is the National Fraud. Information Center's Consumer Assistance Service, which can answer your questions about online fraud and tell you how to file complaints. Call toll-free at 1-800-876-7060.

that the people running the company have made money for shareholders before. For an excellent list of questions you should ask people who are promoting investment products, go to www.sec.gov/consumer/askqinv.htm. Here are some of the questions you should be sure to ask:

- Does this investment fit my style and my goals?

- What return can I expect on my money?

- What is the risk that I could lose some or all of the money I put into this investment?

- How easily can I sell this investment?

- If I were to sell this investment right away, how much money would I get back?

- How long has this company been in business? Has it made money for investors before?

If you have a question or a complaint about a suspicious online ad or promotion, the first thing you should do is contact your ISP or commercial online service. You can file an official complaint with your state attorney general or consumer protection office. You can also send your complaint to the Federal Trade Commission at Correspondence Branch, Federal Trade Commission, 6th Street and Pennsylvania Avenue, NW, Washington D.C. 20580; and the National Advertising Division of the Council of Better Business Bureaus, 845 Third Ave., New York, NY 10022.

Just the facts

- The *Hulbert Financial Digest* is the best way to choose an investment newsletter; it objectively evaluates the best-known newsletters in terms of total return and risk-adjusted return.

- An investment club is a group of investors who pool their money, study investing, evaluate investments, and make investment decisions together.

- Online investors can get investment advice from newsgroups, mailing lists, message boards, and chat rooms.

- Investment scams are widespread online, and online investors should investigate any tip gleaned online before investing their money.

GET THE SCOOP ON...

So many vehicles to choose from ▪ Basic
investment strategies ▪ Investing in actively
managed mutual funds ▪ Special
considerations for bond funds ▪ Things to
know about money market funds

Venturing Out on Your Own

With all the advice available out there, why would you want to choose your own investments? Well, for one thing, you could save yourself a lot of money. No need to pay someone to do for you what you can do for yourself— and you might just do better on your own. After all, who's going to put more time and effort into your portfolio than you? Perhaps the biggest advantage of going it alone is control. You have no limitations. There's no debating with others, no compromising. Just the freedom to build a portfolio and follow a strategy that fit your individual needs and investor personality. Now *that's* freedom.

Of course, that also means a lot of responsibility. Going it alone means taking all the credit and all the blame. There aren't any scapegoats. You'll have to invest more time, too. Doing all your own research and managing your own portfolio is work. But if these things don't deter you, the amount and quality of information you can get on the Web will put you on a level playing field with the pros.

Before you get started, make sure your financial house is in order. If you're in debt, have a negative cash flow, are living paycheck to paycheck, have no emergency savings, or are currently unemployed, you should not be dabbling in the stock market. Review your goals and the time frame in which you want to achieve them. As you create your personal investment strategy, make sure you're in tune with that little inner voice that's always telling you whether something fits you.

Choosing your vehicles

An investment strategy is a policy for what, when, and how much to buy, hold, and sell. First, you must decide what to invest in. Let's review the major investment vehicles you have to choose from:

- Stocks
- Stock mutual funds
- Bonds
- Bond funds
- Bank money market accounts
- Certificates of deposit
- Money market funds
- Options
- Futures
- REITs
- Precious metals

"
The key to your universe is that you can choose.
—Carl Frederick
"

How do you choose? And on what basis? Based on performance, stocks and stock mutual funds have had the best long-term track records. Between 1926 and 1996, stocks returned an average of 10.7

percent (S&P 500); bonds, 5.1 percent (long-term U.S. government); and cash, 3.7 percent (30-day T-bills). Inflation averaged around 3.1 percent during this period. Historically, REITs have returned around 7.0 percent.

Will these rates of return persist? Most likely, yes, over the long-term. Over shorter periods, however, it's anyone's guess. Bonds, for example, outperformed stocks in the 1980s. While stocks should ultimately net you the highest return, they are riskier than bonds, and bonds in turn are riskier than cash investments. Giving up security in the hopes of gaining a higher return is known as the risk/return trade-off. Futures and options, REITs, and precious metals can also be quite lucrative and can provide balance to your portfolio, but the information you would need to invest successfully in these vehicles is beyond the scope of this book.

So if stocks and stock mutual funds are tops, how do you choose between them? If you're inclined to research individual companies and invest only in those that meet your specific criteria, buying stocks could be the best course for you. If you're not interested in picking individual stocks, or if you don't want to put in the time necessary to do this well, you would be better off investing in stock mutual funds. It takes less time to find a good stock fund than a good stock.

If you don't even like the idea of choosing a stock fund for yourself, invest in a stock index fund. Actually, only a fraction of actively managed mutual funds beat the S&P 500 in any given year, so index funds are a solid choice. The Vanguard 500 Index Fund is arguably the best of the lot because of its extremely low expense ratio (about 0.2 percent a year). Call Vanguard at 1-800-871-3879 and check out the fund's specs online at www.vanguard.com (listed first under Our Funds, By Name).

Basic investment strategies

Over time various strategies have been developed for investing in the stock market. Some require you to watch market indexes carefully, monitor prices, and buy and sell frequently; others require you to do next to nothing. While proponents of each strategy tend to argue that theirs is the best, each of the strategies presented here can be effective, if employed diligently. The most important thing is for you to pick a strategy that appeals to you. If you have trouble deciding, create several portfolios and employ a different strategy for each. By trial and error, you will find the strategy that works best for you.

The buy-and-hold

“

It is common sense to take a method and try it. If it fails, admit it frankly and try another. But above all, try something.
—Franklin D. Roosevelt

”

The buy-and-hold, often equated with long-term investing, is the best-known and most widely practiced of all the investment strategies; many other strategies are simply variations on this theme. The buy-and-hold is simple: You buy stocks and hold on to them, whether the share prices go up or down. Buy-and-hold investors sell a stock only if they have reached a goal, such as accumulating the necessary funds for their child's college education, and need to cash in. The beauty of this strategy is its simplicity. You simply buy a stock and hold it, no matter what. It's also the cheapest strategy around—there are very few transaction fees.

But does it work? Quite simply, yes, in the long run. In any given year, the chances of a stock declining in value are great, but as the length of time you have held the stock increases, the chances of the stock price remaining below what you paid for it decline. Table 11.1, based on data from the Vanguard Group, Inc., shows the best and worst returns for stocks over different holding periods between the years 1926 and 1996:

TABLE 11.1: RANGE OF RETURNS ON STOCKS: 1926–1996

Holding Period	Best Return	Worst Return
1 year	53.90%	−43.30%
5 years	23.90%	−12.50%
10 years	20.10%	−0.90%
15 years	18.20%	0.60%
20 years	16.90%	3.10%
25 years	14.70%	5.90%

Over the last 40 years, you would have made an average of 11.4 percent annually if you had been fully invested in the stock market throughout that period. Had you bought the same number of shares of all the stocks in the Dow once a year for the last 30 years when the Dow was at its yearly low, your return would have been 11.7 percent annually. If you had done the same thing but purchased the Dow at its high each year, your annual return would *still* have been 10.6 percent. But if you had not been in the market during the 40 best months of the last 40 years, your return would have been only about 2.7 percent! Buy-and-hold investing requires that you get into the market and stay in.

Historically, buying and holding stocks has generated gains over the long run because the market has always gone up over the long run. But there is no guarantee that this will always be the case, of course. The United States could reach its zenith of wealth and power and, like other great nations

Bright Idea
Buy-and-hold investing requires a strong commitment on your part to get into the market and stay in. Otherwise, you risk losing the benefits of this approach.

before it, crumble. Or, the global economic system could collapse. But if these possibilities seem less than likely to you, the buy-and-hold should continue to work.

The key to using this system, though, is patience. You have to be willing to hold a stock, often for many, many years before you start to see a profit. If you're planning to retire in a couple years and will need a steady stream of income from your investments, being 100 percent invested in stocks, no matter what happens to their value, might not be such a hot idea. It really depends on your time horizon (the amount of time remaining before you'll need the money you are investing.) A basic rule of thumb is 10 years. If you don't have at least that much time to work with, buying and holding may be a bit risky.

Of course, even 10 years—or 20 years—may not be enough to realize serious gains. A person who had invested $5,000 in the S&P 500 at market *peaks* from December 31, 1973, through December 3, 1993, would have amassed $465,397 on a cumulative investment of $100,000. But a person who invested $5,000 a year in the S&P at market peaks from December 6, 1954, through December 6, 1974, would have only $127,168, for less than a 3 percent annual total return.

Investors would have been better off having put their money in a money market fund for this 20-year period. True, those who stayed in the stock market during this period did not lose any money, but with the inflation rate averaging more than 3 percent, how much did they really make? Be careful about all the rosy buy-and-hold statistics you see in the media and in mutual fund literature. Mutual fund companies tend to highlight periods during which the buy-and-hold was particularly effective. The true effectiveness of the strategy, however, will depend on your time horizon and on the idiosyncrasies of the market during the period in which you employ the system. The truth is that the buy-and-hold may not fit your needs or your personality, and you just might be able to make more money with another strategy.

Short-term trading

In stark contrast to the buy-and-hold, short-term trading is an investment strategy that revolves around buying and selling stocks frequently. Short-term traders tend not to hold a stock for long—sometimes a year, but often for only a few months, weeks, or even days. The philosophy behind short-term trading is that you can make more money by trading frequently than by simply buying and holding.

Here's how it works, ideally: You buy 100 shares of XYZ at $50 ($5,000 value); the price drops to $45 ($4,500 value), and you sell; when the share price bottoms at $25, you purchase 180 shares ($4,500 value) and ride the stock up to $75 ($13,500 value) and sell. You're up $9,000. If you had bought the 100 shares of XYZ at $50 a share ($5,000 value), held as it went down to $25 and back up to $75, you would be up only $2,500 ($7,500 value). You did 360 percent better with short-term trading! Now, these numbers do not factor in transaction fees, which will be significantly higher for short-term traders, of course, but if you can make an average of 300 percent more with short-term trading, the additional fees won't hurt one bit.

But can investors consistently make money with short-term trading? Is it really possible to sell at peaks and buy at valleys? How do you know when a stock is at a high or a low? Many short-term traders simply buy a stock they think is going to move up over the near term and establish a goal for the stock's share price. When the stock hits the goal price, they sell. It's that simple. If the stock goes down instead of up, however, they tend to get out of the stock quickly. Short-term traders, then, hope to make money by making a nice profit on the stocks they're right about and lose very little on the stocks they misjudge.

Short-term trading can be very risky because it takes a great deal of discipline to sell losing stocks quickly and to sell winning stocks when they hit your goal. In both cases, emotions come into play. In the case of a stock going the wrong way, the short-term trader, not wanting to sell at a loss, may convince himself that the stock will turn around. Instead, it may just drop further, and he will end up selling at a much lower price. In the case of a stock hitting its target price, the short-term trader may get greedy and decide to hold in the hopes that it will continue to climb. It may do so, of course, but if it then backs down below the goal price, he may decide to hold until it hits the goal again. Instead, the stock may drop from there and keep dropping.

In both of these cases, the short-term trader is actually flirting with the buy-and-hold strategy. He fails to make money because he is unable to commit to one system or the other. Lack of discipline is the downfall of many a short-term trader.

Short-term traders often try to time the market. They attempt to have their money invested long when the market is going up, in cash when the market is moving sideways, and short when the market is moving down. But can anyone predict when the market is going to move up or down? Buy-and-hold advocates, which include the entire mutual fund industry and virtually all financial advisers, say that predicting bull markets and bear markets is impossible, so it's best not to try. Of course, investment professionals have a vested interest in your being fully invested at all times.

In fact, many short-term traders employ market-timing strategies to improve their chances of being in and out of stocks at the right time; long-term investors, defined here as investors who hold securities for at least a year, also do. Why? Some market-timing strategies have helped investors make money. For example, if from 1953 to 1993 you had employed a simple market-timing strategy of investing in the S&P 500 whenever the S&P was above its 150-day moving average and putting your money in a money market fund whenever the S&P was below the moving average, a single $10,000 initial investment would have grown to $1,341,448 by 1993, versus $676,035 if you had used a buy-and-hold. You would have doubled your returns! (A moving average is the average price of a stock calculated over a certain period.) Timing strategies can also significantly reduce risk; this is discussed in some detail in Chapter 13, "Keeping a Lid on Risk."

Dollar cost averaging

Dollar cost averaging requires you to invest a certain amount of money in the stock market at regular intervals. You invest this amount regardless of whether the market is going up, down, or sideways. The amount can be as large or small as you choose, and the interval can be as short or as long as you want. Some people make purchases weekly or monthly; others prefer quarterly, biannually, or even annually. It doesn't matter. What's important is to

Unofficially...
If you're interested in exploring market timing strategies, *Hulbert's Financial Digest* has interesting long-term data suggesting that some market timers are actually quite good at it. Market timing models and other tools for helping investors place short-term trades are part of the world of technical analysis.

invest relatively small amounts of money on a regular basis without fail.

The major advantage of this system is that you buy fewer shares of a stock when the market is up, and more shares when the market is down, reducing the possibility of buying a lot of shares when the price is high. In fact, by using dollar cost averaging, you can make good money on a stock over a given time period even if the price of the stock has not gone up during that period. This phenomenon is illustrated in Table 11.2.

TABLE 11.2: DOLLAR COST AVERAGING IN ACTION

Month	Investment Amount	Share Price	No. Shares Bought
January	$200	$20	10
February	$200	$18	11.111
March	$200	$16	12.5
April	$200	$14	14.286
May	$200	$12	16.667
June	$200	$10	20
July	$200	$10	20
August	$200	$12	16.667
September	$200	$14	14.286
October	$200	$16	12.5
November	$200	$18	11.111
December	$200	$20	10
Total	**$2,400.00**		**169.128**
Total value	**$3,382.56**		
Total gain	**$982.56 (40%)**		

Notice that if the same $2,400 had been invested all at once in January, the total value of the shares in December would have been just $2,400, for a gain of 0. Dollar cost averaging works because over time the average *cost* of all the shares you purchase will be less than the average *price*, assuming that the company or fund you're investing in is fairly solid. The system will not work, however, if the security keeps going down in price, so it's best not to use dollar cost averaging with highly speculative stocks. Even with solid, blue chip companies, of course, there may be periods of precipitous decline in share prices, but it's pretty safe to say that eventually these stocks will recover. Regardless, dollar cost averaging should be employed as a long-term strategy—say, 10 years or more. When used properly, the strategy relieves you of the angst that comes with trying to decide when it's a good time to invest.

Common sense suggests that you should use this system to buy more than one stock at a time because there's always the possibility that the one stock you choose will keep going down in price. Having a portfolio of at least five or six stocks minimizes the chances of this happening. Of course, if you use dollar cost averaging to invest in a mutual fund, a single fund may suffice because all funds hold stock in numerous companies.

For all its merits, however, dollar cost averaging is not a perfect system. The main disadvantage of the system is that it does not tell you when to get out of a stock, only when to get in. You have to decide for yourself when and if you should sell. One of the practical difficulties with dollar cost averaging is that you need the discipline to write a check to yourself every month and actually purchase those shares—and you have to remember to do this. If you're in an investment plan such as a DRIP, have an automatic transfer set up between your bank and a mutual fund company; if you are in an investment club that requires a monthly payment, it's much easier to

Bright Idea
If you're a mutual fund investor, call your fund company and ask if they can help you set up dollar cost averaging. They should be able to arrange for regular deposits to be taken from your bank account, your paycheck, or your money market fund.

maintain this regimen. You could also buy a Treasury bond and use the dividend payments to invest in the stock market whenever you receive a dividend check. This system has the built-in advantage of safeguarding your principal, which is invested in the bond.

The constant dollar system

With the constant dollar system, a cousin of dollar cost averaging, you keep the total amount of money you have invested in stocks constant. The amount should be based on your investment style and goals. At a predetermined interval, you should check the value of your stock investments and either add to them, if their total value has fallen below the set amount, or sell some, if their value has risen. You could use a predetermined percentage change in your portfolio's value instead of a time interval as a basis for buying or selling. The logic behind the constant dollar system is to sell stocks when prices are high and buy when they're low.

Let's look at an example. Say you decide to keep $100,000 invested in stocks at all times and to check on your portfolio's value once a year. At the end of the first year, you discover that your portfolio's value has risen to $115,000. To bring the portfolio's value back to $100,000, you sell $15,000 worth of your stock and invest that money in bonds or something else. A year later you check again, and this time your portfolio's value has fallen to $95,000. Now you have to buy stock, $5,000 worth, to bring the portfolio's value back to $100,000.

Using percentage changes in your portfolios value as a basis for action instead of time periods is a viable alternative. You might decide to buy or sell shares whenever your portfolio is up or down by, say,

10 percent. The advantage of using percentages is that it places some limits on the amounts you'll have to buy or sell at a given time. Using time intervals may require large purchases if your portfolio's value has fallen a great deal over the period.

As with dollar cost averaging, the constant dollar system will not work if the share price of a stock continues to fall. It's best to buy solid issues and make a long-term commitment. The major disadvantage of this system, though, is that unlike dollar cost averaging, you could suffer significant initial losses if you make your original purchases at a market high because you're investing a lump sum of money. By the same token, if you buy your original stocks at a market low, you won't have as many opportunities to buy low in the future. The system works best when the market is trading sideways and share prices are fluctuating above and below the purchase prices. Implementing this system for optimal results, then, would seem to require a bit of market timing.

Dogs of the Dow

The Dogs of the Dow is a simple investment system, one with an impressive long-term track record. The strategy requires you to purchase equal dollar amounts of the 10 Dow stocks with the highest dividend yields and hold them for one year. At the end of the one-year period, you sell any stocks that are no longer among the 10 with the highest dividend yields and replace these with the Dow stocks that have newly entered the top 10. Why the stocks with the highest dividend yields? Dividend yield is calculated by dividing the dividend per share by the price per share. If the share price goes down and the dividend payouts stay about the same, the dividend yield will climb. Thus, Dow stocks with high dividend yields

Timesaver
The advantage of using time intervals is that after you make your investments you can forget about them for a while. Using percentages requires you to monitor your portfolio's value continually.

are thought to be stocks whose share prices have taken a beating and are ready to stage a recovery. Of course, a stock's dividend yield could go up if dividends increased and share price increased less, but this isn't usually the situation.

It's important to hold your Dog stocks for a full year because stocks held for a year or more are considered long-term investments, and long-term capital gains are taxed at a lower rate than short–term gains. Short-term gains are taxed as ordinary income. Long-term gains are taxed at 10 percent if you're in the 15 percent tax bracket, and 20 percent if you're in any other bracket. (Your long-term gains are included when figuring out what bracket you're in.) Many Dogs investors follow the calendar year, buying and selling stocks in late December. If you don't want to figure out the Dogs for yourself, various Web sites will do it for you. Check out www.dogsofthedow.com. There are also many unit trusts to choose from.

Historically, the Dogs of the Dow strategy has performed exceptionally well, earning a compounded annual return of 17.7 percent since 1973, trouncing the Dow, which returned only 11.9 percent over the same period. Over the 30-year period of 1968 to 1998, $10,000 invested in the Dow would have provided a total return of more than $200,000, but the same $10,000 invested in the Dogs of the Dow would have returned more than $800,000! Even with growing notoriety, the system continues to make money: In 1996, the Dogs were up 28.6 percent; in 1997, 22.2 percent; in 1998, 10.7 percent.

A powerful variation on the Dogs of the Dow was developed by Michael O'Higgins and described in his book *Beating the Dow*. The strategy is called, aptly enough, the Beating the Dow 5, but it is also known as the Flying Five, the Small Dogs of the Dow, and the Puppies of the Dow. In the Small Dogs, you invest an equal dollar amount in the 5 stocks with the lowest share prices from the 10 Dow stocks with highest dividend yields. The rationale in choosing the stocks with the lowest share prices is that these stocks have greater upside potential than the stocks with higher share prices; this claim is rooted more in investor psychology than anything else. As with the Dogs, the Small Dogs strategy calls for you to hold the stocks for one year, at which time you must adjust your portfolio. The Small Dogs has actually performed better than the Dogs of the Dow historically, averaging about 20.9 percent since 1973.

Still another powerful variation on the Dogs of the Dow is the Foolish Four, developed by brothers David and Tom Gardner, founders of the Motley Fool Web site (www.fool.com). The Foolish Four has evolved; the current variation was originally known as the RP variation. Going the Beating the Dow 5 one better, the Foolish Four requires investors to purchase only four stocks, and the process of selecting those four is a tad more involved. First, you identify the 10 Dow stocks with the highest dividend yields, as usual. Next, you divide the yield of each by the square root of the price. Then you order the 10 stocks according to the resulting ratio, from highest to lowest, and eliminate the stock at the top of the list. The second, third, fourth, and fifth stocks on your list are your Foolish Four. (If you don't want to do the math, you can get the current Foolish Four from the Motley Fool Web site.) Invest equal dollar amounts in these four stocks, hold them for a year, and then recalculate your Foolish Four and replace

Watch Out!
Not every stock in a Dogs of the Dow portfolio will go up every year, nor will the Dogs outperform the Dow every year. This is a long-term strategy.

any stocks in your portfolio that are no longer in the Foolish Four. While the Foolish Four has been field-tested only for a few years, back-testing shows that this strategy would have generated a compounded annual return of about 24.6 percent over the last 25 years (although only 18.8 percent since 1961).

Why do the Gardners divide the yield by the square root of the price? Interestingly, studies have shown that price volatility (also known as beta) is greater for lower-priced stocks, so dividing the yield by the square root of the price allows you to factor volatility into the stock selection process. Stocks with the highest dividend yields and lowest prices will gravitate to the top of the list.

How is this helpful? Well, if you're fairly sure that a group of stocks is likely to go up in price (remember, you're already working with the 10 Dow stocks with the highest dividend yields), choosing the stocks with the greatest volatility will increase your chances of choosing stocks that will move up dramatically. That is, if all the stocks in a group are expected to move up, those with the highest beta should move up the most. The Foolish Four, then, consists of the stocks with the greatest overall combined levels of dividend yield and volatility. The reason the Gardners drop the top stock on the list is to avoid extremes—they reason that investing in the stock with greatest overall levels of dividend yield and volatility could be asking for trouble.

The thing you need to be careful about in pursuing a Dogs investment strategy at this point is that these strategies have become epidemically popular. Why is this a concern? The Dogs strategies rely on being able to buy stocks that are relatively unpopular and that are benefiting from the turnaround. As the Dogs strategies become more popular, however, so may these stocks, and the underpinnings of the strategy may begin to crumble. Buyer beware.

In fact, if the Dogs advantage were to completely disappear, it would conform to the historical pattern of stock market anomalies disappearing once they become widely known. Michael O'Higgins, by the way, no longer invests in the Dogs. He was quoted in the December 8, 1997, issue of *Time* as saying that Dow Dogs "have become too popular and the market has become too high" for the strategy to keep on working. Louis Rukeyser, the host of the television program *Wall $treet Week,* said on his February 5, 1999, show, "Vast amounts of phony commentary have been paraded on this subject, and mutual funds and unit investment trusts have been formed to exploit the market. But the reality is, as with so many so-called sure-fire theories, that just about the time you hear about it, somehow it stops working."

Another reason to be cautious about Dogs strategies is that back-tested systems often don't produce similar results going forward, and this could be because they lose their edge once they are discovered. The fallacy of data mining, or finding data from the past to support a theory when no cause-and-effect relationship actually exists, may also come into play here. Peter Coy deals with this phenomenon in an article he wrote for the June 16, 1997, issue of *Business Week*. In the article, he cites a study by David J. Leinweber, Ph.D., who found after analyzing a United Nations CD-ROM that the "the single best predicator of the Standard & Poor's 500-stock index was butter production in Bangladesh." Patterns may occur in data by chance that have no predicative value whatsoever.

What's more, historically Dogs strategies have not always worked so well. A study conducted by H.G. Schneider, which appeared in the June 1951 issue of the *Journal of Finance,* documented the results of investing in either 6 or 10 of the Dow stocks selling at the lowest earnings multiples and rebalancing the portfolio once a year. The strategy was actually unprofitable from 1917 to 1933. Sometimes you have to go back farther than 25 years to find the pin that bursts the bubble.

To be sure, the Dow Dogs have beaten the Dow for the last 50 years, with a compounded annual return of 16.77 percent to 13.71 percent, but with greater risk, as measured by volatility. Also, a greater portion of the Dogs return comes from dividends, the taxes on which cannot be deferred and are higher than those in capital gains. The annual rebalancing of the portfolio triggers capital gains taxes. There are also annual transaction costs associated with Dogs strategies.

Indexing

Indexing is an investment strategy that calls for investing in all the securities in a given market index or in a representative sample of securities in an index. There is no buying and selling of individual securities; you simply buy the index or sell the index. Because indexing involves very little portfolio activity and no attempt to outperform a given market, it is said to be a passive investment approach. Active money management involves buying and selling carefully selected securities in an effort to beat the market. The majority of investors practice indexing by buying index mutual funds or unit trusts. The investment manager of these vehicles does his best to reproduce the results of the index represented by the fund.

Indexing, then, is the virtual equivalent of investing in a market itself, and this has some distinct advantages. One is psychological. How often have you checked your portfolio after a big up day on Wall Street, only to find that your particular stocks are down? Indexing ensures that, for the most part, this won't happen. If the market is up, your portfolio will be, too. Another big advantage of indexing is that you know your total return will equal the market's. That's really saying something, considering that the majority of "actively managed" mutual funds do not equal, let alone beat, the market. (The S&P 500 outperforms 75 percent of actively managed equity mutual funds over time.) One reason is that actively managed funds tend to have a portion of their assets in cash and bonds, which, while lowering risk, also reduce returns.

Actively managed funds also have higher transaction fees and fund expenses (including advisory fees, distribution charges, and operating expenses), both of which are taken out of the fund's returns; load funds also charge commissions. All these costs significantly reduce your returns. The average annual expense ratio (the percentage of a fund's assets that goes to fund expenses every year) is 1.44 percent. Annual transaction costs also average between 0.5 percent and 1 percent. Together, these expenses will reduce your true returns by around 2 percent a year.

With their passive investment approach and minimal transactions, index fund managers can keep costs way down, and this means more money for you. (Table 11.3 illustrates how great an impact fund costs can have on your bottom line.) Costs of index funds do vary, however, so you should shop around. As mentioned earlier, Vanguard has some of the most famously inexpensive, high-quality, no-load funds around, and the Vanguard 500 Index Fund has been a stellar performer for many years (18.6 percent compounded annual return over the last 10 years).

TABLE 11.3: THE IMPACT OF FUND COSTS ON A 12 PERCENT RETURN

	Standard Mutual Fund	Low-cost Index Fund
Expense ratio	1.40%	0.20%
Transaction costs	0.80%	0.10%
Loads	0.50%	0%
Net return	**9.30%**	**11.70%**

A final cost advantage of index funds is the tax advantage. Because index funds have a much lower turnover rate than standard mutual funds, which average 77 percent turnover of holdings per year, far fewer capital gains distributions are passed on to the investor. This means fewer taxes. This tax advantage is not reflected in the total return numbers for mutual funds because mutual fund gains are always calculated before taxes.

You can choose from several kinds of index funds. The most popular are the S&P 500 Index Funds; there are also Dow Index Funds, Wilshire 5000 Index Funds, Russell 2000 Index Funds, International Index Funds, and Bond Index Funds. Some investors favor Wilshire indexing because the Wilshire represents 100 percent of all regularly traded stocks in the U.S. stock market, whereas the S&P 500 represents only 70 percent (by value). It's also possible to buy value index funds, which cover all the stocks in an index with share prices the fund manager determines to be below their fair market value, and growth index funds, covering all the growth stocks in a given index.

While the advantages of index funds are many, there are a few things to consider before you invest. First, while index funds will keep pace with the market when it's rising, they will do an equally admirable job of keeping pace on the way down. So watch out below! If you're an aggressive buy-and-hold investor, this is not a problem. But if the idea of riding through the full force of a bear market feels a bit risky to you, and if you're not interested in trying to time the market, you may want to invest a core amount in an index fund and the rest in some actively managed funds. With ownership of shares in an actively managed fund comes the hope of beating the market and the peace of mind that if the market goes down, the fund manager will increase the fund's cash position to cushion the fall.

Other investors use a market timer to help them switch in and out of index funds on buy and sell signals. Mutual funds don't like this much, partly because the more people jumping in and out of a fund, the higher the fund's transactions costs. One reason is that the more a fund's balance fluctuates, the harder it is to manage; another reason is that fund companies just don't want you to take your money out of their funds. To discourage short-term trading, most fund companies allow only a few free trades (switches) in and out of a fund per year.

Investing in actively managed mutual funds

Investing in index mutual funds is a popular and important investment strategy, but indexing is only

Timesaver
Investing in international index funds or actively managed international funds is the best way for most investors to invest in foreign securities because it's still relatively difficult to get all the information you need online to make informed decisions about individual foreign securities yourself.

one of the investment opportunities available to you in the mutual fund universe. Indeed, numerous actively managed funds outperform the index funds. The big advantage of investing in these funds is that you don't have to spend the time, effort, or emotional energy that those who invest in individual securities themselves must spend researching, selecting, and managing a portfolio of securities. The fund manager does all the work and worrying for you. And you can take comfort that your mutual fund manager is a professional (although this does not guarantee that you'll make more money than if you invested on your own, nor does it insulate you from losses).

It's also comforting to know that the money you invest in a fund is automatically diversified, at least within the scope of the fund's investment parameters, because funds invest in a number of securities, not just one or two. By investing a minimal amount in a mutual fund, then, it's possible to enjoy the benefits of partial ownership of a myriad of securities, a much wider array than you could possibly achieve with the same amount of money if you were buying on your own.

Fund type

When choosing an actively managed mutual fund, the first step is to decide what kind of a fund you're interested in. As mentioned in Chapter 4, "Plenty of Investment Vehicles to Choose From," there are a variety of fund types. These are the most common:

- International and global stock funds
- Regional and country funds
- Aggressive growth funds
- Growth funds

- Growth and income funds
- Value funds
- Equity income funds
- Specialty funds/sector funds
- Socially responsible/green funds
- Balanced funds
- Asset allocation funds
- International bond funds
- High-yield bond funds
- Corporate bond funds
- Government bond funds
- Money market funds

Generally, the higher the fund appears on the list, the riskier it is. But the riskier the fund, the higher the potential returns.

Top performers

Having chosen a fund category, you next need to generate a list of top-performing funds within that category. While past performance is no guarantee of future returns, there is a positive correlation between the past and the future. In comparing funds' performances, be careful not to confuse *yield* with *total return*. Yield is a fund's dividend income expressed as a percentage of the fund's current share price; total return is the sum of dividend income and capital gains. So Stock Fund A, with a yield of 5 percent, might look superior to Stock Fund B, with a yield of 3 percent, but when you include increases in share prices (capital gains), Stock Fund B may come out on top. When comparing funds' overall performances, then, look at the total return numbers. When comparing the amount

Bright Idea
Only you (or you and your investment adviser) can find the right types of funds for you, after a careful analysis of your investment style and goals, and a certain amount of trial and error.

of income generated by funds—especially bond funds and money market funds—use yields.

A good place to start this research is with Quicken's mutual fund finder (www.quicken.com/ investments/mutualfunds/finder/). If you choose the Full Search option, you can specify the parameters that are most important to you in a fund, and Quicken will produce a list of funds that meet your criteria. Quote.com (www.quote.com/ mutual_funds/index. html) also provides a nice mutual fund screening tool. Yahoo! Finance's mutual fund top performers page (http://biz.yahoo.com/p/top.html), which lists mutual fund top performers by fund category, is good as well. You also can go to www.fundz.com/ mf/rnk.htm for links to a host of Web sites that rank mutual funds.

Here are some additional online mutual fund screens:

- **SmartMoney.com:** www.smartmoney.com/ si/tools/fundscreen/

- **Forbes.com:** www.forbes.com/tool/toolbox/ lipper/screen.asp

- **Money.com:** www.pathfinder.com/money/ fundfinder/index.html

- **Mutual Funds Online:** www.mfmag.com/ databse.htm

- *U.S.News* **Online:** www.usnews.com/usnews/ nycu/money/mutserch.htm

Then there's *Morningstar Mutual Funds,* a comprehensive report that uses a star system to compare the performances of 1,700 mutual funds on a risk-adjusted basis. *Morningstar* gives five stars to the funds with the highest returns and lowest risk, and one star to those with the lowest returns and highest risk. These rankings are accompanied by full-page reports on each fund. You can subscribe to *Morningstar* online at www.morningstar.com, or call 1-800-735-0700. A year subscription of 24 reports costs $495, but you definitely get what you pay for.

Mutual fund newsletters can also be a good source of fund performance information. Be careful, though, about relying on literature from mutual fund companies for performance data. Fund companies may try to put a positive spin on a fund's performance by reporting only how it did over a favorable time period or neglecting to adjust returns for loads and expenses.

When you get down to the nitty-gritty, be sure that you're comparing funds in the same asset class. For example, there's no way that a top money market fund is going to have a higher average annual total return than a top stock fund, and it would be meaningless to compare them. Stock funds and money market funds have totally different risk/return characteristics. For the same reason, even within the same asset class, it's best to compare funds in the same investment approaches: value with value, growth with growth.

Whatever you do, don't just buy the fund with the highest total return you can find. Just because a fund is among the top performers when you do your research doesn't mean that it will stay there. Performance data, especially risk-adjusted data, is only one indicator of how the fund might do in the future. Focus on the funds in your chosen category that have performed well on a risk-adjusted basis over the longest time period. The longer the period,

Unofficially...
For a list of the
top-performing
green funds,
go to www.
greenmoney.com
and click SRI
Mutual Funds,
then on SRI
Mutual Fund
Performance
Chart. You can
also go to www.
socialfunds.com
and click the
Funds icon to
get very detailed
information on
individual funds.

the more likely the data will reflect how the fund has done during both good and bad markets.

To gauge a fund's risk-adjusted performance, first look at its *alpha*. Alpha is the difference between what a fund actually returned and what it should have returned based purely on the risk the manager took. A positive alpha, then, measures the percent of the fund's return that resulted from skill. The higher the alpha, the better.

Next, look at the fund's *Sharpe Ratio.* The Sharpe Ratio, developed by Nobel Laureate Bill Sharpe, measures how well a fund has performed relative to the risk it has taken by dividing performance figures by standard deviations; as with alpha, the higher the Sharpe Ratio, the better. (Standard deviation measures the amount of volatility of a portfolio by measuring the extent to which individual returns differ from an average.)

Then look at the *R-squared.* The R-squared measures the correlation between a fund's performance and the performance of an index to determine how much of a fund's performance can be explained by the performance of the overall market. The higher the number (ranging from 0 to 1 or 0 to 100), the greater the correlation. The lower the correlation, the better.

All said, performance statistics tend to be more useful for eliminating the funds you shouldn't invest in than determining the ones you should. This is because funds with poor track records tend to continue to perform poorly, whereas exceptionally good funds tend to regress to the mean over time. In any case, you shouldn't pick a fund based simply on its one-year or three-month performance numbers; there is very little correlation between recent past performance and future performance.

Managers matter

Now that you have a list of top-performing funds in your category of choice, it's time to look at management. Favor the funds that have been under the auspices of the same fund manager for a while—ideally the manager who has guided the fund to its current lofty heights. That said, you don't want to exaggerate the importance of the manager—most fund managers who significantly outperform their peers in a particular period do not do so in later periods. They even have trouble beating the market.

What's more, a fund's performance cannot always be attributed to one person anyway because only some funds follow the individual-decision-maker approach; many use a committee approach. In the former case, a star fund manager makes all the major investment decisions; in the latter case, however, the fund manager makes decisions in consultation with a committee or team. The advantage of the committee approach is that when a member of the team leaves, there tends not to be as big of an impact on the future performance of the fund.

The next step in the selection process is to assess the fund manager's investment approach. Does it match yours? These are the most common approaches:

- **Objective-centered investing:** Fund managers who are objective-centered invest only in securities meeting certain clearly defined criteria, such as companies included in the S&P 500 or companies meeting certain environmental standards.

- **Open-objective investing:** Fund managers in this category are not required to follow a

Bright Idea
If the manager of a mutual fund you're interested in has a relatively short tenure with the fund, find out what funds she has managed previously. Examining the data on these funds during the period of her stewardship should shed some light on her style and ability.

specific fund objective and have great flexibility in choosing investments for the fund.

- **Bottom-up method:** Managers examine individual securities in all industries and invest in those securities determined to be the best investments at the present time.

- **Top-down method:** Managers first determine what sectors or industries are currently the strongest, and invest in the best individual securities within those sectors or industries.

- **Proprietary system:** Managers use a multistep stock-screening system that usually takes into account value, risk, and price action.

- **Performance method:** Managers base their investment decisions mainly on past performance—either short-term or long-term, depending on the fund's objective.

- **Value investing:** Managers invest in stocks that they consider to be bargains.

- **Growth investing:** Managers invest in companies that they expect to exhibit greater than average growth over the next several years.

Of all these approaches, probably the most important to distinguish are the value approach and the growth approach. Value funds invest in stocks whose prices have been beaten down and tend to have relatively high dividend yields. (Sound like the Dogs of the Dow? It should. The Dogs is a value-oriented strategy.) Total returns of value funds tend to be less volatile than those of growth funds because a larger portion of the returns of value funds comes from dividends, which are more stable than capital gains, and because share prices are already on the low side, leaving relatively less room for price depreciation. Value funds tend to appeal to more conservative investors and investors who want a certain amount of investment income. Because of their higher taxable dividend payouts, they are often held in tax-deferred accounts.

For an in-depth look at value stock investing, go to www.troweprice.com/mutual/insights/valuinvest. html.

Growth funds invest in stocks that are paying out small or no dividends because almost all earnings are being reinvested in the company to maximize growth. Because a much larger portion of the total returns of growth funds comes from capital gains than dividends, they are riskier than value funds and tend to be favored by aggressive investors. For more information on the ins and out of growth-stock investing, go to www.troweprice.com/mutual/insights/grth.html.

In practice, fund managers usually employ a combination of investment approaches, such as top-down, value investing, or objective-centered, growth investing. While the approaches listed here are the most common, you can also find funds that follow momentum and contrarian approaches and funds that focus on small cap or large cap stocks. Balanced funds and asset allocation funds follow an asset allocation approach, dividing assets among several types of investments—generally stocks, bonds, and cash. Some of these funds use timing models as a basis for deciding the mix of asset classes to be held at a given time. Most fund families offer funds with various risk levels within each fund category, such as aggressive growth, moderate growth, and conservative growth.

You're free, then, to switch to more conservative or aggressive funds with the same investment approach to accommodate changes in your risk-tolerance or time horizon.

Risk assessment

While it's sometimes possible to assess a fund's investment approach from its name, it's best to call the fund and request a prospectus, or look for the information on the fund company's Web site. (For a database containing mutual fund contact information and Web sites, go to Fund$pot at www.fundspot. com/research.htm.) What a fund invests in can change over time, so a fund's name may not be a clear indication of its actual holdings.

Another reason to read the prospectus is to get an idea of how risky a fund is. Remember, risk is not the same thing as risk-adjusted performance. To gauge a fund's risk, first take a look at its year-to-year performance numbers. Fairly low-risk funds should show relatively stable numbers. Riskier funds will show wider fluctuations in total return from year to year. Imagine how you would feel if you were holding this fund if it were to continue to post similar numbers.

Check out the fund's standard deviation numbers, too. The lower the standard deviation, the better. Next, look at the fund's beta. A beta of more than 1 means the fund is more volatile than the overall stock market; a number of less than 1 is less volatile. Now take a look at the fund's holdings (asset classes held and percent of each). Is the fund investing in a lot of derivatives or speculative stocks? Is the fund using leverage? Is it selling short? If so, are you comfortable with that? Because funds are required to reveal their holdings only twice a year, though, it's a good idea to call to confirm or look into this at FundStyle (www.fundstyle.com).

You should also look into whether most of a fund's returns have come from dividends or capital gains. The larger the proportion that have come from dividends, the more stable the fund is likely to be. For example, say two funds have an 11 percent compounded annual return over the last five years. Fund A achieved this return with a portfolio of 50 percent stocks and 50 percent bonds, and Fund B did so with 90 percent stocks and 10 percent bonds. Fund A is probably less risky.

How expensive?

Having weeded out the funds that don't seem to fit your investor personality, you should now have a handful of funds that meet your criteria for fund type, performance, style, and risk. How should you choose among your finalists? Look at expenses. Which of the funds has the lowest expense ratio, transaction costs, and loads? This will be in the prospectus. Ideally, you want a no-load fund with a very low expense ratio. Load funds *rarely* figure loads into their performance figures, so watch out. Don't compare the performances of load and no-load funds until you have subtracted the loads from the load-fund performance figures. (Not only are load funds more expensive, but they also may be riskier. Saddled with loads and high expense ratios, load fund managers may have to take additional risks to achieve competitive returns with no-load funds.)

As a rule, avoid stock funds with an expense ratio of more than 1 percent or bond funds with an

Unofficially...
Because they don't have to conform to the composition of an index, managers of actively managed bond funds can be more selective about the credit quality of the bonds they buy than managers of bond index funds. They can also better control call risk—the likelihood that a lender will call a bond before maturity.

expense ratio of more than .75 percent. If the funds you're interested in have higher expense ratios, set the limit at the sector average (typically, 1.32 percent for large cap funds, 1.58 percent for small cap funds, 1.91 percent for international funds, and 1.08 percent for bond funds). When you reduce returns by expenses (after loads have been taken out), no-load funds often outperform funds with loads. But this is not always the case. Some load funds make up for their sales charges with superior returns and lower risk.

Tax considerations

The final major consideration in choosing a fund is dividends and capital gains distributions. Dividends are generated by the individual securities held in the fund; capital gains are generated by the sale of these securities. Most funds distribute dividends to shareholders monthly or quarterly and distribute capital gains annually, semiannually, or quarterly. All funds distribute some or all capital gains in December; they're required to make distributions by December 31 every year.

Why is this important? If you buy a fund just before the fund declares a dividend or capital gains distribution, you'll get the distribution, but the fund's NAV will be reduced by a corresponding amount, for a net gain of 0. Nevertheless, you *will* have to pay taxes on that distribution—you'll be paying taxes on other people's gains. The best time to get into a fund, then, is just after the fund makes a distribution, and the optimal day to do this is known as the reinvestment date. Call the fund to find out when this is. The day distributions are posted to accounts is known as the record date. (With stocks, the record date is the date by which you have to officially own a stock to be entitled to receive the next dividend; the ex-dividend date is the date from which the seller, rather than the buyer, is entitled to receive the next dividend.)

If you're investing in a tax-sheltered account, you don't have to worry about any of this. If you're in a taxable account, however, and if you want to get into a fund immediately but you know that an *annual* distribution is coming soon, do some fast math. If you're in the 28–31 percent tax bracket, you will pay 2–2.5 percent of your total account value in taxes if the capital gains distribution is 7.7 percent of the fund's assets (1997 average). This means that if the fund rises more than 2–2.5 percent before the distribution, you'll come out ahead.

As a rule, though, buy funds on the reinvest date, and be particularly careful about buying in November or December. Also, stay away from funds with a high turnover rates—more than 80 percent—because these funds will realize more capital gains. In the same vein, the less buying and selling (switching) of funds you do, the fewer personal capital gains taxes you will have to pay from the sale of the funds themselves. A major incentive for limiting switching, then, is to put off having to pay capital gains taxes for as long as possible— the longer you do, the longer your money will be working for you, not Uncle Sam. As the Vanguard Group notes, "early payment of taxes may reduce after-tax returns by up to 3 percent a year."

Even after screening for expenses, you may still have a few funds to choose from. If so, consider factors such as minimum investment, fund family size, number and kinds of funds available, number of free switches per year, and services such as checking,

Moneysaver
Consider avoiding funds with high dividend yields because dividends are taxed at your income-tax rate.

Web account information and access, and customer service availability. How well can this fund and fund family meet your individual investment needs? In the end, follow your gut. Ask yourself which of the funds you like the most. Which do you *want* to buy?

You can buy a mutual fund in one of three ways:

1. Buy it directly from the mutual fund company for no fee (unless there's a front-end load).

2. Buy it through a broker and pay a brokerage fee.

3. Buy it through Schwab's Mutual Fund OneSource program, Fidelity's Funds Network, or from another broker's no-fee funds list.

The advantage of the third option is that you can switch among fund families, not just among funds within a family, for free. You must hold a fund for at least 180 days with these programs, however, to avoid an early encashment fee. The main drawback of these programs is that not all mutual funds participate. In fact, it's not possible to buy all mutual funds through a broker; some fund companies require you to buy shares directly through them. If you can purchase shares of the fund you're interested in for free, consider using dollar cost averaging rather than buying a large dollar amount of shares all at once.

Unofficially...
FundAlarm (www.fundalarm. com) offers free, nonpartisan analysis of how 2,656 funds have performed against their peers and advice on when to sell a mutual fund.

When to sell a mutual fund

The decision of when to sell a mutual fund will depend a great deal on your overall investment strategy, but there are a few guidelines. If the fund changes its overall strategy or starts investing in securities that don't conform to its purported strategy, it's time to tell it goodbye. A good example of this is when a value fund starts investing in growth stocks.

By the same token, if your investment style or goals change, you might want to sell a fund that no longer fits you. Some people switch to more conservative funds as they get older, for instance. Similarly, if after investing in a fund, you feel that it just doesn't fit you like you thought it would—perhaps it's too volatile or not volatile enough—consider switching to another fund. And you just might want to get out of a fund if it isn't behaving the way it's supposed to, such as an equity income fund that is showing more volatility than the average aggressive growth fund—even if that volatility is upward. Don't let yourself get swept up in the increases: The fund's downside moves will probably be more dramatic than you had expected as well.

Buying bond mutual funds

The process of selecting a bond fund is similar to that of choosing a stock fund, but there are some special considerations. When selecting a bond fund, the most important thing to consider is the type and quality of the bonds in a fund. The higher the quality, the lower the volatility of the fund's NAV and yield. This is because the credit ratings of lower-quality bonds tend to fluctuate more than those of higher-quality bonds; when credit ratings change, so do the fund's NAV and yield. To minimize price and yield fluctuations caused by changes in credit ratings, then, stick with bond funds holding high-quality bonds.

Another important consideration in choosing bond funds is maturity. The longer the average maturity of the bonds held in a bond fund, the more the NAV and yield will change when interest rates change. This is because a change in interest rates will have a much greater impact on the relative income received from a long-term bond than a short-term bond. Holding a $1,000 bond with an 8 percent coupon and a two-year maturity will not net you much more than the same bond with a 7 percent maturity. But a $1,000 bond with an 8 percent coupon and a 30-year maturity will yield significantly more than a 7 percent bond with the same maturity. If you want to minimize price and yield volatility, then, buy bond funds containing bonds with shorter maturities. Of course, the trade-off for higher credit quality and shorter maturities is lower yields.

You should also look at the management style of a bond fund before deciding to invest. As with stock funds, your choice is between index funds and actively managed funds. The average bond index funds track an entire bond market index and generally invest in high-quality government bonds of intermediate maturities. It is possible, though, to invest in bond index funds that concentrate their holdings on bonds with long-term or short-term maturities.

Two kinds of actively managed bond funds exist: corporate and government. Corporate bond funds have higher returns but are riskier and often have a greater tax liability. Both corporate and government bond funds come in three average maturities: short-term, intermediate-term, and long-term. Your decision of bond type and maturity should be based on your requirements for risk and return. Consider your goals, risk tolerance, and income needs when deciding what kind of a bond fund to invest in.

Finally, consider municipal bond funds if you want to avoid taxes. You don't have to pay federal taxes on munis, and you may even be able to avoid state and local taxes if the bond fund invests only in

Bright Idea
Consider investing in the Treasury inflation-indexed security, introduced by the U.S. Treasury in 1997. The annual interest paid on the bond remains constant, but the principal is adjusted to keep pace with inflation. This way, when the bond matures, the buying power of your money has increased by an amount equal to the yield on the bond.

municipal bonds issued by your state of residence. Munis may provide you with more after-tax income, depending on the fund's total return and your tax bracket, so they're worth a good look. It's easy to figure out if a muni is a good deal. Divide the muni's yield by the difference of 1 minus your tax bracket to get the muni's taxable equivalent yield. So, if the yield of the muni in question is 4.5 percent, the taxable equivalent yield would be 6.25 percent (4.5% / [1.00 − .28] = 6.25%). This means that any taxable bond meeting your requirements for risk and maturity must yield more than 6.25 percent to be a better deal than the Muni. (See Appendix E for a handy table of taxable equivalent yields.)

Money market funds

Money market funds are pretty much the same from one fund family to the next. They are the safest type of mutual fund and a good place to keep some or all of your money when you don't want to expose it to the risks of the markets. The main consideration with money market funds is whether to buy a taxable or tax-free fund. The former invests in taxable short-term loans to banks, corporations, and the government; the latter invests in tax-free instruments. Taxable funds pay dividends that are subject to federal, state, and local taxes; tax-free funds pay dividends that are exempt from federal taxes—and, in some cases, state and local taxes as well.

Three types of taxable funds exist:

- **General purpose money market funds:** Invest in the short-term debt instruments of large, financially secure corporations and banks.

- **U.S. government money market funds:** Invest in the debt instruments issued by the U.S.

Moneysaver
Because all returns from money market funds are taxed at your tax rate—you get dividends, not capital gains—which ones you decide to invest in should depend on your tax bracket. Compare the total returns you would receive on taxable money market funds after taxes with the returns you would get on tax-free funds, and go with the higher of the two.

Treasury as well as agencies of the U.S. Government.

- **Treasury money market funds:** Invest in direct U.S. Treasury debt instruments (backed by the "full faith and credit" of the U.S. government).

Two types of tax-free funds exist:

- **National municipal money market funds:** Invest in the debt obligations of state and local governments. Dividends are exempt from federal income taxes.

- **Single-state municipal money market funds:** Invest in the debt obligations of state and local governments of a single state. Dividends are free of federal, state, and local income taxes.

If you're trading within a fund family—especially if you're trading frequently—you should probably just choose from among the money market funds your fund family offers. Moving your money to a different family just to get a slightly higher rate would be troublesome, and if there were any charges or commissions involved, this could negate any advantage.

If you have money spread among several fund families, however, or if you are operating within the framework of Schwab OneSource or the Fidelity Funds Network, which allow commission-free mutual fund trading, it's a good idea to comparison-shop. A great site to compare current money market fund rates is IBC Financial Data (www.ibcdata.com/index.html). Click the link that says How to Select a Money Fund. Unless you have $100,000 or more to invest, you should look at the retail funds for individual investors, not the institutional funds for corporations and fiduciaries (someone who holds the funds or property of another in trust, such as a real estate broker). If you do have $100,000 or more to put in a money fund, you could get a slightly higher rate with an institutional fund.

When chasing the highest rate, be watchful of one thing: Some new money market funds use teaser rates to attract customers. These funds absorb most of the fund expenses for a time so that they can post exceptionally high rates. When they've roped enough people in, they institute the regular charges, and the rates come down to earth. A final caution: If you want checking privileges with your money market account, look into it. Some accounts allow you to write only a limited number of checks a month, and others won't allow you to write checks over a certain dollar amount.

Just the facts

- Stocks and stock mutual funds have outperformed bonds and cash investments over the long term, but with appreciably more risk.

- There are many basic investment strategies to choose from, including the buy-and-hold, short-term trading, dollar cost averaging, the constant dollar system, the Dogs of the Dow, and indexing.

- Considerations when purchasing an actively managed mutual fund include fund type, performance, management style, riskiness, expenses, and tax consequences.

- In buying a bond mutual fund, there are certain special considerations, including the quality of the bonds in the fund, the average maturity of the bonds in the fund, and whether you would make more in a municipal bond fund.

- Don't put your money in a taxable money market fund unless your after-tax return would be greater than the return you would get from a tax-free fund.

GET THE SCOOP ON...
Picking stocks using fundamental
analysis ▪ Picking stocks using technical
analysis ▪ Covering your bases with
a combination approach

Picking Individual Stocks

S o you're not satisfied with your mutual fund returns? Even your index fund is underperforming the market? You think you could do better than that 28-year-old managing your aggressive growth fund? Maybe you could—maybe you could do *much* better, as a matter of fact. Table 12.1 shows how much better you might have done if you had been picking your own stocks in the early 1990s.

Even in down markets, there are individual stocks that are advancing sharply. A good example is in 1994, a year when all major market averages were down. While it might be difficult to choose the best stock in a given year, your chances of picking a winner, after some very diligent research, aren't so bad—even in bear markets, when virtually all mutual funds will be following the market down.

So you think you've got some ideas? Great. But realize that picking your own stocks is not just about intuition. It's about backing up your hunches with solid research. That's whole-brain stock-picking.

Your right brain gives you the feeling that a certain stock is ready for take-off, and your left brain corroborates the hunch with data—or it doesn't. That's the key: If your research supports your feelings, invest; if it doesn't, don't. This chapter is about how to ground your hunches in reason, and it looks at the three most common methods of doing that: fundamental analysis, technical analysis, and the combination approach. As with investment styles, the decision as to which approach you take should depend on your investment philosophy and personality.

TABLE 12.1: MARKET AVERAGES VS. INDIVIDUAL STOCKS

Year	Market	Market Average	Best Stock	Average Best 25 Stocks	Worst Stock	Average Worst 5 Stocks
1994	NYSE	−5.8%	**208%**	94.70%	−88%	−74.6%
	AMEX	−11.8%	**1269%**	123.20%	−97%	−86.6%
	NASDAQ	−7.4%	**447%**	187.70%	−100%	−96.6%
1993	NYSE	7.60%	**220%**	145.30%	−97%	−84.4%
	AMEX	16.60%	**445%**	155.80%	−90%	−79.8%
	NASDAQ	12.10%	**458%**	277.80%	−88%	−85.8%
1992	NYSE	5.10%	**266%**	140%	−82%	−75%
	AMEX	−.2%	**188%**	113.70%	−89%	−81%
	NASDAQ	8.70%	**1609%**	318.30%	−92%	−87.4%

Chart courtesy of the On-Line Investment Center: www.the group.net/ invest/select.htm. From information obtained by Fortune, *1/24/94, 1/25/93, and 1/16/95.*

The fundamentals of fundamental analysis

Fundamental analysis is a method for analyzing stocks that revolves around a company's fundamentals—things like revenue, revenue growth, earnings, earnings growth, debt, and price-to-earnings ratio, as well as other factors such as corporate culture, level of competition, and marketing savvy. By examining a company's fundamentals, investors hope to gauge a company's financial stability, form an opinion about a company's future prospects, and finally come up with an intrinsic value for the company—a price per share valuation based on the company's true worth, as opposed to its current market value. (The process of determining the intrinsic value of a security by examining only its numerical, measurable characteristics such as revenues, earnings, and market share is referred to as *quantitative analysis*.)

Fundamentalists believe that all stocks will eventually move toward their intrinsic value. Thus, a stock with an intrinsic value greater than its market value would be expected to move up in price over time (a buy candidate), while a stock with an intrinsic value below its market value would be expected to decline (a sell candidate).

Fundamental analysis rests on the premise that not all information available to the public about a stock is immediately figured into a stock's price, and that investor psychology, which at times is anything but rational, can cause significant price distortions. Fundamentalists believe that these factors make it possible to find stocks that are underpriced.

The major tenets of fundamental analysis run counter to the *efficient market hypothesis*, embraced by the majority of professors of finance at academic institutions. The efficient market hypothesis argues that all available information—any information about a company's fundamentals you can get your hands on—has already been taken into account by the markets and is reflected in the stock's price. The markets are "efficient" in this regard, so no amount of research can net you any advantage whatsoever. Princeton University professor Burton Malkiel develops this argument powerfully in *A Random Walk Down Wall Street*.

Watch Out!
Value investing is not for the lazy. You'll need to dig for information on some companies, especially small companies. You'll also need to monitor your stocks closely so as not to miss the chance to sell them when they move up in price and are no longer undervalued.

Warren Buffett, of course, would disagree. Numerous academic studies have shown that value investing, which rests on fundamental analysis, works. While the debate rages on, it's safe to say that analyzing the fundamentals of a company before you invest just makes good sense. You simply shouldn't buy things, especially expensive things, without checking them out first. Whether or not fundamental analysis will add value to your investments in the long run, it certainly can't hurt—and the only thing it will cost you is time.

Although classic fundamental analysis goes hand in hand with value investing, it can be applied to other investment approaches. Growth investors, for example, also examine companies' fundamentals as a basis for making investment decisions. They simply apply different criteria, often using the same parameters. Because fundamental analysis is generally equated with value investing, however, this chapter discusses it from that angle. For solid guidelines on applying fundamental analysis to growth investing, contact the National Association of Investors Corporation at 877-275-6242, or visit their Web site at www.better-investing.org.

Scrutinizing the balance sheet

While different fundamentalists emphasize different data, all fundamentalists look at certain core indicators, and many of which can be found on a company's balance sheet. A *balance sheet* is a financial report that indicates the net worth of a company (shareholder's equity or common stock equity) at a given time, by showing how much is owned (assets) and how much is owed (liabilities). The balance sheet is divided into three sections: assets, liabilities, and shareholder's equity (with the shareholder's equity being equal to the company's assets minus its liabilities).

Before you can examine a company's balance sheet, you have to get your hands on it. But where? Let your mouse do the walking. Go to FreeEDGAR at www.freedgar.com. Enter the company's name or ticker symbol, and on the next page click View Filings. On the next page, click the most recent 10-Q (quarterly report) or 10-K (annual report). Next, look under Table of Contents on the left margin and click Balance Sheet. From here either select the Excel option, to download a copy of the report as a spreadsheet, or scroll down to view the report online. Balance sheets usually cover only two years of data, so you'll want to download older 10-Ks as well to get a meaningful picture of trends. You should get at least four years of data. Another way to get a company's balance sheets is to call the company and ask to have the last several quarterly and annual reports sent to you.

Now that you have your balance sheets, take a look at the assets. The major asset categories are cash and marketable securities, accounts receivable (money the company is owed), inventories, other current assets, investments in affiliated companies, and plant and equipment. Considering the business, does the allocation of assets seem logical to you? Realize that an automobile manufacturer is going to have a lot of its assets in plant and equipment, whereas a brokerage firm will show more assets in cash and marketable securities. If the amount the company has invested in a particular asset seems unreasonably high or low to you, download the balance sheet of another company in the same industry and compare.

Unofficially...
Value stocks outperformed the broad market from 1977 to 1985, underperformed from 1985 to 1990, outperformed from 1991 to 1994, underperformed in 1995, outperformed again in 1996, and went back to trailing in 1997. The moral of the story: Be patient if your value stocks don't go up right away.

Next, look at the liabilities and then at how much long-term debt the company is carrying. If it's a significant amount, such as 30 percent or more of assets, can you think of a good reason why this might be? For a car manufacturer, long-term debt vehicles could be an excellent way to finance equipment, but that wouldn't be the case for a brokerage firm. Again, if you're suspicious, compare these numbers with those of a competing firm.

The next thing you want to check out is the company's total working capital and current ratio. Working capital, or *net working capital*, is the difference between the company's current assets and current liabilities. It's the cushion that largely determines a company's ability to consistently pay bills and employees and to finance new operations. If net working capital is zero or a negative number, the company is struggling just to make ends meet.

So how much working capital is considered enough? Generally, a company's current assets should be twice its current liabilities. Often this relationship is expressed as a ratio: Current assets divided by current liabilities equals current ratio. As a rule of thumb, then, a company should have current ratio of at least 2.0. But this depends: New companies generally need more working capital than this because they're expanding rapidly, while older, established companies tend to need less. Again, comparing this statistic with that of one or more companies in the same industry will give you some perspective.

Finally, you'll want to look at the trend of the current ratio over time. If it seems to be decreasing, that's not a good sign. You can find current assets, current liabilities, working capital, and current ratio

stats on RapidResearch (www.rapidresearch.com).
Just type in the company's ticker symbol; on the
information page about the company that comes
up, scroll down to Historical Financial Information.

Price-to-book value should be the next item on
your checklist. The book value of an individual asset
is the cost of the asset minus depreciation. In the
case of a company, book value is equal to the shareholder's equity—the total value of all the company's
assets minus all its liabilities. Book value, then, can
be viewed as a company's actual value, and the
extent to which this differs from the company's market value is of great interest to fundamentalists. In
using book value, fundamentalists compare book
value per share to price per share and then compare
this ratio to that of other companies in the same
industry.

You can get a company's book value right off the
balance sheet: It's listed at the bottom as shareholder's equity. To get the book value per share,
divide the shareholder's equity by the number of
outstanding shares. You can find this stat on
RapidResearch's Additional Information page. The
number of outstanding shares will be listed first.
Now divide your book value by the number of shares
outstanding to get book value per share. Finally,
divide the price per share by the book value per
share to get your price-to-book ratio.

The higher this ratio, the more value investors
feel management has added to the company. At the
same time, the higher this number relative to that of
other companies in the same industry, the less
upside potential there tends to be for the price.
Fundamentalists are looking for a price-to-book
value that is *low* relative to the competition. You can

Timesaver
Value investors
would do well
to invest in
companies with
share prices of
more than $5
because cheaper
stocks tend to be
ignored by
analysts, which
could delay their
discovery.

actually find out how a stock's price-to-book ratio compares to that of the industry average on RapidResearch. The figure is expressed as a percent under Co. to Industry (%). Anything over 100 indicates a higher price-to-book ratio than that of the industry as a whole.

Another important ratio to look at is the debt-to-equity ratio, which will give you some idea of how much debt a company is carrying relative to its size. The debt-to-equity ratio is calculated simply by dividing the amount of long-term debt—which you'll find right on your balance sheet—by the shareholder's equity.

Of course, borrowing is not inherently bad. All companies borrow capital; this is what makes it possible for companies to expand and generate even more wealth. And because interest payments on debt are a tax write-off for companies, carrying a certain amount of debt is advantageous. For the most part, though, debt puts a financial burden on a company. As a rule of thumb, don't buy companies with a debt-to-equity ratio of more than 1.0; these companies actually owe more than they own. Further, it's best to go with companies whose debt-to-equity ratios are less than the industry average. You can find a company's debt-to-equity ratio under Historical Financial Information and a company's debt/equity to industry under Co. to Industry (%) on RapidResearch.

Some of the other things you might want to look at include the amount of cash a company holds (listed first under Current Assets) relative to annual sales (which you'll find on the income statement, discussed in the next section). More is better, especially for companies that sometimes want to run in the red during expansionary periods. Also look at return on equity or net income (also found on the income statement) relative to stockholder's equity. Higher is better, of course, and inventory shouldn't be rising much faster than sales.

Tearing apart the income statement

The other core statistics used by fundamentalists to analyze a company can be found on a company's income statement. An income statement is a report of the annual revenues (sales), expenses, and income (the difference between revenues and expenses) of a corporation, usually for two separate years. So while the balance sheet gives a picture of a company's overall wealth, the income statement shows how much money a company is making. You can access a company's income statement the same way you access its balance sheet. Go to freedgar.com, open the most recent quarterly or annual reports (10-Q or 10-K), and then click Income Report. As with balance sheets, remember to download 10-Ks from a few prior years so you can get a longer-term view.

Reading an income statement is not difficult. The first line gives the company's sales or gross revenue, depending on what kind of business it is. This is followed by itemized expenses, which are subtracted from the sales figure to give a net income or loss for the year, listed near the bottom of the report. A loss is indicated by putting the figure in parentheses.

Naturally, you want to see that a company is making money, not losing it. But the net income figure will not always give you the complete picture. A company can record a sale as income as soon as the sale is made, even if it hasn't been paid for in full, so the income statement often includes income that hasn't actually been received yet. Conversely, a company is

Watch Out!
Because of permitted practices for recording expenses, a company can have a positive net income and still go bankrupt. Be sure to familiarize yourself with income statements, so you learn to identify troubling parts of a company's financial picture.

allowed to report expenses for certain items incrementally, even if all the money for an item has been paid out. This is why checking the ratio of current assets to current liabilities on the balance sheet is so important. You can find revenue and net income figures on RapidResearch.

Next, take a look at the earnings per share (EPS), which is calculated by dividing the company's total earnings over a given period by the number of shares outstanding. Ideally, a company's EPS will be higher than the industry average. But it's even more important that a company's EPS be growing. EPS growth is the growth of a company's earnings over time.

To get an idea of the trend in EPS growth, you need to look at a period covering at least 10 years. This means you'll have to download income statements from 10-Q or 10-K reports going back several years. (RapidResearch data goes back only four years.) At or near the bottom of the income statement, you'll find earnings per share. This is sometimes expressed as income per share. Plot a line chart of the company's earnings per share, with years on the x-axis and EPS on the y-axis. The line should be moving up from year to year. If the EPS is moving down or changing erratically, you'll want to avoid this company at the present time. You're looking for steady earnings growth. A particularly good sign is if earnings growth is actually accelerating over time, reflected by a line that curves upward. To evaluate the earnings of the most recent quarter, compare them to those of the same quarter a year ago. This is especially important with cyclical stocks, which may show large seasonal swings in earnings.

The next thing to look at is profit margin. Profit margin is the percentage of total income that is left over after expenses have been covered. It can also be thought of as the percentage of a company's income that is turned into profit. Profit margin is calculated by dividing net income (profit) by gross revenues (sales).

As with EPS growth, it's best to chart profit margin over a period of several years to see if the company has been successful at increasing the margin. You want to avoid firms with steadily decreasing margins, of course. A company can increase its profit margin by increasing sales or reducing expenses, so for a deeper understanding of what's driving a company's profit margin numbers, take a look at these numbers. It's a good idea to compare a company's profit margin to that of a competitor or the industry as a whole. RapidResearch provides profit margin to industry figures and expresses them as a percent. A number over 100 percent indicates a profit margin above that of the industry average; a figure under 100 percent indicates a profit margin below the industry average.

The interest coverage ratio is another important measure of a company's financial situation. The interest coverage ratio measures how many times over a company could pay the interest payments on its debt in a given year, giving an indication of how solvent a company is. A company that is barely able to cover its debt obligations is flirting with bankruptcy.

The interest coverage ratio is calculated by dividing the earnings before interest and taxes (EBIT) by the interest payments. The EBIT simply measures a company's total earnings before taxes and interest payments on debt obligations have been taken out. If the EBIT does not appear as such on the income statement, take the pretax income or total company

Unofficially...
The most frequently quoted data on both domestic and foreign investments comes from Ibbotson Associates (www.ibbotson. com), which publishes its *Stocks, Bonds, Bills and Inflation (SBBI) Yearbook* annually. They also make software products based on their research. Contact Ibbotson at 1-800-758-3557.

income before income taxes, and add the interest payments or interest expenses. (The pretax income figure on income statements does not include interest payments because these are tax-deductible.) Now divide the sum and by the interest payment figure. The resulting number is the interest coverage ratio. Fundamentalists are looking for companies with an interest coverage ratio of 3 or 4; the higher the better. The EBIT is available on RapidResearch.

No analysis of a company's fundamentals would be complete without a look at the price-to-earnings ratio. This ratio indicates the relationship between a stock's price per share and its earnings per share (EPS), giving an indication of how richly priced a stock is relative to how much money a company is actually making. The PE is calculated by dividing the stock's share price by its EPS. Again, earnings per share (or income per share) can be found at the bottom of an income statement. By traditional standards, a stock with a high PE relative to that of the market—or, better, the industry or its own history—is more likely to come down in price (bringing its PE into line with the average PE for the market or the industry) than a stock with a high PE, and a stock with a relatively low PE has greater upside potential. The lower the PE, the better.

But this is not an ironclad rule. A company's current PE could be higher than its historical PE because of rising earnings expectations or some other positive development. Growth stocks, for example, tend to have higher PEs because they're expected to experience better-than-average earnings growth going forward. In fact, a lot of new companies have *no* PE because they don't have any earnings yet. But if such a company's other fundamentals are solid and future expectations for the company are high, it could be an excellent investment. Instead of looking at the standard trailing PEs, which are based on past numbers, many growth investors look at forward PEs, which are based on expected earnings. So, if earnings are expected to grow 100 percent in a year, a stock with a trailing PE of 40 would have a forward PE of only 20. Suddenly the stock doesn't look so expensive. Conversely, a low PE isn't always a good thing. A company that is really struggling could have a low PE because of low earnings and a low price.

It's essential, then, to view a stock's PE in light of its other fundamentals. If these are solid, a low PE is a big plus. PE and PE industry are available on RapidResearch.

You should also take a look at the dividend yield. This is the annualized dividend rate of a stock, calculated by dividing the cash dividend per share by the price per share. Dividend per share is listed at the very bottom of the income statement. If the stock was trading at $50 per share, and cash dividends equaled $1.80 per share, the dividend yield would be 3.6 percent ($1.80 / $50 = .036). The higher the dividend yield, the better. A low dividend yield indicates that a stock has a high price, a low dividend, or both—not good. It's not unusual for many growth stocks, though, to pay no dividends because all earnings are being reinvested in the company. It's best to compare a company's dividend yield, then, with its own history and with the dividend yields of other companies in the same industry. Generally speaking, higher dividend yields are indicative of greater stability and lower risk. They can also indicate lower prices.

Watch Out!
If a fundamental statistic of a company changes significantly, find out why. It could be a fluke. A dramatic change in the PE, for example, could be caused by a one-time charge or taxes.

Historically, the average dividend yield on the S&P 500 has always been above 3.0 percent, but in the 1990s it dropped below 2.0 percent and now stands around 1.3 percent, an all-time low.

Other factors to consider when analyzing a company's fundamentals include these:

▪ **Revenue growth:** The higher the better. As with earnings, look at several years, and compare the most recent quarter's revenues with those of the same quarter a year ago.

▪ **Research and development:** Here you're looking for stable or increasing spending on research and development (R&D) as a percentage of sales, which is especially important for technology companies.

▪ **Tax abnormalities:** Paying too few taxes may indicate that a company is taking write-offs to give their earnings a face lift.

▪ **Changes in the number of shares outstanding:** Stock splits, reverse splits, and the issuing of new stock are not inherently bad, but when a company does any of these things, it's important to find out why.

Moneysaver
Go to www. investorguide. com and click Investing under the Links Directory on the home page menu for lists of links to free (and fee-based) Web sites offering investment information and research tools.

Picking some stocks

As an online investor, the best way to pick some stocks for yourself is to first narrow the field by using an online stock screen. A stock screen is a program that generates a list of stocks based on the parameters you input. Using a stock screen will allow you to create a list of a couple dozen stocks that meet some of your basic criteria. With your list in hand, you can start to analyze each stock's fundamentals and make some selections. Don't rush this process. There's nothing wrong with buying one stock at a time; you don't have to go from a 100 percent cash position to a 100 percent stock position overnight.

The accompanying box gives a list of some good stock screens. Your online broker may also provide a stock screening tool.

Quicken.com	quicken.excite.com/investments/stocks/search
RapidResearch	www.rapidresearch.com
Hoover's Online	www.stockscreener.com
Smart Ratings.com	www.smartratings.com
Stock Selector.com	www.stockselector.com/screen.htm
MarketPlayer.com	www.marketplayer.com
INVESTools	www.investools.com/cgi-bin/free/screening?
The Motley Fool	www.fool.com/Stockscreens/StockScreens.htm
SmartMoney	http://university.smartmoney.com/Departments/StrategicInvesting/StockScreens

After analyzing the fundamentals of the companies on your list, go back to the quarterly or annual reports you have on hand and take a look at each company's cash flow statement (or look on the 10-Q or 10-K on FreeEDGAR). The cash flow statement will show you exactly where a company's cash is coming from and in what quantities, as well as where it's going. When inflow is greater than outflow, cash flow is positive. The best case is when cash flow is positive and growing. If it isn't, find out why not.

The other thing in the annual report you want to look at is management's discussion and analysis of the company. This is where you'll find any explanations of why certain numbers may have changed or

Timesaver
To get the most out of the time you put into your research, make a list of the things you're looking for in a stock before you do anything else. A checklist serves as a rudder, helping you stay on course as you navigate the sea of reports and statistics you'll encounter along the way.

moved in an unfavorable direction. You'll also find out what management's future plans are and possibly any concerns they may have.

If you're still not sure about a stock at this point, step back and try to see the big picture. What do you think of the company's products? Do you think the company can stay competitive? Defend its niche? How's marketing? Management? Corporate culture? Can the company attract and hold on to talented people? What do future prospects look like? Is the company international or planning to be? What about the industry? What do the analysts say? If you have a higher opinion of the company than the analysts do, and you're right, you might pick the stock up (relatively) cheap. Do insiders (directors and senior officers) continue to hold or, better, accumulate stock? Insider buying is much more meaningful than selling because buying means insiders think the stock is cheap; selling often just means the insider needed some cash.

The significance of insider selling depends on what percentage of his position the insider is selling. Check the InsiderTrader at www.insidertrader.com or Yahoo! Finance at http://quote.yahoo.com for the inside scoop on insider trading at virtually all actively traded company. The accompanying table lists some other good free sites where you can find various kinds of information on various companies, as well as overall market news and commentary.

Technical analysis

Technical analysis is a method of analyzing stocks and markets that revolves around price movements and trading volume. It does not involve looking at a company's financial stability, profitability, or future prospects. Technicians focus on prices instead of

COMPANY INFORMATION

Wall Street Research Net	www.wsrn.com
Hoover's Online	www.hoovers.com
Corporate Information	www.corporateinformation.com
Wright Research Center	http://profiles.wisi.com/profiles/comsrch.htm
Dun & Bradstreet's Companies Online	www.companiesonline.com
FinancialWeb StockTools	www.financialweb.com/stocktools
Yahoo! Business & Economy	http://dir.yahoo.com/Business_and_Economy/Companies
CNNfn Web Connection	www.cnnfn.com/resources/referencedesk/companies/search.html
Zack's Research	www.zacks.com/reswizard/irama+rw.html

NEWS AND MARKET COMMENTARY

CNBC Business & *The Wall Street Journal*	www.msnbc.com/news/COM_Front.asp?a
***The Wall Street Journal* Highlights**	www.msnbc.com/news/WSJHIGHLIGHTS_Front.asp
The New York Times (you'll need to register)	www.nytimes.com/auth/login?Tag=/&URI=/yr/mo/day/business
CNNfn	www.cnnfn.com/briefing
Investor's Business Daily	www.investors.com/web_edition/today/welcome.html
***USA Today* Moneyline**	www.usatoday.com/money/digest/md1.htm
Bloomberg.com	www.bloomberg.com/welcome.html
TheStreet.com (subscription required)	www.thestreet.com
Standard & Poor's	www.stockinfo.standardpoor.com/today.htm

Bright Idea
You might want to check out whether a company you're researching offers its employees stock options. A study by Hewitt Associates shows that companies that do so outperform companies that do not.

NEWS AND MARKET COMMENTARY *(cont)*	
ABC News Business Section	http://abcnews.go.com/ sections/business
Yahoo! Business News	http://dailynews.yahoo.com/ headlines/bs
Yahoo! Finance	http://finance.yahoo.com

fundamentals because they subscribe to the efficient market theory. They simply don't believe there's any information available out there that hasn't already been figured into a stock's price. So, no matter how thoroughly you scour a company's balance sheets and income statements, they think, you just won't find any bargains. While technical analysts don't believe that fundamental analysis will add any value to your stock picking, they think examining price trends will.

Behind this belief is the theory that the stock market, while efficient, is not logical. Rather, it is psychological. The theory goes something like this: When a person decides to buy a stock, he expects its price to go up. When he sells, he expects it to fall. So investor's buy-and-sell decisions rest heavily on their expectations about what's going to happen with a stock's price. Now, humans are not machines—they are imperfect, at times unreasonable, often emotional, and relatively unpredictable creatures. This means that their expectations about a stock's price may change with time for reasons that may not be entirely reasonable. In fact, investor's expectations about future prices change in direct relation to the ways in which stock prices themselves change. By gaining an understanding of how certain price movements affect investor psychology, then, it is possible to gain a distinct trading advantage.

What technical analysis boils down to is the belief that it's much more important to determine what investors *expect* a security to sell for in the future than what it *should* be selling for now.

Many opponents of technical analysis state that even if there is a correlation between past and future prices, this correlation in no way implies a cause-and-effect relationship. Analyzing past prices for indications of future prices, then, is the financial equivalent of reading tea leaves. Other say that even if there is a cause-and-effect relationship between past and future prices, it's too slight to base investment decisions on. Proponents of technical analysis counter that price patterns do exist—and appear again and again. Even if we don't understand why they occur, they claim, it's prudent not to trade against them.

> 66
> In individuals, insanity is rare, but in groups, parties, nations, and epochs it is the rule.
> —Friedrich Nietzsche
> 99

Dow Theory

Modern-day technical analysis had its beginnings in Dow Theory, developed by Charles Dow, who cofounded Dow Jones & Company with Edward D. Jones around the turn of the century. There are two parts to Dow Theory. The first part states that there are three types of general price movements: the primary or long-term trend, which takes place over years; secondary movements, which occur over weeks or months and run counter to the primary trend; and daily fluctuations, which can go in either direction but are of little overall significance. The second part of the theory states that the Industrial Average and the Railroad Average (now the Transportation Index) must move in the same direction for a clear market trend to be in place.

Dow Theory also states that when prices move sideways in a range of about 5 percent for several weeks or more, a line (trading range) has been established. If prices then move above this line, they should head higher; if they move below the line, they should head lower. These contentions, of course, apply only if both the Dow Industrials and Transportation Index show the same trend. If they do not, the future direction of prices remains uncertain.

Dow ascribed basic attributes to bull and bear markets that are still used today. The first stage of a bull market, he said, is characterized by low share prices, bad financial reports, and general pessimism. This is when far-sighted investors are actually buying stock. The second stage is characterized by better financial reports, increased activity, and rising prices. As optimism grows, the market becomes overbought, and savvy investors start to sell. The first stage of a bear market is characterized by panic *buying*, even as seasoned investors are selling. Oversupply of stocks caused by the selling leads to a fall in share prices, which leads to the second phase of a bear market: panic selling. In this phase, prices fall hard as more people head for the exits. But unbeknownst to the masses, smart investors have already started to buy again, for this is actually the first stage of the next bull market.

According to Dow Theory, an overbought or pricey market will show weak, dull rallies (low trading volume, poor breadth) but active declines; an oversold market will show the opposite. The ends of bull markets (market tops) are characterized by heavy volume; the ends of bear markets (market bottoms), by light volume.

One of the most important theories to evolve from Dow Theory is Stage Theory, developed by Stan Weinstein, which states that a stock usually moves through four consecutive stages. In Stage 1, the stock price moves sideways, trading in a relatively narrow range. The stock doesn't really advance or decline; it moves back and forth across its 200-day moving average. The stock is said to be "base-building" in Stage 1. Stage 2 begins as the share price rises above its 50-day and 200-day moving averages, usually due to improving conditions at the company. If the stock drops below its 50-day moving average but stays above its 200-day average, it is still considered to be in Stage 2. In Stage 3, the stock tops out and starts to cross below the 50-day and 200-day moving averages. This is when you should sell to lock in profits. Stage 4 is marked by steady decline, the stock price dropping convincingly below the 50- and 200-day moving averages and continuing down until Stage 1 begins again. Never buy a stock that's in Stage 4.

An entire discipline of stock analysis, incorporating some highly sophisticated tools, has grown out of Dow's basic observations. These tools do not enable investors to predict the future direction of prices, but they can increase an investor's chances of making profitable trades.

Support and resistance

One of the most fundamental concepts of technical analysis is *support and resistance levels.* A support level is a price at which the majority of investors consider a stock to be cheap and expect it to rise. When a stock drops to a support level, investors in the stock become net buyers, and the price of the stock tends not to fall farther. A resistance level, by contrast, is a price at which the majority of investors consider a stock to be expensive and expect it to fall. When a stock climbs to a resistance level, investors in the

> 66
> Invest your time before you invest your money. Test your strategy before you risk your money.
> —Equity Analytics, Inc.
> 99

stock become net sellers, and the stock tends not to climb higher. Support and resistance levels result from the forces of supply and demand. As a stock's price reaches a certain high, demand for the stock wanes and supply increases, leading to a subsequent drop in the price; as a stock's price drops to a low, demand increases and supply falls, leading to a rise in the price.

When a stock price penetrates a resistance level, an event known as a breakout or penetration of resistance, there is usually an increase in volume, as more investors buy the stock in anticipation of higher price levels. More investors buy the stock in the belief that the stock is finally succeeding in moving up into a higher trading range, and the increased demand for the stock does, indeed, drive its price upward. If the stock breaks below a support level, an occurrence known as a breakdown or penetration of support, volume also increases as more people sell. More investors sell the stock in the belief that the stock is falling into a lower trading range, and the increase in supply of the stock does, in fact, depress the price.

If the penetration is very strong, the stock may actually "gap up" (or "gap down")—jumping to a new trading range from one session to the next, breaking the continuity of prices. Such occurrences are indicated by a break in the line on the stock's price chart. Breakouts or breakdowns not accompanied by higher volume may not last, with prices retreating back to former levels. Figure 12.1 shows a breakout for eBay above the $100 level in March 1999. Notice how volume, shown by the lower chart, explodes.

To use support and resistance levels, draw horizontal lines connecting recent high or lows. One strategy is to buy when the share price is near the

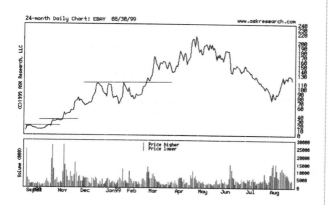

Figure 12.1: A breakout in eBay stock.

support line and sell near the resistance. Another is to wait until the stock dips below the resistance line and then buy in anticipation of higher prices.

The trend is your friend

A trend is a consistent movement in prices in a certain direction, either up or down. Technicians look for trends in stock prices because they believe that there is a tendency for prices moving in a certain direction to continue to do so. A rising trend line is defined by successively higher lows; a falling trend line is defined by lower highs. Figure 12.2 shows a rising trend for Microsoft from October 1998 through February 1999.

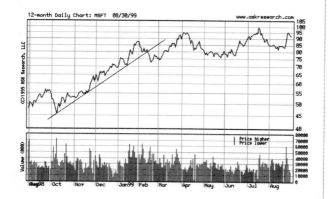

Figure 12.2: A rising trend in Microsoft stock, October 1998 to February 1999.

When a stock rises above a falling trend line, a change in trend to the upside may have begun, indicating that a growing number of investors are expecting higher prices. If a stock falls below a rising trend line, a change in trend to the downside may be underway, indicating that an increasing number of investors expect lower prices. As with penetration of support and resistance levels, penetration of trend lines should be accompanied by an increase in volume. If not, prices may fall back into line with the old trend. Figure 12.3 shows how the rising trend line for Callaway Golf was broken in May 1999 and led to much lower prices.

Figure 12.3: Callaway Golf, May 1999.

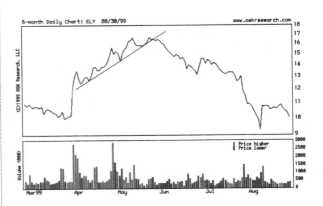

To use trend lines, draw a line connecting recent highs, if a stock is moving down, or connecting lows, if it's moving up. If the stock remains on an uptrend, consider buying. If the stock is on a downtrend, consider waiting to purchase shares until the stock has bottomed and starts to head up again.

Moving averages
As mentioned previously, a moving average is the average price of a security over a given period of time. Some of the more common periods are 25

days, 50 days, and 200 days. Longer time periods are used to reflect long-term trends. To calculate a moving average of a stock, you must first choose the time period. Next, add up the stock's closing prices for each of the days in the time period and divide by the number of days in the period. The resulting number is the moving average of the stock for that time period as of the last day of the period.

The moving average represents the average investor sentiment about a stock as reflected by its price over a given period. If the current price is above the moving average, it shows increasing bullishness for the stock among investors. If the current price is below the moving average, it shows increasing bearishness. Figure 12.4 shows the 50-day and 200-day moving averages for Amgen, a drug company, between August 1998 and August 1999.

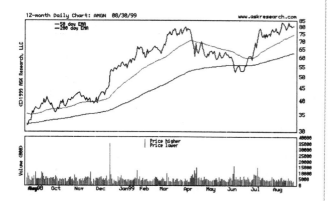

Figure 12.4:
Moving averages (50-day and 200-day) for Amgen stock.

To use a moving average, draw the moving average on a chart of the stock with an online charting program or investment software. To try it out, go to Yahoo! Finance (http://quote.yahoo.com), enter a ticker symbol, click Chart, and then click Moving Averages in the lower-right corner of the chart. When a stock price falls below the moving average you're using, sell. When it rises above it, buy. As with support and resistance lines and trend lines, however, if penetration of a moving average is not accompanied by a rise in volume, it may very well be temporary.

If you want to trade short-term price changes, use a short-term moving average. If you want to trade only long-term changes, use a long-term average. Be careful, however, about trading with a short-term moving average, such as a 25-day average. If a stock is moving sideways, you may get *whipsawed*. A whipsaw occurs when the price crosses the moving average signaling you to buy or sell and then crosses back again soon, signaling you to do the opposite. Whipsaws tend to generate losses and additional commission fees. Using a long-term moving average, such as a 200-day average, will help you avoid whipsaws, but it will also get you in and out of trend changes later. On upmoves, then, you'll miss more of the climb; on downmoves, you'll be selling at a lower price.

These are the most fundamental of technical tools, those which all online investors should be familiar with. But there are dozens more. For example, the moving average convergence divergence (MACD) measures the difference between the 12-day moving average and the 26-day moving average. The higher the 12-day average relative to the 26-day, the better for the stock because more recent sentiment is increasingly bullish.

Stochastics measure closing prices of a stock in relation to their proximity to daily highs and lows over a period. Technicians have found that stocks in an uptrend tend to close closer to their daily highs; those in a downtrend close closer to their lows. If

Bright Idea
Powerful short-term buy and sell signals can be generated by using two moving averages on the same chart, such as a 10-day and a 30-day. A buy is signaled when the 10-day average crosses above the 30-day average and both moving averages are pointing upward. A sell is signaled when the 10-day average crosses below the 30-day average and both are headed down.

stocks in an uptrend start closing closer to their lows (or those in a downtrend closer to their highs), this may signify an imminent change in direction for the stock's share price.

Relative strength or relative strength analysis compares the performances of various stocks or industries to each other (or to indexes) to determine which are performing the best at any given time. Those that are performing well relative to the market are said to have high relative strength.

Investors who use relative strength as a basis for making buy and sell decisions buy stocks in industries with high relative strength and sell these stocks when the stocks' relative strength starts to fall. The theory is that if a stock's performance is strong relative to that of the market, it will continue to be, and if a stock's relative strength begins to fall, it will do so before the price does.

Relative strength is commonly measured by dividing a stock's current price by its price a year ago, dividing the current S&P 500 level by its level a year ago, and then dividing the stock's price-change fraction by the S&P's. A value above 1.0 means that the stock shows relative strength over the last one-year period—it has moved up faster than the S&P. A value below 1.0 shows relative weakness. The best way to get a quick idea of which stocks or industries are showing the greatest relative strength is to purchase specialized software, such as Telescan Analyzer (go to http://software-guide.com/cdprod1/swhrec/017/915.shtml), or subscribe to a service or newsletter (such as *The Chartist*) that ranks stocks or industries on a relative-strength basis.

While relative strength is a powerful tool, however, it does not take risk into account. Often stocks that move up faster than the market as a whole during bull markets move down faster during bear markets. Of course, stocks that move down the least during a bear market display high relative strength and are often the stocks that lead the charge in the ensuing bull market.

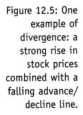

Unofficially...
Relative strength is not the same thing as the Relative Strength Index (RSI), which is used as a contrary, not a momentum, indicator.

The number of indicators used by technical analysts is extensive, and you certainly don't have to master them all. In fact, while it's a good idea to familiarize yourself with as many as you can, many successful traders only use one or two of their favorite indicators to trade by.

Technicians have a host of technical indicators at their disposal to confirm price trends, but in some cases the indicators fail to do so, a situation known as a divergence. One example is when a stock is hitting new highs, but the statistics show a clustering of closing prices near daily lows; another is when the stock market itself is climbing to new highs, but the advance/decline line is falling, as shown in Figure 12.5.

Figure 12.5: One example of divergence: a strong rise in stock prices combined with a falling advance/decline line.

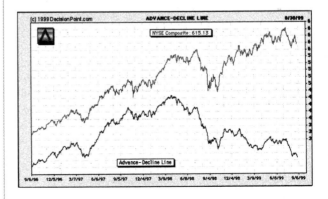

Usually divergences resolve themselves by prices falling into line with the indicators. Another type of divergence, however, occurs between indicators themselves, when one gives the opposite indication of another. Divergences among indicators may indicate a forthcoming change in direction for a stock or a market.

It has probably become apparent by now that all of the indicators used by technicians appear on charts. Indeed, charts and charting are essential to technical analysis. The following is a list of free charts you can access online:

- **StockCharts.com:** www.stockcharts.com
- **EquityTrader:** www.equitytrader.com
- **Ask Research:** www.askresearch.com
- **BigCharts:** www.bigcharts.com

Applying technical analysis to the broad market

In addition to analyzing individual securities, technical analysts also evaluate the direction of the overall market and adjust their market exposure accordingly—a practice referred to as market timing. If a technician determines that the market trend is up, the market is a buy; if the trend is down, the market is a sell. When the trend changes from down to up, the technician says the market has given a buy signal; if the market trend turns down, he says the market has given a sell signal.

Technicians use three kinds of indicators to analyze the market: monetary, momentum, and sentiment.

Monetary indicators

Monetary indicators focus mainly on trends in interest rates. As mentioned earlier, falling rates are favorable for stocks and bonds; rising rates are unfavorable.

Unofficially...
Before advising anyone to buy a particular security, most technical analysts will first try to confirm that the broad market is moving up and then that the individual security is. A rising market puts the wind at the back of individual securities, so to speak, whereas a declining market forces them to fly into the wind.

Momentum indicators

Momentum indicators look at price trends. In determining market momentum, technicians apply many of the same indicators to the market that they do to individual securities, including support and resistance levels, trend lines, moving averages, and so on. But they also apply indicators that they can't apply to individual stocks, including new highs to new lows, advancers versus decliners, and the number of stocks above their 200-day moving average—all of which are said to measure breadth—or the number of issues doing well at a given time. Because all major market indexes, with the exception of the Dow, are weighted by market capitalization, it's possible for an index to rise even if only a few large cap stocks in the index are doing well. In a healthy bull market, however, market advances should be broad-based, involving a large number of stocks.

The number of new highs to new lows is a market indicator that looks at the ratio of stocks hitting their all-time highs to those hitting their all-time lows each day. Using the daily figures, technicians can chart this ratio. When the chart is rising, indicating that the all-time highs are outpacing the all-time lows, the market tends to head higher. The same can be said when the number of advancing issues exceeds the number of decliners. (The chart of this indicator is known as the advance/decline line.) When a large or ever-increasing number of stocks are above their 200-day moving average, chances are good that the market will continue to rise. Breadth indicators should always move in tandem with prices. If the market is heading higher but breadth indicators are heading lower, you have a divergence, which often signifies an imminent change in market direction. Divergences are not infallible, but they do provide valuable warning signs.

Sentiment indicators

Sentiment indicators measure investor expectations (and emotions), and one of the most basic is the put/call ratio. The *put/call ratio* is the number of outstanding put contracts divided by the number of outstanding calls; the moving average of the ratio is also charted. A *put,* as you recall, is a contract that gives you the right to sell a stock at a certain price by a certain time in the future. Buyers of puts profit when the stock falls, allowing them to purchase the stock low and sell it at the higher put price. A *call* is a contract that allows you to buy a stock at a specified price within a specified period. If the stock rises, you can buy it at the cheaper call price.

Because the movement of individual stocks is influenced by the movement of the broad market, investors tend to buy more calls when they think the market is headed up and more puts when they think it's headed down. (It's also possible to buy puts and calls on the market itself.) The put/call ratio, then, measures the amount of pessimism relative to optimism in the market at a given time. In deference to Dow Theory, technicians consider this a contrary indicator, one that suggests prices will do the opposite of what most investors expect. So when the put/call ratio rises above a certain level, the number of puts to calls being high, market sentiment is thought to be excessively pessimistic, which is bullish because prices may be overly depressed. If the ratio falls below a certain level, investors are overly optimistic, which is bearish.

For similar reasons, the number of investment advisers who are bullish on the stock market is also a contrary indicator. When the number of bullish advisors rises above a certain number, market sentiment is thought be excessively optimistic, which is bearish. When the number of bulls falls, it's bullish.

To learn more about these and other indicators, check out the following sites:

- www.equis.com/free/taaz/ inttechnicalanalysis.html

- http://members.aol.com/indivstr/ styles-technical-analysis.html

- www2.hawaii.edu/~rpeterso/finbkmrk.htm

- www.e-analytics.com/tutor2.htm

Before placing a trade, some technical analysts also take into account what's called seasonality, or seasonal indicators. In a broad sense, *seasonality* is the same thing as cyclicity, the tendency for the performance of stocks to be affected by different seasons. In a more specific sense, however, seasonality is the historical bias for the market as a whole to do better or worse than usual on certain dates, days of the week, and months of the year. Historically, November, December, and January have been the best months of the year for the stock market; May, September, and October have been the worst. (The 1929 and 1987 crashes both occurred in September/ October.) In general, the spring and fall are often disappointing, while summer often brings a "summer rally"; winter brings "The Santa Claus Rally" and "The January Effect." The days surrounding Christmas, New Year's Day, and Thanksgiving are particularly good.

Bright Idea
Consider glancing at Art Merrill's *The Behavior of Prices on Wall Street* and Yale Hirsch's *Don't Sell Stocks on Monday*. They demonstrated the statistical validity of seasonal indicators.

Advantages and disadvantages

One of the potential advantages of technical analysis is that it helps you avoid serious losses to your portfolio. While fundamentalists refuse to sell a stock unless certain fundamentals worsen, technicians will sell not long after a stock turns down, regardless of the reason, only to pick it up again later if it starts to rebound.

Let's look at an example, which should remind you of the short-term trading discussion in Chapter 11, "Venturing Out on Your Own." Say you bought 50 shares of XYZ at $100 per share, and the stock went up to $125 before starting down. Following technical analysis, you sell at $119 because the stock has broken below its 25-day moving average. Down, down, down it goes, bottoming around $85. At this point, you're up $950, but the fundamentalists who also bought 50 shares at $100 per share are down $750. Now imagine the stock starts coming back. As the price rises above its 25-day moving average, you pick up 50 shares again at $90 and ride the stock back up to $125. You made an additional $1,750 on this move, for a total of $2,700. The fundamentalist is up only $1,250. The technical approach limited your losses and maximized your gains. Of course, you paid double the transaction costs, but the extra $1,450 ought to cover it.

Ideally, this is how technical analysis works, but like most things in life, it's not always so effective in practice. As mentioned in the discussion of moving averages, if a stock is trading sideways, and you're jumping in and out in accordance with a sensitive trend indicator, you're definitely going to lose money, whereas the fundamentalist will not. Also, if the stock shoots up suddenly, you're going to get in

Unofficially...
Keep in mind that many seasoned, knowledgeable investors maintain that you cannot time stocks or the market, and any attempt to do so will only hurt your returns in the end.

late and quite possibly miss out on the major part of the move. The fundamentalist will profit fully. In fact, technicians are almost always late getting in because their indicators don't turn positive until the stock has already started its ascent.

A number of stock-screening tools are available online geared toward technical analysis. Be fore-warned, though, that these may be difficult for the beginning online investor because they require deeper knowledge of technical indicators:

- www.alphachart.com/scan.html

- www.investorama.com/iqc_scan.html

- www.iqc.com/research/customscan.asp

The combination approach

While buy-and-hold index investors and academi-cians may scoff at the whole notion of stock analysis, the majority of serious, successful investors sub-scribe to one form of analysis or another. The best methods generally involve a combination of both the fundamental *and* technical approaches.

How does one combine the two? One approach is to start by using a stock screen that employs gen-eral fundamental or technical criteria to generate a list of potential stocks for your portfolio. Go through the list, first examining each of the stock's fundamentals to narrow the list further. Next, pull up the price charts of the stocks you're still inter-ested in, and examine them on technical grounds. If a stock's fundamentals are solid but its share price is in a tailspin, hold off. Time your entry.

Another approach would be to first look at the overall market on technical grounds and confirm a bullish trend, and only then screen for individual stocks and analyze them. If the overall trend is bearish, you might not buy stocks at all. For a stock screen that combines both the fundamental and technical approaches, go to Vector Vest at www.vectorvest.com/stockreport/index.phtml?vvnumber=1036.

While it makes sense to consider technical factors in purchasing a stock, the decision to sell based on technical or fundamental data will depend on your investment philosophy and the degree to which you consider yourself a fundamentalist or technician at heart. The approach to stock analysis you end up taking, in the end, should come down to what feels right.

Just the facts

- Fundamental analysis involves evaluating stocks based on their fundamentals—factors such as price-to-earnings ratio, debt-to-equity ratio, and management.

- Technical analysis involves evaluating markets and securities based on price movements and volume changes.

- A combination approach involves evaluating stocks and markets based on both fundamental and technical factors.

Watch Out!
If you encounter data in your research that seems a bit unusual, it could be highly significant, or it could be a mistake! Don't assume that all the information you find is 100 percent accurate. If you're surprised by a figure, double-check it with another source.

GET THE SCOOP ON...
Asset allocation ▪ Buying bonds to reduce
risk ▪ Stops put a floor under a security ▪ Using
put options as hedges ▪ Market timing
▪ Avoiding risky investments and strategies

Keeping a Lid on Risk

Chapter 13

It's nice to be right. Back in May 1998, you had a hunch about America Online (AOL), did some research, bought 100 shares at $21 per share, and have watched the stock move up and up. With its share price around $130 by the fall of 1999, you're up well over $10,000 and feeling no pain. It's Thursday; you're at work and at around 1:00pm, a colleague comes into the office and announces nonchalantly, "The stock market is crashing." "What do you mean?" you ask. "The market is in a tailspin," he says. "It was down 400 points at noon." You shrug it off, figuring that it's just more of the same volatility that has characterized the market for months now. Remember the golden rule: Buy on dips. On your way home, you flip on the car radio only to hear that the market really did crash, closing down over 1,000 points, at 9,600! AOL was slammed for a 40 percent loss, closing at $78.

You quickly recall that the huge drop in April 1997 was followed the next day by an equally huge rally. So, you actually think about buying some more shares. But you don't. And you're glad the next day that you didn't, because this time is different. Against a backdrop of recent Fed tightening and overseas economies struggling, the tumble has a dire effect on investor psychology. During after-hours trading that night, the selling continues, and overseas markets plunge in sympathy with ours. When the market opens Friday, the selling contin-ues in earnest. Trading is suspended at noon because an SEC market circuit breaker kicks in as the market hits 8640 (down 10 percent). An hour later trading resumes, and the market moves lower, to close at 8550. AOL is off another 30 percent for the day, closing at $54.5. In two days you've lost 70 percent of your profits! And this is only the *begin-ning* of the bear market.

Market uncertainty

A likely scenario? Perhaps not. Possible? Absolutely. Market valuations, such as price per book, price per dividends, and price-per-earnings ratios for the broad market are at *all-time historical highs,* indicating that stocks are overvalued. And the market is long overdue for a real bear. A bear market is defined as one that loses 15 percent of its value as measured by a market index, such as the S&P 500. The average length of time between bear markets is 3.1 years. Thus, historically, bear markets occur fairly often. But as of mid-August 1999, there has been only one correction that meets the formal definition of a bear market since July 1990. This was the correction that took place from mid-July 1998 to the end of August 1998, when the S&P fell 19.3 percent.

The period of decline, however, was only 1.5 months, compared to a historical norm of 1.5 *years* for the average bear market, and the usual effect of bringing valuations back down to reasonable levels did not occur. Most bears are also much more severe, taking prices down an average of 36.5 percent. No, this was no bear market. This was just a temporary pullback.

Yeah, but mutual funds are designed to shield investors from the full brunt of a bear market, aren't they? No way. While individual stocks can go up during a bear market, the more stocks in a portfolio, the more closely the portfolio will mirror the performance of the major indexes. Growth and aggressive growth funds are designed to go up *more* than the indexes, and because the stocks in these funds are more volatile than average, these funds will also go down more than the indexes in a bear market. In the average bear market when the S&P loses 36.5 percent, the average index fund will lose 36.5 percent, and the average growth fund will lose more than 50 percent of its value. Stock mutual funds are not bear market safe havens.

The risk of bear markets and significant downturns in individual securities is always with us. High-risk investments do not equal high returns, not even over the long run. They may increase your chances of making more than average over time, but they don't *guarantee* it. And with the riskiest of investments, you may simply lose your money—all of it. The objective of the savvy online investor, then, is to look for ways to put a lid on risk while keeping potential returns high. This chapter explores ways to do just that.

The ins and outs of asset allocation

Asset allocation (or diversification) is the global allocation of investment assets among different asset classes (such as stocks, bonds, and cash) and different securities within each class. This is done to minimize

Watch Out! Don't assume that blue chip stocks won't get hit as hard as other stocks in a bear market. In the 1973–1974 bear, Coca-Cola lost 70 percent of its value, GE lost 60 percent, GM lost 66 percent, Pepsico lost 67 percent, and Walt Disney lost 85 percent.

risk and maximize return. Asset allocation is based on Modern Portfolio Theory, developed by Nobel prize winners Harry Markowitz, Merton Miller, and William Sharpe in the early 1950s. This theory shows how "optimal portfolios" can be constructed that offer the maximum possible expected return for a given level of risk. With a specific goal in mind, requiring, perhaps a 10 percent average return over the next 10 years, an investor can construct a portfolio that mixes various assets in a proportion that will maximize her chances of achieving that goal. If she were to put all her money in stocks, her portfolio after 10 years might be up—and up much more than 10 percent—but it also might be way down. If she skillfully mixed stocks, bonds, and cash, however, the risk of her portfolio being down after 10 years would be significantly reduced, while the chances of it being up at a value near her goal would be greatly increased.

So, a stock investor can diversify into some bonds and cash to reduce risk; a bond investor can diversify into some stocks to increase returns. Of all the investment techniques employed by investors, this mixing of asset classes most strongly influences portfolio performance. In fact, studies have shown that investment policy (the selection of asset classes and their weights) accounts for more than 90 percent of the variability of portfolios' risk and return, while investment strategy (timing and selection of individual securities within each asset class) accounts for only 10 percent.

Modern Portfolio Theory rests on the observation that not all types of investments behave the same way at the same time. When stocks rise, for example, money market instruments tend to fall. If any two given investment types tend to behave in a similar way at any given time, they are said to have a positive correlation; if they behave in an opposite way, they are said to have a negative correlation. If they behave in neither a similar nor a dissimilar way, they have no or low correlation. The central idea of diversification is to construct a portfolio of assets with negative or low correlations to each other so that when some are declining in value, others may be rising. Asset allocation also takes into account the inherent risk levels of different asset classes. By mixing high-risk assets with low-risk assets, you can further modify a portfolio's overall risk level, adjusting it to one that is best-suited to your goals and investor personality. Ideally, asset allocation produces smooth, if not spectacular, returns from year to year.

Real-world asset allocation

Asset allocation generally comes down to allocating your assets among three asset classes: stocks, bonds, and cash. Cash includes savings accounts, CDs, money market accounts and funds, and Treasury bills. You should always consider throwing international stocks and bonds into the mix as well. While international stocks themselves are riskier than domestic stocks, they may actually lower the risk of your portfolio because they often show a low correlation to U.S. markets. What's more, international securities may improve your bottom line because the performance of overseas stock and bond markets is often better than those in the United States. (In recent years, however, foreign markets have been far too closely correlated with our own to provide real diversification, and U.S. markets have outperformed overseas markets.)

Watch Out!
While international stocks, small cap stocks, high-yield bonds, and other securities with higher-than-average risk can reduce portfolio volatility and increase returns, most investors should limit the sum total of these investments to no more than 30 percent of their total portfolios.

Splitting your money between two domestic stocks in the same industry, then, would not constitute thorough asset allocation. These stocks would tend to show a relatively high positive correlation and would tend to move up and down in unison. Having a portfolio containing a number of domestic stocks, some international stocks and bonds, and some cash would constitute adequate asset allocation, however, because these investments would tend to show a relatively high negative correlation and different risk levels.

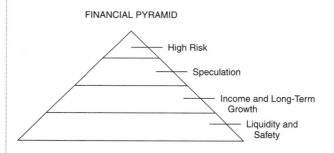

FINANCIAL PYRAMID

High Risk

Speculation

Income and Long-Term Growth

Liquidity and Safety

In theory, the idea of selecting investments with no or low correlations is sound; in practice, however, it is difficult because the performance correlations among various types of investments is not set in stone. Some years foreign stocks may run up with domestic stocks; other years they may not. Some years domestic bonds may move up in unison with domestic stocks; other years domestic stocks and bonds may go in opposite directions. Because the future performance of individual asset classes relative to each other is so hard to predict, real-world asset allocation revolves around determining the percentage of assets that an investor should invest in *each* of the major asset classes more than choosing among them. These percentages are based on the historical risk levels associated with each asset class.

The financial pyramid provides a useful visual model for how an investor should conceive of asset allocation in a general sense. The base of the pyramid is built with low-risk investments, which also constitute the largest segment of the portfolio; the next level consists of higher-risk investments, which make up a smaller percentage of the whole than the base; and the top level of the pyramid contains the highest-risk investments, comprising the smallest segment of the pyramid overall. The pyramid may be said to have a solid foundation, built on strong, safe, dependable securities. While sound in structure, the financial pyramid does not take individual differences into account, which could result in altogether different geometry. The portfolios of the most aggressive investors could look like an inverted pyramid, in fact.

Age (and time horizon) is often the primary factor used to determine differences in individual asset allocations. Young investors—those in their teens, 20s, and 30s—should generally have a high percentage of their assets in growth investments, such as stocks. Over the long term, these investments historically net the highest returns. There's also plenty of time to make up for any mistakes or mishaps.

Middle-age investors need to start thinking about preserving capital because there would be less time to make up for substantial portfolio losses caused by overexposure to high-risk investments. Nevertheless, middle-age investors should continue to pursue growth investments because they have not achieved their goals yet.

TABLE 13.1: BASIC ASSET ALLOCATIONS FOR RETIREMENT FUNDS

Youth	Middle Age	Retirement
70–80% stocks	50% stocks	10% high-dividend stocks
10–20% bonds	40% bonds	80% bonds
10% cash	10% cash	10% cash

Retired investors need to emphasize capital preservation because they will be relying on a steady stream of income from their investments to live on. However, these investors may want to keep a small portion of their portfolio in growth investments to help offset the effects of inflation. Table 13.1 gives some basic asset allocation parameters for the three major stages of life:

In addition to age, an investor must consider his own individual risk tolerance in determining his portfolio's asset allocation. Young investors who are also conservative should put a smaller percentage of their assets in speculative stocks than young aggressive investors.

The process of diversification can and should be taken beyond diversification among asset classes to diversification *within* asset classes. With stocks, you should try to diversify among companies in different size categories—small cap, mid cap, and large cap—depending on how much risk you want to take. The smaller the company, the riskier. With bonds, diversify among those with different quality ratings and maturities.

As risk tolerance and time horizon increase, the recommended percentage of stocks and higher-risk securities in a portfolio also increases. As risk tolerance and time horizon decrease (with age, usually), the recommended percentage of stocks and higher-risk securities decreases. We don't just see a higher

Bright Idea
If you're married, consider diversifying across both your assets as if they were in one account. For example, his 401(k) could be invested in a growth fund, hers in an international stock fund, his savings in a bond fund, and hers in a money market fund.

proportion of stocks, then; we also see a higher proportion of higher-risk stocks.

The final stage of diversification takes place on the level of the individual securities in your portfolio. If you have decided to invest 20 percent of your assets in domestic large cap stocks, for example, owning several large caps will protect your portfolio from a huge loss if one of them should go down the tubes. Don't buy large caps that all have a high positive correlation or that share the same risk characteristics. If you're going to buy Ford, for instance, think twice before also buying GM. If people stop buying cars, the entire auto industry will suffer. Why not buy Ford and Merck, a drug stock, whose fate is not closely correlated with that of Ford? If you're set on buying more stock in a given industry, though, consider buying shares of a different company rather than more shares of the same company—buy 100 shares of GM rather than 100 *more* shares of Ford.

Diversifying with mutual funds

A good way to diversify your stock holdings is to buy stock mutual funds. Just make sure you know what the fund is investing in. A specialty fund, which invests in a specific industry, will not provide any cross-industry diversification. Mutual funds are particularly good for investing in overseas markets because researching and selecting foreign stocks on your own is difficult. Global and international fund managers have the resources and the expertise to do this competently. Some investors invest the core of their assets in mutual funds and a small percent in individual securities.

Investing in mutual funds is also a good way to diversify your bond holdings. Because bond mutual funds are professionally managed, you don't have to worry about call options or staggering maturities

Unofficially... If you're interested in diversifying overseas through stocks rather than mutual funds, consider buying shares of U.S. companies with a large percent of total revenues coming from overseas markets— companies such as Foster Wheeler, Vishay Technology, Boeing, Beckman Instruments, Duracell International, and Caterpillar.

(which we'll talk about later) or trying to monitor the bond's price, which may not be that easy. It's all done for you by someone who really knows what he's doing.

You can apply the same asset allocations to fund categories that you would to individual securities. For example, if you decided to go with an allocation of 70 percent stocks, 20 percent bonds, and 10 percent cash, you could simply put 70 percent of your money in stock mutual funds, 20 percent in bond mutual funds, and 10 percent in money market funds. As with individual securities, you should also try to diversify *within* each asset (fund) class. The types of funds you choose should be a function of your risk tolerance. Table 13.2 shows the relative riskiness of the major types of stock and bonds funds, with risk decreasing from top to bottom:

TABLE 13.2: RISK LEVELS OF FUNDS

Stock Funds	Bond Funds
Sector	International
Aggressive growth	High-yield
Small cap growth	Multisector
International	Corporate
Global	Government mortgage
Growth	Short-term corporate/treasury
Growth and income	
Equity income	

If you want to invest in actively managed funds, one value or growth fund and one corporate or government bond fund could suffice. But a more thorough approach would be to diversify across the parameters of geography, company size, industry, and investment style as well as asset class. You might own separate funds, then, that specialize in small cap stocks, mid cap stocks, large cap stocks, foreign stocks, growth investing, and value investing, for a total of six stock funds, in addition to your bond fund and money market fund holdings. As for bond funds, some investors should consider high-yield funds in addition to the investment-grade varieties. Just for fun, you could also throw some focus funds into the mix. Focus funds generally invest in a fund manager's top 15 to 30 picks. Don't forget emerging market funds, gold funds, real estate funds, utility funds, and the like. Because these special funds tend to show low correlations to standard domestic growth funds, they can (while volatile in their own right) paradoxically lower the overall risk of your portfolio.

Carefully selecting a large number of funds for your portfolio is time-consuming, and if you buy too many, you will have trouble keeping track of them all. There's also the danger of overdiversification, which is discussed next. An alternative would be to invest in an all-in-one fund such as the T. Rowe Price Price Spectrum Growth Fund, which invests in a well-diversified group of eight T. Rowe Price equity funds. Going this route will save you time and simplify your life. The drawback? You just might eke out a better overall return if you had picked your own funds from a broader universe.

Another way for mutual fund investors to diversify simply, of course, is to bag actively managed funds altogether and buy index funds. If you're an index fund investor, buying one stock index fund and one bond index fund will provide adequate diversification. For investors combining index and actively managed funds, two index (a stock and a bond) and two actively managed (a stock and a bond) would be necessary for adequate diversification. Mutual fund investors who hold only sector

Bright Idea
If you're a conservative investor, purchase mutual funds that include income among their main objectives, such as equity income funds. Funds that emphasize income tend to show more moderate price fluctuations than funds that do not.

funds or small cap or large cap funds may not be adequately diversified because funds with specialized holdings are riskier than those that invest across a wide spectrum of industries.

Finally, as with the asset allocation of individual securities, the final stage of asset allocation with mutual funds is to make sure you're diversified on the level of individual securities. Get a prospectus or call the fund company to find out what kinds of securities they're actually investing in. Or, as always, check online.

The limitations of asset allocation

For all its benefits, asset allocation should not be taken too far. You don't want to be overdiversified. Studies have shown that while adding securities to a portfolio always reduces risk, a portfolio of only 5 to 10 holdings eliminates 80–90 percent of the risk of having only one. So, there is a point beyond which diversification may actually diminish returns without a commensurate reduction in risk. This may occur when an investor who really does have four or five good ideas dilutes the returns of those core holdings by investing in an additional four or five companies or funds that he really doesn't know much about—only for the sake of diversification. Clearly, finding a balance between diversification and concentration is important. To avoid overdiversification, some mutual funds, such as the Oakmark Select Fund, own fewer than 20 securities, with only 5 of those accounting for more than 50 percent of the fund's value.

Asset allocation is not the holy grail of investing. It does not eliminate market risk; it reduces portfolio risk. And there is a trade-off here. By keeping a certain percentage of your assets in bonds, cash, and other nonstock assets, you will be sacrificing a certain amount of profit potential in exchange for lower risk and more consistent portfolio returns. If your goal is simply to make as much money as you possibly can, if you have a very high risk tolerance, and if you have plenty of time to work with, asset allocation may not be a relevant strategy for you. You should probably be 100 percent invested in stocks. On the other hand, if you have specific financial goals and time horizons, and if your tolerance for risk has limits, asset allocation is something you should employ.

Determining your portfolio's asset allocation

The first step in choosing the mix of asset types for your portfolio is to clearly identify your goals and your time horizons for achieving those goals. With a clearly defined goal and time horizon, you can determine the average rate of return you will need to achieve the goal. Second, review your risk tolerance (see Chapter 6, "Inner Investing").

Third, decide on a mix of investments (an asset allocation) that will maximize your chances of achieving the necessary rate of return, and a mix that fits your investor personality. The mix should include both foreign and domestic investments from various asset classes and various types of assets within each asset class. There are several sites on the Internet designed to help you determine your ideal asset allocation mix. Keep in mind, however, that some sites tell you how to diversify only among mutual funds; others tell you how to diversify only among *their* mutual funds. The following online asset allocation planners give general asset allocation recommendations:

- http://personal100.fidelity.com:80/ planning/investment/content/peterlynch/ strategy/assetalloc.html?ref=design

> ❝
> Don't put all your eggs in one basket.
> —Old Italian proverb
>
> Put all your eggs in one basket and watch that basket.
> —Mark Twain
> ❞

- www.smartmoney.com/ac/retirement/investing/index.cfm?story=retireinvest
- www.smartmoney.com/si/tools/oneasset
- www.schwab.com/SchwabNOW/SNLibrary/SNLib093/SN093frame.html
- http://cbs.marketwatch.com/funds/mf_portindex.htx?source=htx/http2_mw

If you feel a little uncomfortable about determining the best asset allocation mix for your portfolio by yourself, consider consulting an investment adviser. A good investment adviser will help you clarify your goals, your time horizons, your risk tolerance, and the optimal mix of assets for your portfolio.

When you have settled on an asset allocation and invested accordingly, you should plan on rebalancing your holdings at least once a year because contributions made to your portfolio during the year and different rates of return for each asset class will alter the original percentages of the assets in your portfolio. There are two ways to rebalance: sell some of the assets in the asset classes that have exceeded their allocation percentages, or buy additional assets for the asset classes that have fallen below their allocations. The latter method is preferable because you're adding to your savings and avoiding capital gains taxes. If the amount needed to bring an asset class back up to its allocation level is sizable, you can do it in installments. Also, always consider any fees that may be associated with rebalancing, such as loads.

Fixed-weighting vs. dynamic

While the importance of asset allocation is accepted by virtually the entire investment community, there is some controversy as to how it should be implemented. Many investment professionals subscribe to a relatively static approach, advocating a fixed weighting of asset classes for a portfolio based on the historical returns for each asset class and the needs of the investor. That is, once an investor has determined his long-term goals and risk tolerance, he should calculate an investment mix to achieve those goals and maintain that mix until his goals are achieved.

Other investment professionals argue that asset allocation should be dynamic—that even if an investor's goals and risk tolerance do not change significantly over time, the percentage of assets allocated to each asset class should change to reflect market conditions. That is, an investor should re-allocate his assets every so often to favor those markets that appear most attractive at a given time. You may want to increase your exposure to the stock market, for example, based on the outlook for stocks in the coming year or on your current comfort level. The outlook for stocks can be based on your own research or on that of an investment professional, an investment newsletter, or a market timer with a proven track record. The *Value Line Investment Survey,* for example, makes recommendations for what percentage of your portfolio should be invested in stocks at any given time, and these percentages do not change that often. Another possibility would be to buy a tactical asset allocation mutual fund, which makes asset allocation adjustments based on market conditions for you.

Obviously, the dynamic approach involves a certain amount of market timing, and if this is not something you believe in or feel comfortable with, you should go with the fixed-weighting approach. If you're interested in the dynamic approach, however,

Watch Out!
Frequent changes in your asset allocation may negate the intended smoothing of returns that results only from holding a balance of different asset classes over time. Just as important, frequent buying and selling will drive up your costs and capital gains taxes.

you should set up certain guidelines for yourself, such as how often you allow yourself to make adjustments. You won't want to give yourself too much leeway here, because making frequent adjustments could negate any real asset allocation. As you switch in and out of investments at will, you may find yourself back among the legions of seat-of-the-pants investors who sell stocks just when they should be buying them—exactly what establishing an asset allocation and maintaining it is designed to prevent.

Once a year is not too often to review your asset allocation. But if you decide to adjust your portfolio, you'll want to avoid making dramatic changes based on emotion rather than reason. Generally, the extent of adjustments should be moderate, designed to maintain the basic structure of the original allocation, which is based on a variety of mostly long-term factors, not current market conditions. If your original allocation was 65 percent stocks, 25 percent bonds, and 10 percent cash, for example, you might move to 50 percent cash, 40 percent bonds, and 10 percent cash if the market looks pricey. Maintaining an asset allocation for at least a year ensures that all securities you sell will be taxed as long-term capital gains.

Buying bonds to reduce risk

Buying bonds or bond funds is an integral part of effective asset allocation because the interest payments from bonds can offset losses from stocks in your portfolio. Bond prices generally show a positive correlation with those of stocks, so the portfolio risk reduction resulting from holding bonds does not come from capital appreciation; it comes from the dividend payouts. When buying bonds to reduce portfolio risk, then, focus on dividends. If your goal is capital appreciation, not diversification, remember that stocks beat the pants off of bonds in a falling-interest-rate environment.

Bonds can be a bit confusing. If you need a review of the basics, take a look at Chapter 4, "Plenty of Investment Vehicles to Choose From." In a nutshell, you need to know seven things about a bond before you buy it: kind, credit rating, maturity, face value, coupon (or yield), price, and yield-to-maturity. As with other investments, the more risk you take with bonds, the more money you stand to make—or lose. As a rule, the lower the credit quality and the longer the maturity, the higher the YTM, but the greater the chance that the issuer will default, costing you your expected interest payments, if not your principal.

While lower credit quality always means higher YTM, longer maturity does not. Usually, bonds with longer maturities command higher YTMs, but if the market is anticipating a recession and lower rates to follow, long-term bonds may offer *lower* rates than short-term bonds. This is because an increasing number of investors think that now may be the last chance to lock in rates at current levels before they plunge. The increased demand for long-term bonds enables issuers to knock down yields without hurting the bonds' attractiveness. Under these circumstances, a bond investor who buys a short-term bond with an 8 percent yield will be out of luck in a year if he has to reinvest at 5 percent, but the long-term investor will be sitting pretty with his bond, which he bought at 7.5 percent.

To get a clear picture of how bonds of comparable quality but different maturities are selling in relation to each other, you need to take a look at the yield curve. The yield curve is a line graph—usually curved, not straight—described by different government bond yields for different maturities. The x-axis is maturity; the y-axis is yield. The figure below is a graph of a normal yield curve.

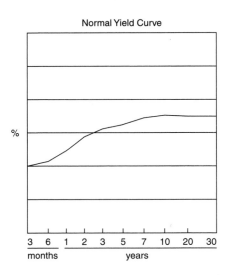

Normal Yield Curve

Notice how the curve slopes gradually upward, indicating higher rates for longer maturities. An inverted yield curve slopes downward, just the opposite of the normal curve, indicating higher short-term rates than long-term rates. An inverted yield curve is a bad omen for the stock market; a steep or normal curve is good. When a normal curve flattens out (sometimes it gets bulges a little in the middle), the curve often turns into a fully inverted curve.

Selecting bonds for your portfolio
Choosing bonds that are appropriate for your portfolio is, first and foremost, a question of your goals

and time horizons; next, a question of your risk tolerance; and, finally, a question of which bonds will give you the best return for the amount of time you have and the risk you're willing to take. If you need a high return and you have a lot of time and a high risk tolerance, high-yield bonds may be appropriate for you. If you need a moderate return, you're retiring in three years, and you have a low risk tolerance anyway, Treasuries would be better.

While the basics of choosing bonds are clear, you need to be aware of some special considerations. First, while long-term Treasuries should logically provide a better YTM than intermediate-term Treasuries, this isn't always the case. Over the past 30 years, there have been many periods when Treasury notes outperformed Treasury bonds. And notes, having much shorter maturities, are much less volatile (risky) than bonds. What does this mean for the individual investor? Buy notes.

You can buy Treasuries through your broker or through the government's Treasury Direct program for no fee. Go to the Bureau of Public Debt online at www.treasurydirect.gov and download the application form. You can also go to the Federal Reserve's Web site at www.ny.frb.org/pihome/treasdir, or call the Federal Reserve Bank nearest you and ask to be mailed an application to open a Treasury Direct account. While you can buy Treasuries directly from the Treasury through this program, you'll need a broker to sell them, if you decide not to hold them to maturity. Of course, the broker will charge you a commission. Treasury notes with maturities of two or three years have a $5,000 minimum purchase requirement; those with 10-year maturities have only a $1,000 requirement. Accounts

Bright Idea
If you're interested in buying bonds for capital appreciation, wait until interest rates seem to be peaking. Also consider buying a bond with a shorter maturity, one that you wouldn't mind holding to maturity, just in case rates continue to go up.

with a balance of $100,000 have an annual mainte-nance fee of $25, but smaller accounts have no fee whatsoever.

Although government agency bonds offer gen-erally higher rates than Treasuries, they are hard to get your hands on. For the most part, you can get them only through brokers, which means having to pay a fee. This nullifies most of the advantage of the higher rates. If you have an account worth more than a million dollars, however, you may be able to negotiate lower brokerage fees, which could make buying agency bonds a better deal than Treasuries. You may also want to consider municipal bonds. Because of the lower yields, you should buy munis only if you're in a high tax bracket and have enough money to diversify among bonds of several different municipalities (in case of a default). Because munis run in lots of about $25,000, you will need upwards of $100,000 to get started. If you don't have that kind of bread, you can always purchase shares of a municipal bond fund.

Zero coupon bonds are called zeroes because they don't have a coupon; that is, they don't pay out any interest. Instead, they are sold at a deep dis-count, and the interest accrues. In exchange for let-ting the government keep your loan *and* your interest payments until the bond matures, you get a higher YTM than with other Treasuries. However, you have to pay taxes each year on the accrued inter-est. Because zeroes are issued by the federal govern-ment, they are safe, and for this reason, could be said to reduce risk. But because zeroes do not pay out any interest along the way, they will not provide the same kind of cushion to your portfolio that other bonds will. It's best to invest in zeroes if you have a relatively low risk tolerance and want to be absolutely sure that you'll have a certain amount of money waiting for you after a certain period of time. Don't use zeroes as a diversification tool.

Then there are corporate bonds. While corporates offer the highest rates, remember that all the interest you earn is taxable at all levels: federal, state, and local. You also have to pay your broker, and the bond dealers as well, a commission. On top of all the taxes and charges, call provisions make it possible for issuers to call corporates at any time. Companies tend to call their bonds when interest rates go down and the bond's value increases. All these things conspire to diminish the real value of corporate bonds. Before buying corporates, try to figure out what your after-taxes, after-charges return will be.

Use a ladder

While the risk that the bond issuer will default is a real possibility when you invest in speculative bonds, default is not a major concern when you invest in high-quality bonds. The primary concern with investment grades is interest rates. Interest rate risk is the risk that interest rates will rise after you buy a bond, driving down the price of your bond and leaving you wishing you had waited to make the purchase. If you own a short-term bond and interest rates rise, the real dollar loss in terms of what you will make versus what you would have made at the higher rate is minimal. The bond will mature shortly, and you will be able to reinvest at the higher rate. If you own a long-term bond, however, the difference could be significant. You'll be stuck at the lower rate for years (unless interest rates drop again or you sell the bond at a loss). This is why long-term bonds are considered riskier than short-term bonds, and why the prices of long-term bonds fall more than those of short-term bonds when interest rates climb.

Now, the more bonds you own with the same maturity, the greater the interest rate risk. If all your bonds constituting a major portion of your portfolio's value mature at the same time, and if you're forced to reinvest all that money at a much lower yield than before, the negative impact on your portfolio's rate of return would be profound.

The best way to protect yourself from interest rate risk is to ladder your bonds. Laddering bonds means buying bonds so that they mature one at a time, at even intervals (with maturities spaced out evenly like rungs on a ladder). The way to do this is to buy equal amounts of bonds with incrementally increasing maturities. You could buy bonds maturing every year, every other year, every three years, or at even larger intervals.

Let's say you laddered your bonds to mature yearly—in two years, three years, four years, five years, and six years—starting two years from now. When the two-year bonds matured, you would take the money and buy another bunch of six-year bonds. You would repeat this action the next year and the next, indefinitely. By laddering your bonds, you can reinvest at a higher rate if interest rates rise, but you can keep most of your portfolio invested at higher rates if they fall. Laddering your bonds lessens interest rate risk by allowing you to continually reinvest part of your bond portfolio at current rates.

Use stops

Having looked at how to control risk through the selection of different asset types, it's time to examine a key money management strategy—the stop loss. Chapter 9, "Setting Up an Account," defined a stop as an order to buy or sell a stock if a certain price is hit. Stops can be used to limit losses and lock in profits. Stops are not used by buy-and-hold investors, nor are they employed by pure fundamentalists. Stops are generally used by investors who subscribe to technical analysis or a combination of fundamental and technical analyses, or by investors who just can't stomach large downside fluctuations in their investments.

To keep it simple, this discussion is limited to stops placed on stocks bought long. The same principles, however, can and should be applied to stocks sold short. Typically, a stop is placed 10–20 percent below a stock's current price, and the stock is sold if it hits its stop or if it closes below its stop, depending on your policy. If you're placing stop orders with an online broker, the order will be activated as soon as the stop price is hit. If you're using mental stops (stops you keep in your head or, more likely, on paper), however, it's up to you whether you sell when the stop is hit, when the stop is violated, when the stock closes at or below the stop, or only when the stock closes below the stop.

Deciding where to place a stop is more of an art than a science. The idea is to try to place a stop at a price that, if hit, would indicate a change in trend to the downside. One method is to simply place a stop below a stock's most recent low. Most stocks on a solid uptrend show a pattern of higher highs and higher lows. If a stock's price drops below the previous low, then, this could indicate a change in trend and a good time to sell. Placing a stop below the most recent low is the equivalent of placing a stop below the most recent trend line.

> **"**
> A small loss, when realized, becomes an opportunity for profit elsewhere. It gives you the chance to turn a liability into an asset, instead of just sitting there praying that your old stock will come back.
> —Martin Zweig
> **"**

Another simple method for using stops is to sell any stock that drops a certain percent in price. You might choose 10 percent, 15 percent, or 20 percent. Regardless of the individual qualities of the stocks in your portfolio, any stock that dropped a certain percent would be sold. Again, you could include intraday price movements or base your calculations solely on closing prices.

Most investors, however, set stops for each stock in their portfolio on an individual basis. To individualize a stop, you need to print out or draw the stock's one-year price chart, and actually draw in resistance lines, trend lines, and moving averages. Often, as you know, when a stock breaks below one of these lines, it's a sign of a change in trend. A good place to put a stop, then, would be just below one or more of these lines. But which? And should you use the most recent resistance line? If you're using moving averages, which one should you go by? The 50-day? The 200-day? Both? These are questions only you can answer because how you go about placing your stops is largely a question of style.

You should take a stock's volatility into account, though, in placing a stop. Volatile stocks require looser stops. Take a look at the stock's price history. If 20–25 percent corrections (pullbacks) in price are common (high beta) as the stock advances, you probably won't want to place a stop 10 percent below the stock's current price. Chances are good that your stop will get hit on a normal pullback, and you'll be prematurely stopped out of your position. On the other hand, if a stock shows little volatility (low beta), you probably won't want to place a stop 20 percent below the current price. You'll probably end up getting stopped out later than necessary.

A final consideration is your comfort level. Maybe you just wouldn't feel comfortable placing stops a full 20 percent below a stock's current price. Your comfort level also may vary depending on how bullish or bearish you are at a given time. If you're feeling bearish, you might use relatively tight stops; if you're feeling bullish, you'll want looser stops.

After you have placed a stop (assuming that your stock moves up), you have to decide when to move it. A stop you move up behind a stock as it moves up in price is called a trailing stop. Let's look at an example that incorporates all the principles of stops we have talked about so far. After a comprehensive analysis of XYZ's fundamentals and price action, you decide to purchase 50 shares of the stock at $100 per share. You note that XYZ is a fairly volatile stock (beta 1.3) and has shown corrections of 20 percent after surges in price before continuing up. You are currently neutral to bullish on the market. Based on all these factors and the fact that you're comfortable with the idea, you decide to place a stop about 20 percent below XYZ's current price. A drop in price greater than that, you reason, could signify a general change in the direction of the stock rather than a temporary correction. You draw in trends lines, lines of resistance, and moving averages and then decide to set your stop at $79, just below a major resistance line for the stock at $80, 21 percent below the current price.

Over the next few sessions, XYZ climbs to $104, $106, and then $110, putting it a full 27 percent above its stop. Should you move up your trailing stop at this point? Probably not yet—better wait and see how far XYZ pulls back on the inevitable correction. Over the next few sessions, XYZ moves up to

$112 and then begins "backing and filling" as it drops to $110, $107, $105, and $100 before turning around and shooting straight up to $110 and then $112 again. (Backing and filling is the tendency for a stock on a healthy uptrend to move down in price after a large run-up before resuming its climb.)

Having corrected to $105 and then resumed its ascent, XYZ has established a new higher low, and a certain amount of support at this price. Now is a good time to move the trailing stop up. Because the stock's general volatility hasn't changed, and because you're still neutral to bullish on the market, you decide to move the stop up to a price, again, around 20 percent below XYZ's current price. You take another look at the chart, trend lines, lines of resistance, and moving averages, and decide to place the stop at $89, just below a recent low and 20.5 percent below the current price of $112.

Over the next several months, XYZ continues to move up, and you happily and diligently move the trailing stop up behind it. Then, the inevitable happens. At $154, XYZ starts to falter and slide, and slide and slide some more, approaching and finally hitting your trailing stop at $123. You sell at $123 for a 23 percent gain on the trade. Over the next several months, you watch, safely on the sidelines, as XYZ continues to move lower, below your purchase price. Using trailing stops enabled you to lock in profits that would otherwise have turned into losses. Of course, you didn't get out at the high; you actually left 20 percent on the table. But you wanted to give XYZ room to correct if it was just preparing to take off on a new leg of its rocket shoot. You might have set the trailing stop on XYZ at around 10 percent instead of 20 percent, but then you might have gotten stopped out

Unofficially...
As a stock continues to climb, some investors employ ascending stops. An ascending stop is a trailing stop that is gradually tightened as a stock's run lengthens. Such a stop might initially be placed 20 percent below a stock's price and then move to 15 percent, 10 percent, and 5 percent, as the momentum of the stock's advance appears to wane.

early, causing you to miss out on most of the run-up. And if XYZ had stopped falling at $125 and started back up again, you might have ended up making a great deal more than you did. (One of the drawbacks of stops is that you never get out at the high.)

There will be times when just after you get stopped out of a position, the stock turns on a dime and shoots straight up, and you will be wishing mightily that you had given the stock more room to breathe. But there will be many other times when you lock in profits and watch the price subsequently fall and fall, seemingly without end. There certainly is a trade-off when using stops, but if you're not a buy-and-hold investor, then using stops is a must. You can review how different types of stop orders can be used both alone and in combination in Chapter 9.

Use a market timer

While the idea of trying to time the market is an anathema to mutual fund companies and professional investment advisors alike, varying degrees of market timing and technical analysis are, in fact, employed by most investment companies and investors. Mutual fund managers, for example, adjust the percentage of assets they hold in cash within a certain framework based on their *outlook* for the market. This means that if they are bullish, they will have a larger percentage of assets in stocks than if they are bearish. This is market timing, pure and simple. Mutual fund companies have actually created tactical asset allocation funds whose raison d'être is to provide investors with mutual funds that will make significant adjustments to asset allocation based on perceived market risk. Let's face it—these are market-timing funds! In all fairness, however,

Moneysaver
As with stock funds, the total return of asset allocation funds and balanced funds is significantly influenced by fund costs. On the whole, funds with lower expense ratios are able to generate higher total returns.

the managers of tactical asset allocation funds are not deciding whether to invest in stocks at all based on their market projections; they are only adjusting the fund's asset allocation.

But the principal is the same: Market timing can help reduce portfolio risk. The goal of market timing is to increase your chances of being fully invested during bull markets and only partially invested or on the sidelines during bears. The central advantage to effective market timing over the buy-and-hold, then, is the reduction of your losses or, if you don't sell, "drawdown." Table 13.3 shows how recouping a loss requires a gain of greater, not equal, magnitude.

TABLE 13.3: GAINS NEEDED TO RECOVER LOSSES

Loss	Gain Needed
−5%	5.26%
−10%	11.11%
−20%	25%
−30%	42.86%
−40%	66.67%
−50%	100%
−60%	150%
−70%	233.33%
−80%	400%
−90%	900%

Table 13.3 lends mathematical certainty to the cold reality that it's harder to erase losses than it is to acquire them (kind of like gaining and losing weight). Investors who employ some form of market timing believe that an ounce of prevention is worth a pound of cure.

Many investors devise their own market timing strategies. Those who use technical analysis may watch the charts of indexes, applying Dow Theory, stage theory, and various technical tools to gauge the general trend of prices. Technicians often buy in two distinct circumstances: either when momentum is good or when blood is flowing in the streets. Fundamentalists may look at the valuations of the overall market to determine whether it's pricey or cheap. Other investors use a combination of these approaches. While some investors will invest all or none of their portfolio's assets in stocks, based on the results of their market assessment, many investors will use the results to gauge overall market risk and adjust their asset allocation accordingly.

If you're interested in following the advice of a professional market timer or an investment adviser who gives good buy and sell signals, subscribe to the *Hulbert Financial Digest*. Hulbert does periodic issues on the best market timers and ranks all newsletters on a timing only basis in the newsletter's Long-Term Performance Ratings Report.

If you are a buy-and-hold investor, from one perspective, even you are employing a kind of random timing system, based on the fact that you have to buy at some point and sell at another. While buy-and-hold has worked well over the last 20 years due to a stampeding bull market (interrupted only a couple times by short-term technical bears), the stock market can trade sideways or down for periods of 10 years or more. During times like this, the buy-and-hold may not work as well.

Keep in mind, too, that while it's all well and good to say you're a buy-and-hold investor when stocks are on the up and up, your mettle will be tested in a prolonged bear market, when your portfolio starts showing major-league losses and the media is trumpeting the collapse of the world economy. You might start thinking that you should get out with what little you have left before you lose it all. The emotional pain of a bear market has historically proven to be too much for the average investor to bear, and most jump and run with terrible losses at or near the bottom, just when they *should* be holding. You might call this the hold high, sell low strategy.

So ask yourself, "Will I have the strength and the discipline to hold for the duration of an extended bear market?" It's important, as you know, that once you have earmarked certain funds to be invested according to a certain strategy, you stick to that strategy, even if things start going sour. Deviating from a strategy arrived at by careful consideration in the heat of the moment is the hallmark of unsuccessful investing.

Bright Idea
If you are a buy-and-hold investor and the going gets tough, just remember—the longer you hold an investment, the more likely it is that you will earn a positive return.

The options option

One of the most advanced techniques for controlling risk is to buy stock options. A stock option is a contract that gives you the option to buy (call option) or sell (put option) 100 shares of a stock at a specified price within a certain period of time. There are also index options that give you the option to buy or sell an index at a certain price by a certain date. What is the advantage of a owning an option? If you buy a put option that gives you the option to sell 100 shares of a stock at $100 by a certain date, and the stock goes down to $80, you can buy 100 shares of the stock at $80 and use the put option to sell them at $100, for a gain of $2,000. This will come in handy if you actually own 100 shares of the stock and the price plummets from $100 to $80—the option will cover your loss. So, you buy a put option to cover a long position when you're concerned that the stock might go down, but you don't want to sell and forfeit the opportunity for further gains.

As mentioned before, the average investor should consider only *buying* options. Selling or "writing" options is very risky and requires specialized knowledge. For the sake of simplicity, this discussion is limited to buying puts, and only as hedges on long positions, not as speculative instruments. The same principles, however, apply to buying calls to hedge short positions.

When you buy a put option, you are said to be "long the put." The party who writes or sells the option is "short the put." A put option consists of four major components: the underlying security, the expiration date, the strike price, and the price (or "premium"). The underlying security, of course, is the stock you have the right to sell; the expiration date is the date by which you have to sell, if you're going to; the strike price is the price at which you can sell the security; and the price is how much you pay for the option. For example, an IBM November 100 put costing $350 is a put option to sell 100 shares of IBM at $100 per share by the end of November, selling for $350. The price of the option is actually $3.5 or $3^1/2$ (100 shares × $3.5 per share = $350).

Factors affecting an option's price

The price of this option is dependent on several factors, including the current price of IBM, the strike price of the option, the time remaining on the option, and the volatility of IBM. Why would the current price of IBM and the strike price affect how much you pay for the option? Well, if you have an option to sell IBM at $100 per share and IBM is currently at $90, the option is obviously more valuable than if IBM is currently trading at $110. If IBM is at $90 and you have an option to sell at $100, you could buy the option and turn right around and sell IBM at a profit. On the other hand, if IBM is currently at $110, you could sell IBM only at a loss with this option. When a put option's strike price is above the current price of the underlying stock, the option is said to be "in the money." When the strike price is below the current price, the option is said to be "out of the money." When the strike price is equal to the current price, the option is said to be "at the money."

Watch Out!
It's best to use put options as hedges only when you're concerned about an imminent correction. Continually hedging with puts will cut seriously into your annual returns.

The amount of time left on the option will also affect how much you have to pay for it. An option with only a month remaining before expiration won't cost as much as an option with four months left. Think of an option as insurance: You're going to pay more for four months of insurance than one month. The volatility of IBM will also affect the price of the option. The more volatile a stock is, the greater the chance its price will zig and zag (possibly down), so the more you'll have to pay for a put option. The price might also be affected by interest rates and the dividend yield of the stock. Higher rates would put downward pressure on stocks and make put options in general more expensive. Stocks with a low dividend yield may be more volatile and expensive (growth stocks) than average, making put options for those stocks more expensive.

Saving money on out-of-the-money puts

Buying an out-of-the-money put is like using a stop, except that you have to pay for the put, and the put will definitely limit your downside risk to the amount defined by the strike price. A stop limit order is not always filled, and a stop market order can be filled well below the stop price if the stock is moving downward quickly.

Should you buy out-of-the-money puts? Yes. The idea of using puts as hedges is not to eliminate risk but to control it. Buying puts with a strike price close to, at, or over the current price will give you superb protection against a price decline, but you'll have to pay a great deal for them. To keep costs down, it's sensible to buy out-of-the-money puts that will limit any losses to a reasonable amount. Depending on your risk tolerance, you should probably be looking at puts with strike prices between 10 percent and 20 percent below the current price of the stock.

When to sell your put

Three things can happen when you buy a put option. The first is that the stock will actually continue to rise. In this case, the best thing for you to do is simply hold onto the put as insurance against an unexpected reversal of fortune or until it expires as worthless. You'll be out the money you paid for the insurance, but the increase in the stock's price may offset this.

The second scenario is that the stock will move sideways. Again, you *should* just let the option expire worthless.

The third possibility is that the stock will go down. In this case, when should you exercise your option? Ideally, you would exercise it when the stock's price hits its lowest point. But how do you know when the price has bottomed? You don't. If you're a die-hard technician, you could use technical indicators to try to determine the best time to sell, but you will never be 100 percent sure. And by exercising the option before expiration, you could be taking yourself out of a position too soon—the price might recover. The best policy, then, is to hold onto the put until expiration day, exercising it then if doing so will defray a loss in the stock.

When you exercise a put, you actually sell your shares at the strike price of the put. So if you bought an IBM November 100 put to cover 100 shares of IBM, and IBM was down at 80 on November 30, you would exercise the put on November 30 and sell your 100 shares of IBM at $100/share. You'd be out of the position, but you would also have spared yourself a loss of $2,000.

If, while you're holding a put, you think the stock has bottomed, or you feel that the stock's downside risk has abated, you could sell the put option itself. If the underlying stock is down from when you bought the put, the value of your put will be up. This is because the strike price, if it were still out of the money, would be closer to the current price than it had been when you bought the put. And the closer the strike price to the current price, the more downside protection the put provides. Conversely, if the stock has gone up, the value of your put will be down.

Let's go back to our example of the IBM November 100 put, which you bought at 3.5. If IBM's share price drops, the price of the put option will rise. If the put's price rises to, say, 10, and you sell the put at that point, you would make $650 ($1000 − $350 = $650). Even if the value of the put goes down, selling it for something before expiration would be better than letting it expire worthless.

Gauging the best time to sell a put is very difficult, and should not be tried unless you have a good deal of experience. The important thing to keep in

Moneysaver
If you really want to lock in a substantial profit on a put option but continue to cover your long position, you can sell the first put and buy a new put with a lower strike price.

mind when you buy puts as hedges is the reason you bought them in the first place: insurance.

Avoid risky investments and investment strategies

Recognizing what investments and investment strategies are inherently risky and why will help you further limit portfolio risk. The strategies and investments discussed here are not categorically unprofitable; on the contrary, they can be quite lucrative. However, they are inherently risky. As a rule, unsophisticated investors should avoid them.

Margin revisited

Buying on margin is risky because you're investing with money you have borrowed, in addition to your own money. It's not so difficult to pay back money you have borrowed, unless you lose some of it. Then you have to pay it back out of your own money. If you invest $10,000 in XYZ and buy $5,000 more on margin, and if the stock goes down 50 percent, you haven't just lost $5,000 from your original $10,000; you've lost $2,500 from the $5,000 you borrowed. You pay back $2,500 from the remaining margin money and $2,500 from your own money. So, you've actually lost $7,500 or 75 percent on the trade, not just 50 percent. See how margin works? On top of all the money you have to pay back, you have to pay interest on the money you borrow as well. Ouch!

Buying on margin adversely affects investor psychology. If you're fully margined and the stock market starts going down, the pressure to sell (too soon) will be much greater than if you weren't investing on margin. Margin fear is compounded if you're over-invested in a single stock. Inexperienced investors should stay away from margin because they'll have a great deal of difficulty keeping their emotions in check during price drops.

Selling short can get hairy

Selling short is selling shares that you borrow (from a broker) with the idea of buying them back later at a lower price, returning the shares, and pocketing the difference between what you sold them for and what you bought them back for. You sell short when you think the price of a security is going to go down. For example, you might sell 100 shares of XYZ short at $60 per share, buy them back at $50 per share, return the borrowed shares to the broker, and walk away with a $1,000 profit. Selling short can be very profitable, if you know what you're doing. Most investors who sell short analyze a company's fundamentals and its price history and sell the stock short if they think the company is headed downhill, if they think the stock is overpriced, if they think the share price is in a downtrend, or any combination of the three.

Now, because a broker is actually lending you the shares you're selling, the broker will require you to have equity in your account equal to at least 50 percent of the value of the shares you're borrowing. This ensures that you will be able to cover the cost of repurchasing the shares if the share price goes up. The broker wants to make sure he gets his shares back. If the stock does go up in price, and up and up, and if your account equity as a percentage of the repurchase cost drops too far, the broker will ask you to deposit more money. If you can't come up with the funds, the broker will buy back his shares at that point using the funds from the original short sale plus the additional funds necessary from your account. You will be out of the trade and out of a chunk of change.

Watch Out!
Selling short is riskier than buying long to the extent that the stock market has a historical upward bias. A sell-short-and-hold strategy definitely won't work.

On the other hand, if you are able to supply the funds the broker asks for, you will be able to stay in the position, but keep in mind that the potential loss from a short sale position is unlimited. The price could keep on rising until the day you die, literally. (The potential loss of a long position is limited, however, because a stock price can't fall below 0.) While it's true that some sophisticated investors make good money shorting and may even short stocks to hedge their long positions, you really shouldn't get into selling short until you've built up a successful track record in both up and down markets trading stocks long.

Bright Idea
Always use protective stops when you're selling short. If you don't stop yourself out of a losing position, your broker surely will.

Averaging down is not a sure thing

Averaging down is the practice of buying more shares when a stock you own goes down in order to average the loss and position yourself to make back your money and then some when the stock recovers. Let's look at an example. Say you buy 50 shares of XYZ at $50 per share and the stock drops to $40. You buy an additional 50 shares at $40, which makes your average loss only $5 per share, instead of $10. When the stock climbs back to $50, you're up $500 on the shares you bought at $40 and up 0 on the original shares, for a gain of $500. Even if the stock doesn't come back to your original purchase price, you can make money by averaging down. In the example, if XYZ had come back to only $46, you'd still be up $100 overall.

Averaging down *can* work. The problem is that it just doesn't always. The inherent flaw of the system is that you're throwing money after a stock that's moving in the wrong direction. The stock has negative momentum. How do you know if the stock has bottomed when you buy more shares? There's always the possibility that, as you average down and average down some more, the stock will just keep heading south, perhaps settling into a lower trading range. By averaging down, all you have done is compounded the original mistake—you're down far more than you would have been if you had just bought and held the original shares. Even if the stock does come back part way, it may not come back far enough for you to get out of the hole you've dug for yourself. You'll also have a lot of capital tied up in a stock that's going nowhere fast; you'll be over-invested in one security or industry.

Before you decide to average down, you should research the company all over again. Make sure you still think it's a solid buy. Definitely don't average down if you have lost faith in the company, if you think the price is falling for fundamental reasons. Also avoid averaging down during bear markets. The strategy is more defensible if the broad market is rising and your stock appears to be going through a temporary correction. This strategy is not one to pursue unless you're a seasoned investor who is fully aware of the risks—and even then, it's sketchy.

Penny stocks and IPOs can cost you a bundle

Penny stocks are usually defined as stocks with a share price of less than $5, less than $4 million in real assets, and a brief operating history. Stocks are introduced into the market through initial public offerings (IPOs), and at the time of their IPOs, most stocks fit the definition of penny stocks. Investors who buy penny stocks are hoping to get a piece of the next Microsoft or Amazon.com in its incubative period, just before the share price explodes upward. More often than not, however, the average investor is unable to get the stock at its opening price, buys shares after it has already shot up, and watches helplessly as the share price heads for the cellar.

The fact of the matter is that the majority of penny stocks don't do all that much, sporting low share prices because—well, because they just ain't worth a whole lot. There's serious quality risk here because these are fledgling businesses, and many of them will eventually go bankrupt. Fraud is also a major problem with penny stocks. Brokers who act as principals (who actually own shares) rather than purely as agents may not get you the best prices because of a conflict of interest, and market makers who have a monopoly on a penny stock may hype the stock. When the market makers stop creating buzz about the stock, demand for the issue abates, and the stock takes a dive.

In addition to quality risk, investors in penny stocks face the danger of falling victim to the low-price delusion. This is the belief that if a stock is selling for "pennies" already, it can't go much lower—and even if it does, you can't lose much. Exposing the delusion for what it is usually dispels it once and for all. If you buy 4,000 shares of ABC for $2 per share, and the stock drops to $1 per share, you lose $4,000, no two ways about it. And this happens all the time to amateur penny stock investors. In fact, it's easier to lose money in penny stocks than in more expensive issues because penny stocks are more volatile.

Some people do make money in penny stocks by investing in real start-ups. If you're truly interested in penny stocks, do your research. Learn as much as you can about the company before you invest. Get literature about and from the company. Also check

> **"**
> A loss never bothers me after I take it. I forget it overnight. But being wrong—not taking the loss—that is what does damage to the pocketbook and to the soul. Of all the speculative blunders, there are few greater than trying to average a losing game. Always sell what shows you a loss and keep what shows a profit.
> —Jesse Livermore
> **"**

out the broker-dealer, by all means. For more information on how to go about investing in penny stocks, go to http://mosl.sos.state.mo.us/sos-sec/penstk.html. But don't dabble in penny stocks until you have some experience investing in established companies under your belt.

Insider trading can backfire

Insider trading is the practice of placing trades based on material, nonpublic information about a company, usually by people "inside" the company who have access to such information. In general, insider information is any information that, when disclosed to the public, could affect a company's stock price. If you are privy to insider information about a company and trade on this information or pass it on to others who trade on it, you're breaking the law, and if you're caught, you'll have to give up any money you made (or avoided losing), plus a penalty. But why? What's the big deal, anyway? No one can predict the direction of prices for securities, right? So what difference does it make if I place a trade based on some inside information? The SEC states it best: "Insider trading undermines investor confidence in the fairness and integrity of the securities markets."

If you ever do gain access to privileged information about a company—such as your own—and think you could get away with placing a trade, just know that the SEC awards bounties to informants who help them nail people for insider trading. You never know who might squeal on you. Then there are the shysters. The information you think is legit may not be. You'll feel like such a hot shot, placing your insider trade, until the stock tanks, and you realize that you have just fallen for the oldest trick in the book—the

Unofficially...
It's a good idea to avoid stocks with high insider selling coupled with high PEs. Stocks experiencing heavy insider buying, however, may be ripe for purchase.

pump and dump. No, this is not the way to make money in stocks. If you want to incorporate a more legitimate form of insider information into your investment strategy, check on what company insiders are doing with their shares. Many research sites have information on insider trading activity, such as the InsiderTrader at www.insidertrader.com or Yahoo! Finance at http://quote.yahoo.com. (With Yahoo!, type in any stock ticker and then click Insider.)

The dark side of after-hours trading

After-hours trading is the trading of securities after 4:00pm (EST), when the markets officially close. Until recently, only institutional investors such as mutual funds and pension funds could trade after hours, and after-hours trading was limited to electronic trading networks (ECNs) such as Instinet and Island ECN. But the exchanges have started vying for a piece of the after-hours action. The Nasdaq computer systems are already open from 8am to 5:15pm, and brokers are allowed to trade outside regular market hours. Recently Nasdaq decided to give individual investors access as well between 4pm and 5:15pm Nasdaq also has plans for an actual second trading session, which will run from 5pm or 6pm until 9pm (EST).

Not to be outdone, the New York Stock Exchange is also planning to expand hours, with a morning session beginning at 5am (EST) (but not until June 2000) and an evening session from 5pm (EST) to as late as midnight. The Chicago Stock Exchange also has approved a plan to allow the trading of selected issues between 3pm and 5:30pm Central Standard Time.

After-hours trading affords investors the opportunity to make profitable trades after hours, as stock

> **“**
> No one can earn a million dollars honestly.
> —William Jennings Bryan
> **”**

prices are affected by late-breaking news announcements, economic data, and other information that was not made available until after the close. But after-hours trading is riskier than trading during regular trading hours because, with relatively low volume, after-hours markets are not as liquid. This means that orders may not be filled as quickly or as easily because there are fewer buyers and sellers. There will also be fewer market makers after hours, meaning less competition and wider spreads between bid and ask prices. Market makers will be able to buy shares for less (the ones you're selling) and sell shares for more (the ones you're buying). Lower liquidity also means higher volatility, the effect of news being concentrated rather than diffused across a large trading volume.

Of course, how liquid a stock is after hours depends on the stock. Popular issues are quite liquid. To protect investors from excessive volatility in after-hours trading, Nasdaq is allowing only limit orders. The Chicago Stock Exchange is following suit. Don't concern yourself with after-hours trading until you've got trading during regular hours figured out.

Day trading: Not to be entered into lightly

Day trading—entering and exiting all positions in a single day, win, lose, or draw—is all the rage. Day traders will buy a stock, watch it as it moves up, and dump it as soon as it starts to head down. Day traders usually buy large quantities so that they can realize substantial profits from small moves in a stock. To be a successful day trader, you need speed because you're trying to get in and out of positions at a certain price before it changes, which essentially means getting your trade off before the next guy does.

To do be able to do this with any consistency, you'll need the fastest quote system and the fastest order-entry system in town. Forget your 56K modem, and forget the cable modem, too, if you're really serious about making money. You'll need a dedicated telephone line (T1 or fractional T1) or a satellite system. You'll also need to use an electronic direct access trading system (EDAT), such as SuperDOT, InstiNet, or Island, which are offered by professional trading firms; you really shouldn't use online brokers for day trading. You'll need first-rate charting and technical analysis software as well. Having the best equipment will put you ahead of 99 percent of the home day traders out there and put you on an almost level playing field with the pros.

If you don't want to front all the money for the equipment, you could join a day trading brokerage operation, which will supply you with everything you need. These firms don't require any money up front. You just need to have the minimum start-up capital, usually at least $25,000. You pay the firm a fraction of what you make on your trades.

Most day traders are unsuccessful (translation: they lose a lot of money). One reason is that they're competing with professional market makers, trying to make money on small intraday movements of a stock's price. Unfortunately, market makers are professionals with much more experience. Often, the day trader isn't able to get his order in before the market maker makes his trade at a price, and the day trader misses the market. (Day traders use limit orders.) So day traders have to move *fast!* They have to see the stock move, analyze and evaluate the move correctly, and type in their order immediately,

Timesaver
Macintosh users will find the range of real-time software necessary for successful day trading to be pretty slim. Look into getting at least a 486/66MHz PC running Windows, with 16MB of RAM. Ideally, though, you would have a Pentium processor with 32MB of RAM and a 1GB hard drive.

with no mistakes. If their quotes or orders are delayed by even a few seconds, or if their reaction time (or typing) is slow, their order will not get filled and they will lose money.

The other big reason day traders lose money is lack of discipline and emotional stability. Many unsuccessful day traders have trouble taking losses. They just can't bring themselves to close out losing positions consistently, and so they end up losing more than they should. Another problem is greed. Second-rate day traders often have trouble locking in gains when a stock is up because they want to give the stock a chance to run higher. Thus, gains often turn into losses. Insufficient study also plagues the unsuccessful day trader. To excel, a day trader always needs to be striving to learn and improve.

You shouldn't day trade without the proper equipment and a sufficient knowledge base. And you shouldn't even *think* about day trading unless you're an experienced, disciplined position investor (investors who buy and hold stocks for more than a day). If you don't know what you're doing, day trading will wipe you out faster than the casinos. Day traders who don't get wiped out in the first year usually don't make real money for another year or so after that.

These are some basic rules of thumb followed by most day traders:

- Have a strategy and stick to it.
- Always use limit orders.
- Always use stops.
- Focus—trade only five or six stocks at a time.
- Buy stocks that are rising.
- Sell stocks short that are falling.

- Don't buy stocks that are down.

- Don't short stocks that are up.

- Never hold positions overnight.

For useful articles and information on day trading, check out the following sites:

- www.daytradingstocks.com/
  lessonsandeducation.html

- www.careerdaytrader.com

- www.futuresmag.com/library/daytrade97/
  daytrdcontents.html

- www.daytraders.com

- www.tigerinvestor.com

Use your common sense

All investors should follow some basic rules of thumb to avoid unnecessary risks. Perhaps the most important rule is to develop a strategy and stick with it, even if the going gets tough. Strategies can be reviewed, of course, but it's best to do this at predetermined intervals (such as once a year), not whenever you feel like it. If you have made a trade based on a certain strategy, follow through with that strategy. Never change strategies in the middle of a trade.

People often change their carefully thought-out strategies because they get emotional (they panic—another no-no). Successful investors stay cool in the clutch. Emotional-style investing, where you make impulsive decisions that run counter to reason, will not pan out in the long run; this will take you down. Your reason should be firmly planted in the driver's seat at all times.

It's not a good idea to rush investment decisions. You may want to place a trade quickly, but you

Watch Out!
It's a basic rule of thumb not to invest in things you don't understand. If you don't feel that you understand how an investment works and the risks involved, don't make the trade. Invest your time before you invest your money, and figure it out first.

shouldn't feel that you're not absolutely sure that this is what you ought to be doing right now. When in doubt, don't. You're prone to make mistakes when you rush—*stupid* mistakes that could cost you a lot of money.

Regarding investment strategies you come up with yourself, it's a good idea to test them out on paper before you put money behind them. If they still look good after you paper-test them, put a small amount of money behind the strategy and then increase or decrease the amount gradually based on how the strategy actually performs. Sometimes strategies that work great on paper don't pan out in the real world because of unforeseen difficulties and drawbacks that come to light only when implemented.

This is a list of other generally accepted investment principles, some of which have already been discussed:

- You should establish an emergency fund consisting of safe, short-term investments that you can access or liquidate at any time for unexpected expenses. You should not put all your savings in stocks and bonds.

- The percentage of assets you have in stocks should increase with wealth but decrease with age.

- Tax-free investments should be held outside retirement accounts; heavily taxed investments should be held within.

- You should diversify your assets across asset classes and diversify your equities across industries and companies.

Just the facts

- Asset allocation is the process of dividing your assets among different asset classes to achieve a desired return with the least amount of risk.

- Stop orders limit risk by setting a price at which a stock is to be sold.

- Put options limit risk by allowing you to profit from downmoves in a stock (or index) below a specified price.

- Market timing is the process of adjusting asset allocation based on an evaluation of market risk at any given time.

- Buying on margin, selling short, averaging down, trading penny stocks, after-hours trading, and day trading carry special risks and should be avoided by unsophisticated investors. Insider trading is illegal.

- All investors should follow several rules of thumb to limit risk. The most important of these include formulating a strategy and sticking to it, basing decisions on reason instead of emotion, and not investing in anything you don't understand.

Defending Your Wealth

GET THE SCOOP ON...

Tax strategies for stock investors ▪ Minimizing the mutual fund tax bite ▪ Taxes on other investment vehicles ▪ Deducting your investment expenses

PART V

Handling the Spoiler: Taxes

Chapter 14

Successful online investing is not just about how to make money; it's about how to hold on to it. It's about having a good offense *and* a good defense. The less you give away in the form of losses, costs, and taxes, the more you'll end up with. It's that simple—and easier said than done.

Of all the forces working to diminish the online investor's take-home pay, none is more insidious than taxes—always there, lurking in the background, waiting to strike. Taxes are our worst enemy, and to do effective battle, you must possess the weapons of awareness and knowledge. You must be aware of how each trade you make will affect your taxes, and you must be knowledgeable about how to minimize this effect. The first step in gaining tax awareness is to understand that you must always be thinking about taxes when you invest, not just when you file your returns. The next step is to get into the habit of considering an investment's tax implications along with its immediate costs every time you place a trade.

The knowledge you'll need to cut your taxes down to size will come from study, but the material has become convoluted. In a successful effort to balance the budget, the government raised taxes several times during the 1980s and 1990s and, in the process, made the tax laws much more complicated. The laws concerning capital gains taxes, in particular, became much more involved with the passage of the Taxpayer Relief Act in 1997 and the Internal Revenue Service Restructuring and Reform Act of 1998. Congress seems to have realized that the growing complexity of the tax laws is a problem and, hopefully, will simplify the tax code in the years to come. In the meantime, all we can do is roll up our sleeves and hash through it. This chapter is designed to do that for you.

Stocks and taxes

Believe it or not, common stock is one of the best tax shelters around. No matter how much the value of a stock goes up each year, you don't have to pay taxes on the capital appreciation until you sell. You could hold a stock for 20 years or more, enjoy a 1,000 percent return, and still not owe the government taxes on the capital gain until you sell. The beauty of the tax deferral is that the entire capital gain stays put in your investment, contributing to the size of your returns and the growth of your position's value. A long-term stock investment feeds on itself, so when the tax bite finally does come, it comes out of a much larger pie than if you had had to pay taxes all along the way.

As you know, your total return from a stock includes both dividends and capital gains. You can do nothing about dividends. They will come, and you will have to pay taxes on them every year. Dividends are taxed at the same rate as regular income—end of story. If you want to keep the taxes you pay on stock dividends low, you have stay away from stocks that have high dividend yields. Try growth stocks.

Capital gains are different. First, you control when they are realized because you control when your stocks are sold. You might decide to sell a stock in January of next year instead of December to push the capital gains tax forward a year. Or, you might decide to use an installment sale, selling your position off bit by bit to spread the capital gain out over several years. The second big difference between capital gains and dividends is the rate at which capital gains are taxed. Capital gains realized after a period of a year or less are short-term capital gains and, like dividends, are taxed at your income-tax rate. But capital gains realized after a period of more than a year are long-term capital gains and are taxed at a lower rate. You must hold a stock for *more* than a year (at least a year and a day) for the capital gain to qualify as long-term. If you sold a stock on February 2, 2000, for more than you had purchased it on February 2, 1999, the capital gain would be considered short-term.

The holding period of a stock is based on the trade date, which is the date your order is filled, not the settlement date, which is the date the securities are actually moved in or out of your account (usually three days later). The holding period doesn't begin until the day *after* you buy a stock. So if you purchase a stock on October 10, the holding period begins on October 11; on November 11, you have held the stock for one month, on December 11, for two

Moneysaver
You'll save money on taxes if you buy stocks long because capital gains on short sales will always be short-term.

months, and so on. The holding period ends on the trade date, which is the day your shares are actually sold, not the settlement date, which is the day cash from the sale is placed in your account.

The amount of a capital gain is determined by your "basis" in a stock—generally, how much you paid for the stock plus the brokerage fee. (If any changes occur to your basis, as in the case of a merger, your basis is referred to as an adjusted basis.) Just think of your basis as the total amount you have invested in your shares. So, if you bought $5,000 worth of XYZ and paid your broker a commission of $25, your basis in XYZ would be $5,025. If several months later you sold all of your shares of XYZ for $6,000 and your broker charged $25 again, your sale proceeds would be $5,975, and your capital gain would be $950 ($5,975 – $5,025). Your capital gain in a stock, then, is calculated by subtracting your basis from your sale proceeds. For information on how to determine your holding period and basis for stocks obtained other than by direct purchase, such as through DRIPs, inheritance, gifts, and company stock options, surf on over to the Fairmark Press Tax Guide for Investors at www.fairmark.com/stockbas/index.htm.

No matter what tax bracket you're in, long-term capital gains on stocks will be taxed at lower rates than short-term gains, dividends, and regular income. If you're in the 28 percent tax bracket or higher, the rate on your long-term capital gains is 20 percent; if you're in the 15 percent tax bracket, the rate is 10 percent. Now, it's possible to have some of your capital gains taxed at 10 percent and some at 20 percent. For example, if you're a single filer, and your income is $22,000, and you have $5,000 in long-term capital gains, the first $3,750 of your capital gains will be taxed at 10 percent and the remaining $1,250 will be taxed at 20 percent. Why? Because $25,750 is the upper boundary of the 15 percent tax bracket (for 1999). Your capital gains beyond $3,350 put you up into the 28 percent bracket, where capital gains are taxed at 20 percent. (Long-term capital gains are figured in after your other taxable income has been calculated.)

So, the more you make, the more of your money is taxed at higher rates—this is the meaning of a graduated tax system. The highest level at which your income is taxed is called your marginal tax rate. Table 14.1 lists tax brackets for 1999 based on taxable income and filing status.

Watch Out!
A stock split doesn't change the holding period of or your basis in a stock. The new shares are considered to have been in your possession from the purchase date of the original shares, and the dollar value of your investment doesn't change.

TABLE 14.1: 1998 TAX BRACKETS (TAXABLE INCOME)

Filing Status	15%	28%	31%	36%	39.60%
Single	Up to $25,750	$25,751+	$62,451+	$130,251+	$283,151+
Married filing separately	Up to $21,525	$21,526+	$52,026+	$79,276+	$141,576+
Married filing jointly	Up to $43,050	$43,051+	$104,051+	$158,551+	$283,151+

Another capital gains rate break will take effect in 2001. Stocks purchased in 2001 and held for more than five years will be taxed at 18 percent for investors in the 28 percent tax bracket and above, and taxed at 8 percent for investors in the 15 percent bracket.

Why are there so many incentives to invest in stocks for the long term? The government is trying to encourage long-term investment in companies because it's good for the economy. Obviously, there are some major tax advantages for long-term investors. If you're a short-term trader, crunch some numbers at the end of the year to see if you're really making out better than you would if you held all your stocks for at least a year and a day.

Keeping good records is essential if you are to optimize when to take capital gains and capital losses. For both purchases and sales, you should be sure to record the name of the company and its ticker symbol, the trade date, the number of shares traded, the price the shares traded for, and the commission you paid.

Making the most of capital losses

Now, what about those rare cases in which you sell at a loss? When you sell a stock for less than you bought it, you have a capital loss on your hands. Capital losses are first used to offset any capital gains you have for the year—short-term capital losses offset short-term gains, and long-term losses offset long-term gains. For example, if you have $7,500 in long-term capital gains and $2,000 in long-term capital losses, you subtract the losses from the gains to get a net long-term capital gain of $5,500 for the year.

If your long-term capital losses exceed your long-term capital gains, or if your short-term losses exceed your short-term gains, or both, after using a portion of the losses to offset all the corresponding gains, you can deduct the excess losses (up to $3,000) from your taxable income. If you have both excess long-term losses and excess short-term losses, use the excess short-term losses first to offset your income. Any short-term or long-term losses you don't use up can be carried forward to the following year.

Let's take an example. Let's say your long-term capital gains for the year are $4,000, and your long-term capital losses are $12,000. Your short-term gains

Unofficially...
While we would like to believe that expert investors rarely suffer losses, this is simply not true. All investors, even Warren Buffett and Peter Lynch, make mistakes, experience bad luck, and lose money sometimes. What separates the men from the boys is how they handle their losing positions.

are $2,000, and your short-term losses are $4,000. First, use the losses to offset the gains. This leaves you with $8,000 in long-term losses ($12,000 – $4,000) and $2,000 in short-term losses ($4,000 – $2,000). Next, use the excess losses to offset up to $3,000 in income, starting with the short-term losses. So, offset $2,000 of the $3,000 in income with all the remaining short-term losses, and use $1,000 of the remaining $8,000 long-term losses to offset the last $1,000 in income, leaving you with $7,000 in long-term losses. Carry this $7,000 in long-term losses forward to next year.

Watch out for wash sales

Let's say you bought XYZ at $100 more than a year ago, and it's down around $75 now. You aren't ready to cry uncle, but you'd like to claim the loss to offset your long-term gains for the year. Wait a minute! What if you sold the stock and bought it back real quick? Then you could claim the loss without giving up the position. A neat idea, except for the fact that the government doesn't allow it. Selling and repurchasing a security for reasons other than trying to make a profit on the trade is considered a *wash sale*, and the wash sale rule states that you can't claim a capital loss on any security you repurchase within 30 days of selling it. You have to wait until the 31st day. Why? The government just doesn't want the investing public creating all kinds of phony capital losses to get out of paying taxes.

If you unwittingly sell some shares and repurchase them within 30 days, however, you will not suffer a fate worse than death. The loss will be added to the basis of the repurchased shares, so you will be able to claim the loss later when you sell. To illustrate, say you bought 50 shares of XYZ at $100 per

Bright Idea
One way to get around the wash sale rule is to replace the shares you sell with shares of a very similar stock, such as replacing shares of GM with shares of Ford. Go to www. jsonline.com/ business/arm/ 980921averaging downtechniqu. asp to learn about another technique called "doubling up."

share, and the price dropped to $80 per share. If you sold the shares at $80 and repurchased at $80 within 30 days, you would not be able to claim the loss. But the $20 per share loss would be added to the basis of the repurchased shares, so your basis in those shares would not be $80; it would be $100, as if you had never sold them. Your loss would be intact, and so would your holding period. The period of time you had held XYZ before the sale would be included in the holding period for the replacement stock.

The complete wash sale rule states that you can't claim a loss on the sale of stock purchased less than 31 days *before or after* you sell it if the purpose of the purchase is to replace the stock you sold. The wash sale rule doesn't apply if the stock you buy isn't replacement stock. For example, if you buy 100 shares of XYZ at $60 on April 1 and sell all the shares at $55 on April 15, you are in a position to claim a loss on shares you purchased less than 31 days before you sold them. This situation, however, does not trigger the wash sale rule because the shares you purchased on April 1 were not replacement shares. For additional rules pertaining to wash sales, such as buying and selling different numbers of shares and wash sales with short selling, refer to the Fairmark Press Tax Guide for Investors at www.fairmark.com/ capgain/ws101.htm.

Capital gains strategies

The main thing to keep in mind with capital gains taxes is that the longer you put off selling a stock with a gain, the better. It's really that simple. Buy-and-hold investors, who are deferring capital gains taxes and minimizing brokerage commissions, are making the most of this rule of thumb. Of course, if you're following a strategy that calls for you to sell a stock, you shouldn't abandon your strategy to avoid the capital gains tax. The importance of a smart tax strategy rarely outweighs the importance of a well-conceived investment strategy. But the tax implications of your strategy should be taken into account when you formulate it, and tax efficiency should be considered when you implement it.

While the general rule is to put off as long as you can selling shares that are up, the opposite tends to be true in the case of losses. Imagine that you have a $5,000 short-term capital gain and a $5,000 long-term capital gain in the same year. If you also had a short-term position that was down $5,000, you might want to go ahead and sell that position before it becomes a long-term loss. Why? As a short-term loss, it will offset the short-term gain, which would be taxed at a higher rate than the long-term gain. By taking the short-term loss to offset the short-term gain, you'll have to pay the lower tax only on the long-term gain.

As a rule, you want to avoid taking long-term capital gains in the same year as long-term losses because you're better served when the losses are used to reduce taxable income rather than long-term capital gains. Why? Again, your regular income is taxed at a higher rate than your long-term gains.

Let's take a look at an example. Let's say your taxable income for the year is $35,000, your long-term capital losses are $3,000, and you're currently holding a long-term winning position that's up $3,000. If you close out that position, the capital loss will offset the gain, and you will pay 28 percent on $35,000, or $9,800. If you wait to close out the position until next

Unofficially...
If you simply cannot get your hands on all the information you need to calculate your capital gains taxes, such as the original purchase price or date, you are permitted to estimate, within reason.

year, however, the $3,000 loss will be deducted from
your $35,000 taxable income, leaving $32,000, and
you'll pay only $8,960 in taxes. Next year, when you
take the $3,000 gain, you'll pay 20 percent on the
$3,000 or $600. So, your total tax on the same
money spread over two years would come to $9,560,
for a savings of $240.

You might want to take a *large* long-term loss in
the same year as a large gain, however, if you don't
want to pay a lot of capital gains taxes in a single
year. If you had a $30,000 capital gain coming, tak-
ing a $20,000 loss the same year as the gain would
leave a net gain of only $10,000, the taxes on which
might be more manageable than those on $30,000.
If you took the $20,000 loss the following year, how-
ever, you could not use it to offset the $30,000 gain
because you can't carry a loss backward. If you didn't
have a large capital gain to offset the $20,000 loss in
the year you took it, you could deduct only $3,000 of
it from your income, leaving $17,000. It could take
you years to use up that remaining $17,000, and you
would have to keep track of how much remained
each year and remember to use it.

How to sell partial positions

If you own shares of the same stock purchased at different times, and if your strategy calls for you to sell
some of the shares, selling winning shares you've
held for more than a year will yield a tax advantage.
At the same time, you'll want to consider selling the
shares showing the smallest gain, regardless of when
you bought them. Your decision about which losing
shares to sell should depend on which, if any, gains
you want to offset. If you have no gains, long-term or
short-term losses can be used to offset income.

If you want to sell only some of the shares of a stock you own, not all, and if you do not specify which shares you want your broker to sell, the first-in-first-out (FIFO) rule automatically applies. FIFO means the shares you bought earliest are sold first. For example, if you bought 50 shares of XYZ in August, 50 shares in September, and 50 shares in October, and you decided to sell 75 shares in November, as far as the IRS is concerned, you would be selling all 50 of the shares bought in August and 25 of the shares bought in September. You can't decide later, say at tax time, that the shares you meant to sell were any other than the earliest you purchased. Realize that if you sell the shares you purchased earliest first, you are more likely to realize a larger capital gain than if you sell more recently purchased shares because the older shares were probably cheaper.

If you want to sell some of your shares in a stock, but not the shares you bought earliest first, you need to specify to your broker which shares you want to sell. This is known as the specific ID method. This method lets you sell the highest-cost shares first, keeping your capital gains taxes down. Of course, if you haven't held the highest-cost shares for a year, the capital gains from the sale of these shares, however minimal, will be taxed at the same rate as your regular income. To avoid this, you might choose to sell the highest-cost shares that you've held for at least a year.

To sell shares using the specific ID method, indicate to your broker how many shares of what company from which lot. For example: "Please sell 40 shares of XYZ from the lot purchased on January 23, 1999." Some brokers will be confused by this kind of

Watch Out!
It's important not to think of capital losses as desirable things just because they can be used to defray capital gains taxes. Capital losses do not save you money—they are still losses!

order, thinking you're actually asking them to locate the very shares you purchased on such-and-such a date and sell them. In fact, all the broker has to do is sell the number of shares you specify at the price you indicate and e-mail or mail you a confirmation within a reasonable amount of time that acknowledges which shares you intended to sell. At the very least, you should keep your own written record of the request, although this may not be enough to satisfy the IRS in an audit.

If you're using an online broker, right after you send in your order, send an e-mail specifying which shares you want to sell, and include your order number. (The order number will be on the online confirmation that confirms the placement of your trade.) Print out your e-mail and file it, and ask for an e-mail acknowledgement of your specific request. (Just don't let them mistake your e-mail for an additional order!) Even if your online broker refuses to send you a personal e-mail confirmation, *your* e-mail requesting the confirmation and specifying the shares you intended to sell should suffice if you're ever audited.

Mutual funds and taxes

As with stocks, the buying and selling of mutual fund shares generates capital gains and losses. If you buy a fund with a NAV of $12.85, for instance, and sell all your shares in that fund later at $13.75, you will realize a capital gain. If you sell the shares in the fund for less than you paid, you will realize a capital loss. This is true even if you switch or exchange from one fund to another *in the same fund family*. When you make an exchange, you are not just transferring funds; you are selling one fund and buying another using the proceeds from the sale of the first fund. While you may not have to pay any fees or loads, switching

Timesaver
If you hold stock certificates for different lots of a stock you purchased at different times, simply send the broker the certificate for the shares you wish to sell. If your certificate covers a number of shares bought at different times, however, you will have to specify which shares you want sold and get a confirmation acknowledging this.

between funds in the same fund family is a taxable event. Money market funds are the exception because money market funds are designed to maintain a NAV of $1 per share. Selling shares in a money market fund, then, will not generate capital gains or losses. Writing a check against a fund that requires some of your shares to be sold is also a taxable event, except, again, in the case of money market funds.

The basic rules for capital gains for stocks apply to mutual funds. When you sell shares of a mutual fund that you have held for a year or less, the capital gain or loss generated by the sale is short-term. When you sell shares held more than a year, the gain or loss is long-term. As with stocks, short-term capital gains from mutual funds are taxed at the same rate as ordinary income; long-term capital gains are taxed at 10 percent for investors in the 15 percent tax bracket and at 20 percent for investors in the 28 percent bracket and above. Short-term losses offset short-term gains; long-term losses offset long-term gains; and excess capital losses can be used to offset up to $3,000 of income a year, with any remainder to be carried forward to the following year.

As with stocks, keeping careful records of all your mutual fund transactions is key to accurately reporting capital gains and losses to the IRS. Most mutual fund companies will mail three forms to you in January, where applicable, to help you out:

- **IRS Form 1099-DIV:** This form reports all the ordinary dividends and capital gains distributed to you by each fund you owned shares in during the previous year.

- **IRS Form 1099-B:** This report is a record of all your sales of shares (but not purchases) during the previous year.

Watch Out!
Whether you realize it or not, you pay income taxes throughout the year in the form of withholding taxes, taxes withheld from your paychecks. If your withholding does not cover at least 90 percent of your tax liability, you have to send the IRS estimated tax payments four times a year or face a penalty. For more information about estimated taxes, check out www.fairmark.com/estimate/index.htm.

■ **IRS Form 1099-R:** This form reports all the distributions you received from retirement accounts, such as IRAs, during the previous year.

Don't let fund basis throw you

To calculate a capital gain or loss from a mutual fund, you need to determine your basis in the shares you're selling. This is relatively easy if you purchased all your shares in the fund at the same time, and if you haven't received any dividends or capital gains. For example, say you buy 100 shares of no-load XYZ at $32 per share on March 5, 1999, and decide to sell all shares at $40 per share on April 5, 1999. Your basis in XYZ is simply $3,200 (plus brokerage fees). Your sale proceeds are $4,000 (minus brokerage fees), and your short-term capital gain is $800 (minus brokerage fees for buying and selling).

Things get a little more complicated when you hold on to your mutual fund shares for a while, having opted to reinvest all dividends and capital gains. Under these conditions, every time the fund generates a dividend or a capital gain, the proceeds are used to buy you additional shares of the fund, and these new shares have a different basis than the original shares you bought. Why? Because your basis in a block of shares is determined by the share price and the date of purchase. If you yourself purchase additional shares of a fund frequently, as in the case of dollar cost averaging, you will own many blocks of shares, each block with a different basis. For example, say that you buy 100 shares of no-load XYZ at $26 per share on June 6, 1999, and an additional 100 shares three months later at $28 per share—your basis in the original shares would be $2,600, but your basis in the additional shares would be $2,800. The fact that not all your shares have the same basis is important when you start selling shares because a logistical problem arises in calculating capital gains. What is the basis of the shares you're selling?

But most investors don't worry (or even think) about any of this. They just sell however many shares they want, when they want. And this is fine. But it's good to understand what you're actually doing and to realize the consequences and options before you. According to tax law, if you don't specify which shares you want sold when you submit a sell order, as with stocks, the first-in-first-out (FIFO) rule applies. The shares you sell will be the ones you bought first. However, if you specify which shares you mean to sell and get a written confirmation of that intent from your broker or mutual fund company, then those are the shares you can claim that you sold on your tax return. As with stocks, this is called the specific ID method.

Remember, we're talking only about how purchases of blocks of shares in a single fund at different times can affect your calculation of capital gains. The actual buying and selling of shares by the fund is a no-brainer. If you buy 100 shares of Fund X at $30 per share, buy 50 more shares a month later at $40 per share, and sell 30 shares a month after that at $50 per share, the fund just buys and sells the shares. It's very straightforward. The complexity arises only in which shares you should indicate, for tax purposes, that you intended to sell.

The disadvantage of the first-in-first-out (FIFO) method is that you're always selling the shares that are most likely to generate the largest capital gains

Moneysaver
If you plan to sell shares in a fund that you've held more than 12 months, do so before the December dividend. This way, your entire capital gain from the sale will be a long-term gain.

(because you've held them the longest). And while the specific ID method does allow the greatest control in planning your taxes, it may just be too time-consuming and troublesome for you. So, to make figuring out capital gains on mutual funds with multiple purchases of shares easier to calculate, the IRS has devised two averaging methods: the single-category method and the double-category method.

When using the single-category method, you simply add up the basis of each of the blocks of shares you own (the cost of all the blocks of shares plus commissions) and divide by the total number of shares you own. The resulting number is your average basis per share, or basis per share. You then use this number to calculate capital gains on the sale of any shares.

For example, if you calculate your basis per share to be $8.95 and you sell 50 shares, your basis in those 50 shares is $447.50 plus commissions ($8.95 per share × 50 shares = $447.50). If you sell the 50 shares at $13.40 per share, your sales proceeds are $670 minus commissions, for a capital gain of $222.50, minus the commissions for buying and selling. Shares are sold on the FIFO basis, so how long you have held the oldest shares in your account at any given time will determine whether their sale will generate long-term or short-term capital gains. While the system of selecting which shares are sold first is the same as the FIFO method, however, the way the shares' basis is determined is different. Most mutual fund companies that provide statements that include cost basis calculations for shares you have sold use the single-category method.

The double-category method also allows you to use average basis per share to calculate capital gains, but this method lets you control whether you're realizing long-term or short-term capital gains with a sale. With the double-category method, you add up the bases for all the blocks of shares you've held in a fund for a year or less, and then you add up the bases for all the blocks of shares you've held for more than a year. You then calculate the average long-term basis per share by dividing the total long-term basis by the total number of long-term shares. You also calculate the average short-term basis per share by dividing the total short-term basis by the total number of short-term shares. As with the specific ID method, when you use the double-category method, you should specify to your broker which shares you want to sell and get a confirmation of this.

Let's look at an example of the double-category method in action. Say you decide to sell 50 fund shares of XYZ from a lot purchased June 19, 1997. First, send your broker a sell order saying "Please sell 50 shares of XYZ from the lot purchased on June 19, 1997." Second, get your confirmation. Next, to calculate your capital gains tax, add up the basis of all the blocks of long-term shares you have, and get your total long-term basis; let's say it's $3,786. Then you divide your total long-term basis by the total number of long-term shares you own (say, 150), and get your average price per long-term share: $25.24. Your basis in 50 long-term shares, then, would be 50 × $25.24 = $1,262. If the current share price is $38, you'll make 50 × $38 = $1,900 on the sale. Your long-term capital gain would then be $638 ($1,900 − $1,262), and your capital gains tax would be 20 percent of that, or $127.60.

The double-category method and the specific ID method are considerably more complex than the

Moneysaver
If only part of the dividends you receive come from interest on Treasuries or other government obligations, you may be able to avoid paying state and local taxes on that portion of your dividends. You can do this only with certain funds, though. Typically, a fund must have at least 50 percent of its assets in vehicles that are exempt from state and local taxes.

single-category or the FIFO method. Of all the methods for calculating your capital gains mentioned here, the single-category method probably will provide the most advantages with the fewest hassles for most investors. Whichever method you choose, though, be careful not to mix and match. While it's perfectly okay to use different methods with different funds, you cannot use different methods with the same fund. For example, you cannot calculate your capital gains on Fund X using the single-category method one year and the double-category method the next. If you elect to use an averaging method with a fund, you should attach a short note to your tax return the first year that you own the fund stating the averaging method you have used to calculate your capital gains for that fund.

Handling mutual fund dividend payouts

Calculating the capital gains generated from selling shares is the biggest headache in figuring out the taxes you owe on your mutual funds each year. But what about dividends? A mutual fund pays shareholders dividends, generated by the underlying securities the fund holds, so that the fund doesn't have to pay taxes on them—the shareholders do. Both interest income and short-term capital gains are distributed to the fund's shareholders as ordinary dividends and are reported on Form 1099-DIV, *Dividends and Distributions,* which is sent to shareholders between January and March. (The fund retains capital losses and uses them to offset capital gains that are not distributed.) You won't receive a 1099-DIV if you don't owe any taxes on a fund or if you received less than $10 in dividends, although you will owe taxes on *any* dividends you received, even if it was only a couple bucks.

You must report both the short-term capital gains and the interest income, which are lumped together in these dividend payouts as a unit. You cannot separate the short-term capital gains out of the dividend and offset them with short-term losses. The dividend is indivisible, and the entire amount is taxed at the same rate as your regular income. Also, you must pay tax on all the dividends you receive from your mutual funds each year, even if you have elected to have your dividends reinvested. Your tax liability is not contingent on actually receiving a check in the mail.

The exception to the rule is if you are invested in tax-free money market funds, tax-free bond funds, or Treasury bond funds, in which case the dividends received are wholly or partly tax-exempt. These dividends are referred to as exempt-interest dividends and are reported on a separate statement from the 1099-DIV. But you still must report these dividends on your tax return. Depending on the fund and your income, the dividends may be taxable in part, may not be exempt from state or local income taxes, may increase the tax you pay on your Social Security income, and may be subject to the alternative minimum tax (AMT). (The AMT is a tax designed to ensure that high-income taxpayers pay a certain minimum amount of tax no matter what. For the basics on the dreaded AMT, check out www.fairmark.com/amt/index.htm.)

If a mutual fund has long-term capital gains generated by the sale of some of its underlying holdings, it will distribute these gains to shareholders as capital gain distributions or capital gain dividends. These long-term capital gains are designated as part of the fund's dividend. The total long-term capital gain distribution will be reported on Form 1099-DIV in Box 2a. (It will be broken down into subcategories in boxes 2b, 2c, and 2d.)

You must report the capital gain distribution part of the dividend as a long-term capital gain on your tax return—whether or not you have held the fund for more than a year. Any long-term capital gains generated by tax-exempt funds are also taxable as long-term gains. (It's the interest income that's tax-exempt.) Capital gain distributions received through mutual fund dividend distributions are taxed at the rate of 10 percent for investors in the 15 percent tax bracket, and 20 percent for those in higher brackets.

Now, just to make things interesting, some funds use capital gain *allocations,* which are different from capital gain dividends or capital gain distributions. When a mutual fund makes a capital gain allocation, the fund keeps the capital gain, apportioning some of it to your account, and pays a tax on it for you (with your money). Mutual funds report capital gain allocations on Form 2439, *Notice to Shareholder of Undistributed Long-Term Capital Gain;* allocations do not appear on 1099-DIV. If you get a capital gain allocation, you should report the gain on your tax return as a long-term capital gain, claim a tax credit for the tax paid for you by the mutual fund (because they usually pay too much), and adjust your basis in the fund. For instructions on how to do all this, surf on over to www.fairmark.com/mutual/cgalloc.htm.

As if that weren't enough, there are also occasions when mutual funds make dividend payments called return of capital distributions or nontaxable distributions. These are not ordinary long-term capital gains, nor are they ordinary dividends or

Watch Out!
Make sure you fill out the tax computation on the back of Schedule D on your tax return. It's necessary to do this to make sure you're paying the right tax on your capital gains.

exempt-interest dividends. They are actually a return of some of the money you originally invested in the fund.

Return of capital distributions are listed in box 3 on Form 1099-DIV. You do not have to report your nontaxable distributions on your tax return (unless they exceed your basis in the fund, in which case you report the difference between the distribution and your basis as a capital gain on Schedule D). All you *do* have to do is adjust your basis. When you get a return of capital, you're getting some of your original investment back, so your basis in the fund goes down. If you're using the single-category averaging method, just subtract the nontaxable distribution from your total basis to get your adjusted basis. If you're using another method, you have to subtract the nontaxable distribution from your total basis and divide by the total number of shares you own to get your adjusted basis per share. You then multiply the number of shares in a given block by this number to get your adjusted basis in that block of shares.

Finally, if you own shares in a country, regional, global, or international fund, or any fund that holds overseas stocks, that allocates foreign taxes to its shareholders, you can do one of two things: deduct the foreign taxes paid by the fund, or claim a foreign tax credit. Taking the foreign tax allocation as an itemized deduction is quick and easy—you just enter the amount (in addition to any other foreign tax allocations you may have received) on line 8 of the 1040 tax form. A fund's foreign tax allocation will be reported in box 6 of Form 1099-DIV.

Claiming the foreign tax as a tax credit is a bit more complicated, but it will usually net you a bigger savings. (Tax credits tend to save you more than

Unofficially...
Mutual funds are allowed to treat dividends declared during the last three months of one year, but not distributed until January of the following year, as belonging to the earlier year.

deductions because credits come directly off your tax, not just your taxable income.) To figure out your foreign tax credit, you need to fill out Form 1116, which is a bit complicated. If your foreign taxes are $300 or less, you do not have to fill out this form, but you will need to follow the instructions on the form to properly claim the credit.

Mutual funds have wash sales, too

If you buy shares in a mutual fund just before an ordinary dividend payout and sell the shares right afterward, you can claim a short-term capital loss, which you can use to offset an equal amount of short-term capital gains. Remember, when a mutual fund pays out a dividend, the fund's NAV goes down by the amount of the dividend. But if you receive a capital gain distribution or allocation shortly after you buy a fund and then sell the fund at a loss, you cannot claim a short-term capital loss on the fund because the distributions you received are considered long-term, and you would be getting an unfair tax advantage.

Let's look at an example: Say you buy 100 shares of Fund Z at $30 per share, and soon it pays out a capital gain dividend of $1.80 per share, which you receive. Even though you have held the fund only a short while, you must report this gain as a long-term gain (because it is). After the distribution, the NAV of your fund drops to $28.20, and you sell the fund planning to claim a short-term capital loss. But you can't! In doing so, you would be trying to reduce the amount on which you have to pay the higher rate, when you broke even with a gain that you'll be paying the lower rate on.

You can claim a short-term capital loss only when you sell your mutual fund shares at a loss if you've held the shares for more than six months. The government feels that a decline in the share price of a fund after six months will generally be the result of changes in the value of the fund, not just the result of dividend payouts. If you sell a fund you've held six months or less at a loss, the government insists that you treat the portion of the loss equal to the capital gain distributions and allocations you received as a long-term capital loss, and only the remainder as a short-term loss.

This rule also applies, of course, when you receive exempt-interest dividends, such as those distributed by municipal bond funds. The IRS won't let you buy shares in such a fund just before a distribution, receive your tax-exempt interest, and then turn around and sell the fund at a loss to claim a short-term capital loss. The dividend you received is not taxable, so you have no right to use the drop in the NAV caused by distribution of the dividend to offset any of your taxable gains. Only the portion of the drop in price not caused by the exempt-interest dividend can be used as a short-term loss. Again, these restrictions no longer apply after six months.

How to choose tax-efficient funds

How do you find the most tax-efficient funds? Clearly, some types of funds are more likely to generate taxable income and capital gains than others. Stock funds, for example, will generate more taxable income and capital gains than municipal bond funds will. The fund types that create the least tax liability include taxable money market funds, tax-exempt money market funds, tax-exempt bond funds, and state tax-exempt bond funds.

Among the taxable stock and bond funds, those that generate relatively few ordinary dividends (taxed at the same rate as your income) would offer

Unofficially...
Among the things that increase the likelihood of being audited is not reporting income you received that *was* reported to the IRS; this includes investment income. Remember, your broker is required by law to furnish the IRS with a 1099 form every year, detailing your investment earnings. For more information on how to avoid an audit, go to www.smartmoney. com/ac/tax/ index. cfm?story=audit.

a tax advantage. Growth funds, which tend to pay out few, if any, dividends, fit this description. Value funds and equity-income funds, which tend to hold stocks with high dividend yields, and taxable bond funds, which make substantial interest payments, would carry a larger tax liability than most growth funds. Think about holding funds that generate a lot of taxable dividends in tax-exempt accounts, such as your IRA and 401(k), and hold funds that don't in taxable accounts.

But fund type is not the sole determinant of a fund's tax efficiency. In fact, funds within the same category show wide discrepancies in tax efficiency. This phenomenon can be explained by the fact that some fund managers are simply better at minimizing tax liability than others. And we have a means to compare: the tax-efficiency ratio. This is the ratio between a fund's after-tax and pretax returns. You can think of it as the percentage of a fund's pretax return that you actually get to keep. *Morningstar* has starting ranking mutual funds on the basis of tax efficiency, giving funds a tax-efficiency rating.

The factor thought to be most influential in determining a fund's tax efficiency is the fund's turnover rate. The turnover rate is the percentage of a fund's securities that are sold each year. A fund with a 60 percent turnover rate sells securities equaling 60 percent of the fund's average net assets a year. (The average U.S. stock mutual fund has a turnover rate of 88 percent.) The higher the turnover rate, the more capital gains being realized and distributed to you, and the more taxes you have to pay.

All other things (such as performance) being equal, then, you should favor funds with lower turnover rates. Some financial analysts, however, argue that there's no relationship between turnover and tax efficiency. They say that funds with low turnover now are simply holding stocks that will have to be sold eventually, generating massive capital gain distributions when they are. What to do? Give more weight to a fund's tax-efficiency ratio than to its turnover rate.

If you don't want to spend a lot of time researching, you could just invest in a tax-managed (or tax-efficient) fund. These funds are managed to minimize taxable income and capital gains by using a variety of strategies, such as indexing, holding all shares for a minimum period such as 18 months, investing in stocks with low dividend yields, and assessing fees to shareholders for early redemptions. Tax-managed funds usually require an initial investment of at least $10,000, but this may be changing. T. Rowe Price now offers such a fund with only a $2,500 initial investment requirement. Of course, you could always go with an index fund, which tend just to hold the stocks in the index they track.

Taxes on other vehicles

As with stocks, when you sell a bond at a higher price than you buy it for, you will realize a capital gain; if you sell it for less, you will incur a capital loss. If you have held a bond for a year or less when you sell it, your gain or loss will be short-term; if you've held the bond for more than a year, you'll have a long-term gain or loss. The rates and rules are the same as for stocks. Dividends generated by bonds are also treated the same way as those for stocks, with the exception of tax-exempt bonds, whose dividends are tax-free. The main difference between stocks and bonds is not in the treatment of dividends and

Bright Idea
If you have a fairly large taxable portfolio, consider putting it (at least part of it, anyway) under the management of your bank's trust department. Unlike mutual funds, which pay out distributions automatically every year, bank trust departments have the expertise to create income and taxable gains at the optimal times for you.

capital gains, but in the proportion. Bonds tend to show comparatively smaller amounts of capital appreciation and depreciation than stocks, but relatively larger dividend payouts.

Long put options (puts bought as hedges) follow the same rules as stocks and bonds for determining short- and long-term capital gains, with the one-year mark determined by the holding period of the put. If a long put expires, it will result in a short-term capital loss if you held it for a year or less, and it will be considered a long-term capital loss if you held it for more than a year. The loss is equal to the cost of the option plus the commission you paid the broker.

If you sell a put option, you will realize a short- or long-term capital gain or loss, depending on whether you held the option for more than a year. If you exercise a put option, you must first subtract the price of the put and the commission fees from the amount realized from exercising to determine your sale proceeds. If your sale proceeds exceed your cost basis, you will pay taxes on a short-term or long-term capital gain, depending on whether you held the underlying stock for more than a year. If your basis exceeds your sale proceeds, you can claim a short-term or long-term capital loss, also depending on how long you held the underlying stock.

For information on how to handle taxes on the stock options your company gave you (known as company or corporate stock options, incentive stock options, or ISOs), check out SmartMoney.com at www.smartmoney.com/ac/tax/index.cfm?story=options, or the Motley Fool at www.fool.com/school/taxes/taxes24.htm. For information on special tax breaks for day traders, click over to www.smartmoney.com/ac/tax/index.cfm?story=daytrading or http://tigerinvestor.com/articles/

TJ2_3_8_99.html. For a review of taxes on traditional and Roth IRAs and 401(k)s, take another look at Chapter 7, "Setting Goals and Formulating a Game Plan."

Deduct your investment expenses

You should deduct all the investment-related expenses you can from your taxes every year. These expenses include things such as money you spent for professional investment advice, investment newsletters, investment-related legal and accounting fees, the portion of your ISP charges equal to the fraction of time online you devoted to investing, the percentage of the yearly depreciation of your computer equal to the percentage of time you used the computer to manage and transact your investments, and anything else you can think of. You cannot deduct broker's commissions, though, which are already incorporated into the basis of your securities, lowering the amount of your taxable gains on a dollar-for-dollar basis. You also cannot deduct costs related to investing in tax-exempt securities. (There's no justification for deducting an expense for purchasing a security whose dividends you're not going to pay taxes on anyway.) You can also forget trying to deduct travel and other expenses related to attending shareholder's meetings.

Be sure to deduct the interest charges on your investments, though. Margin account interest is the most common source of investment interest expenses, but any interest charged on short positions—not to mention the interest you might be paying on loans used to purchase or carry investment property—can be deducted. Investment interest expenses can be deducted to the extent of your net investment income—your total investment income

Bright Idea
The most important overall tax strategy you can employ is to defer income, generally earned income such as salary and bonuses. You don't have to pay taxes on deferred income until you receive it, which has the dual advantage of lowering your taxes now and letting you grow that income on a tax-deferred basis.

minus directly connected *noninterest* investment expenses. If your investment interest expenses for the year exceed your net investment income, the excess can be carried forward to future years.

All investment-related expenses are calculated on the tax form "Schedule A—Itemized Deductions" in the section entitled "Job Expenses and Most Other Miscellaneous Deductions." For the items you list in this section to contribute to your itemized deductions, however, they must total more than 2 percent of your adjusted gross income (AGI) (basically, your income minus a few major expenses, such as alimony payments, moving expenses, and retirement plan contributions). If 2 percent of your AGI is greater than all your miscellaneous deductions, you get no deduction in this department. If your miscellaneous expenses are greater than 2 percent of your AGI, you can deduct the difference—that is, your total miscellaneous expenses minus 2 percent of your AGI equals your allowed deduction for job expenses and most other miscellaneous deductions.

Believe it or not, this 2 percent floor screens out most investors. But even if your miscellaneous expenses exceed 2 percent of your AGI, your miscellaneous expenses plus your other itemized deductions may not come to more than your standard deduction. Even if you do claim your itemized deductions because they exceed your standard deduction, you could end up having to pay an AMT, which would force you to pay the money you thought you had saved writing off all those blasted investment expenses! The people who *can* benefit from writing off investment expenses tend to have incomes low enough not to trigger the AMT, but investment expenses high enough to push their overall miscellaneous deductions well above 2 percent of their AGI.

If you can manage to claim trader status for yourself instead of investor status, you can deduct much more. Traders can deduct 100 percent of both interest and noninterest investment expenses—they are not subject to the 2 percent AGI floor. The reason is that the IRS views traders' investment expenses as business expenses because trading securities is essentially a trader's full-time job.

To meet the definition of a trader, you don't have to be a day trader, but you do need to log a lot of hours trading, engage in a lot of trading activity, and make short-term (not long-term) trades. Holding any stocks for more than a year could disqualify you. If you're still not sure if you're a trader or an investor, take a look at the Fairmark Press Tax Guide for Investors' article on the subject at www.fairmark.com/traders.htm.

Just the facts

- Long-term capital gains are realized on securities sold after more than a year and are taxed at a lower rate than short-term capital gains and dividends, which are both taxed at the same rate as regular income.

- Long-term capital losses can be used to offset long-term capital gains, short-term losses, short-term gains, and excess capital losses—up to $3,000 of income a year.

- The long-term capital gains tax rate for investors in the 15 percent tax bracket is 10 percent; the rate for those in the 28 percent bracket and above is 20 percent.

- Unlike stock investors, mutual fund investors will receive capital gains distributions every year from the sale of stocks in the fund.

- Investors who sell bonds, options, or any other type of investment for more than they bought them will have to pay a capital gains tax, even if the investments are tax-exempt vehicles.

- Investment interest expenses and noninterest investment expenses can be deducted from your adjusted gross income.

GET THE SCOOP ON...
Health insurance—a priority ▪ Disability
insurance ▪ Ways to save on your auto
insurance ▪ Homeowner's insurance—more
than just a good idea ▪ Don't overdo
your life coverage

Insurance: The Fortress Around Your Finances

Chapter 15

Having adequate insurance is a rampart against losing your nest egg. It's there just in case, to cover those major, unexpected expenses that would otherwise come out of your savings. But you don't have major, unexpected expenses, you say? You're almost never sick, and when you are, you just sleep it off and you're fine. You're a safetynik. You've never had a car accident. That's great, and you may very well be doing something right, but you *still* need to protect yourself against the possibility of something bad happening. If you don't, one unexpected accident, illness, or lawsuit could wipe you out.

Buying insurance is just another form of risk management. It should not be viewed as a cheaper way of paying for the things in your life that you don't like to pay; it should be thought of as a way to pay for things *not* in your life that could ruin you if

517

they were. Insurance is a protective stop, if you will, against catastrophic loss. All types of insurance, then, are really a form of savings insurance.

All online investors should carry adequate health, disability, auto, and homeowner's (or renter's) insurance. But exactly what you should buy—and how much—depends on your personal situation and, to some extent, on your risk tolerance level. If you have a very high tolerance for risk, you may feel comfortable carrying a minimal amount of insurance, but if you have a low risk tolerance, you won't feel comfortable unless you're covered to the teeth. Trying to save money on insurance payments without regard for your comfort level will have a negative impact on your quality of life.

But, as in investing, the more you try to eliminate risk in insurance, the more you'll probably end up paying. You want to avoid being overinsured. To be sure, all kinds of available insurance policies are geared toward the paranoid and have little practical value. (Have you ever heard of alien-abduction insurance?) The goal in buying insurance is to buy only what you need and not pay too much for it.

You've gotta get health insurance

First things first—health insurance. Why is health insurance first? Well, because there really isn't anything more important in your life than your health—no, not even money. How much is five minutes of life worth? How many times have you heard, "When you have your health, you have everything"? It's a cliché, perhaps, but it's true nonetheless. Our health is the foundation of everything we do—work, play, travel. You don't want to make a fortune investing online and not be healthy enough to enjoy it.

Unfortunately, health problems visit us all from time to time, often with increasing frequency as we get older. And medical costs, rising without rhyme or reason, add insult to injury. Nowadays, a broken arm or leg or a minor illness that requires a couple of days in the hospital can set you back thousands of dollars if you're not insured, to say nothing of a major illness or a serious injury. If you're poor, you may get a certain amount of treatment at little or no cost, but you might not get the best treatment available. Most people who lack insurance, however, will just be saddled with debt for years to come. And if you have the cash, you'll have to fork it over.

Many people get health and dental coverage through work. If you do, great. You're all set. Check out the policy, though, to make sure you know exactly what it covers, what the maximum benefit is, and whether there are any deductibles or co-payments. The maximum benefit is the maximum amount the insurance company will pay out under the policy. The deductible is the total amount you have to pay for accidents or illnesses per year before the insurance company will pay anything. The co-payment is the percent of the bills you have to pay per year after you've paid the deductible. After the total dollar amount of your medical bills (minus the deductible) reaches a certain amount in a year, the insurance company will pay 100 percent, up to the maximum benefit of the policy.

Let's take an example. Say you have a policy with a $500 deductible and a 20 percent co-payment on the first $5,000 (meaning, after the deductible), and after that the company will pay 100 percent up to a total of $5 million. And say your total bill for an illness comes to $3,200. You must pay the first $500 by yourself and 20 percent on the remaining $2,700, or

$540. Your total payout for the illness would be $1,040. The insurance company's total payout would be $2,160 (80 percent of the $2,700). If you got sick or injured again in the same year, however, there would be no deductible and you would pay only 20 percent on up to $2,300 ($5,000 – $2,700). Remember, deductibles and co-payments put *yearly* limits on your medical expenses; your payments are cumulative. After 12 months, however, your payment totals are reset to zero, and you have to start over.

Examining your health insurance options

If your employer does not provide you with health insurance, or if you're self-employed, you will need to purchase private insurance. While group plans—the kind offered by companies to their employees—cannot reject you for health reasons or refuse to cover pre-existing conditions, private plans can—and will. (Pre-existing conditions are chronic health conditions a policyholder suffered from before she obtained her policy.) Also, group plans generally must meet more stringent state and federal guidelines about the coverage they provide subscribers than private plans, so be careful to check out what you're getting before you sign on to a private plan.

Two major categories of private health insurance exist: traditional and managed care. Traditional health insurance plans, also known as indemnity or fee-for-service plans, let you go to any doctor or hospital you want when you're sick or injured, and will even cover you if you decide on your own to go see a specialist. After you pay your deductible, the insurance company pays usually about 80 percent, not of the total bill, but of what they believe is "reasonable and customary" for the services provided. This amount is referred to as the allowable amount. So, if

Bright Idea
If you're an independent contractor and are paying higher rates for private health insurance that won't cover your pre-existing conditions, consider working part-time for someone else. Some companies, such as courier companies and security services companies, offer part-time workers (usually those who work at least 20 hours a week) full group dental and medical plans.

your doctor charges more than the allowable amount, you have to pay 100 percent of the difference, plus your 20 percent co-payment on the allowable amount. After a certain total dollar amount in medical bills, however, the insurer will pay 100 percent of the allowable amount, up to the maximum benefit, but you will still have to pay the difference between the allowable amount and the amount your doctor actually charged.

With some traditional health insurance plans, you have to pay the doctor, and the insurance company pays you back. With others, the doctor sends the bill directly to the insurance company. You pay a monthly, quarterly, or annual premium (charge) to carry the insurance. The amount of the premium varies with your age, the size of deductible, and the maximum benefit. The lower the deductible and the higher the maximum benefit, the higher your premium.

Managed care health insurance plans differ from traditional health insurance plans in that managed plans offer reduced costs if you restrict yourself to a network of participating doctors and hospitals, and they penalize you if you don't. Some managed care plans won't let you see doctors outside the network at all. Three kinds of managed care plans exist: preferred provider organizations (PPOs), point-of-service plans (POSs), and health maintenance organizations (HMOs).

> **Preferred provider organizations** have made arrangements with a network of doctors to provide you with reduced rates. The doctors in the PPO network must conform their charges to what the PPO says is "reasonable and customary," which means lower bills for you. A PPO will provide you with coverage if

Moneysaver
If you enroll in a managed health insurance plan, always get a network doctor's office to send the bill to the insurance company rather than paying up front. The insurer will determine an allowable amount that could be less than the original charge.

you see a doctor outside the network, but you may have to pay a larger deductible, pay the doctor up front, and wait for the PPO to reimburse you—and, of course, pay the difference between the allowable amount and the actual charge. PPOs tend not to pay for preventive care services—things such as nutrition workshops or programs to help you quit smoking. Exclusive provider organizations (EPOs) are a kind of PPO that requires you to foot the entire bill if you venture outside the network.

Point-of-service plans differ from PPOs in that, while you're free to roam among the doctors in a POS network, you must first go to a primary care physician (PCP) in the network, who will refer you to specialists in the network, as necessary. If your PCP refers you to an out-of-network doctor, your POS will probably pay for it, but if you go to an out-of-network doctor on your own, the POS won't pay as much. POSs tend to be a bit cheaper and cover more preventive medicine than PPOs.

Health maintenance organizations require you to see the doctors in the network or pay the entire cost of treatment yourself. If you want to see a specialist, you must be referred to one in the network by your primary (HMO) physician. You may also need to get visits to the emergency room preapproved. The trade-off for the total inflexibility of HMOs is very low or no co-payments and excellent coverage for preventive care services and health-improvement programs.

Alternative insurance for special situations

Consolidated Omnibus Budget Reconciliation Act insurance (COBRA) is available to you if you have quit or been fired from a job recently, and you were covered under your previous employer's health plan. (You're not eligible if you were fired for gross misconduct.) COBRA gives you the right to continue to get coverage under your former employer's group health plan for up to 18 months after you leave the job. The major problem with COBRA is that it's expensive. With most employer-sponsored group plans, your employer pays a chunk of the premium, and the rest comes out of your pretax pay. Under COBRA, however, you pay the entire premium yourself. Generally, only people who are already sick and using their employer's insurance at the time they leave the company sign on with COBRA. These are people who know they won't be able to find coverage for ongoing (pre-existing) conditions with a private insurer.

If you're looking for work and expect to find a job within the next six months, consider short-term health insurance, which will give you coverage for one to six months. Short-term plans are nonrefundable, so if you find a job before your policy expires, you won't get a refund on the remaining coverage. On the other hand, short-term plans are not renewable, so if you were to develop a serious illness while on such a plan, you couldn't extend it; when the policy expired, your sickness would become a preexisting condition. This is true even if you hadn't signed up for the maximum allowable term originally and decided to continue with the same shortterm policy; you'd have to reapply, and any illnesses or injuries you were treated for under the original

Watch Out!
When you allow an insurance policy to lapse, you put yourself at risk for losing coverage of pre-existing conditions. A recurrence of an illness covered under your previous policy may not be covered if you let the policy lapse and sign up again or buy new insurance with a different company.

policy would now be considered pre-existing conditions. These policies also are very strict about pre-existing conditions going in—most short-term insurers won't cover any condition you've suffered from within the last five years.

What's more, eligibility requirements are stringent. You'll probably be denied if you've ever been turned down for other health insurance, suggesting that you might have serious health problems if you work in a hazardous industry, such as construction, or if you engage in any high-risk activities, such as rugby or rock climbing.

With some short-term plans, you're restricted to doctors in a network; with others, you're not, but you'll lose some of the benefits of staying in the network if you venture outside it. Rates for short-term plans depend on the deductible you choose, generally ranging between $250 and $2,000. After you pay the deductible, the insurance company will typically pay 80 percent on the next $5,000 and 100 percent after that, up to the maximum benefit of the policy. A policy with a $2,000 deductible and a maximum benefit of $2 million would cost around $60 per month.

If you don't expect to find a job within the next six months, or if you're working as an independent contractor, and you're healthy, you should consider high-deductible or catastrophic health insurance. Unlike short-term plans, these policies do not place a limit on length of coverage. Your coverage continues for as long as you pay your premiums. High-deductible health insurance policies are designed to cover only serious (translation: expensive) illnesses or injuries. They're not the right kind of insurance for people who get sick a lot or for people who aren't comfortable with having to pay 100 percent of their minor medical bills. Most catastrophic health insurance plans come with large deductibles—some as high as $15,000—but cover you well after you've paid the deductible. A typical plan might have a $5,000 deductible but pay 100 percent after that, up to a maximum benefit of $5 million.

With some high-deductible plans you're restricted to doctors in a network; with others, you're not, but you'll lose some of the benefits of staying in the network if you see an out-of-network doctor. Because of the large deductibles, you can get very low premiums on catastrophic plans. Some of these policies cost less than $25 per month. The higher the deductible you're willing to assume, of course, the lower the premium, but the higher the risk to your assets. Some high-deductible plans actually have reasonably *low* deductibles, some as low as $500. If you can find such a plan, there would no reason to go with a short-term plan. Unlike short-term plans, high-deductible plans generally offer 100 percent coverage (no co-payments) after you pay the deductible and also afford you the option of continuing your coverage indefinitely if you need to.

If you've left your employee status for good and actually started your own business, you may qualify for a group plan in your own right. By law, insurance companies can't exclude people in a group from a group plan for health reasons and must cover policyholders' pre-existing conditions. To qualify for a group plan, however, you'll have to prove you're a legitimate business, and that's not easy. Most insurers will want to see a business license, payroll records, and quarterly wage and withholding reports (DE-6 forms), among other items. They'll

Bright Idea
You can sometimes get cheap, comprehensive health insurance through an organization you belong to. Inquire at any clubs or associations you're a member of, and contact your college alumni association, which may offer some kind of health insurance for graduates.

also expect anyone in the group looking for coverage to work full-time, or at least 30 hours a week, and will want to see that the business has been in operation for at least three months.

If none of the options for health insurance discussed thus far appeals to you, consider setting up a medical savings account (MSA) if you're self-employed or in a company with fewer than 50 employees. An MSA lets you combine a tax-deductible savings account with a high-deductible insurance policy. You use the money in the savings account to pay the deductibles when you get sick or injured or to pay for any health expenses not covered by your policy.

You could also contact your state insurance department (or go to www.insure.com/states) about guaranteed issue policies, which are state-sponsored health insurance plans. Guaranteed issue policies tend to be cheaper than individual plans but more expensive than group plans. You have to meet certain conditions to qualify. If you're over 65, you may qualify for Medicare, a federal plan that pays for certain hospital and medical expenses. (Some people buy Medigap insurance to supplement Medicare.)

If you're determined to cut costs to the bone, you could look into Medicaid, another federally funded medical benefits program that pays some medical expenses, although you have to meet poverty-level income standards to be eligible. You can always try local clinics, which often charge next to nothing for basic medical care, but you may have to prove your low-income status. If you have to go to the hospital for something serious, and if you're not actually poor, you'll need to have health insurance.

Moneysaver
Cancer insurance, critical illness insurance, and long-term care insurance are supplemental insurances and should not be purchased in lieu of basic health insurance. Supplemental health insurance policies tend to be very expensive and very limited in what they cover, and they may not be necessary.

Buying yourself some insurance

How should you go about buying health insurance for yourself? First, determine your needs and consider the major health insurance options (previously discussed).

This is a list of questions you need to ask yourself when you're looking for health insurance:

- Do I get sick or injured often?
- How much coverage do I need?
- How much of a deductible can I afford to pay?
- Do I mind paying a large deductible?
- Do I mind being limited to a network of doctors?

Next, do some comparison-shopping, using the Internet as one of your tools. Prices for the same product for the same person can vary as much as 50 percent from one insurer to the next. These are the main questions you need to ask your potential insurer when looking at different health insurance policies:

- How much is the premium?
- Are there any discounts?
- How much is the deductible?
- Is the deductible per malady or per year?
- What are the co-payments?
- What is the maximum benefit?

Contact an insurance agent to assist you. Good agents are knowledgeable about a wide range of health insurance products and can be an invaluable resource in finding the policy that will best fit your needs at the best price. But know that there are two types of agents: independent and exclusive.

Independent agents do not work for any one company. They are knowledgeable about a variety of policies from a number of companies, and they are free to recommend the policy at the company they think best fits your needs. Exclusive or captive agents sell only the products of a certain insurance company, and while these agents know the products offered by that company backwards and forwards, they cannot offer you policies offered by other companies that might be a better deal or that might suit you better. Insurance companies pay agents; you don't, and the commissions the insurance companies pay agents should not be reflected in the price of policies. However, because insurance companies generally pay independent agents more than exclusive agents, you might want to comparison-shop a little.

After looking at a policy's coverage and price, you'll want to evaluate the quality of an insurer's customer service. How quickly does the company process claims? Is the procedure for filing a claim simple? Ask your agent, or call the insurer and ask someone in the customer service department what the average turnaround time is for claims. If they won't or can't tell you, it's not a good sign. Ask family and friends if they know anything about the insurer, and check out online discussion groups and chat rooms. You can also call your state insurance department's consumer services division to see if any disciplinary action has been taken against your agent or the insurance company in question, or check out www.insure.com/states/index.html.

You should also check the financial strength or claims-paying ability of the company you're thinking of buying a policy from. You can check an insurer's credit rating with your agent or independently with any of the following ratings services:

Unofficially... Insurance companies have been reluctant to sell policies directly to consumers for less because they're afraid of angering their agents. Rumor has it, though, that cracks in the old system have begun to appear. When you've decided on a policy, see if there's a way you can buy it directly from the insurer—via phone, mail, or the Internet—at a discount.

- **Moody's Investor's Service:** Free ratings. Call 212-553-0300.

- **Standard & Poor's:** Five free ratings per phone call: 212-208-1146. You can also e-mail them for ratings at ratings@mcgraw-hill.com.

- **Duff & Phelps Credit Rating Company:** Free ratings. Call 212-908-0200, or e-mail hotline@dcrco.com.

- **A.M. Best:** Charges $4.95 per rating and $2.95 for a phone call. Call 1-800-424-2378, or e-mail customerservice@ambest.com.

- **Weiss Ratings:** Charges $15 per rating. Call 1-800-289-9222 or 561-627-3300, or e-mail wr@weissinc.com.

Weiss is the only ratings service that doesn't charge insurance companies to list the insurer's ratings; Weiss just lists them. This is important because insurance companies can and do ask to have their names removed from listings if their ratings start to drop. Because Weiss is not charging to list, faltering insurance companies can't get their names pulled from the list. Another interesting way to find out an insurance company's financial strength rating is to call and ask for it. If they are not forthcoming with this information, you had better stay away.

Don't pass on disability insurance

Disability insurance replaces a portion of your regular income if you get sick or injured and can't work for a period of time. These policies cover both physical and mental disabilities. Unless you're able to support yourself without working, you really need to get yourself some disability insurance.

You can get disability insurance in one of five ways: through your employer, Social Security, workers' compensation, the state, or an insurance company. Your employer may offer disability insurance to employees through a group disability plan, but in most cases the payments you receive from these plans approach only about 60 percent of your regular salary. To qualify for Social Security, you have to be totally incapacitated, and the payments are tiny. Workers' compensation will kick in only if you're injured on the job, but most disabling injuries occur outside of work. State programs are insufficient.

Given the inadequacy of the programs already in place, buying individual disability insurance for yourself is important. But how much should you buy? First, you need to determine what benefits you would be entitled to in the event of a disabling illness or injury. Then you need to subtract this amount from what you would need to maintain your current standard of living. The difference is the amount of disability insurance you need to purchase. Disability payments you receive from insurance your employer pays for (workers' compensation) are taxable. Payments received from your private disability insurance policy are not.

Private disability insurance policies come in all shapes and sizes. With any policy, the premiums are based on your age, sex, health, occupation, income, duration of coverage, and type of coverage you select. You have to get a physical exam from a physician or other medical professional approved by the insurance company as part of the application process. The delay before the benefits are to begin, also known as the elimination period, also affects the premium. Disability insurance payments generally don't begin for at least a month to as long as a year after you become disabled. The longer the

Bright Idea
Ask your employer if you can trade in your company disability policy for cash. If your employer agrees, use the proceeds to buy private disability insurance because benefits on private insurance are not taxed.

delay, the lower the premium. The average delay is three months.

Traditional disability insurance plans offer what's known as "own-occupation coverage." These plans compensate you based on the average salary for your occupation if you're unable to perform the job you had when you became disabled. "Modified occupation" or "reasonable occupation" policies are less expensive, but they pay out only if you're unable to work at *any* job that's suitable for your training, education, and experience. If you're able to find work in your field but at a lower salary, these policies pay a "residual disability" benefit, supplementing your income up to 60 percent of what you used to make. For example, if you used to make $50,000 a year, but after getting injured you could earn only $20,000, your modified occupation disability insurance would pay you up to $30,000 (60 percent of $50,000) a year for every year the policy was in effect. Even cheaper than modified occupation policies are "any occupation" policies. These plans pay out only if you can't work at all.

After choosing the type of disability insurance you prefer, you need to decide on the riders you want on your policy. A rider is a special provision that is added to a policy to expand or limit the benefits of the policy. For example, some policies have riders stipulating that benefits (and premiums) will increase automatically to keep pace with inflation. Other policies have riders that give you the option to increase your coverage later, without having to get another medical exam. You may also be able to get a lifetime benefit rider, which guarantees that your disability payments will continue beyond age 65, when most disability policies expire, or a return of premium rider, which

Moneysaver
If you expect to be out of work only a month or two, it's best not to tap your disability insurance because your future premiums may go up significantly. Instead, try to get paid sick leave from your employer or live on your savings for a while.

allows you to get back some of the premiums you put into the policy plus a return on investment (unless you actually make a claim, in which case the return on investment would be zeroed).

The more riders you decide to attach to your basic policy to expand your coverage, the higher the premium will be. At least try to get a policy that is guaranteed renewable so that the insurer cannot cancel the policy for any reason other than your not paying the premiums, and a policy that is not cancelable, so they can't raise the premium.

Check out the following Web sites for more information on disability insurance:

- **American Disability Association:** www.adanet.org.

- **American Association of People with Disabilities:** www.aapd.com.

- **National Organization on Disability:** www.nod.org.

Automobile insurance is a must

While auto insurance requirements vary from state to state, most states require all drivers to carry a certain amount of liability insurance. Liability insurance covers the damage to other people's property and the medical expenses of others (including the people, other than immediate family, in your car) resulting from an accident you caused. Specifically, the property damage coverage includes the cost of replacing all the possessions of others you damaged or destroyed through an accident. The bodily injury coverage includes the medical bills and lost wages of those you hurt. Liability insurance will also pay for legal bills if you're sued and, depending on the policy, funeral expenses for anyone you kill.

Choosing how much insurance to carry

Of course, how much your insurance company will actually shell out if you cause an accident is contingent on the maximum benefits, or limits, of your policy. The higher the limits, the higher the premiums. Liability insurance limits are described with a series of three numbers, such as 30/60/20. If your liability policy has limits of 30/60/20, your insurance company will pay a maximum of $30,000 for the injuries to any one person (other than yourself) per accident, a maximum of $60,000 for the injuries to *all* other people per accident, and a maximum of $20,000 for the damage to other people's property per accident.

Clearly, these amounts may not be enough to cover the actual costs of an accident, and the people you hurt could very well sue you for more—and win. That's why it's so important to carry enough insurance, not just the minimum amount required by your state (for state minimums, go to www.insure. com/auto/minimum.html).

But how much is enough? You should carry at least enough liability insurance to cover your net worth. If you have a net worth of $100,000, you should carry at least $100,000 per person and $300,000 per accident for medical, and at least $50,000 for property (that's 100/300/50). Half a million dollars, bodily injury and property damage combined, is generally the maximum coverage you can get on an automobile insurance policy. If you're worth more than that, you should look into buying an umbrella insurance policy to supplement your auto liability coverage. Umbrella policies are pure liability policies that kick in only after your auto liability has been completely exhausted.

While you may not be legally required to carry any kind of auto insurance other than liability, you should consider picking up some uninsured/underinsured motorist insurance because the number of uninsured and underinsured drivers has been steadily increasing. This insurance covers medical and funeral expenses for you and your family when a car accident is the other driver's fault and when the perpetrator is underinsured or uninsured, or is a hit-and-run driver. These policies also tend to cover you and your family if any of you is involved in an accident as a cyclist or a pedestrian. This type of insurance costs only about $40 a year for $100,000 of coverage and serves as an excellent supplement to your health insurance, which may not cover everything. If you're injured in a car accident, your health insurance company will start to pay for your medical expenses only after all your auto insurance is used up.

If you really want to save money on auto insurance, don't buy anything but liability insurance and maybe uninsured/underinsured motorist coverage. But you really should think about buying medical payment insurance, too—also referred to as personal injury protection insurance (PIP) or no-fault insurance. Medical payment insurance will cover your own medical bills, up to the limits of the policy, no matter whose fault an accident was. If the accident wasn't your fault, your insurance company will pay your medical bills under your medical payment policy and then try to recover the money from the other driver's insurance company. Medical payment insurance is quite cheap and is great to have if you aren't carrying much health insurance, as injuries related to automobile accidents can be quite expensive. If you have good health insurance and a good disability

Watch Out!
Avoid insurance companies that use common law arbitration for disputed claims; it is not binding. If you win a decision under common law arbitration, the insurer can then file a civil suit, and civil suits can take years to come to trial.

policy as well as underinsured/uninsured motorist coverage, however, you may be able to forgo it.

The next thing to consider is whether to get collision insurance or comprehensive insurance. Collision insurance covers the damage to your own car, regardless of whose fault an accident was. If you're driving an expensive new car, this is a must. If you're driving an old model (more than five years old), though, you may not want to bother. Check the value of your car in the Kelley *Blue Book* (www. kbb.com), which is what the insurance companies all use. This is the amount you would get back if you filed a claim.

Comprehensive insurance covers any damage done to your car resulting not from an accident but from events such as fire, flood, or vandalism. Comprehensive plans also cover your car and any personal property inside your car against theft. You may have to pay a higher premium, however, if you want to cover things you've added to the car, such as expensive stereo speakers, after you bought it. Whether you should get comprehensive insurance is a judgment call. Again, check the *Blue Book* value of your vehicle, but if it's more than five years old, you may want to pass. If you're worried about theft, you could just get a car alarm; if you're concerned about vandalism, rent some garage space. By the same token, if you already have a car alarm and park in a garage, your comprehensive premium would be reduced. If you do decide to get collision or comprehensive insurance or both, go with the highest premium you can afford.

You can get several supplemental types of auto insurance, but these are definitely not essential. Rental reimbursement covers the cost of having to

Unofficially...
If you lend your car to someone, that person is covered under your insurance policy. If the driver has an accident while driving your car, your insurance company should pay. However, if a certain person drives your car often, you should include that person on your policy. Otherwise, that person would probably be covered the first time he had an accident in your car, but not the second.

rent a car if your car is stolen or damaged. Towing and labor coverage reimburses you for having to get your car towed and repaired if it breaks down. Auto replacement coverage covers the cost of repairing or replacing your car, even if doing so costs more than the car was worth before it was damaged. Full glass coverage covers the cost of broken windows or windshields.

How to save money on auto insurance

The first thing you can do to save money on your auto insurance is review your current policy and make sure it still fits your needs. You may not need that collision insurance anymore, or maybe you could comfortably raise your deductibles. Your situation may have changed in ways that make you a lower risk for the insurance company, and if you want to be rewarded with lower rates, you have to mention these things to your agent and ask for a discount—your agent isn't likely to call you up and ask you.

If you've gotten married, your rates should come down. If you've moved to a rural location from an urban one, they should come down. If you've had a clean driving record for the past three years, they should come down. And they also should come down if you've stopped smoking (insurance companies consider this a distraction and an indication that you may be prone to other high-risk behaviors), if you drive less than 7,500 miles a year (because you're not on the road all that much), and if you've retired—especially early. If your kids have moved out, requiring them to get their own insurance, make sure you take them off your policy and have your rates reduced. If you are the kid, getting good grades in school and taking a driver's education class should trim your premiums. The most important thing for kids, though, is to get onto their parents' policy. This saves you a bundle.

Here are some other ways to lower your premiums:

- Insure all your cars with the same company and ask for a discount for doing so. Or, insure your cars and your home through the same company and ask for a really big discount.

- Take a defensive driving course.

- Choose your car carefully—mid-priced conservative cars and economy cars cost less to insure than expensive sports cars. Vehicles that come with safety features such as air bags and antilock breaks also are cheaper to insure.

- Stop driving to work. Insurance companies charge lower rates if you carpool, use mass transit, or find some other way to get to and from the office every day.

The most important thing is to make sure your agent knows you're looking to reduce your premium and that you're shopping around. Saying as much may be especially effective if your policy is up for renewal because some companies, eager to keep your business, will give you a renewal discount. If your agent knows you mean business, he's more likely to give you the best rates he can. When you've got your agent's best offer, go ahead and call up some other agents to see what they're charging for the identical coverage. If your agent is an exclusive agent, you want to be sure to call up some independent agents at this stage. Independent agents often have an unsurpassed knowledge of the market and are aware of deals you would never find out about on your own.

Bright Idea
If you're married, make sure both your names are on your automobile insurance policy. If you ever do get divorced, the person whose name is not on the policy will no longer be covered.

After you've spoken to some agents, do some exploring on your own. Hop on the Internet and go to InsWeb at www.insweb.com, a free site that lets you generate a list of insurers that meet your criteria at the best prices. Then surf on over to AM Best, also a free site, at www.ambest.com/resource/insdir.html. AM Best ranks nearly 6,000 insurance companies from superior to poor, based on financial strength, operating performance, and market profile. Next, call a few companies that sell policies directly via 1-800 phone numbers, such as Geico (1-800-841-3000), Amica (1-800-242-6422), American Express (1-800-535-2001), USAA (1-800-531-8100), and 20th Century (1-800-443-3100). Because these guys aren't using agents, they have less overhead and can often make you a better deal than the likes of State Farm or Allstate. If you have any moving violations or accidents within the last three years, however, the big guys might be cheaper.

Homeowner's insurance

If you own a home, what's to insure? Well, the house itself, for one thing—it could burn down. Depending on where you live, your house could even get swept up in a tornado. To put it mildly, losing your house would be a tough blow to your finances. Even if the damage to your house caused by, for example, lightning or a hurricane wasn't total, the cost of repairs could be huge.

So, the first reason to buy homeowner's insurance is to cover your house itself—the structure. What else? Well, things *inside* your home could also be damaged, destroyed, or stolen—furniture, jewelry, electronic equipment, and so on. If you came home from a well-deserved vacation and found that your house had been ransacked, you'd be glad your

Watch Out!
Pay your premiums on time. Some insurance companies will drop you if you're late with your auto insurance payments. It will be that much harder to get another company to cover you if you were dumped by your last insurer for nonpayment of premium.

possessions were covered. Anything else? Well, let's say a visitor to your home fell down the stairs and sustained serious injuries. She could hold you liable, and you'd want to be covered.

There are seven categories of homeowner's insurance:

1. **HO-1:** This is the most basic policy, covering your house and personal property against losses from 11 "perils": fire or lightning, windstorm or hail, explosion, riot or civil commotion, aircraft, vehicles, smoke, vandalism or malicious mischief, theft, damage by glass or safety glazing material that is part of a building, and volcanic eruption.

2. **HO-2:** This policy covers everything the HO-1 policy does, plus six additional perils: falling objects; weight of ice, snow, or sleet; water damage from home utilities; water damage from appliances; and damage from electrical surges.

3. **HO-3:** This policy is the all-in-one package, covering *all* perils except for the ones specified in your policy—usually flood, earthquake, war, and nuclear accident.

4. **HO-4:** This is renter's insurance. Because you don't own the building you rent, this policy covers only your personal property against the 17 perils covered in HO-2 policies.

5. **HO-5:** This policy covers your house and all your personal belongings fully. (Most policies place limits on the amount of coverage you get.) Few insurance companies offer this policy anymore.

6. **HO-6:** This is condominium insurance. It covers your personal property against the 17 perils

of HO-2 and any parts of the building you have a stake in.

7. **HO-8:** (Interestingly, there is no HO-7 policy.) This a basic policy like HO-1, covering your house and personal property from 11 perils. The difference is that this policy covers the cash value of your home and damaged or stolen items, not the cost of replacing them.

Most homeowners have HO-2 or HO-3 policies, but some people carry one of the others. It's possible to get only partial coverage, too—say, for the house itself, but not for the personal property.

How much homeowner's insurance do you need? Conventional wisdom says you should buy only enough to cover 80 percent of the cost of rebuilding your home because the chances of your house being completely destroyed are very slim. But if you want to play it safe, you'll go for 100 percent, especially if you live in an area with a history of floods or violent storms.

Now, there are actually two types of homeowner's insurance: cash value and replacement cost. The former is cheaper but will pay out only what your house (or an item) was worth at the time it met its demise; the latter is more expensive but will pay for the cost of rebuilding your house or replacing an item. Cost replacement policies usually will not pay more than 120 percent of the face value of the policy, however. If you go with a replacement policy, it's important to get periodic estimates of the cost of rebuilding your home. As the estimated cost goes up, you'll want to consider buying more insurance. You can buy an inflation rider, which will make increases in the policy's maximum benefit at the rate of inflation, but you'll still want to get those periodic estimates.

As for personal property, most homeowner's policies cover your possessions up to 75 percent of the face value of the policy, although 50 percent is more common. The best way to ensure that you have enough coverage for your things is to take an inventory of every single item in your house and record what it would cost you to replace it. Then make sure you get a homeowner's policy that will cover the replacement cost of all your possessions, not the cash value. Also, because insurance companies place limits on coverage for certain items, such as antiques, oriental rugs, fine art, silverware, jewelry, and home office equipment, you may need to buy a rider to cover these items individually.

As for liability coverage, most homeowner's policies come with $100,000 to $300,000 in coverage. Just make sure that your policy covers your net worth. If you're worth more than $300,000, you should look into getting an umbrella insurance policy to supplement the liability coverage in your homeowner's policy.

Do you know what a home warranty is?

While homeowner's insurance covers the cost of damage and destruction to your house and belongings, it does not cover the cost of repairing or replacing things that just break down. This is where home warranties come in.

Here are some of the things that might be covered by a home warranty:

- Plumbing
- Heating
- Air-conditioning
- The electrical system
- Washing machines

Watch Out!
Most homeowner's policies do not cover the cost of having to meet new building codes that may have cropped up since your house was originally constructed. If codes in your area have changed, try to get a policy that will cover the cost of meeting the new codes in the event that you need to get your house rebuilt.

- Dryers

- Ovens

- Refrigerators

For a little extra, you can get smaller items covered as well—things such as garbage disposals, doorbells, and built-in electric fans.

Home warranties run about $350–$400 a year plus $35–$50 per incident. To make a claim, you call a number and the warranty company sends out a contractor to fix the problem. You pay $35–$50 for each problem, and the warranty company pays the rest. There are caps on coverage for certain types of repairs, however, such as hot water heating systems.

It's essential that you check out a home warranty company before you do business with them. Ask your real estate agent if he can recommend some good companies. Check to see if a company you're looking at is a member of a professional organization that requires its members to meet certain standards. You can also contact the Better Business Bureau or your state insurance department's consumer services division for information about a company.

Get the life insurance you need

Life insurance provides money to a beneficiary if you die. The only reason you should buy life insurance is to provide your dependents with enough money to get by in your absence. If you and your spouse have already paid off the mortgage, put your kids through college, and receive a steady, adequate investment income, you don't need life insurance. On the other hand, if you're in mid-career, still paying off the mortgage, raising three kids, and trying to pay down some hefty credit card debts, you definitely need life insurance.

Two categories of life insurance exist: term life and permanent life (often referred to as "whole life"). Term life covers your life for a set period of time. Permanent life covers your life for life *and* establishes a forced savings reserve for you, which is invested on a tax-deferred basis. There are three kinds of permanent life insurance: whole life, universal life, and variable life.

- **Whole life policies** require fixed premium payments and tend to invest the savings part of your policy or the cash value in bonds and mortgages.

- **Universal life policies** allow you to vary the death benefit and premium payments of your policy and tend to invest your cash value in money market funds.

- **Variable life policies** require fixed or variable premium payments, depending on the policy, and allow *you* to decide how the cash value portion of your policy is invested. You can choose among a limited number of stock, bond, and money market funds managed by the insurance company.

Most online investors should buy term insurance, for two reasons. First, term insurance will get you through the period in your life when prematurely dying would leave your loved ones in dire straits. Two, term insurance is cheaper—*much* cheaper—than permanent insurance. Permanent policies carry annual premiums 9 to 10 *times* those of term policies. A term policy costing something like $340 a year could offer the same death benefit as a permanent policy costing $3,000.

Why the huge discrepancy? Permanent policies are really forcing you to save for your retirement on top of paying for life insurance.

> **"**
> I detest life-insurance agents; they always argue that I shall some day die, which is not so.
> —Stephen Leacock
> **"**

Bright Idea
Since life insurance premiums are largely determined by your age and the state of your health at the time you purchase the policy, consider getting a policy *before* you have kids if you're planning on starting a family in the not-too-distant future.

The bulk of your premiums are going to your savings reserves under the policy. Why isn't the forced savings thing a good thing? Because you can invest your own money for a better return and at lower cost than your insurance company can. The facts are that insurance companies often won't even tell you exactly how much of your premium is going to insurance and how much toward investment, future investment returns are not guaranteed, and a sizable portion of your return on investment is eaten up by high charges and commissions. Online investors don't have time for this nonsense.

There are only a couple situations in which you should consider getting a permanent policy. One is if you're wealthy and are concerned about your kids having to pay horrendous taxes when they inherit your estate. You can take care of this by setting up an insurance trust in which the death benefit of your permanent insurance policy goes to pay off the taxes on your estate when you die. You might also want to consider a permanent policy if you're in your 40s or 50s and are just starting a family. Why? Because chances are higher that you'll have dependents and major financial obligations until your final days. You won't want your life insurance running out.

If your term policy runs out, though, and you still want coverage, can't you just buy a new term policy? Not necessarily. Not without getting another medical exam. As part of the application process, insurance companies require you to get a complete physical, conducted by a physician or other medical professional who is approved by the insurance company. The company uses the results of the physical to decide whether to cover you and at what rates.

Insurance companies have three rating classes: standard, which is the lowest; select, which is the middle; and preferred, which is the highest. If you're rated preferred, you will get the best rates. But if you're rated standard, having been found to be in poor health or suffering from a life-threatening disease, you will be refused coverage. So, being older and possibly in bad health, you might have trouble buying additional life insurance when your term policy runs out. If you're concerned about this eventuality, buy a convertible term policy that allows you to convert to a permanent policy without having to get another physical exam when your term policy expires.

Two types of term life insurance policies exist: level term and annual renewable. Level term policies charge you the same premium over the life of the policy; annual renewable policies increase premiums as you get older. But the premiums for annual renewable policies start out much lower than those for level term. Still, you'll probably find the best deals among the level term policies. To find those deals, search the Net and work the phones. You can start your Web research with a visit to any of the following sites:

- **Quotesmith.com:** www.quotesmith.com

- **Quickquote:** www.quickquote.com

- **InsWeb:** www.insweb.com

- **Quicken InsureMarket:** http://insuremarket.com

Just the facts

- The two major kinds of health insurance are group plans and private plans; the two kinds of

Watch Out!
Don't dump your permanent life insurance policy if you've already paid thousands of dollars into it over several years. Make sure you know how much you'll get back first. Based on the policy's cash value build-up schedule, it might be better to hold on to your permanent policy, at least for a while.

private plans are traditional and managed care;
and the three kinds of managed care plans are
preferred provider organizations (PPOs),
point-of-service plans (POS), and health maintenance organizations (HMOs).

- High-deductible policies are an excellent alternative for healthy people, and short-term and
COBRA policies can be useful for people
between jobs.

- Disability insurance replaces a portion of your
regular income if you get sick or injured and
can't work.

- The one kind of auto insurance you must have
is liability insurance, which covers bodily injury
to others and damage to other people's property resulting from a car accident that you
caused.

- Homeowner's insurance covers damage to your
house, the possessions in your house, theft of
these possessions, and injuries sustained by
other people on your property.

- Buy life insurance only if you have dependents;
generally, buy only term insurance, which covers your life for a limited period of time.

Glossary

10-K See *Form 10-K.*

12B-1 fee A fee charged by some mutual funds to cover the costs of promoting and marketing the fund and compensating brokers.

401(k) plan An employer-sponsored retirement plan that allows employees to put a certain amount of pretax pay into a retirement savings account. Many employers will match a portion of the employee's contributions, which are invested on a tax-deferred basis.

after-tax return The rate of return on an investment after adjusting for taxes.

alpha Measure of the risk-adjusted performance of a stock or mutual fund. A positive alpha indicates superior performance to the market; a negative alpha indicates inferior performance.

annual report A report on the financial condition of a company, produced annually. The 10-K is an expanded version of the annual report.

annuity An insurance product that makes guaranteed regular payments to the owner for a fixed period, usually for life, in exchange for a prior single payment or series of payments to the insurance company.

appreciation A rise in value or price of an asset.

ask The lowest price a seller is willing to accept for a security; also referred to as the ask price, the asked price, or the offer price.

ask price See *ask*.

asset Anything that an individual or a corporation owns that has value.

asset allocation The division of investment funds among different asset types, such as stocks, bonds, and cash equivalents, to minimize risk in achieving financial goals.

average An arithmetic mean of the prices of a group of stocks, meant to represent the overall movement of a market or some part of it. Unlike an index, an average is not weighted.

average annual gain An inflated measure of return, which does not take into account the effect of compounding.

average maturity The average maturity of the debt securities held by a mutual fund.

back-end load A sales charge most load mutual funds charge an investor when he sells shares. This charge may decrease or be eliminated the longer shares are held.

balance sheet A financial statement that reports a company's assets, liabilities, and net worth at a given time.

balanced fund A mutual fund that invests in both stocks and bonds, providing more upside potential than most bond funds and carrying less risk than most stock funds.

basis The total amount an investor pays for a security, including the price of the security plus any commissions.

basis point   One-hundredth of 1 percent (0.01%); used to refer to yields on bonds.

bear   An investor who believes that a significant decline in the stock market is imminent.

bear market   A market in which prices fall, usually by 20 percent or more, over a period of months or years.

beta   A measure of how volatile a stock or mutual fund is relative to the market. A stock with a beta of 1.2 is 20 percent more volatile than the market; a stock with a beta of .8 is 20 percent less volatile.

bid   The highest price a buyer is willing to pay for a security; also referred to as the bid price.

bid-ask spread   The difference between the bid and the ask prices.

bid price   See *bid.*

block   A large quantity of stock purchased at a given time, usually thought to be 10,000 shares or more.

blue chip stock   Stock in a stable, financially sound company that has a track record of paying dividends in both good markets and bad.

bond   A security that obligates the borrower of a certain amount of money to repay the loan at or before a certain date and to pay interest payments periodically along the way (although some bonds require the borrower to pay the loan and all interest on the loan at maturity).

bond fund   A mutual fund that invests primarily in bonds.

broker   A licensed agent who charges a commission to execute the public's orders to buy and sell securities; also referred to as a stockbroker or a broker-dealer.

bull   An investor who believes that a significant rise in the stock market is imminent.

bull market   A market in which prices rise over a period of months or years.

buy-and-hold   An investment strategy in which an investor buys stocks and holds on to them, through good markets and bad, until he needs to cash them in or until his financial goals are met.

call option   An option contract that gives the holder of the option the right to purchase a specified number of shares of the underlying stock at a certain price by a certain date.

capital   Money or property that can be used to produce wealth.

capital appreciation   A rise in the market price of an asset.

capital gain   When a security is sold for a profit, the difference between the sale proceeds and the investor's cost basis in the security.

capital loss   When a security is sold at a loss, the difference between the sale proceeds and the investor's cost basis in the security.

cash value   The current market value of an asset.

churning   Excessive trading of a client's account to generate commissions.

close   The end of a trading session in a given market.

closed-end mutual fund   See *investment trust.*

commission   The fee charged by a brokers to buy and sell securities on behalf of investors.

commodity   Any staple product, as in agriculture or mining, traded on an exchange or in the cash market (where they're bought and sold for cash and delivered immediately). Examples include metals, grains, oil, and meats.

compounded annual return   An accurate measure of return, which takes into account the effect of compounding.

compounding The phenomenon whereby the earnings on an asset generate their own earnings when invested.

confirmation A statement that documents the specifics of a trade, such as price, quantity, and trade date, sent to an investor following a trade.

contrarian An investor who goes against the crowd, tending to buy when most investors are selling and to sell when most are buying.

convertible A security, such as preferred stock, that can be exchanged for another security, such as common stock, if the owner so chooses.

correction A temporary decline in a market or in a stock's price that occurs during a general rise.

cost basis See *basis*.

coupon The interest rate paid on a fixed-income security, such as a bond; also referred to as the coupon rate.

cyclical (stock) A stock whose price tends to rise and fall with the economy.

day trading Entering and exiting all positions in a single day.

deduction An expense subtracted from adjusted gross income when determining taxable income.

depreciation The decrease in the value of an item over time.

derivative A security, such as an option, whose value is based on the value of an underlying security.

discount The amount by which a bond is selling below its face value.

distribution A payment to shareholders of a dividend or capital gain.

divergence When two or more indices or indicators show conflicting trends.

diversification Spreading investment capital across a variety of investments to reduce the impact of any one security on the overall performance of your portfolio.

dividend   A payment by a corporation to its shareholders, usually a share of the company's earnings, in cash or additional stock.

dollar cost averaging   A investment system whereby an investor buys a fixed dollar amount of a security at regular intervals so as to purchase fewer shares when the price is high and more shares when the price is low.

Dow   Short for the Dow Jones Industrial Average, an index measuring the collective performance of 30 of the largest companies in the United States.

earnings   Profits.

EDGAR   Acronym for Electronic Data Gathering, Analysis, and Retrieval. The Security and Exchange Commission's electronic database containing the financial reports and information that all publicly traded companies are required to file with the SEC.

equity   (1) A stock. (2) The value of a company's assets minus its liabilities—shareholder's equity.

exchange   A marketplace where stocks or futures and options are traded.

ex-date   See *ex-dividend date*.

ex-dividend date   The date from which the last announced dividend for a given stock will not be received by a new purchaser. This is two days before the record date.

execution   Completing an order to buy or sell a security. Compare with *settlement*.

exercise   To use an option to buy or sell the underlying security.

expense ratio   The percentage of a mutual fund's assets that are spent to manage the fund; also referred to as the operating expense ratio (OER).

expiration date The last day on which an option may be exercised.

face value The amount of money the issuer of a bond must repay the bondholder on or before the maturity date; also referred to as par value.

fixed-income investment Investments that generate a fixed amount of interest, such as bonds, certificates of deposit, and preferred stock.

Form 10-K A report filed annually by a company with the Securities and Exchange Commission, giving a detailed breakdown of a company's financial condition.

Form 10-Q A report filed quarterly by a company with the Securities and Exchange Commission, containing important financial information for the past quarter.

front-end load A sales charge most load mutual funds charge an investor when he buys shares.

fund A professionally managed portfolio of securities.

fundamental analysis A method of stock analysis that revolves around analyzing a company's fundamentals, such as revenues, earnings, expenses, assets, liabilities, debt, management, competitiveness, and so on, in an attempt to determine whether the stock is underpriced.

fund family An investment company that sells shares in and manages various mutual funds with different objectives.

fund objective A mutual fund's stated objective, always given in the prospectus.

futures Contracts that obligate a buyer to buy and a seller to sell a certain number of shares of a specific stock or other financial instrument, or a certain amount of some product, such as sugar, wheat, or soybeans, at a certain price on a future date; also referred to as *commodities.*

going long   Buying and holding stock.

going short   Selling stock short.

growth stock   A stock of a company that is expected to grow at a relatively rapid rate.

hedge   To offset the risk of one investment by purchasing another, usually a derivative such as an option, with the opposite orientation.

high-yield bond   A bond with a speculative credit rating, generally BB or lower, and a correspondingly high yield; also referred to as a junk bond.

index   A statistical measure, usually weighted for market capitalization, of the collective price movements of a group of securities that are meant to represent the overall movement of a market or some part of it.

index fund   A mutual fund that attempts to match the performance of a market index by purchasing a large number of the securities in that index.

indicator   (1) A measure that provides data on the state of the economy; also referred to as an economic indicator. (2) A technical analysis tool designed to give some indication of the future price movements of markets or individual securities.

industry   A distinct category of business activity.

inflation   An increase in the price level of goods and services.

initial public offering (IPO)   A company's first sale of stock to the public.

insider trading   The illegal practice of buying and selling publicly traded stocks by people with privileged information about the company.

instrument   A legal document specifying some right or obligation.

interest The amount a borrower pays a lender for the use of the borrower's money, usually expressed as an annual percentage of the amount borrowed.

investment company A company engaged primarily in the business of investing in other companies. There are two kinds: the closed-end, or investment trust; and the open-end, or mutual fund.

investment trust (1) A fund with a fixed number of shares that are bought and sold on the open market for a price, influenced by supply and demand for the shares, that may be above or below the fund's NAV. (2) A closed-end investment company.

investment vehicle A type of investment.

IRA Individual retirement account; an investment vehicle with various tax advantages that allows an investor to contribute up to $2,000 a year.

Keogh plan A qualified tax-deferred retirement plan that can be set up by a self-employed individual who is not incorporated or by someone who earns extra income outside her regular job.

leverage The use of borrowed capital to invest or finance a business.

liability A debt.

limited partnership A partnership (a business owned by more than one person, each of whom is referred to as a partner) with two kinds of partners: limited partners, who invest in the business but who don't get involved in managing it and who cannot lose more than they invest; and general partners, who are responsible for managing the business and who have unlimited personal liability for its debts.

limit order An order to buy or sell a stock only at a specified price or better.

liquidity The ease with which an asset can be converted to cash without a significant loss in value. A large number of buyers and sellers and high trading volume provide high liquidity.

load   A sales charge incurred with the purchase of certain securities or with the sale.

load fund   A mutual fund that charges investors a fee to buy or sell shares.

long owning securities   An owner of a stock is said to be "long the stock."

long-term investor   An investor who holds stocks he owns for a long time, usually many years.

margin   The use of money borrowed from a broker to purchase securities (buying "on margin").

margin account   A type of account with a broker in which the broker agrees to lend a customer a certain amount of money for the purchase of securities. The loan is collateralized by the security; if the value of the security drops sufficiently, the customer will be asked to either deposit more cash or securities in the account or sell some of the stock.

margin call   A demand for a customer to deposit money or securities with a broker when the equity in the customer's account as a fraction of the equity plus the debt declines below a minimum standard set by the SEC, the exchange on which the security is traded, or the brokerage.

market capitalization   The total dollar value of a company's stock, calculated by multiplying the share price by the number of shares outstanding.

market cycle   The period defined by the two latest highs or lows on the S&P 500. Traditionally, a market cycle is said to be complete when the S&P is 15 percent below the most-recent high or 15 percent above the most-recent low.

market maker   A broker-dealer on the NASDAQ system who makes a market in a particular security by remaining consistently willing to buy and sell shares of the security, making money on the bid-ask spread.

market order   An order to buy or sell a security at the best price currently obtainable on the market.

market timing   Adjusting market exposure with changes in perceived market risk, usually by examining recent price and volume data, monetary policy, and market valuations in a historical context.

maturity   (1) The length of time until a debt instrument must be paid off by the issuer. (2) The date on which a debt instrument comes due and must be paid off.

minimum purchases   The minimum amount required to open a new account with a mutual fund (minimum initial purchase), or the minimum amount required to make additional deposits in a mutual fund account (minimum additional purchase).

money market   The market for high-quality, short-term debt instruments, such as CDs and Treasury bills.

money market fund   A mutual fund that invests only in short-term debt instruments.

mutual fund   (1) A professionally managed investment vehicle that pools investor's money and invests, according to its objective, in stocks, bonds, money market instruments, or other securities, or some combination thereof. A mutual fund issues and redeems shares on demand at the NAV, which is not influenced by supply and demand for shares, but only by the changing value of the securities held by the fund; also referred to as an open-end fund. (2) An open-end investment company.

net asset value (NAV)   The dollar value of one share of a fund, calculated by adding up the value of all the fund's holdings and dividing by the total number of shares. For a mutual fund, the NAV usually represents the fund's market price. For a closed-end fund, the market price may vary significantly from the NAV.

net worth   The amount by which an individual or company's assets exceed liabilities. In the case of a company, this is also referred to as shareholders' or stockholders' equity.

no-load fund   A mutual fund that does not charge investors a fee for buying or selling shares of the fund. Some no-load funds charge 12b-1 fees, however, to cover the costs of selling and marketing shares. True no-load funds have neither sales charges nor 12b-1 charges.

NM   Abbreviation for Not Meaningful.

NMF   Abbreviation for No Meaningful Figure.

odd lot   Fewer than 100 shares of a stock traded.

offer price   See *ask.*

opening   The beginning of a trading session.

option   A contract giving an investor the right to buy or sell something—often a specified number of shares of stock—at a set price on or before a given date.

par   See *face value.*

payment date   Date on which a stock dividend or bond interest payment is scheduled to be made.

point   In the case of shares of stock, a point means $1; in the case of bonds, a point means $10; in the case of market averages, point is used to indicate one whole number change on the index.

portfolio   The collective investments held by an individual or institution.

position   The amount of a security an individual or dealer controls.

preferred stock A class of stock that pays a specified dividend and gives the holder a claim, prior to that of common stockholders, on assets in the case of bankruptcy. Appealing mainly to corporations, which get a tax break on the dividend income, preferred stock generally pays less income than bonds of the same company and lacks the price appreciation potential of the company's common stock. Preferred stockholders do have voting rights.

premium The amount by which a bond or preferred stock sells above its face value, or the amount by which a closed-end fund sells above its NAV.

price The cost of one unit of an investment, such as the cost of one share of a stock or mutual fund, one bond, or one options contract.

price, 52-week high The highest price a stock traded at in the last 12 months.

price, 52-week low The lowest price a stock traded at in the last 12 months.

price-earnings ratio A ratio traditionally used to determine how expensive a stock is by comparing its share price with the earnings of the company. The ratio is determined by dividing price per share by earnings per share for the past 12 months.

primary market The market in which new securities issues are traded before they go to the exchanges.

prime rate The interest rate that commercial banks charge their most creditworthy customers, generally large corporations, to borrow money.

principal (1) The amount owed on a debt instrument. (2) The amount invested. (3) The person for whom a broker executes an order. (4) A dealer who buys or sells for his own account.

prospectus The document that lays out the business plan for a new business, or the detailed information about an existing one that an investor needs to make an informed decision about whether to buy stock. In the case of mutual funds, a prospectus describes the fund's objectives, risks, and other essential information.

proxy A document providing shareholders with the information they need to vote on matters to be covered at an upcoming stockholders' meeting.

put option An option contract that gives the holder the right to sell a specified number of shares of the underlying stock at a certain price on or before the expiration date of the contract.

quotation (or quote) The bid and ask prices of a security at a given time.

rally A significant rise in the prices of securities or in the price of an individual security.

range See *trading range*.

rate of return See *total return*.

real-time quotes Stock prices that reflect the actual price of the stock at the moment the quote is given; not delayed.

record date The date by which a shareholder must officially own a stock to be entitled to the next dividend payout. A buyer of a stock will not officially own the stock until the settlement date.

redemption charge See *back-end load*.

REIT Real estate investment trust, a type of company that invests the pooled funds of investors in real estate.

replacement cost The cost of actually replacing an asset.

return See *total return*.

reverse stock split A decrease in the number of outstanding shares and a proportionate increase in the price per share, maintaining the value of all positions; done in the hopes of attracting more investors.

risk The probability that the value of an investment will fall.

risk-reward tradeoff The tendency for returns and the potential for losses to increase with increasing risk.

rollover The reinvesting of funds in such a way as to avoid having to pay taxes.

Roth IRA A type of IRA in which contributions are not tax-deductible, but withdrawals are tax-free.

round lot Generally, 100 shares of stock or multiples of 100.

S&P 500 A weighted index consisting of 500 of the largest publicly traded stocks, most of which are blue chips.

SEC The Securities and Exchange Commission, the primary federal regulatory agency of the securities industry.

secondary market The market where investors purchase securities from other investors rather than from the issuers of the securities. Most trading takes place on the secondary market and includes all the exchanges and the bond markets.

security A certificate that proves ownership of an investment, often stocks or bonds.

selling short Borrowing shares of stock from a broker and selling them with the idea of repurchasing them later (and returning them to the broker) at a lower price than you sold them.

settlement When payment is made for a trade.

settlement date The date on which payment is made to settle a trade. For stocks traded on U.S. exchanges, settlement occurs three business days after the trade takes place. For mutual funds, it's one day.

share One unit of ownership in a corporation, mutual fund, or limited partnership.

shares outstanding   Shares of a corporation's stock that are publicly traded.

share repurchase   The buying back by a company of its own shares on the open market to reduce the supply of the shares and to elevate the price.

short-term trader   Short-term traders buy and sell stocks frequently, tending not to hold on to a stock for long, especially if it starts going down in price.

short sale   See *selling short*.

specialist   A member of the New York Stock Exchange who makes a market for certain securities, buying and selling shares and making money on the bid-ask spread. A specialist is expected to buy and sell for his own account as necessary to counteract temporary imbalances in supply and demand, and thus prevent wide swings in the prices of the stocks he is handling.

speculation   Making high-risk investments in the hopes of realizing very high returns.

split   The dividing of the outstanding shares of a corporation to create more shares, and the proportional lowering of the price per share to make the stock look affordable to more investors.

stock   Ownership interest in a company.

stockholder's equity   See *net worth*.

stock exchange   See *exchange*.

stock screening   Narrowing the choices of stocks to invest in by screening out those that do not meet certain criteria.

stock split   See *split*.

stop order   An order to buy or sell a stock at the best price available when a given stop price is hit; also referred to as a stop market order.

stop limit order   An order to buy or sell at a specified price or better when a given stop price is hit.

street name The name in which a stock is recorded, usually the broker's rather than the owner's, when the stock is held by the broker to facilitate subsequent transactions.

switching Moving money from one mutual fund to another in the same fund family, usually at no commission if done directly through the fund family.

tax deferral Legally postponing paying taxes on income earned in the current year until sometime in the future.

technical research Analysis of the market and stocks based on price movements and volume rather than on fundamental factors.

term The length of time until the issuer of a debt instrument must pay back the lender the full amount of the loan; also referred to as term-to-maturity.

total return The return on an investment, including all dividends and capital appreciation or depreciation, over a period of time, usually a year.

trade A transaction in which one party buys a security from another party.

trade date The date on which a trade occurs. Stock trades generally are settled (paid for) three business days after the trade date; for mutual fund trades, this is one day.

trading range The high and low prices for a security during a period of time; also referred to as *range*.

transaction costs Costs incurred when buying or selling securities.

Treasuries Essentially risk-free U.S. government debt obligations that are exempt from state and local taxes. There are three kinds of Treasuries: Treasury bills, Treasury notes, and Treasury bonds.

trend   The general direction of the market or the price of a security.

trust   A legal instrument in which a person or institution holds the right to manage property or assets for the benefit of someone else.

turnover rate   In mutual funds, the percentage of a fund's total assets that were sold in the previous year.

underlying security   The security an option owner has the right to buy or sell if she exercises the option.

underwriter   An investment dealer who buys all or part of a new securities issue from a company and sells the securities to the public at a slightly higher price.

unit investment trust   An investment vehicle with an investment portfolio whose composition is fixed.

value stock   A stock that appears, after a thorough analysis of its fundamentals, to be undervalued.

valuation   Determination of the current worth of an asset or company.

vehicle   See *investment vehicle*.

volatility   The extent to which the market price of a security fluctuates.

volume   The number of shares or options contracts traded in a security or an entire market during a given period.

wash sale   IRS rule that basically prohibits an investor from claiming a loss on any security he repurchases within 30 days of selling it.

weighted   Adjusted to give more weight to stocks of companies with larger market capitalization.

yield   The percentage paid on a stock in the form of dividends, or the rate of interest paid on a bond or note.

yield curve A line chart showing the relationship between yields and maturities for a set of similar bonds, usually Treasuries, at a given point in time.

yield to maturity (YTM) The total return an investor will receive on a bond, note, or other fixed-income security if he buys and holds the security to maturity. The calculation for YTM is based on the coupon, the length of time to maturity, and the price of the security. The calculation assumes that the coupon interest paid over the life of the bond will be reinvested at the same rate.

zero coupon bond A security that does not pay out interest but that is sold at a deep discount and will mature at its face value.

Resource Guide

Top financial web sites

ABC News Business Section	http://abcnews.go.com/sections/business
AMDG+ Daily Stocks Search Engine	www.dailystocks.com
Bloomberg.com	www.bloomberg.com/welcome.html
CBS Market Watch	cbs.marketwatch.com/news/newsroom.htx
CNBC Business & *The Wall Street Journal*	www.msnbc.com/news/ COM_Front.asp?a
CNNfn	www.cnnfn.com
CyberInvest.com	www.cyberinvest.com
Fool.com Finance and Folly	www.fool.com
Hoover's Online	www.hoovers.com
Individual Investor	www.individualinvestor.com
INVESTools	http://investools.com
InvestorGuide	www.investorguide.com
Investor Home	www.investorhome.com
InvestorLinks	www.investorlinks.com
Investor Services	www.investorlinks.com/service.html
Market Guide Inc.	www.marketguide.com/MGI

MoneyCentral	moneycentral.msn.com/investor/home.asp
The New York Times	www.nytimes.com/auth/login?Tag=/ &URI=/yr/mo/day/business
RapidResearch	www.financialweb.com/rapidresearch
Silicon Investor	www.siliconinvestor.com/index.gsp
SmartMoney.com	www.smartmoney.com
Standard & Poor's	www.stockinfo.standardpoor.com/today.htm
StockHouse.com	www.stockhouse.com
The Dismal Scientist	www.dismal.com/economy/releases/ new_home.asp
TheStreet.com	www.thestreet.com
The Wall Street Journal Highlights	www.msnbc.com/news/ WSJHIGHLIGHTS_Front.asp
Wall Street City	www.wallstreetcity.com
WSJ.COM	www.wsj.com
Yahoo! Business News	http://dailynews.yahoo.com/headlines/bs
Yahoo! Finance	http://quote.yahoo.com
Zack's Investment Research	www.zacks.com

Arbitrators

American Arbitration Association (AAA)

www.adr.org
Corporate Headquarters
335 Madison Av., 10th floor
New York, NY 10017-4605
Phone: 212-716-5800
Customer service: 800-778-7879
Fax: 716-5905

The Chartered Institute of Arbitrators

www.arbitrators.org
24 Angel Gate, City Road
London EC1V 2RS
Phone: 44-0171-837-4483
Fax: 44-0171-837-4185
e-mail: info@arbitrators.org

International ADR
www.internationaladr.com/am.htm
P.O. Box 870
Washington, D.C. 20044
e-mail: info@internationalADR.com

Calculators

Bloomberg.com: Retirement Calculator
www.bloomberg.com/pwealth/new_retire.
cgi?template=money_calcr99.ht

Hugh's Mortgage and Financial Calculators
www.interest.com/hugh/calc

Kiplinger.com
Calculators:
www.kiplinger.com/calc/calchome.html

Money Advisor/Financial Calculators
www.moneyadvisor.com/calc

Registered Education Savings Plan Calculator
www.retireweb.com/respcalculator.html

Retire on a Bundle
worldi.com/calcltee.htm

Certificates of deposit

Bank-CD Rate Scanner
http://bankcd.com

Bank Rate Monitor
www.bankrate.com/brm/default.asp

FISN Nationwide Certificate of Deposit Service
www.fisn.com

rate.net
www.rate.net/index.htm

Consumer organizations

Advocacy Institute (AI)
1707 L St., NW Suite 400
Washington, D.C. 20036
Phone: 202-659-8475
Fax: 202-659-8484
e-mail: ai1@adzinst.org

Alliance Against Fraud in Telemarketing (AAFT)
c/o National Consumers League
701 K St. NW, Suite 1200
Washington, D.C. 20006
Phone: 202-835-3323
Fax: 202-835-0747

Alliance for Consumer Rights (ACR)
132 Nassau St., 2nd Floor
New York, NY 10038
Phone: 212-349-9204; 212-608-2310

American Council on Consumer Interests (ACCI)
University of Missouri
240 Stanley Hall
Columbia, MO 65211
Phone: 314-882-3817
Fax: 314-884-6571
e-mail: acci@mizzou1.missouri.edu

Americans for Legal Reform (HALT)
1319 F St. NW, Suite 300
Washington, D.C. 20004
Phone: 202-347-9600
Fax: 202-347-9606

Bankcard Holders of America (BHA)
524 Branch Dr.
Salem, VA 24153
Phone: 701-389-5445

Center for Consumer Affairs (CCA)
161 W. Wisconsin Ave., Suite 6000
Milwaukee, WI 53203
Phone: 414-227-3250
Fax: 414-227-3267

Center for the Study of Responsive Law (CSRL)
www.essential.org
P.O. Box 19367
Washington, D.C. 20036
Phone: 202-387-8030
Fax: 202-234-5176

Conference of Consumer Organizations (COCO)
www.essential.org
Box 158
Newton Centre, MA 02159
Phone: 617-552-8184
Fax: 617-552-2380

Consumer Action (CA)
116 New Montgomery St., Suite 233
San Francisco, CA 94105
Phone: 415-777-9648

Consumer Hot Line
Phone: 415-777-9635
Fax: 415-777-5267

Consumer Federation of America (CFA)
1424 16th St. NW, Suite 604
Washington, D.C. 20036
Phone: 202-387-6121
Fax: 202-265-7989

Consumers Education and Protective Association International (CEPA)
6048 Ogontz Ave.
Philadelphia, PA 19141-1347
Phone: 215-424-1441
Fax: 215-424-8045

Consumers Union of United States (CU)
101 Truman Ave.
Yonkers, NY 10703
Phone: 914-378-2000
Fax: 914-378-2900

National Association of Consumer Agency Administrators (NACAA)
1010 Vermont Ave. NW, Suite 514
Washington, D.C. 20005
Phone: 202-347-7395
Fax: 202-347-2563
e-mail: nacaa@essential.org

National Consumer Law Center (NCLC)
18 Tremont St., Suite 400
Boston, MA 02108-2336
Phone: 617-523-8010
Fax: 617-523-7398
e-mail: hn0639@handsnet.org

National Consumers League (NCL)
1701 K St. NW, Suite 1200
Washington, D.C. 20006
Phone: 202-835-3323
Fax: 202-835-0747

National Insurance Consumer Organization (NICO)
414 A St. SE
Washington, D.C. 20003
Phone: 202-547-6426
Fax: 202-547-6427

Public Citizen (PC)
1600 20th St. NW
Washington, D.C. 20009
Phone: 202-588-1000

Public Citizen Litigation Group (PCLG)
1600 20th St. NW
Washington, D.C. 20009
Phone: 202-588-1000

Public Interest Research Group (PIRG)
218 D St. SE
Washington, D.C. 20003
Phone: 202-546-9707
Fax: 202-546-2461
e-mail: uspirg@aol.com

Public Voice for Food and Health Policy (PVFHP)
1101 14th St. NW, Suite 710
Washington, D.C. 20005
Phone: 202-371-1840
Fax: 202-371-1910
e-mail: pvoice@ix.netcom.com

Southwest Research and Information Center (SRIC)
P.O. Box 4524
Albuquerque, NM 87106
Phone: 505-262-1862
Fax: 505-262-1864

Credit bureaus
Equifax
www.equifax.com
P.O. Box 740241
Atlanta, GA 30374-0241
Phone: 800-685-1111; 770-612-3200
For Georgia, Vermont, or Massachusetts:
800-548-4548
For Maryland: 800-233-7654

Experian (Formerly TRW)
www.experian.com
P.O. Box 949
Allen, TX 75013-0949
Phone: 888-397-3742

Trans Union Corporation
Consumer Disclosure Center
www.tuc.com
P.O. Box 390
Springfield, PA 19064-0390
Phone: 800-916-8800; 800-682-7654; 714-680-7292

Debt and bankruptcy

American Consumer Credit Counseling
www.consumercredit.com
24 Crescent St.
Waltham, MA 02453
Phone: 800-769-3571
Fax: 781-893-7649
e-mail: help@consumercredit.com

Debt Counselors of America (DCA)
www.dca.org
Phone: 800-680-3328
e-mail: counselor@dca.org

Consumer Credit Counseling Service (CCCS)
www.cccsintl.org
4600 Gulf Freeway, Suite 500
Houston, TX 77023-3551
Phone: 800-873-2227; 713-923-2227

Credit Counseling Centers of America
www.cccamerica.org
Phone: 800-493-2222

Dividend reinvestment plans

Dividend Reinvestment Plans
www.drp.com

DRIP Central
www.dripcentral.com

InvestorMap.com (stock dividend reinvestment programs)
http://investormap.com/stock-drips.htm

The Moneypaper, Inc.
1010 Mamaroneck Ave.
Mamaroneck, NY 10543
Phone: 800-388-9993; 914-381-5400
Fax: 914-381-7206

Netstock Direct
www.netstockdirect.com

Exchanges

American Stock Exchange
www.nasdaq-amex.com
86 Trinity Place
New York, NY 10006
Phone: 212-306-1000

Nasdaq-Amex
www.nasdaq-amex.com

The Nasdaq Stock Market
33 Whitehall St.
New York, NY 10004
Phone: 212-858-4000

New York Stock Exchange
www.nyse.com
20 Broad St., 5th Floor
New York, NY 10005
Phone: 212-656-2772

Financial planners

American Institute of Certified Public Accountants (AICPA)

www.aicpa.org
1211 Avenue of the Americas
New York, NY 10036
Phone: 888-777-7077

Institute of Certified Financial Planners (ICFP)

www.icfp.org
3801 E. Florida Ave., Suite 708
Denver, CO 80210-2544
Phone: 800-322-4237; 303-759-4900
Fax: 303-759-0749

International Association for Financial Planners (IAFP)

http://mediasource.com/iafp_home.htm
Suite B-300
5775 Glenridge Dr., NE
Atlanta, GA 30328-5364
Phone: 404-845-0011
Fax: 404-845-3660

Government agencies and financial regulators

Federal Reserve Bank of New York

www.ny.frb.org
33 Liberty St.
New York, NY 10045-0001
Phone: 212-720-6134

Federal Reserve Board

www.bog.frb.fed.us

Federal Trade Commission

CRC-240
Washington, D.C. 20580
Phone: 877-382-4357

FTC/Bureau of Consumer Protection
www.ftc.gov/ftc/consumer.htm

Investor Protection Trust
www.investorprotection.org
e-mail: ipt@investorprotection.org

North American Securities Administrators Association (NASAA) www.nasaa.org
10 G St., NE, Suite 710
Washington, D.C. 20002
Phone: 202-737-0900

Securities and Exchange Commission (SEC)
www.sec.gov
SEC Headquarters
450 Fifth St., NW
Washington, D.C. 20549
Phone: 202-942-7040 (Office of Investor Education
and Assistance)
e-mail: help@sec.gov

Insurance

4Insurance
www.4insurance.com

Insurance Quote.net
insurancequote.net

Insurance Shopping Network
www.800insureme.com

Investor Services
www.investorlinks.com/service-insurance.html

Quicken InsureMarket
www.insuremarket.com

Quotesmith.com, Inc.
www.quotesmith.com

SafeTnet
www.safetnet.com

The Insurance Link
www.inslink.com

Investment clubs

National Association of Investors Corporation
www.better-investing.org
P.O. Box 220
Royal Oak, MI 48068
Attention: (Dept. Name)
Phone: 877-275-6242 (toll-free); 248-583-6242

The World Federation of Investors
www.wfic.org
711 W. Thirteen Mile Road
Madison Heights, MI 48071
Phone: 810-583-6242
Fax: 810-583-4880

Investor education

The Alliance for Investor Education (AIE)
www.investoreducation.org

American Association of Individual Investors
www.aaii.org/invbas
626 N. Michigan Ave.
Chicago, IL 60611
Phone: 800-428-2244

American Association for Retired Persons (AARP)
www.aarp.org/indexes/money.html
601 E St., NW
Washington, D.C. 20049
Phone: 800-424-3410; 202-434-2277

National Association of Investors Corporation (NAIC)
www.better-investing.org
P.O. Box 220
Royal Oak, MI 48068
Attention: (Dept. Name)
Phone: 877-275-6242; 248-583-6242

SEC Office of Investor Education and Assistance
www.sec.gov/oiea1.htm

Legal resources

American Bar Association
www.abanet.org
750 N. Lake Shore Dr.
Chicago, IL 60611
Phone: 312-988-5000

LawForum
www.lawforum.net/service.htm

Nolo.com
www.nolo.com
950 Parker St.
Berkeley, CA 94710
Phone: 800-728-3555
e-mail: cs@nolo.com.

Rominger Legal
www.romingerlegal.com

Online banking

AAAdir World Banks
www.aaadir.com
e-mail: webmaster@aaadir.com

FiTech, Inc.
P.O. Box 953218
Lake Mary, FL 32795-3218
Phone: 407-302-0435
Fax: 407-302-0436
e-mail: fitech@mybank.com

MyBank Directory
www.mybank.com

Online Banking Report
www.onlinebankingreport.com/fullserv2.shtml
5025 25th Ave. NE, Suite 1146
Seattle, WA 98105
Phone: 206-517-5021

Taxes

1040.com
www.1040.com

Armchair Millionaire Tax Center
www.armchairmillionaire.com/tax

Fairmark Press Tax Guide for Investors
www.fairmark.com/index.html

Form and Publications IRS
www.irs.gov/forms_pubs

NetTax '9X
www.nettax.com

Tax and Accounting Sites Directory
www.taxsites.com

TradersAccounting.com
www.tradersaccounting.com

Recommended Reading List

All-time classics

25 Investment Classics: Insights from the Greatest Investment Books of All Time by Leo Gough (Editor).

The Art of Speculation by Philip L. Carret.

The Battle for Investment Survival by Gerald M. Loeb.

Beating the Street by John Rothchild and Peter Lynch.

Common Stocks and Uncommon Profits by Philip A. Fisher.

Extraordinary Popular Delusions and the Madness of Crowds by Charles MacKay.

A Fool and His Money: The Odyssey of an Average Investor by John Rothchild.

The Go-Go Years: The Drama and Crashing Finale of Wall Street's Bullish '60s by John Brooks and Michael Lewis (Introduction).

The Great Crash 1929 by John Kenneth Galbraith.

How I Made $2,000,000 in the Stock Market by Nicolas Darvas.

The Intelligent Investor by Benjamin Graham.

Manias, Panics and Crashes: A History of Financial Crises by Charles P. Kindleberger.

Market Wizards: Interviews with Top Traders by Jack D. Schwager.

The New Market Wizards: Conversations with America's Top Traders by Jack D. Schwager.

One Up on Wall Street by Peter Lynch.

The Only Investment Guide You'll Ever Need by Andrew Tobias.

A Random Walk down Wall Street by Burton Gordon Malkiel.

Reminiscences of a Stock Operator by Edwin Lefevre.

The Robber Barons: The Great American Capitalists, 1861[nd]1901 by Matthew Josephson.

Security Analysis by Benjamin Graham and David Dodd.

The Stock Market Barometer by William Peter Hamilton.

Technical Analysis of Stock Trends by Robert D. Edwards and John Magee.

Understanding Wall Street; Third Edition, by Jeffrey B. Little and Lucien Rhodes.

The Warren Buffet Way: Investment Strategies of the World's Greatest Investor by Robert G. Hagstrom, Jr.

Where the Money Grows: An Anatomy of the Bubble by Garet Garrett, Christopher M. Byron (Foreword).

Bonds

Bond Markets, Analysis, and Strategies by Frank J. Fabozzi.

Duration Analysis: Managing Interest Rate Risk by Gerald O. Bierwag.

Fixed Income Mathematics by Frank J. Fabozzi.

The Handbook of Currency and Interest Rate Risk Management by Robert J. Schwartz and Clifford W. Smith, Jr.

The Handbook of Fixed Income Securities by Frank J. Fabozzi.

The Handbook of Interest Rate Risk Management by Jack K. Francis and Avner Wolf.

A History of Interest Rates; Third Edition, by Sidney Homer and Richard Sylla.

Interest Rate Swaps by Carl R. Beidelman.

The Random Character of Interest Rates by J. E. Murphy.

Personal finance

Get a Financial Life: Personal Finance in Your Twenties and Thirties by Beth Kobliner.

Making the Most of Your Money: Smart Ways to Create Wealth and Plan Your Finances in the '90s by Jane Bryant Quinn.

Twenty-five Myths You've Got to Avoid If You Want to Manage Your Money Right by Jonathan Clements.

The Wall Street Journal Lifetime Guide to Money: Everything You Need to Know About Managing Your Finances—For Every Stage of Life by *The Wall Street Journal*'s Personal Finance Staff.

Your Next Fifty Years: A Completely New Way to Look at How, When, and If You Should Retire by Ginita Wall and Victoria F. Collins.

Stocks

101 Investment Lessons from the Wizards of Wall Street: The Pros' Secrets for Running with the Bulls Without Losing Your Shirt by Michael Sincere.

Buying Stocks Without a Broker by Charles B. Carlson.

Getting Started in Stocks; Third Edition, by Alvin D. Hall.

The Gorilla Game: An Investor's Guide to Picking Winners in High Technology by Geoffrey A. Moore, Paul Johnson, and Tom Kippola.

How to Buy Technology Stocks by Michael Gianturco.

How to Pick Stocks: America's Leading Mutual Fund Managers Tell How They Do It by Fred W. Frailey.

It's When You Sell That Counts: A Must-Have Book for Anyone Who Owns Stocks by Donald L. Cassidy.

Martin Zweig's Winning on Wall Street by Martin Zweig.

The Money Masters by John Train.

The Motley Fool Investment Guide: How the Fool Beats Wall Street's Wise Men and How You Can Too by David and Tom Gardner.

The Motley Fool's Rule Breakers, Rule Breakers, Rule Makers: The Foolish Guide to Picking Stocks by David and Tom Gardner.

Reminiscences of a Stock Operator by Edwin Lefevre.

Stocks Bonds Options Futures: Investments and their Markets by Stuart R. Veale (Editor).

Stocks for the Long Run: A Guide to Selecting Markets for Long-Term Growth by Jeremy J. Siegel.

The Unemotional Investor: Simple Systems for Beating the Market by Robert Sheard.

What Works on Wall Street: A Guide to the Best-Performing Investment Strategies of All Time by James O'Shaughnessy.

Why Stocks Go Up (and Down) by William H. Pike.

You Can Be a Stock Market Genius: Uncover the Secret Hiding Places of Stock Market Profits by Joel Greenblatt.

A Zebra in Lion Country: Ralph Wanger's Investment Survival Guide by Ralph Wanger with Everett Mattlin (Contributor).

Important Documents

List of online filing services

The Internal Revenue Service (IRS) has joined with various private companies to enable taxpayers to file their tax returns online. All these services are cheap, and some are free if you qualify. Go to www.irs.gov/elec_svs/partners.html for more information. If you need help filing, you can get a list of authorized IRS e-file providers with offices near you.

This is a list of the major authorized IRS e-file providers:

- **SecureTax.com:** www.securetax.com
- **Intuit's Quicken Tax Freedom Project and WebTurboTax:** www.intuit.com/turbotax/irsinfo.html
- **UDS ELECtroTAX:** www.udstax.com
- **TaxACT.com:** www.taxact.com/efile/index.asp
- **Kiplinger TaxCut:** www.taxcut.com/1040ez/index-irs.html
- **H&R BLOCK.COM:** www.hrblock.com

- **Jackson Hewitt Tax Service:** www. jacksonhewitt.com/ctg/cgi-bin/JacksonHewitt

Personal finance worksheets

PERSONAL NET WORTH WORKSHEET

ASSETS

Cash

      Cash on hand   _____

      Cash owed   _____

      Bank accounts   _____

      Brokerage account cash   _____

      Money market accounts   _____

      Certificates of deposit   _____

Securities

      Stocks   _____

      Bonds   _____

      Mutual funds   _____

      Options   _____

      Other   _____

Retirement plans

      Company pension plan   _____

      401(k) or Keogh plan   _____

      IRAs   _____

      Expected Social
        Security benefits   _____

Insurance

      Life insurance cash value   _____

      Annuities (cash value)   _____

Real estate

      House   _____

      Vacation home   _____

      Other properties   _____

      Land   _____

      REITs   _____

Personal property

    Cars _____

    Computer equipment _____

    Electronic equipment _____

    Jewelry _____

    Furniture _____

    Antiques/art/collectibles _____

    Other _____

TOTAL ASSETS _____

LIABILITIES

Real estate

    Primary mortgage _____

    Second mortgage _____

    Vacation home mortgage _____

    Home-equity loan _____

    Investment property loan _____

Installment debt

    Car loans _____

    Student loans _____

    Furniture loans _____

    Charge accounts _____

    Other _____

Other loans

    Loans against securities
        (margin debt) _____

    Loans against
        insurance policies _____

    Loans against
        retirement plan _____

    Other _____

Current bills

    Rent _____

    Utilities _____

    Credit cards _____

PERSONAL NET WORTH WORKSHEET *(cont.)*

    Medical   _____

    Dental   _____

    Alimony   _____

    Other   _____

Taxes

    Income tax   _____

    Property tax   _____

    Other   _____

Other liabilities   _____

TOTAL LIABILITIES   _____

NET WORTH
(Total Assets – Total Liabilities)   _____

PERSONAL CASH FLOW WORKSHEET

INCOME

    Job

        Salary   _____

        Commissions   _____

        Bonuses/profit sharing   _____

        Interest income   _____

    Investment income

        Dividends   _____

        Capital gains realized   _____

    Retirement income

        Pension   _____

        Social Security   _____

    Insurance income

        Life insurance   _____

        Annuity   _____

    Other

        Alimony/child support   _____

        Gifts   _____

    Appreciation in home   _____

    Miscellaneous   _____

        TOTAL INCOME   _____

EXPENSES

    Deductions from salary

        Federal income tax   _____

        State income tax   _____

        Social Security   _____

        Company savings plan   _____

        Health/disability
insurance   _____

        Other   _____

    Housing

        Mortgage or rent   _____

        Utilities   _____

        Homeowner's insurance   _____

        Phone bill   _____

        Heating bill   _____

        Property taxes   _____

        Daily upkeep   _____

        Repairs and improvements   _____

    Transportation

        Car operation and
maintenance   _____

        Auto insurance   _____

        Depreciation of car   _____

        Car rentals and leasing   _____

        Public transit and taxis   _____

    Other

        Food   _____

        Clothing   _____

        Tuition   _____

    Health

        Health insurance   _____

        Disability insurance   _____

PERSONAL CASH FLOW WORKSHEET *(cont.)*

Life insurance _____

Doctors _____

Hospitals and tests _____

Dentists _____

Medicines _____

Debt repayment

Credit cards _____

Car loans _____

Student loans _____

Other _____

Entertainment

Vacations _____

Shows and musical
performances _____

Dining out _____

Movies and videos _____

Books/magazines/online _____

Gambling _____

Other _____

Other expenses

Alimony/child support _____

Child care _____

Charitable contributions _____

Gifts _____

Miscellaneous _____

TOTAL EXPENSES _____

CASH FLOW
(Total Income – Total Expenses) _____

Reading the stock page

52 Weeks					Yld		Vol				Net
Hi	Lo	Stock	Sym	Div	%	PE	100s	Hi	Lo	Close	Chg
$56^3/_4$	$25^1/_2$	AFLAC	AFL	0.3	0.7	23	6263	46	$44^1/_2$	$45^1/_{16}$	$+ {}^{11}/_{16}$

52 Weeks Hi Lo: This field indicates the highest and lowest prices per share for the stock during the last 52 weeks (one year). In this example, the high for the stock over the past 52 weeks was 56¾, and the low was 25½. The 52-Week hi/low may give you an indication of how volatile the stock is. The greater the difference between the prices, the more volatile the stock probably is.

Stock: This field gives the company's name, often abbreviated. In the example, the company's name is AFLAC.

Sym: Abbreviation for symbol. This field gives the stock's ticker symbol. In the example, the symbol is AFL.

Div: Abbreviation for dividend. This field gives you the annual dividend payout amount in dollars per share. Stocks with higher dividend yields tend to be more stable in price. In the example, AFLAC pays shareholders 30 cents per share a year.

Yld%: Abbreviation for percent yield, but commonly referred to as dividend yield. The dividend yield is calculated by dividing the dividend by the closing price. In the example, the dividend yield is 0.7 percent, meaning that AFLAC pays shareholders ⁷⁄₁₀ of 1 percent in dividends a year.

PE: Abbreviation of price-to-earnings ratio. The PE is calculated by dividing the stock's closing price by the company's annual earnings per share. Generally speaking, the lower the PE, the better, although some high-flying growth stocks have justifiably high PEs. In the example, the PE is $23 per share.

Vol 100s: Abbreviation for volume (divided by 100). Volume is the number of shares of a stock that were traded the previous market day. Generally, high volume in a stock shows that it is popular and liquid.

Unusually high volume may indicate a rally or a correction in the stock. To get the actual number of shares traded, multiply the number in this field by 100. If the number is followed by a small z, however, the number is the actual number of shares traded and should not be multiplied by 100. In the example, 626,300 shares were traded (6,263 × 100).

Hi: The highest price the stock traded at the previous market day. In the example, the high for AFLAC was $46 per share.

Lo: The lowest price the stock traded for the previous market day. In the example, the low for AFLAC was $44.50 per share.

Close: The last price the stock traded at the previous market day. In the example, the closing price for AFLAC was $45 1/16 per share.

Net Chg: Abbreviation for net change. This net change tells you how much a stock rose or fell the previous market day. Net change gives a short-term indication of the direction of a stock's price. In the example, the share price of AFLAC rose 11/16 (or about 69 cents).

Reading the mutual fund page

Name	NAV	Net Chg	YTD%ret
Acorn Funds:			
AcornInt	26.5	+0.16	+28.1

Name: This field gives the name of the investment company (mutual fund company or fund family) and underneath that, the name of the specific mutual fund. In the example, the name of the investment company is Acorn Funds and the name of the mutual fund is AcornInt, the abbreviation for Acorn International Fund.

NAV: Abbreviation for net asset value. The net asset value is calculated by dividing the value of all the shares held by the fund by the total number of shares held by the fund. In the example, the NAV is $26.50 per share.

Net Chg: Abbreviation for net change. The net change is the amount the NAV changed the previous market day. In the example, the NAV of the Acorn International Fund was up 0.16, or 16 cents per share.

YTD%ret: Abbreviation for year-to-date percent return. The YTD percent return is the change in the value of a fund from January 1 of the current year to the present. This number includes any distributions made during the current year. In the example, Acorn International is up 28.1 percent so far this year.

Important Statistics

Valuation levels at all-time highs

KEY RATIOS AT MARKET HIGHS

Date	S&P 500	PE	Price per Dividend	Dividend per Yield
5/29/46	19.25	22.4	29.6	3.38%
6/15/48	17.06	9.3	20.1	4.98%
3/20/56	48.87	13.3	25.9	3.87%
1/5/60	60.39	17.8	32	3.13%
12/12/61	72.64	23	35.6	2.81%
2/9/66	94.06	17.9	33.2	3.01%
11/29/68	108.37	18.3	35	2.86%
4/28/71	104.77	20.4	33.9	2.95%
1/11/73	120.24	19.6	37.9	2.64%
9/21/76	107.83	11.8	27.6	3.62%
11/28/80	140.52	9.4	22.2	4.50%
10/10/83	172.65	13.7	24.2	4.12%
8/25/87	336.77	22.9	38.1	2.62%
7/16/90	368.95	17	30.3	3.30%
2/2/94	482	23.6	37.9	2.64%
7/17/98	1186.75	30	73.8	1.35%
7/1/99	1380.96	36	82.5	1.21%

Make more money by avoiding taxes

THE POWER OF PRE-TAX, TAX-DEFERRED COMPOUNDING

	After-Tax/ Taxable Earnings; Example: Bank CD	After-Tax/ Tax-Deferred Earnings; Example: Roth IRA	Pre-Tax/ Tax-Defer. Earnings; Example: 401(k)
Invest income	$10,000	$10,000	$10,000
After taxes	$7,200	$7,200	$10,000
5 years	$10,193	$11,596	$16,105
10 years	$14,430	$18,675	$25,937
15 years	$20,429	$30,076	$41,772
20 years	$28,922	$48,438	$67,275
25 years	$40,945	$78,010	$108,347
30 years	$57,966	$125,636	$174,494
35 years	$82,063	$202,337	$281,024
40 years	$116,178	$325,866	$452,592

The figures in this chart are based on an annual return of 10 percent, with all returns reinvested and taxed as regular income at a rate of 28 percent.

How likely are you to get audited?

AUDIT RATES FOR VARIOUS TAX RETURNS

FORMS 1040, 1040A, 1040EZ	% Audited in Fiscal 1997
Income of $25,000 to less than $50,000	0.7
$50,000 to less than $100,000	0.77
$100,00 and over	2.27

Schedule C (Sole Proprietorships)	% Audited in Fiscal 1997
With gross receipts less than $25,000	3.19
$25,000 to less than $100,000	2.57
$100,000 and over	4.13

Estate-Tax Returns	% Audited in Fiscal 1997
Gross estates of less than $1 million	6.83
$1 million to less than $5 million	18.88
$5 million and over	47.43

Source: Internal Revenue Service, 1997 Data Book.

The income figures are based on total personal income before deductions, losses, and other adjustments. The percent audited figures are based on returns filed in 1996.

Going with taxable or tax-free investments

DETERMINING TAXABLE EQUIVALENT YIELDS

Tax-Free Yields:	4%	4.50%	5%	5.50%	6%	6.50%
Tax Rate:						
15%	4.71%	5.29%	5.88%	6.47%	7.06%	7.65%
28%	5.56%	6.25%	6.94%	7.64%	8.33%	9.03%
31%	5.80%	6.52%	7.25%	7.97%	8.70%	9.42%
36%	6.25%	7.03%	7.81%	8.59%	9.38%	10.16%
39.60%	6.62%	7.45%	8.28%	9.11%	9.93%	10.76%

The figures in the cells under the "Taxable Equivalent Yields" heading show you how much you need to make on a taxable investment (based on your tax bracket) to equal the yield of a corresponding tax-free investment. These figures take only federal income taxes into account, not state and local taxes or alternative minimum tax.

The *Unofficial Guide*™ Reader Questionnaire

If you would like to express your opinion about investing online or this guide, please complete this questionnaire and mail it to:

The *Unofficial Guide*™ Reader Questionnaire
IDG Lifestyle Group
1633 Broadway, floor 7
New York, NY 10019-6785

Gender: ___ M   ___ F

Age: ___ Under 30   ___ 31–40   ___ 41–50
___ Over 50

Education: ___ High school   ___ College
___ Graduate/Professional

What is your occupation?

_____

How did you hear about this guide?
___ Friend or relative
___ Newspaper, magazine, or Internet
___ Radio or TV
___ Recommended at bookstore
___ Recommended by librarian
___ Picked it up on my own
___ Familiar with the *Unofficial Guide*™ travel series

Did you go to the bookstore specifically for a book on investing online?   Yes ___   No ___

Have you used any other *Unofficial Guides*™?
Yes ___   No ___

If Yes, which ones?

_____
_____
_____

What other book(s) on investing online have you purchased? _____

_____
_____

Was this book:
___ more helpful than other(s)?
___ less helpful than other(s)?

Do you think this book was worth its price?
Yes ___ No ___

Did this book cover all topics related to investing online adequately?
Yes ___ No ___

Please explain your answer:

_____
_____
_____

Were there any specific sections in this book that were of particular help to you? Yes ___ No ___

Please explain your answer:

_____
_____
_____

On a scale of 1 to 10, with 10 being the best rating, how would you rate this guide? ___

What other titles would you like to see published in the *Unofficial Guide*™ series?

_____
_____

Are Unofficial Guides™ **readily available in your area?** Yes ___ No ___

Other comments:

_____
_____
_____
_____

Get the inside scoop...with the *Unofficial Guides*™!

Health and Fitness

The Unofficial Guide to Alternative Medicine
ISBN: 0-02-862526-9 Price: $15.95

The Unofficial Guide to Conquering Impotence
ISBN: 0-02-862870-5 Price: $15.95

The Unofficial Guide to Coping with Menopause
ISBN: 0-02-862694-x Price: $15.95

The Unofficial Guide to Cosmetic Surgery
ISBN: 0-02-862522-6 Price: $15.95

The Unofficial Guide to Dieting Safely
ISBN: 0-02-862521-8 Price: $15.95

The Unofficial Guide to Having a Baby
ISBN: 0-02-862695-8 Price: $15.95

The Unofficial Guide to Living with Diabetes
ISBN: 0-02-862919-1 Price: $15.95

The Unofficial Guide to Overcoming Arthritis
ISBN: 0-02-862714-8 Price: $15.95

The Unofficial Guide to Overcoming Infertility
ISBN: 0-02-862916-7 Price: $15.95

Career Planning

The Unofficial Guide to Acing the Interview
ISBN: 0-02-862924-8 Price: $15.95

The Unofficial Guide to Earning What You Deserve
ISBN: 0-02-862523-4 Price: $15.95

The Unofficial Guide to Hiring and Firing People
ISBN: 0-02-862523-4 Price: $15.95

Business and Personal Finance

The Unofficial Guide to Investing
ISBN: 0-02-862458-0 Price: $15.95

The Unofficial Guide to Investing in Mutual Funds
ISBN: 0-02-862920-5 Price: $15.95

The Unofficial Guide to Managing Your Personal Finances
ISBN: 0-02-862921-3 Price: $15.95

The Unofficial Guide to Starting a Small Business
ISBN: 0-02-862525-0 Price: $15.95

Home and Automotive

The Unofficial Guide to Buying a Home
ISBN: 0-02-862461-0 Price: $15.95

The Unofficial Guide to Buying or Leasing a Car
ISBN: 0-02-862524-2 Price: $15.95

The Unofficial Guide to Hiring Contractors
ISBN: 0-02-862460-2 Price: $15.95

Family and Relationships

The Unofficial Guide to Childcare
ISBN: 0-02-862457-2 Price: $15.95

The Unofficial Guide to Dating Again
ISBN: 0-02-862454-8 Price: $15.95

The Unofficial Guide to Divorce
ISBN: 0-02-862455-6 Price: $15.95

The Unofficial Guide to Eldercare
ISBN: 0-02-862456-4 Price: $15.95

The Unofficial Guide to Planning Your Wedding
ISBN: 0-02-862459-9 Price: $15.95

Hobbies and Recreation

The Unofficial Guide to Finding Rare Antiques
ISBN: 0-02-862922-1 Price: $15.95

The Unofficial Guide to Casino Gambling
ISBN: 0-02-862917-5 Price: $15.95

All books in the *Unofficial Guide*™ series are available at your local bookseller.